4 August 1914 saw the British declaration of war on Germany and, in his 'digs' in Hampton, Middlesex, nurseryman James Sadler resolved to enlist to serve and play his part in what was to become known as the Great War 1914–18. 28 August 1918 saw the same man, now infantryman Sgt. James Sadler M.M, being stretchered away from the battlefield at Hardecourt aux Bois in France, his part in the conflict complete. During the interim period, James Sadler had seen action on a number of the major battlefields on the Western Front, including Armentières, Ploegsteert, Loos, the Somme, Arras, the German Offensive of 1918, and the Allied advance in the final 100 Days.

In *Gardener to Fusilier: The story of James Sadler M.M., 9th Royal Fusiliers (Service) Battalion, 1914–18*, his son, James Sadler, takes the record that his father made as he convalesced in the family home in Swanage on return from France, and combines this with his own research into his father's experiences. These are coupled to those of the 9th Royal Fusiliers (Service) Battalion, the unit in which his father served during that period, forming part of Kitchener's First Army in the 36th Brigade and the 12th (Eastern) Division. The story of one infantryman's experiences are intertwined with those, often brief, details given from his Battalion's War Diary, giving insight into what he and his comrades faced in the campaign.

This account not only includes the first-hand recall of the thoughts and aspects of facing battle, but also includes one man's personal comments on what he was asked to undertake, those whom he served with and under and the, often ignored, aspects of the routine and drudgery which were also part of the experience. *Gardener to Fusilier* makes no attempt to generalise about the British Tommy of the First World War; it aims at being the honest recall of one man and his fighting unit in a conflict which, even today, leaves its mark on our society and world.

A qualified Mechanical Engineer, James Sadler is retired following a teaching career which spanned over 30 years, much of which was spent as the Head of Mathematics at a large Comprehensive School in Wiltshire. Born in Twickenham, Middlesex in 1947, James grew up to realise that his father, also James, had played a full part as an NCO infantryman in a major action in world history, the First World War. James, senior, died in 1951, aged 61, leaving personal records in the form of two handwritten books relating his experiences as part of Kitchener's First Army, with the 9th Royal Fusiliers (Service) Battalion, 1914 to 1918.

From his mother, the younger James was to learn that it had always been his father's wish for these to see publication. In bringing this wish to reality son, James, has carefully researched the time his father spent on the Western Front, transcribing his father's work along with the War Diaries of the 9th Royal Fusiliers.

A member of the WFA, James has a keen interest in the many aspects of the First World War and a number of visits to the battlefields of northern France have enabled him to link the personal aspect of his father's recollections with those of the Battalion, the 36th Brigade and 12th (Eastern) Division.

Like his father who, in 1914, enlisted from his lifetime occupation as a gardener/ horticulturalist, James is a keen gardener and sportsman with major interests in cricket (an E.C.B. Qualified coach), rugby and football; his relaxation also takes in amateur photography and music. James has three married sons and lives, with his partner, in the Dales area of North Yorkshire.

GARDENER TO FUSILIER

THE STORY OF JAMES SADLER M.M., 9TH ROYAL FUSILIERS (SERVICE) BATTALION, 1914-18

This book is dedicated to my Family, and in particular the memory of my Father,
Royal Fusilier G321 Sgt. James Sadler M.M. (1890-1951), who I was never really to
know and a most wonderful Mother,
Winifred Elizabeth Sadler (1909-2003)
to whom Liz and I owed so much.

GARDENER TO FUSILIER

THE STORY OF JAMES SADLER M.M., 9TH ROYAL FUSILIERS (SERVICE) BATTALION, 1914-18

Edited by James Sadler

Foreword by Professor Peter Simkins

Helion & Company

Helion & Company Limited
26 Willow Road
Solihull
West Midlands
B91 1UE
England
Tel. 0121 705 3393
Fax 0121 711 4075
Email: info@helion.co.uk
Website: www.helion.co.uk
Twitter: @helionbooks
Visit our blog http://blog.helion.co.uk/

Published by Helion & Company 2015
Designed and typeset by Farr out Publications, Wokingham, Berkshire
Cover designed by Paul Hewitt, Battlefield Design (www.battlefield-design.co.uk)
Printed by Lightning Source Limited, Milton Keynes, Buckinghamshire

Text © James Sadler 2015
Images © as individually credited
Maps drawn by George Anderson © Helion & Company Limited 2015

ISBN 978-1-910777-22-0

British Library Cataloguing-in-Publication Data.
A catalogue record for this book is available from the British Library.

For details of other military history titles published by Helion & Company Limited contact the above address, or visit our website: http://www.helion.co.uk.

We always welcome receiving book proposals from prospective authors.

Contents

List of illustrations   vii
List of maps   ix
Abbreviations   x
Foreword by Professor Peter Simkins   xii
Preface   xv
Acknowledgements   xvi
Maps   xvii
Introduction   xx

1   Start of the Journey, August 1914   24
2   Training: August 1914–May 1915   27
3   May to July 1915 – Off to France and the Trenches   30
4   July to September 1915 – Armentières: Life in the Front Line and on Reserve leading up to the Battle of Loos   39
5   September and October 1915: The Battle of Loos   58
6   October 1915: The Action of Hohenzollern Redoubt – Part 1   72
7   November–December 1915: The Action of Hohenzollern Redoubt – Part 2   78
8   January to February 1916
    The early months – still in the Loos Battlefield Area   94
9   January to March 1916: Further Action on the Loos Battlefield   100
10   March–June 1916: The return to France and the time leading up to The Battle of the Somme   121
11   The Battle of the Somme, June and July 1916 – Arrival in the Area, More Preparation, Attack at Ovillers   134
12   The Somme Battlefield, July and August 1916: After the Ovillers Action, on to Pozières   156
13   The Somme Battlefield, August and September 1916: On from Pozières, Rest and in Reserve at Agny   172
14   The Somme Battlefield, September–October 1916: From Agny and back into Action at Transloy Ridges in October   187
15   The Somme Battlefield, October 1916: The Battle of the Transloy Ridges   194
16   The Somme Battlefield October–December 1916: From the Transloy Ridges to the Reserves Lines and the Lead-up to Christmas   205
17   January 1917: the Arras sector. A New Year but more assault preparations   214
18   April–May 1917, Arras: The Attack starts Easter Monday then moves to Monchy le Preux. Leave. Cambrai   229
19   May 1917–February 1918: From Arras to England and back again, Becoming an Instructor   247
20   March–April 1918: Selected for a Draft and back to France again. Facing the German Offensive – Operation Michael   253

21 April–July 1918: Retreat   268
22 August 1918: Advance Towards a Decision   281
23 August–September 1918: Driving the Enemy back   295
24 27-28 August 1918: Advance and Wounding   308
25 28 August 1918: Onwards Christian Soldier, Wounded. Out of the
        War and Recovery prior to Discharge   315
26 September–November 1918
        Advance Towards Armistice: the War to end all Wars reaches a Conclusion   321
27 1919: A Footnote: After the Armistice: the 9th Royal Fusiliers (Service)
        Battalion disbanded   323

Appendices
I   Outline of the organisation of the Army into which Private G321 J.
        Sadler enlisted in 1914   325
II   Seniority of Rank in the Army into which Private G321 J. Sadler enlisted in 1914   326
III James Sadler M.M.'s position in the British Army 1914–18   327

List of illustrations

29th March 1937: James marries Winifred Elizabeth Ashby in All Saints
    Parish Church, Hampton, Middlesex.   xxi

Sgt. James Sadler's drawing of the Royal Fusiliers crest which he uses at
    the opening of the first of his two handwritten books recounting his
    experiences in The Great War.   xxii

Royal Fusilier G321 L/Cpl. James Sadler's drawing of the Military Medal
    awarded following the Battalion's Action at Ovillers on The Somme,
    7th July 1916.   xxii

James Sadler's identity tag.   xxiii

James Sadler's medal cluster.   xxiii

Mary and Alfred, the mother and father who awaited the return of their
    son, James, in Swanage.   25

James's handwritten account of his Battalion's 1st Visit to the Trenches: June 1915.   33

Ploegsteert Wood.   38

The Artois area of North East France, 1915-16. (George Anderson)   56

James's handwritten account of Action on the Loos Battlefield. September/
    October 1915.   61

James's handwritten account of action seen near the Loos Battlefield: Xmas Day 1915.   91

Craters formed by the blowing up of four mines on 2 March 1916 under
    German trenches in the Hohenzollern Redoubt by the 36th Brigade,
    12th Division. The 8th and 9th Battalions, Royal Fusiliers attacked
    after the mines went up and the 7th Battalion, Royal Sussex with the
    11th Battalion, Middlesex Regiment were in support. Copyright IWM Q 64053   105

James's handwritten account of action seen at the Hohenzollern Redoubt:
    Oct.1915-March 1916.   109

James's handwritten account of action seen leading up to the 1st Battle on
    the Somme. June 1916.   135

Ovillers battlefield today.   139

James's handwritten account of Action seen at Ovillers during the Battle on
    the Somme: 7th July 1916.   145

Derelict German Trenches at Ovillers, looking towards Albert. July 1916.
    Copyright IWM.   150

9th Royal Fusiliers. War Diary records James Sadler M.M.   162

Site of Pozières, August 1916. Copyright IWM (Q4078).   166

Pozières battlefield today.   168

Major General F.D.V. Wing CB, CMG, GOC 12th Division, March–
    October 1915. Killed in Action at the Battle of Loos 1915.   178

Major General H.W. Higginson, CB, DSO, GOC 12th Eastern Division.
    April–November 1918.   178

Commanding Officers under whom James Sadler M.M. served.   178
Captain G.L. Cazalet DSO, CO 'A' Company, 9th Royal Fusiliers
    throughout the Somme campaign.   178
Major M. E. Coxhead CO 9th Royal Fusiliers June 1916–May 1917.   178
The Transloy Ridges today.   192
Arras. Wellington Barracks/Caves. The memorial to the 12th (Eastern)
    Division) from which the Division were to attack on the 9th April 1917.   216
Battle of Arras, 9 April 1917. British infantry moving up to the front line in
    support of the initial advance. Copyright IWM (Q 5115).   232
Aveluy today.   261
Morlancourt today.   280
Hardecourt aux Bois, Chimp Valley.   313
Hardecourt aux Bois.   313
A Ward in the Southampton War Hospital at Netley where James was
    treated for his wounds on return to England in Aug/Sept 1918.   317
James Sadler's Medal Card as held in the National Archives.   318
James Sadler entry recorded on a page in the Roll of Individuals awarded
    Great War medals. The exact dates which James saw action on the
    Western Front are given here. It is extremely poignant to note the
    details relating to L.Cpl. William Spry, the first soldier recorded on this page.   319

List of maps

The Western Front. (George Anderson) xvii

Campaign in Artois. (George Anderson) xviii

The Somme Battlefields – 1916. (George Anderson) xix

Ploegsteert. (George Anderson) 37

Loos. (George Anderson) 59

The quarries at Hulluch. (George Anderson) 63

Bethune, Sailly la Bourse and Vermelles. (George Anderson) 70

Hohenzollern Craters. (George Anderson) 73

Hohenzollern Redoubt Craters. (George Anderson) 79

Sketch from the 9th Royal Fusiliers War Diaries showing map of craters
formed by mining at Hohenzollern Redoubt. (George Anderson) 113

Ovillers, 3rd to 7th July 1916. (George Anderson) 140

Map of advance at Ovillers by the 9th R.F. on 7 July 1916. 141

Pozières August 1916. (George Anderson) 163

Geudecourt Trenches on the Transloy Ridges. (George Anderson) 195

The Arras Front 1917. (George Anderson) 215

The Battle of Arras. (George Anderson) 233

Monchy-le-Preux. (George Anderson) 236

The Scarpe. (George Anderson) 242

Albert, March 1918. (George Anderson) 259

The country around Albert. (George Anderson) 262

Morlancourt through to Hardecourt-aux-Bois: the advance August 1918.
(George Anderson) 285

Abbreviations

A.A.	Anti-Aircraft
Adj.	Adjutant
A.M.P.	Army Military Police
Bde.	Brigade
Bn. or Batt.	Battalion
B.M.	Brigade Major
C.C.S.	Casualty Clearing Station
Co. or Comp.	Company
C.O.	Commanding Officer
Cpl.	Corporal
Capt.	Captain
Col.	Colonel
C.R.E.	Commanding Royal Engineers
C.S.M.	Company Sergeant Major
C.T.	Communication Trench
C.Q.M.	Company Quartermaster
C.Q.M.S.	Company Quartermaster Sergeant
Div.	Division
D.S.O.	Distinguished Service Order
D.S.M.	Distinguished Service Medal
E.A.	Enemy Aircraft
F.A.	Field Artillery
G.C.M.	General Court-Martial
G.S.	General Supply
G.S.O.	General Staff Officer
G.H.Q.	General Headquarters
G.O.C.	General Officer Commanding
G.O.C.in.C.	General Officer Commanding-in-Chief
H.A.	Heavy Artillery
H.E.	High Explosive
H.Q.	Headquarters
H.V.	High Velocity
L/C or L/Cpl.	Lance Corporal
Lieut. or Lt.	Lieutenant
2/Lieut or 2/Lt.	Second Lieutenant
Lt.Col.	Lieutenant Colonel
L.G.	Lewis Gun
L.of.C.	Lines of Communication
M.C.	Military Cross
M.G.	Machine Gun
M.G.C.	Machine Gun Corps

M.M.	Military Medal
Maj.	Major
O.in C.	Officer in Charge
O.R.	Other Ranks
Pte.	Private
R.A.	Royal Artillery
R.A.M.C.	Royal Army Medical Corps
R.A.S.M.C.	Royal Army Special Medical Corps
R.E.	Royal Engineers
Regt.	Regiment
R.G.A.	Royal Garrison Artillery
R.F.A.	Royal Field Artillery
R.F.C.	Royal Flying Corps
R.S.M.	Regimental Sergeant Major
Sgt.	Sergeant
S.A.A.	Small Arms Ammunition
S.P.	Strongpoint
S.R.	Special Reserve
T.C.	Tank Corps
T.M.	Trench Mortar
T.M.B.	Trench Mortar Battery
W.O.	Warrant Officer
V.C.	Victoria Cross

Foreword

Ever since the late 1970s, when I started to undertake research for my book *Kitchener's Army*, I have had a special interest in the story of Britain's New Armies in the Great War. Moreover, having been born and bred in West London and, later, having lived for many years in Sussex and East Anglia successively, I have devoted much attention, in particular, to the 12th and 18th (Eastern) Divisions – the two New Army formations raised principally in London and the Home Counties. Hence I am both pleased and honoured to have been invited to contribute this Foreword to James S. Sadler's fine edition of the diaries and recollections which his own father – also named James – kept of his service with the 9th Royal Fusiliers (a battalion of the 12th Division) from 1914 until a few weeks short of the Armistice.

Despite its unpromising beginnings in 1914 when, like its sister formation (the 18th Division), it suffered, as a newly-raised unit, from inevitable inexperience and from shortages of all kinds, the 12th Division had a distinguished in the 1914-1918 conflict. After crossing to France in late May-early June 1915, it first big action was at The Quarries, near Loos, in October that year. On the Somme in 1916, it had a series of tough fights at Ovillers in July, at Pozières and Ration Trench in August and at Bayonet and Grid Trenches, near Gueudecourt, in October. The following year the Division was heavily involved in the Battle of Arras in April and May and in the Battle of Cambrai in November and early December. On the opening day of the Battle of Arras (9 April) – in a scenario which was exceedingly unusual at that stage of the war, its troops captured a large number of German field guns in the open in Battery Valley.

In the spring of 1918, the 12th Division played a crucial role in blunting the German March offensive and in halting the enemy's advance along the line of the River Ancre near Aveluy, north of Albert. Finally, in the victorious Allied 'Hundred Days' offensive from August to November 1918, the Division had five prolonged spells in the line or in action. It took part in the initial phases of the BEF's crushing success at Amiens between 8 and 13 August, and then in the recapture of the old 1916 Somme battlefield between 22 and 30 August, Sadler himself being seriously wounded at Hardecourt on 28 August, during this period. Thirdly, it was in action at Nurlu, north-east of Péronne, from 4 to 8 September. Next, from 18 to 30 September, it was engaged in the intense struggle for Epéhy, in the outlying defences of the Hindenburg Line, before pressing on to the main Hindenburg Position along the St Quentin Canal. Last but not least came the Division's fifth period of operation in the Hundred Days, this time in Artois where, from 6 to 29 October, the formation carried out a number of outstanding, and sometimes tactically brilliant, minor attacks during an advance from the Lens-Arras area to the banks of the Schelde, a distance of 32 miles.

While it had its share of failures and setbacks, the Division was, on the whole, among the most solid and reliable fighting formations in the BEF. During the Somme offensive in 1916, for example, it had a success rate, in opposed attacks, of just over 63 per cent. In the Hundred Days in 1918 its success rate was even higher at 69.5 per cent, only half a percentage point lower than the Guards Division. If probably not regarded as an élite formation, the 12th clearly had a combat reputation which was sufficiently good for it to be selected to take part in the BEF's key opening assaults at Arras (9 April 1917), Cambrai (20 November 1917) and Amiens (8 August 1918), as well as the decisive attack on the Hindenburg Line in September 1918. With the exception of the Battle of Cambrai, when he was in the UK, and in the weeks after he was wounded in late August 1918, Sadler was involved, with the 9th (Service) Battalion of the Royal Fusiliers, in almost all of the above actions, rising from the rank of Private to Acting Company Sergeant-Major and winning the Military Medal in the process. However, for all his distinguished service, Sadler was not alone in feeling the strain of frequent operations. In August 1918, as he fought his way again over the old Somme battlefield, he was 'even more sick of the war as we had been over this ground before...'

Overall, according to the Divisional History, the 12th Division incurred 48,143 casualties during the Great War, including 435 officers and 6,077 other ranks killed, 1,415 officers and 31,646 other ranks wounded, and 255 officers and 8,315 other ranks missing. Thus its units had to be constantly regenerated, especially after major actions, as fresh drafts of reinforcements and casualty replacements had to be absorbed and trained. It is perhaps worth noting in passing that on 28 August 1918, when Sadler was wounded, the 9th Royal Fusiliers – in clearing Faviere Wood, occupying Hardecourt and seizing 16 German machine-guns – contained some 350 recruits aged eighteen-and-a-half to nineteen-and-a-half, who had been in France barely a week but managed to overcome Fusilier battalions of a Guard Grenadier regiment from the German 2nd Guard Division. The fact that divisions such as the 12th succeeded in maintaining high standards of performance on the battlefield, in spite of recurrent heavy losses, undoubtedly owed much to the guidance and leadership offered by those experienced officers and NCOs who had somehow survived and so gave their formations at least some stability and continuity as well as upholding the unit's traditions and ethos.

James Sadler's own story perfectly illustrates this latter point. He appears to have been basically proud of holding non-commissioned rank, describing the conflict as 'a war run by the NCOs', although in his diaries and reminiscences he also frankly discusses the responsibilities *and* the limitations – together with the advantages – of being a non-commissioned officer.

In this connection, it almost certainly helped the 12th Division *and* the 9th Royal Fusiliers that they both enjoyed relative stability and continuity at senior command levels. The Division had only three commanders during its time on the Western Front. Major-General F.D.V. Wing, a gunner, led the Division from March 1915 until he was killed by a shell near Loos on 2 October 1915. The longest-serving commander of the Division was Major-General Arthur Scott, another gunner, who next held the post until late April 1918. From then until the Armistice the Division's GOC was Major-General Harold Higginson, formerly a brigade commander in the 18th Division and one of the most gifted tacticians in the BEF. The 36th Brigade, in which the 9th Royal Fusiliers served throughout the war, was commanded, from November 1916 onwards, by C.S.'Bingo' Owen, a colourful character who had previously commanded the 6th Royal West Kents in the Division's 37th Brigade since late 1915. Alan Thomas, who served under Owen in the Royal West Kents, portrayed him as 'The Fire-Eater' with 'an eye as a crystal, a tongue as sharp as a razor and a command of language that a sailor would have envied'. Alan Thomas added: 'He never left you guessing: in conversation as in action, he went directly to the point. Toughness was all...' Owen was still only 39 at the start of the Hundred Days in 1918.

At battalion level, Sadler's three principal commanders were Lieutenant-Colonel S. Gubbins (August 1915-June 1916), Lieutenant-Colonel G.C.R. Overton (June 1916-July 1917) and Lieutenant-Colonel W.V.L. Van Someren (July 1917 onwards). Here too the turnover of battalion commanders was not high. All those battalion commanders named above were awarded the Distinguished Service Order while Van Someren also won the Military Cross. Of Lieutenant-Colonel Overton, who seems to have been Sadler's platoon officer at an earlier stage, Sadler wrote: 'I would say that it is unlikely that there was ever a more gallant officer to have served in France'. But Sadler was by no means uncritical of his superiors, writing of one Company Commander in 1917: 'In all honesty, I would not have allowed him to take a dozen boys on a school outing'.

The fascination of Sadler's recollections is that they do not only cover the major battles. What is equally appealing about this book is that James Sadler also deals with the small details of daily life in a British infantry battalion on the Western Front, including references to routine trench warfare, holding the line, raids and patrols, route marches, working parties, training, church parades, food, billets and leave. All of this adds depth to the narrative elements of the book and increases our knowledge of the minor, and often boring and arduous, daily events and tasks which were the common lot of other ranks in the BEF in France and Belgium.

Peter Simkins

Hon, Professor of Western Front Studies, University of Wolverhampton

and Hon. President, Western Front Association

Preface

Having read Max Arthur's book recounting the experiences of British soldiers in the aftermath of Great War, I found myself retracing my father's wartime experience on the Western Front from enlistment in August 1914 to severe wounding in August 1918.

Those who died are, more often than not, commemorated on war memorials throughout Great Britain. Conversely, those who returned, many scarred by the experience, have received no official commemoration. It is to these men and women who, like my father, returned to disappear back into family and community life that this book is dedicated; the backbone, in fact the vast majority, whose Great War service was never told.

My father's recollections and experiences were recorded in two handwritten diaries compiled whilst convalescing in the family home in Swanage. These have, for the past century, remained an unread family heirloom until I took it upon myself to transcribe them for publication.

In this way I feel I have learnt that much more about my father who, having "made it" through the conflict returned home, like so many others, to resume civilian life. I was four when he died in 1951. Having never really known him, it is my sincere hope that the following pages will portray Sergeant James Sadler MM as the man he was and why I am so proud to be his son. Proud of the campaigns, battles and actions in which he took part and proud of those veterans who, like him, fought and returned home to resume their lives in the country they fought for.

The research I have undertaken has led to a fascination with the men who served during 1914-18. Hardships were not always associated simply with the front line and there was a great deal of routine and tedium to endure. My father's account of his wartime service reflects this and the treasured camaraderie that means so much to a soldier. To this end, Sergeant Sadler's memoir will be juxtaposed with entries from the 9th (Service Battalion) Royal Fusiliers war diary. My only hope is that the reader will gain some insight into the experiences of a Kitchener volunteer whose country needed him.

James S. Sadler
January 2013

Acknowledgements

I would wish to express my sincere gratitude and thanks for the support and contributions of the many people who have, both knowingly and unknowingly, helped in bringing this work to fruition. Although it is perhaps wrong to be selective, in this instance I would like to acknowledge, in particular, the following:-

The National Archives who granted me the permission to quote, freely, from the Crown Copyright Document, WO/95/1857. This source and Crown Copyright status of the references and information obtained from this Document are gratefully acknowledged.

Richard and Jonathan Porter of Chevasse Farm in Hardecourt-aux-Bois whose interest and encouragement served as a guide and greatly assisted me in my desire to continue with the relevant research.

Professor Peter Simkins, OBE, for his encouragement and for showing himself to be so interested in the work and so willing to contribute the enclosed Foreword.

Harry Cartledge, my brother-in-law and very dear friend, whose guidance helped lead me towards finding Helion as a publisher for the work.

Duncan Rogers of Helion & Co. Ltd, to whom I am greatly indebted for having the faith in accepting the work for publication.

The Staff at Helion & Co. Ltd who have played such an important part in bringing the work to publication, which has included some fine design work and editing.

The Fusilier Museum at The Tower of London particularly Stephanie Killingbeck, who were so approachable and helpful with regard to aspects of my research.

The Imperial War Museum for granting, following payment, the rights to use the photographic images which are duly credited where this material is incorporated.

The History Staff at The George Ward School and St. Augustine's College in Wiltshire whose interest helped me to keep researching and working towards the conclusion of the work.

Dave Gale, a very dear and long-standing friend since junior school days, whose initial interest helped to make me aware of the significance of the part which people, such as my father, played in The Great War and which led me to believe that the recall of his experiences deserved to be heard.

My three great sons Paul, Ben and Tom and their families who have followed the progress as the work has developed and of whom their Grandad James would have been so proud.

Finally my dear partner June who has been so consistently supportive in helping me as I have worked towards completing the task of fulfilling my father's wish that his experiences would be recognised.

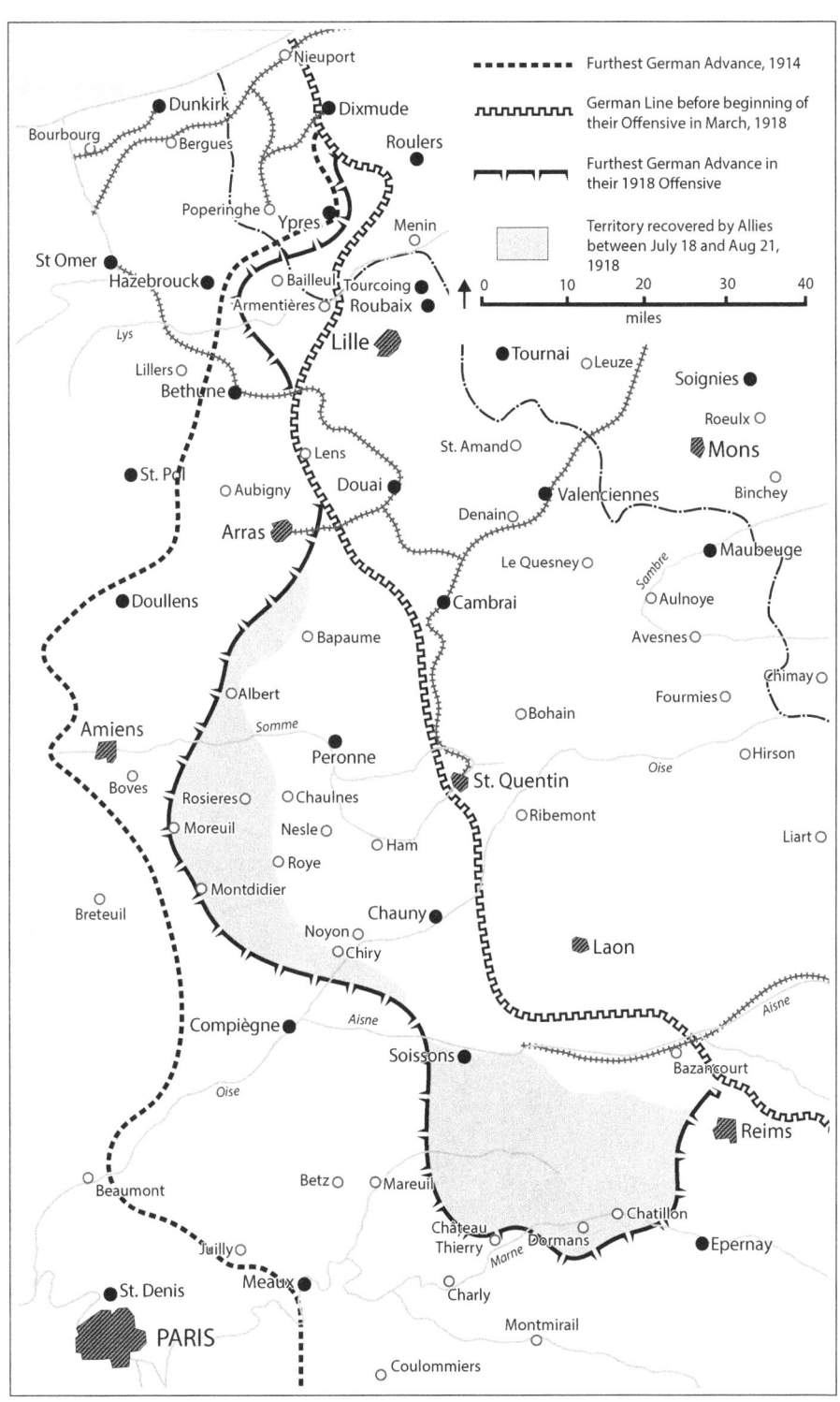

Legend:

- ▪▪▪▪▪▪ Furthest German Advance, 1914
- ⌐⌐⌐⌐⌐⌐ German Line before beginning of their Offensive in March, 1918
- ⌐⌐⌐⌐ Furthest German Advance in their 1918 Offensive
- ▨ Territory recovered by Allies between July 18 and Aug 21, 1918

0 10 20 30 40
miles

Nieuport, Dunkirk, Dixmude, Bourbourg, Bergues, Roulers, Poperinghe, Ypres, Menin, St Omer, Hazebrouck, Bailleul, Tourcoing, Armentières, Roubaix, Lille, Lys, Lillers, Bethune, Lens, St. Amand, Tournai, Leuze, Soignies, Roeulx, Mons, St. Pol, Aubigny, Douai, Valenciennes, Binchey, Arras, Denain, Le Quesney, Maubeuge, Sambre, Doullens, Bapaume, Cambrai, Aulnoye, Avesnes, Chimay, Albert, Bohain, Fourmies, Amiens, Somme, Hirson, Peronne, Oise, Boves, Rosieres, Chaulnes, St. Quentin, Moreuil, Nesle, Ribemont, Liart, Ham, Roye, Breteuil, Montdidier, Chauny, Laon, Noyon, Chiry, Compiègne, Aisne, Aisne, Oise, Soissons, Bazancourt, Reims, Beaumont, Betz, Mareuil, Chatillon, Chateau Thierry, Dormans, Marne, Epernay, Juilly, Meaux, Charly, St. Denis, Montmirail, PARIS, Coulommiers

The Western Front. (George Anderson)

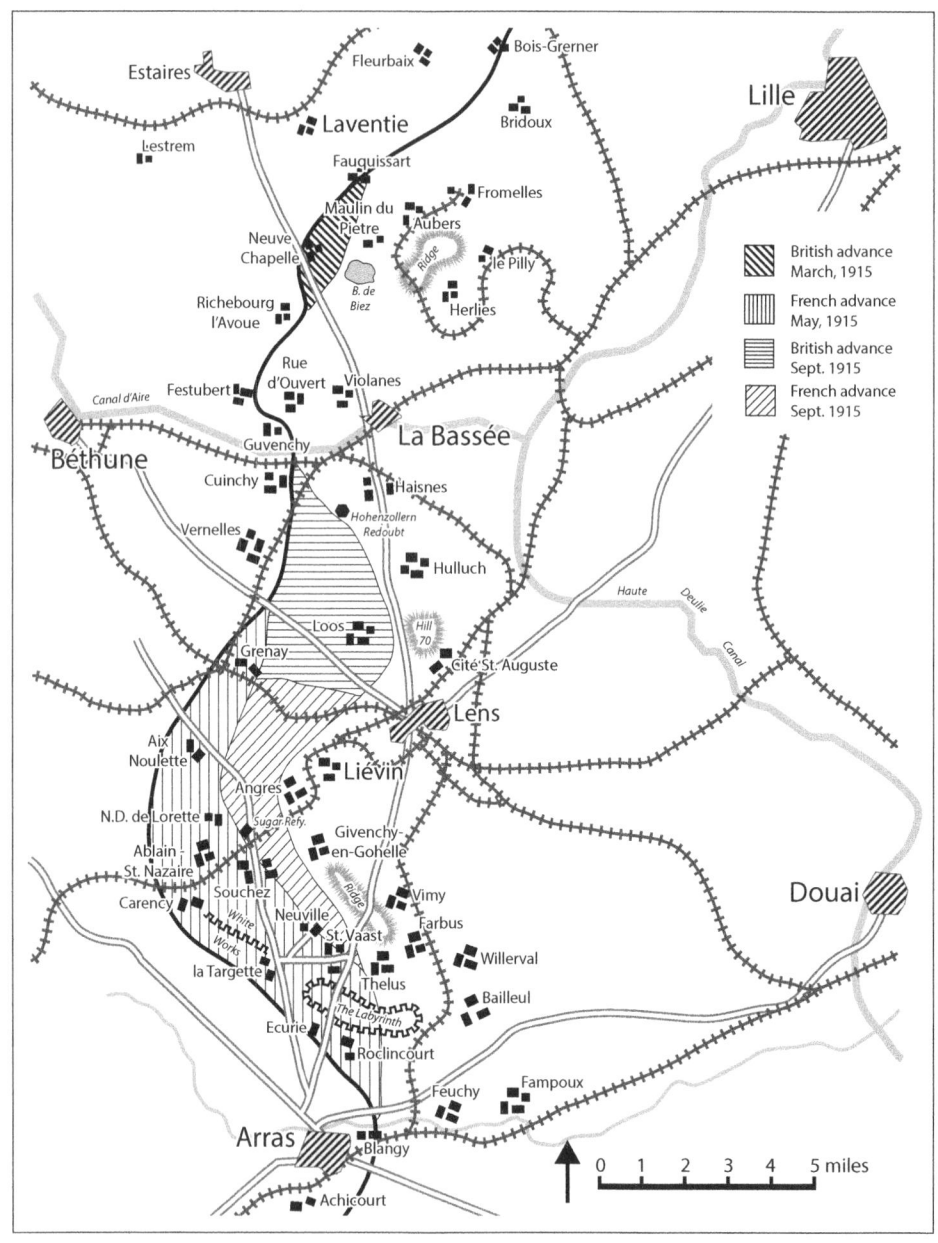

Campaign in Artois. (George Anderson)

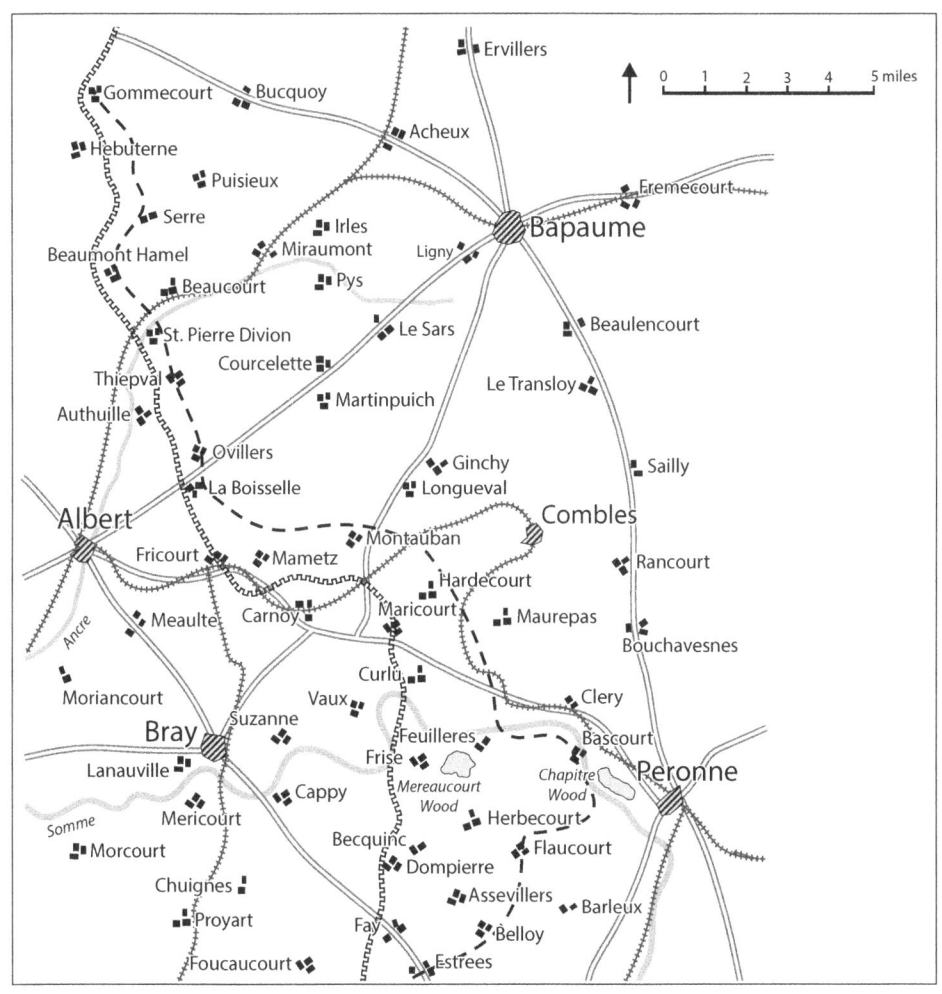

The Somme Battlefields – 1916. (George Anderson)

Introduction

The two untitled canvas-bound books lay around our family home in Hampton and Hampton Hill. I say lay around, this would be doing an extreme disservice to my mum, Winnie – Winifred Elizabeth Sadler – who fondly kept them along with four campaign medals in a special wee spot in her wardrobe; retained these keepsakes along with fond memories of her husband, my father, one James Sadler, whose name they had chosen I should bear on seeing first light of day in July 1947. Clearly, Mum, as I readily came to realise during my childhood, had been and still was deeply in love with Dad. She would do everything possible to nurture and raise my older sister Liz and I in his absence. I'd like to think she recognised the tremendous job she did prior to her passing in 2003.

Returning to the idea of being part of a fatherless family, I was very uncertain what this meant. As a very young boy, I soon became aware that we were somewhat different than the families of my schoolmates and friends. They all had fathers; Liz and I did not. What we had this was this wonderful person who happened to be our Mum; highly capable, talented and always ready to love or accept love in return. However, the wartime journals of my Father's military service were to be a vital link with a man I barely knew. Having passed away in late December 1951, it was some time before I fully comprehended what this loss meant to our family. Bit by bit, my mum pieced together what Dad had been like as a man and, on occasions, related his life experiences to children keen to know but unable to inquire. It was around this time that she introduced me to the canvas- bound journals and war medals.

The opening page of the first volume stated that what followed were the personal recollections of Sergeant J. Sadler MM: His Life and Adventures of the Great War from 13th August 1914 until 6th August 1916. The second covered his experiences from 7th August 1916 to autumn 1918. Initially, this detail meant very little to me but I soon came to realise that a great world war had occurred during the early part of the twentieth century. Dad had enlisted and fought through this conflict. Now, within my hands, I read of his experiences for the first time. It was a genuine link to a seminal period of his life; one which, at a later stage in my own life, I developed a deep interest in.

Mum pointed out that my father's medals had been awarded during the period of active service related in the journals. As our discussions turned to the "books", which I now refer to as his diaries, she stated that Dad expressed the wish that they might one day be published. The layout of the pages was such that he left, opposite each page, a page to be transcribed in his words and, if necessary, spelling and grammatical corrections if required. Dad was not, Mum observed, a literary man but she recognised that the considerable effort taken to record his wartime experiences deserved a larger audience.

Born in 1890, James hailed from what I consider to be a fairly ordinary family background; a late Victorian family in which respect, love and consideration were bywords. His father was employed as a reporter for a Swanage publisher; his grandfather had served the Thames community of Sonning as a lock Keeper and parish clerk. Dad was to spend the majority of his working life in horticulture and agriculture, an occupation to which my eldest son, Paul, is also devoted. Returning to the content of Dad's diaries and what I felt

29th March 1937: James marries Winifred Elizabeth Ashby
in All Saints Parish Church, Hampton, Middlesex.

should be done in regard to transcription; I made several abortive attempts until 2002. It was then that I began to formulate a suitable format; one which Dad would hopefully have approved of; one which would provide a unique but meaningful account of what was a very small part of the Great War experience.

Reading through the diaries, I soon became aware that Dad did not always record dates and locations relating to his time in France during 1915-18. These were important details that I surmised he would have wanted to include. Thus I made the decision to examine the relevant battalion (9th Royal Fusiliers) war diary housed in the National Archives. In doing so, I discovered things Dad had missed. At the same time, I decided that his personal account would stand unaltered, barring minor spelling and grammatical adjustments, to be juxtaposed alongside the Battalion diary. The latter, I subsequently realised, contained scant accounts when compared to men's personal experiences, but gave sufficient evidence of locations, combat and dull routine which is often ignored when recounting Tommy's experience during the First World War. Indeed, there were longish periods during which units spent in support and reserve. Dad's recollections tended to overlook time spent with working parties, training and practice. What follows, therefore, are first-hand accounts of Armentières, Loos, the Hohenzollern Redoubt, Somme, Arras, Kaiserschlacht and the Hundred Days.

I feel certain that if Dad and those he fought with and against could be granted one wish, it would be that the inhumanity they sometimes experienced would never happen again. Sadly it has and still does. Are we any the wiser for this and was it and is it worthwhile? Having been

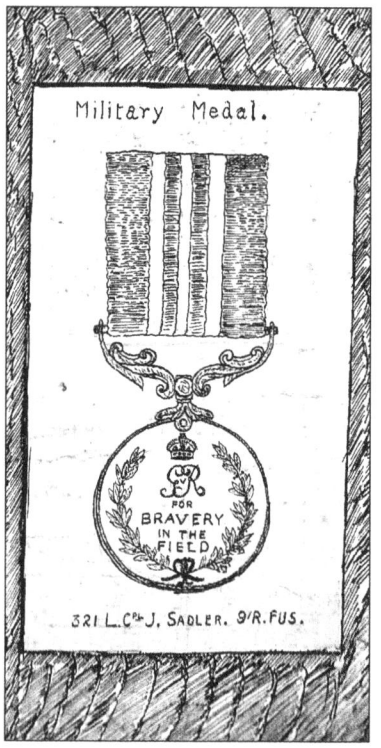

Sgt. James Sadler's drawing of the Royal Fusiliers crest which he uses at the opening of the first of his two handwritten books recounting his experiences in The Great War.

Royal Fusilier G321 L/Cpl. James Sadler's drawing of the Military Medal awarded following the Battalion's Action at Ovillers on The Somme, 7th July 1916.

blessed with the time and inclination to research my father's story and explore the battlefields of France and Flanders where he served, I feel that I have in some small way fulfilled a duty to Dad. Unable to share the experience, I feel certain his spirit was with me during subsequent travels. Indeed, I will never forget the moment I found the very place (Hardecourt aux Bois) where he was wounded in August 1918. His presence was certainly with me; how could it be otherwise?

Reflections on my first visit to Hardecourt aux Bois

I arrived carrying the memoires of my Dad,
Acting Sergeant. Major James Sadler MM.
9th Royal Fusiliers No. 321. 1914-1918
Injured at Hardecourt aux Bois: 28th August 1918. Died: 29th Dec. 1951 Aged 61.
As I leave, his son, James Sadler, 62 years old,
I leave carrying my memories of Hardecourt Aux Bois, knowing that my Dad
would have been pleased with all that I have had the privilege to see.
The land appears to smile now.

James Sadler's identity tag.

James Sadler's medal cluster.

We thank you for your generous hospitality and the
warm welcome which you have given us.
Our stay has been truly memorable.
Thank you so much.

I was here today
And the land smiled.
You who lie here
Did not die in vain

What you gave so many years ago
Blessed the soil
Where you now rest
And so long will the memory remain.

And so I thought on,
And so I thought long,
For what you gave
Your time, love and toil
Is locked here
You will be remembered.

Safer will be our journey
Fuller will be our lives
For you have given to us
A land which will forever smile.

For this sacrifice
We give our thanks

1

Start of the Journey, August 1914

From the place of his lodgings, 1 Brickingham Villas on the Hanworth Road in Hampton, Middlesex, on the evening of 8th August 1914, twenty-three-year-old James Sadler (born 4th September 1890 in Christchurch, Hampshire) set out on his bicycle – he never learnt to drive – to make the five mile or so journey to Hounslow Barracks. He was on a mission that would firmly determine not only his whereabouts for the next four years but, as for so many others, would change his outlook and more than likely, the course of his life forever. His was a similar journey that would be made by millions of other men from all different classes and walks of life. They would come from all over England, the U.K and all areas of the British Empire, united in one common aim; to fight for the freedom and the cause which they firmly believed in. Many did not return home, James Sadler was to be one of the fortunate ones who saw their commitment through until 1918 and who would live to be able to recount his thoughts and experiences which would forever accompany the decision he was about to make. He was heading off to Hounslow Barracks to enlist for King and Country.

James, the second of four children, left the family home in Swanage, Dorset. Leaving behind his father, Alfred Joseph, mother, Mary Elizabeth, two brothers Alfred J. and Harold Arthur and sister, Bertha Mary, "Dolly", and ventured to Hampton where he secured employment as a market gardener at a local nursery, a position he was to return to a few years hence.

Mobilisation was ordered on 5th August 1914. Two days later, on 6th August, Parliament sanctioned an increased Army strength of 500,000 men. Lord Kitchener, the newly appointed War Minister, also decided to raise a New Army of volunteers and issued his first call to arms. This was for 100,000 men aged 19 to 30, at least 1.6m (5'3") tall and with a chest size greater than 86cm (34 inches). All men interested in enlisting - unless they chose to enter the Territorial Force - could now enlist on "general service" terms, which meant full time service for three years or for the duration of the war, whichever was longer. Gardener James Sadler took notice:

1. WHY I ENLISTED IN 1914. First Attempt to Join – Night of Mobilisation. Second Attempt to Join – August 9th 1914. Third and Successful Attempt – August 13th 1914.

Why I enlisted into the Army on the starting of War was because I had always said to my fellow workers that, if it was Germany who started war on England then I would, at once, join up on the outbreak of war.

With that, my first attempt to join the Army was on the night of mobilisation when I called at Hounslow Barracks and offered my services for my country. Owing to the fact it was a very busy time, with the calling up of old Reservists, very little notice was taken of me. Anyhow, I received an offer that I could make myself comfortable on a bed of straw. I told the Recruiting Sergeant that I could very well

Mary and Alfred, the mother and father who awaited
the return of their son, James, in Swanage.

do without that as I only lived a mile or so away. The next day when doing my usual daily work, a chum of mine, being an old reservist, was called away to join his old Regiment, "The Royal Berkshire". With that he came over to wish me goodbye and after wishing him the same, I passed the remark that I would not be long in following him.

The cause of the mounting conflict which was to become known as the Great War of 1914-18, requires a volume in its own right but it can be concluded that James was well-aware of the background which led to Great Britain and its Empire to go to War. The declaration of war with Germany had been made on 4th August with the following announcement by Prime Minister Herbert Asquith;

Owing to the summary rejection by the German Government of the request made by His Majesty's Government for assurances that the neutrality of Belgium would be respected, His Majesty's Ambassador in Berlin has received his passport, and His Majesty's Government has declared to the German Government that a state of war exists between Great Britain and Germany as from 11pm on August 4th.

Committed to serving his country, James eagerly sought out what he considered the best course of action. Based on the next part of his recollections, he appeared a little unaware that it required little more than a signature and the minimum of preparation and training.

2. WHAT IS THE BEST REGIMENT? The Royal Fusiliers

The same day I took another trip to Hounslow to join the R.G.A. (Royal Garrison Artillery); I was told that I could only join the R.G.A. by doing seven years with the Colours and five on the Reserves. This did not suit me as I only wished to serve during the duration of the War, not expecting the War to last as long as it did.

With this answer regarding the R.G.A., I approached the recruiting sergeant and said, "What is the Best Regiment to join?" his answer being "The Royal Fusiliers". I, at once, decided to join and after going through the different stages to become a soldier, within a few days, I was selected for a draft to Dover, no doubt for reinforcements for the regular battalions already serving at the Front. That day I was allowed 24 hours leave before having to return to the Barracks at 9 o'clock on Monday morning. So pleased was I that I should soon be of assistance to the Army in France, I returned to the Barracks quite two hours before time.

All went well until I met some of the old soldiers who were on the same Draft as me. This finished up by us going to have a farewell drink and, with that, missing the Draft. Having not at that time being served out with uniform and there also being, at that time, a great rush to join the Army, my papers were put aside and could not be found when needed. With that being the case I became a free man once more.

James was not included in the draft scheduled for transit on the 10th August. And it does appear somewhat odd that he considered that he could be posted to France as a raw recruit:

My second attempt then to join the Army was on the 13th August, already being at the Barracks since the first date (9th August). This time all went well, I was passed fit and given a uniform and sent over to the huts on Hounslow Common where I spent the night. The next day we marched to the Railhead and took the train, not knowing at the time where we were going to finish up.

If provided with a uniform at this stage, he can be regarded as immensely fortunate; not only in the allocation thereof, but to discover that it was a good fit! Having enlisted, the next four years would be an experience bringing both highs and lows. Indeed, James was to participate in many battles and concurrent events that formed part of the broad spectrum of the Western Front. On both sides, boys became men. Thousands of men perished or returned unscathed or damaged in mind and body to return to a world that would never quite be the same again. James was to find that, despite enlisting, full of enthusiasm, for a task which it was widely considered would be over by Christmas 1914, he would be required to follow a course of training lasting up to six full months during which he would travel across Southern and South East England whilst learning the soldier's trade. All of this culminated with embarkation for France in April 1915. Far from reaching its anticipated conclusion in December of 1914, the conflict bogged down in position warfare. The Great War was entering the "Trench Warfare" Stage and it was during this time that James, in his newly acquired rank of No. G.321 Pte. Sadler of 'A' Company, 9th Battalion Royal Fusiliers found himself, along with thousands of other volunteers, in "Kitchener's Army".

2

Training: August 1914–May 1915

Where, in fact, the en-trained and newly enlisted soldier volunteers were heading for was Battalion training, which was initially to be at the Colchester Barracks in Essex. James now took up his place as part of the 9th Royal Fusiliers, formed as Battalion, on August 15th 1914. The draft to which he was attached was under the direct command of one Officer, (Lieutenant T. G. Cope) and with 100 O.R.'s (Other Ranks) they left the depot at Hounslow bound for Colchester in company with a similar draft under Lieutenant D. E. Estill. At Colchester they were to form the 8th and 9th Battalions Royal Fusiliers, respectively. It was here also that a Lieut. -Colonel J. C. Robertson was appointed as the first C.O., (Commanding Officer) of the 9th. Battalion. The Battalion was stationed in Sobraon Barracks before moved moving to Shorncliffe in Kent (October) and then on to Folkestone in December.

James picks up his story prior to departure from Hounslow:

3. COLCHESTER, SANDLING, FOLKESTONE. Will the War be Over?

Later that night we arrived at Colchester where two Battalions of Fusiliers were formed, these being the 8th and 9th Battalions, two of the first Battalions of Kitchener's Army.

After doing a few hard weeks of training we left for Sandling Camp, not a great distance off where we started getting our hands used to trench digging out.

After we had finished our turn at that we left for Folkestone where we were made very comfortable in private houses, the people making a great fuss of us.

For all of that; we may not have seemed very pleased at the time, our only wish being to get across to France. The remark being passed that "the War will be over before we get out there".

On leaving Folkestone we had the "pleasure" of our first trying march. This took us a week where we lived only on Bully Beef and biscuits.

Leaving Folkestone, we marched to Aldershot and on arriving there we were stationed in the married quarters at North Camp where we finished our training in the way of Divisional Training.

Final Brigade/Division training was undertaken at Aldershot from 20th February 1915. It was during this time that they were joined by cavalry, motor machine gun battery, sanitary and veterinary sections and, on the Brigade's "trying" long march from Folkestone to Aldershot, inspected by Lord Kitchener.

Stationed at Ramillies Barracks, training at Aldershot concerned with developing a real sense of pride in the battalion as a unit and its relationship with other units. Here the recruits of Kitchener's Army underwent basic training including rifle and bayonet drill and small unit tactics. However, there were times when the soldiers were to take matters into their own hands as they endeavoured to maintain a certain "standard of living"; something which they were most unlikely to experience once they had been posted to France.

To this end, Army discipline was occasionally overlooked, as Pte. Sadler explained in two related incidents:

4. ALDERSHOT. Getting into Mischief.

Whilst at these quarters we got to be experts at "taking" electric globes. (Electric light bulbs).

The married quarters were supplied with electric lights and when the globe was of no further use, another one had to be found.

At that time we didn't mind if it had to be taken from a Picture Palace, from the front of a Butcher's Shop or even from the front gate of the Detention Barracks. The last place mentioned was our last hope but the "globe" was usually "won "by us. It was taken with the assistance of two men, one stopping and talking to the Sentry, waiting until the Sentry was as far from the gate as possible, where the man would then strike a match so that it would not be noticed when the electric light went out. By this time, the other man would have the "globe" and be some distance off. Whilst stationed at North camp we also had a shilling stopped from our wages for damages done to a wooden and unused cook house; the wood taken from the Cookhouses being used to light our fires. Before we left for the Front only the tin roofs could be found lying on the ground.

Battalion training was nearing an end; service in France was fast approaching. James recorded his unit's final days at Aldershot as follows:

Finishing our training on 28th May 1915; after that date it was full marching orders only. Kit inspections took place and every man was checked to see that he was fit for active service. Just before leaving we were served with a little box of chocolate, this chocolate was to act as emergency rations to be eaten as a food or crushed and made into cocoa. On the last day of May, we paraded late in the afternoon to march to the railway siding where we were soon got onto the train and off to Folkestone. We arrived at Folkestone at 10 o'clock that night and were then marched on to the boat to start our journey to France.

The 9th Royal embarked for France on the "S.S. Victoria". Its strength at this stage was Officers:-30, O.R. (Other Ranks):- 925.

Battalion and Division Organisation

The 8th and 9th Battalions of the Royal Fusiliers were, along with the 7th Royal Sussex and 11th Middlesex Battalions to form the 36th Brigade part of the 12th (Eastern) Division in Kitchener's Army.

Under the administration of Eastern Command, the Division came into existence as a result of Army Order No. 324, issued on 21 August 1914, which authorised the formation of the six new Divisions of K1. All formed from volunteers. The 12th (Eastern) Division then comprised the following infantry brigades:

35th Brigade: 7th Battalion, The Norfolk Regiment; 7th Battalion, The Suffolk Regiment; 9th Battalion, The Essex Regiment; 5th Battalion, Princess Charlotte of Wales's (Royal Berkshire Regiment) ; 1st Battalion, The Cambridge Regiment.

36th Brigade: 8th Battalion, The Royal Fusiliers (City of London Regiment); 9th Battalion, The Royal Fusiliers (City of London Regiment); 7th Battalion, The Royal Sussex Regiment; 11th Battalion, (The Duke of Cambridge's Own) Middlesex Regiment.

37th Brigade: 6th Battalion, The Queen's Own (Royal West Surrey Regiment); 6th Battalion, The Buffs (East Kent Regiment); 7th Battalion, The East Surrey Regiment; 6th Battalion, The Queen's Own (Royal West Kent Regiment).

Pioneers: 12th Battalion, The Northamptonshire Regiment.

Note: A more detailed indication of the structure of the Troops within the British Army and of the position of G321 Pte. James Sadler at this stage can be found in Appendix 1.

3

May to July 1915 – Off to France and the Trenches

On 31st May 1915 the 9th Royal Fusiliers embarked on their long anticipated journey to France. Months of position warfare awaited them but, in truth, there was little real knowledge amongst the so called "Other Ranks" as to where exactly where they would be deployed or what they had to face. This was, truly, to be an adventure for the majority of the men, most of whom had probably travelled little, if at all, outside of England thus far. These men were the first battalions of Kitchener's Army whose impending arrival had long been awaited by the BEF (British Expeditionary Force). Their fighting ability would be under the close scrutiny of surviving veterans who had been set the initial task of halting the Germans in 1914. At this point, as they journeyed from Aldershot to France, the Battalion's diarist commenced to record their experience until disbandment in 1919:

Battalion War Diary:

31st May 1915 ALDERSHOT.
6.40pm.: H.Q. left Aldershot with 2 Companys (Coys). Transport left 10. 05am. 30/5/15 for Southampton. 6.55pm.: 2 Coys. left Aldershot. (H.Q. and the 4 Coys were to travel to France via Folkestone).

1st June 1915 BOULOGNE
12.25am Arrived Boulogne. Under canvas at Ostrohove Camp.

Sadler account:

5. BOULOGNE Light Refreshments on the Journey.
On this journey we found our little blue box of chocolate, which we had been issued with, very acceptable and when we had finished the journey, there were not very many of them left. They came in very useful when crossing the Channel to prevent hunger setting in.
   Arriving at Boulogne at 11.45 we fell in to march to the Rest Camp, passing through the City at 12.15 by the Cathedral clock.
Arriving at the Rest Camp we were ordered into tents to rest for the night.

Battalion War Diary:

2nd June 1915. BOULOGNE.
1 30 pm: Joined train from AUURE containing transport. Arrived with Unit Complete at ARQUES. 4 45am: By road to billets at WIZERNES.

Sadler account:

5. BOULOGNE. (cont.) Marching and entraining. First impressions.

The next morning we were again served out with Iron Rations, this time Bully Beef and biscuits also a tin containing tea and sugar, which soldiers know so well. These are very acceptable when no other food can be had. This time we were warned that it would be a Service Crime if eaten without orders.

Once this had been done we marched around the City with our Band, the French people turning out in large numbers to witness the sight. We were one of the first three of Kitchener's Divisions to arrive in France.

After this there were many French girls at our Camp to greet us and because of this we started to learn little bits of the French language.

Nothing very excitable happened on our first day in France. After getting warned that Zeppelins were on the road, the order came to "fall-in".

After parading again we were marched to the Station to go further up towards the Line. Lying around in the station for about six hours getting very cold, led many to thinking of just what we would like to do to "Old Fritz".

At last our Train arrived, Fire Engines and many Saloons, Goods Vans and Horse Boxes.

After we were counted into parties of 40 we were allowed to enter our Saloon. Many had to stand throughout the journey and it did not need much straw to keep us from shaking about.

After we had been stopping and starting for a few hours we, at last, arrived at Arques near St.Omer; here being told not to mention anything about our train ride in our letters home.

Battalion War Diary:

3rd June 1915.WIZERNES.

Route March. Training in use of respirators.

4th.June 1915.WIZERNES.

Training in rapid loading, use of respirators.

5th June 1915.WIZERNES – HAZERBOUCK

Left WIZERNES 6 55am. Arrived HAZERBOUCK bivouacked. Many men fell out as the marching was irregular owing to the cutting of the column at level-crossings while trains passed. The men had trained all winter and found that the heat, the extra load and the pavé (French for pavement) were trying.

6th June 1915

Left HAZERBOUCK 6 25am. Arrived La BECQUE 1 00pm. Close billeted in farms. Marching much improved.

Sadler Account:

6. ST. OMER. Our Terrible Marches.

Staying in a Paper Factory at Wizernes, near St.Omer, for two days, 3rd and 4th June, enabled us to pick up a little French from the workmen at the factory and on June 5th. we started marching towards the Line, spending two nights at different Farms on the road. We had two terrible marches to do over the rough cobbled roads of France with Full Marching Order and carrying blankets etc. Also with the terrible heat it was simply killing. We arrived at our resting-place, the outhouses of a Farm, in the afternoon, dying for a drink. No water was to be found but for a large pond a distance off. We spent a short time bathing and refreshing ourselves. Afterwards we watched one of our Officers shooting at fish in the pond. The next day we set off on our march again, towards night finishing up at another Farm, this time within shell range from The Front.The only thing which happened here was a German Shell came over and cut down one of the trees near our Farm. This was the first one any of us in the Battalion had seen burst. The next day we set off for La Becque on our way to Armentières, stopping there a day or so, before preparing for our first trip to the Trenches.

Battalion War Diary:

7th, 8th and 9th June1915
Billeted at La BECQUE.

10th June 1915.
Left La BECQUE. Arrived La Chappelle d' Armentières – 9 20am. Billeted.

Attached to 81st .Brigade for instruction in Trench Warfare. 2 30pm: Officers lectured by GOC of 81 st. Battalion. 3 30pm: Officers of "A" and "B" Companys and Machine Gun Officers shown round the Trenches. 8 30pm: "A" and "B" Companys entered the Trenches and were attached to 2nd Gloucester Regiment and 1st Royal Scots respectively for twenty four hours. H.Q. attached to 1st. Royal Scots.

11th June 1915.
"C" and "D" Companys instructed in parading for Trench duty and on taking over trenches etc. 8.45 pm. "C" and "D" Companys paraded for 24 hours duty in Trenches, taking place of "A" and "B" Companys. 9th. R.F.'s Military Transport Officer, Signalling Officer and Machine Gun Officer instructed under corresponding Officers of 2nd GLOUCESTERS.

Sadler Account:

1. Armentières. 1st Trip to the Trenches.

After spending our first night here, a very remarkable day followed. This day was spent having various Orders read out to us and also being warned not to stand around in groups owing to the place being shelled at various times. We had different Crimes and Sentences read out to us, starting with "so and so" who had been shot for leaving his Post. Someone else had had a certain punishment for missing the parade at The Trenches. We began to wonder what was going to happen next, or

James's handwritten account of his Battalion's 1st Visit to the Trenches: June 1915.

if they considered that we were out there for the good of our health. At dark on this night we paraded for our first trip to The Trenches, "Standing To" for a good time again having Orders read out to us about making noises whilst on the road to The Trench. We were ordered not to talk or whisper or make any noise of any sort. At last we marched away by Platoons to the Trenches. On the road we passed several Platoons of Jocks, Scottish Relieving Troops who naturally shouted out, "What Lot?" When another lot of Jocks passed us the same thing happened, "What Lot?" again not a whisper from us until the remark was passed, "It must be the Deaf and Dumb lot!" On arriving at The Front Line Trenches we found we were quite alright. Germans somewhere but some distance off.

8. Armentières. 1st Trip to the Trenches.

These Trenches were called The Daily Mail Trenches and were used as a proper rest camp for tired Troops.

Here we had the past news of the War knocked into us and we quite agreed that the men holding The Trenches had had a terrible time since the outbreak of the War. The men here were from the 2nd Gloucester Regiment and they had been out at the Front since the beginning of The War. The things that most took our fancy were the German Verey Lights which they sent up occasionally. Of course we could not make out why fireworks were being used to light the place up for a great distance; our eyes could not be kept off of these "Star" lights. One or two little things happened on our first day such as a bag of grass being thrown into the Trenches on top of us. This making us think, at that time of day, that we had enemy visitors arriving. Afterwards we found out that our men had been out cutting grass from the front of our Trench, collecting it in sand bags so that the Verey "Star" Lights would not catch it on fire due to the weather being so dry. On our first day in The Trenches there was no action to report on our front and so after a rifle inspection and after wishing our new comrades the best of luck; we left for Armentières once more. This time we stayed in a much-knocked about part of the town and we could not keep our eyes off the houses that had been so damaged.

Battalion War Diary:

12th June 1915
9 00 am. "A" and "B" Companys instructed in Trench Duties etc. Officers and NCO's lectured on Gas Precautions.

13th June 1915.
8.45 pm. "A" and "B" Companys went into trenches for 24 hours.

14th June 1915.
9.00 am. "C" and "D" Companys lectured on Trench duties etc. Officers and NCO's lectured on Gas Precautions.

Sadler Account:

Having spent the night at this village, the next day we set off for our second visit to The Trenches, 13th June, this time at a different part but not far from our first visit. This time our comrades were from the 1st Royal Scots.

9. Armentières. Two Shells and "Stand To".
Having got quite used to Verey Lights and other items, all went well until around midnight when the Germans sent over two shells. This was a very unusual occurrence at this time of night at these Trenches. The Order was passed along to "Stand To" but after a little while, with nothing more happening, the Order came along to "Stand Down". The next morning, the Germans started shelling the village at the rear. This again took our fancy with the noise of the shell travelling through the air and, on bursting, sending a cloud of red dust and smoke very high into the sky. We soon found out that we were able to tell when shells were coming. With little much of importance happening we left for the village again knowing, we thought, quite enough to now be able to take Trenches on our own. Next day, 15th June, we left to take over a certain part of the British Front, doing another short march and including rifle inspection, kit inspection etc. ... On arrival, nothing of great excitement happened only that late one night, rapid fire from rifles was heard at the Front Line. With that alarm we had to parade, full marching order, at the

Alarm post.

When we started to march away, the firing died away and we were not required.

Battalion War Diary:

15th June 1915.

"A" and "B" Companys lectured on Trench duties. 3 30pm Battalion marched out. Arrived La BECQUE 7 05pm.

16th to 24th June 1915. La BECQUE.

Battalion exercised in marching, musketry, bomb throwing etc. Officers reconnoitred PLOEGSTEERT WOOD.

25th June 1915.

Left La BECQUE arrived ROMARIN 9 15pm. Billeted. Machine Gunners attached to 11th Middlesex for duty in the Trenches.

26th June 1915. ROMARIN.

Officers reconnoitred trenches in Le BIZET area.

27th June 1915. Le BIZET – GRAND RABECQUE

9.30 pm. "D" Company took over Trench 95, Le BIZET area. Battalion left ROMARIN 8.15 pm, arrived GRAND RABECQUE Farm 9.15pm. Telephone communication established with "D" Company. Bomb proof shelter constructed at DESPIERRE Farm for Battalion HQ.

Sadler Account:

10. PLOEGSTEERT. Very Close to the Germans.

On the following Sunday 27th we were "told off", (ordered/commanded), for working parties which all soldiers were to become so well acquainted with. Myself, I was "told off" for repairing an old farmhouse which was to be used for Battalion Headquarters. So I spent the Sunday doing a little sandbagging and only getting troubled occasionally by stray bullets from the German Front Line.

Battalion War Diary:

28th June 1915. Le BIZET

8.45 pm. Battalion HQ moved to DESPIERRE Farm. 9.15 pm. "C" Company took over MONMOUTH HOUSE and Trenches 1, 2, 3, & 4, subsequently renumbered 96,97,98 and 99, from 6th Queens Regiment. 9.45 pm. "B" Company took over Trenches 5 & 6, subsequently renumbered 100 & 101, from Queens Regt. and Support Trenches near OBSERVATION FARM from same Regt. 1 Platoon of "A" Company took over supporting point "7 TREES" from Irish Fusiliers and 1 platoon, Support Trench of No. 95, then vacant. 2 Platoons and reserve Machine Gunners remained at GRAND RABECQUE Farm.

29th June 1915.Le BIZET Area

2.30 am. "D" Company holding FORT of No. 95 Trench came under heavy fire and lost 1 Officer and 3 men. (Casualties: 1 Officer & 3 men killed, 3 wounded). 3.30 pm. GRAND RABECQUE Farm, ESSEX HQ Farm and GUNNER Farm were shelled. Enemy snipers very active. One was killed in a tree by Lt. E.H.Knott, Sniping Officer. 6.15 pm. Burial Party near ESSEX HQ Farm. Shelled by Enemy 8.15 pm. No casualties.

30th June 1915. Le BIZET Area

Sniping prevalent. Much work was done to make trenches safe throughout. (1 man wounded). 10 00 pm. Intelligence Officer, under orders of Colonel, arrested 3 men in ESTAMINET A LA DEMI LUNE under suspicion of being spies. Court set up by AMP (Army Military Police) of 12th (Eastern) Div.

1st July 1915. Le BIZET Area

Defences of MONMOUTH HOUSE improved. German corpses found whilst digging. German sniper brought down from trees opposite No. 100 Trench by Corporal Dade. Enemy machine gun located.

2nd July 1915. Le BIZET Area

Enemy Machine Guns were exceptionally active. Opposite No. 100 Trench an old man with grey beard and also a man wearing a British Khaki Jacket were seen in Enemy Trenches. Sniping by enemy – not so active. A good way of subduing sniping is found to be to take 1 or 2 Machine Guns away behind the trenches and to sweep lots of trees and sniper houses in enemy lines.

3rd July 1915. Le BIZET Area

3.30 am. Enemy Trench and Crater opposite FORT bombarded by our Trench Howitzers. Damage done to parapet, wire and a snipers post in crater. 8.15. am. No. 95 trench bombarded by enemy's artillery – (1hr). 9.30 am. Nos 90-101 trenches bombarded by enemy artillery – (1hr). Our Artillery replied late owing to bad communication with Batteries as R.A., (Royal Artillery), telephones being moved at the time. 6. 00pm. Battalion relieved by 11th Middlesex Regiment. Battalion marched by Platoons to PLOEGSTEERT – ARMENTIERS ROAD thence, by Company, to OOSTHOVE FARM.

Sadler account:

10. PLOEGSTEERT. (cont.) Very Close to the Germans.

On the 28th June we took over our new Trenches this time at "Plug Street", (Ploegsteert).

These Trenches were altogether different to the other two Trenches that we had visited.

At this part of the Line, the Trenches were very close together; at some parts being only a few yards from the German Trenches. Certain parts of these Trenches were made into very strong Forts that held machine guns.

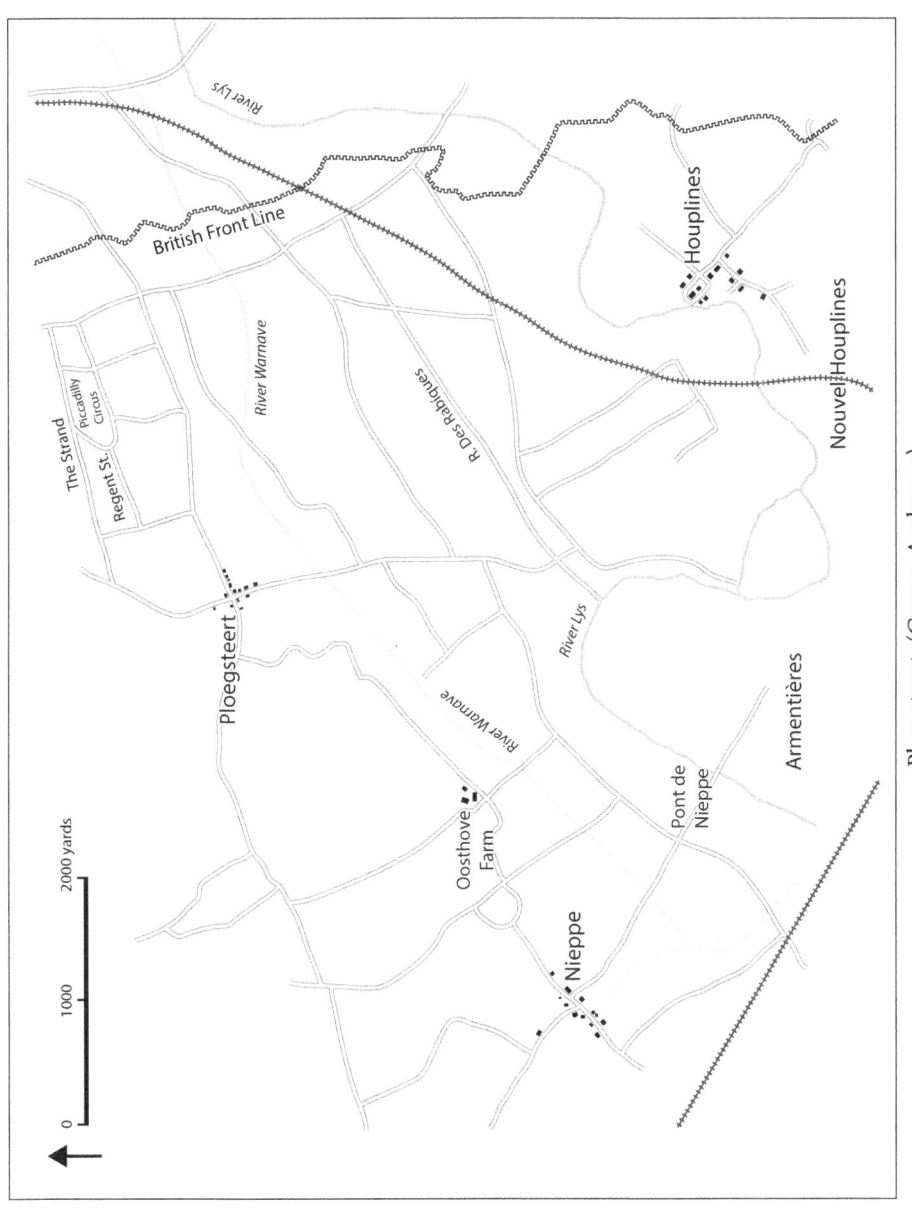

Ploegsteert. (George Anderson)

Ploegsteert Wood.

>   At these Trenches one had to be very careful of German snipers. As soon as
> anyone's head was seen above the Trench in daylight, a bullet was awaiting it.
> At these Trenches we got our first casualties.

these as mentioned in the Battalion's Diary on 29th June.

11. PLOEGSTEERT. Playing a game on Fritz.

Owing to one or two "games" which we managed to play on the Germans, we
made them pay for our casualties. On about the second day at these Trenches we
planned to work the following game. Being close enough to throw tins of our Bully
Beef into the German Trenches and, with them having got to like Bully Beef very
much, we planned to throw over our empty tins made into bombs. The bombs we
used to make up in our spare time, as there were not many "up to date" bombs
about at this stage. The "good news" would soon spread along the German Lines,
far enough to get a little crowd to wait for this "dainty". The Germans clearly did
not know that we used such things to make bombs with and they got really taken
in. I expect they took a great dislike to our Bully Beef afterwards. With our "clever"
bombers we were able to repay his "clever" snipers for our casualties. After doing
our time here we again left for a little village at the rear. (Oosthove Farm).

Having spent their first extended period in the front line trenches, 9th Royal Fusiliers
had sustained the loss of comrades and, more than likely, began to appreciate the task for
which they had enlisted was not going to be an easy one.

4

July to September 1915 – Armentières: Life in the Front Line and on Reserve leading up to the Battle of Loos

Faced with an extended stay in the trenches about Armentières , 9th Royal Fusiliers had certain duties to perform in what could be termed as routine trench warfare. The nature of the defences and the work which it was required to do is recalled by James over the next few pages of his diary. So many days were spent on working parties and so many in reserve at Armentières or Chapelle d'Armentières.

Sadler Account:

12. TRENCHES NEAR TO ARMENTIÈRES. "Stand To".

The Trenches we were in were called "Breast-work" Trenches, built from the ground upwards owing to so much water being around and the low-lying country.

The Trenches were built with sandbags and strongly built up in front with soil.

With thousands of sandbags, the Trenches were kept in good repair and with Trench Boards laid down they were made very comfortable.

At these Trenches there were little shelters or dugouts which, although not strong enough to stop a bullet, were very comfortable as it was normally very quiet at that time of day.

The work in the Trenches was carried out in the following way.

I will, so as to help my readers to understand, describe the work from "Stand To" on one day to "Stand To" the following day. "Stand To" is the early hours of the morning, one hour before daybreak, when every man has to be woken up and has to take his position in case of a sudden attack from the Enemy. At this time of the War, this was the time selected by the Germans to attack and they also frequently carried out attacks at dusk in the evening. The sentry who was on duty at "Stand To" had to keep a sharp lookout as everyone else is ready to be called at a moment's notice.

13. TRENCHES NEAR TO ARMENTIÈRES. "Stand Down". Rifle Inspection. Breakfast. Work and Dinner.

When light enough, the Order is passed along to "Stand Down". An Officer must send this and the Officer's name must be sent with the message. At "Stand Down" and now, with the light of day, only two sentries were needed. Rifle inspection is also taking place at "Stand Down". After this inspection comes breakfast but with little rest to be had as the Trenches had to be got perfectly clean by 9 o'clock. All match stems and fag ends had to be collected up and the Trench Boards dusted with sandbags so as to keep too many flies from collecting. The flies were a great trouble to us in warm weather. Breakfast was a very easy meal to prepare only having a small piece of bacon to fry and a canteen of tea to make. With two or three sharing with each other, this meal was soon prepared. Next came inspection of the Trenches by the Company Officer and if it was not perfectly clean- Look Out!! 9 o'clock having arrived work starts. All men, except the two sentry groups, start work, doing repairs to the Front Line and, at that time, the Support Lines as well. Jobs also included making a shell-proof dug-out for Company H.Q. and also there were carrying parties' etc … This type of work was carried on until 12 or 12.30 when it was time for Dinner.

TRENCHES NEAR TO ARMENTIÈRES. Dinner. Rest. Tea. "Stand To".
Dinner was the hardest meal of the day to prepare, especially if dainties, (sweets/cakes), were included.

If, in the afternoon, men were able to get time off to rest, more time could be spent in getting Dinner ready; including the "dainties"

Our Dinners were a piece of Beef, fresh at this stage of the War, or nearly always so. This used to be fried in the lid of our canteen. Then we were supplied with potatoes which we made into chips and fried in the fat from the meat. If we were unable to get fat from the Beef, our small supply of butter was used. To make the "dainties", which I mentioned, if time allowed, these were made with our hard Army biscuits soaked in water for some time. These were then warmed up and our small supply of jam was used to sweeten this. When finished this was called "French Pudding" After Dinner, the men who had been working in the morning were, if lucky, able to get a little rest. Next came Teatime. Getting Tea ready was very simple, as there was only tea to be made with the other "dainties" being bread, jam and cheese. If short of bread, it was a case of dipping the hard biscuits into water and toasting them in front of a fire where, if possible, we were able to get them as nearly soft as bread. After Tea and before "Stand To", another rifle inspection took place.

14. TRENCHES NEAR TO ARMENTIÈRES. Myself- A Company Barbed Wirer
As soon as "Stand To", arrived more sentries were "told off", (Ordered or Commanded), for duty. As more sentries were needed at night, other men would be "told off" for different working parties such as for the repairing of the front of the Trenches. By the cover of darkness, also, grass-cutting parties were told off for cutting the grass in front of the Trenches and Barbed wire parties were formed. Barbed wire was used so that the enemy could be noticed if trying to advance and the Company's Barbed Wiring Party would get out to start repairing or putting up fresh wire.

I was one of the Company's barbed wirers in these Trenches, only doing one hours work in the morning and then taking charge of the wiring party at night. At this stage of the war I was still a Private in the Ranks.

As soon as it was dark or moonlight, the wiring party would be called together and told to collect up Iron or Wooden stakes and rolls of wire ready to go into "No-Man's Land", No Man's Land being the strip of ground which ran between Our Front

Line and the German Front Line. This area was of little use to either side. It was a very dreary place to work in. On getting our stakes and wire out to the position for work we would commence by knocking in the stakes. There were not the Screw Stakes available, which were to be found later in France as the War went on.

16. TRENCHES NEAR ARMENTIÈRES. Knocking in Stakes noiselessly and Running Wire Along.

In No- Man's-Land, anyone working there had to get the stakes knocked in without letting the Germans know, otherwise they made things very unpleasant for us. They would start sniping, judging where we were by the sound of the knocking or they would send out a strong Patrol to "cheer" us up. Another thing that the Germans would do is, on hearing the knocking, they would, at daylight; look for the fresh work and the next night would have a fixed rifle set on that position. On starting work the following night we might then be greeted with a supply of bullets or machine gun fire. The knocking in of the stakes or poles therefore had to be done quietly. Placing several sandbags on top of the stakes to deaden the sound usually resulted in us doing this quite easily. Both stakes and pickets were driven in this way and then came the running along of the wire which also had to be done without making a sound. This was achieved by two men wearing leather gloves and using Pick handles which were slipped through the wooden frames of the rolls of barbed wire.

Slowly the wire was unrolled, as needed; using the leather gloves. Then there was the French Concertina wire which would also be used. With this being very springy, it would mean that one was able to put up a good wire entanglement.

17. TRENCHES NEAR ARMENTIÈRES. Different Things. Picking the Best Party

If one is fresh to the "game" of putting barbed wire up, it can be very trying because, in such a dreary place as No Man's Land, anyone is likely to imagine many different things.

One can imagine seeing things which do not exist, as I have known when I have been in charge of wiring parties which have been supplied with new men. More than once I have heard men call out to "look out, something ahead" and to then have found out afterwards that they were quite correct but that it was nothing dangerous, only a large weed standing higher than the other weeds. A new "hand" to the job, by doing this, may stop the party's work for some time and also give other new "hands" a real fright. I have known men to keep their eyes fixed on a standing object such as a high weed or a wooden or iron stake and, with the tricks which the dreariness of No Man's Land played on them, it appearing to them to walk and get closer towards them. With these one or two things mentioned, anyone should see that a party of handpicked men was best for this job. The following are different things I used to be careful of when wiring. When I was leading a large party on the job of wiring, I would "tell off" one man to keep close to us with our rifles so that it was possible to have them handed to us at a moment's notice. It was not possible to get on very quickly with rifles slung across the back.

18. TRENCHES NEAR ARMENTIÈRES. Laying Still When Sounds Are Heard,

Sometimes we had to stop work because of movements, heard in the grass, which no doubt would have been a German Patrol. These Patrols would crawl out as far as possible in the long grass but, on coming into contact with the shorter grass and on noticing a large wiring party, they thought it advisable to get away instead of causing too much excitement. The next night we would have to be careful in case the Front was swept with machine gun bullets. I have known times, at the place which I am writing about , when we have had to lay down, rifles up to our shoulders, safety catches forward, ready to fire at the first moving object and then to have had Rats running over our backs. There was no chance of knocking them off because of the movement which that would have caused. Another thing which makes it hard for a wiring party is when we have our own Patrols cruising about in No Man's Land, One has to wait until the Patrol is close enough to challenge. There was always an anxious time waiting to know if it was one of ours or a German Patrol. I did not consider that it paid to let a German Patrol get too close with his Trench Dagger, unless one had his rifle up to his shoulder, with finger on trigger, ready for any rush that might be made by the Enemy..

19. TRENCHES NEAR ARMENTIÈRES German Games.

There were different "games" which the Germans carried on with to get our Sentries to fire and which would then lay them open to the German snipers who were waiting to carry out their game of "life-snatching". At these Trenches there was a fair amount of rifle firing done. A very old game of the Germans was to wave a spade above their parapet so as to cause our sentry to fire. Whilst the sentry was getting ready to fire a "clever" German sniper from another direction would be waiting for his chance to kill. If our sentry missed the shovel, or if he hit but the German did not hear his own sniper, he would wave the spade to signal a washout, thus causing the sentry to fire again. Owing to us being told much about these German snipers and about how we should change our position after each shot was fired, we made this game of "life-snatching" very hard for the German snipers. Another "game" of the Germans was to carry on work in front of his Trench during daytime. Usually one of them would be digging a trench which would be deep enough to cover a body at night-time. He would work all day at that. All that it was possible for us to see was the German's arms, his spade and the soil. This used to draw our fire because, if we hit a German arm, we knew that he would be put out of action.

20. TRENCHES NEAR ARMENTIÈRES. Catching a German Working Party.

Being a very hard target to hit, whilst we were firing at this, we had to be very careful of their snipers.

At this stage of the War, shells were not plentiful enough to stop the Germans from working. However on one day, looking over our Trench, I noticed moving objects passing through a square, cut low in the parapet of the German Trench. I reported this to my Platoon Officer and this was in turn reported to the Staff Officer.

The next night a machine gun and a team of ours went out into No-Man's Land, setting their guns at close quarters, On them hearing much moaning, and from the cries of the wounded Germans who had been caught by the machine gun fire, we knew that much damage had been done. The hole in their parapet was soon closed up and no use made of it again. We had managed to get our own back at this "game".

Battalion War Diary:

16th to 21st July HOUPLINES – In the Trenches at Houplines.

16th July 1915. HOUPLINES.
Night quiet except "listening" Patrol shelled in front of No. 83 Trench. Work of improving defences line commenced. Work for improvement of Trenches commenced. (1 man slightly wounded).

17th July 1915. HOUPLINES.
Night quiet, heavy rain. Patrol from No. 81 Trench reached German Wire and encountered enemy working party. Patrol from No. 82 Trench reconnoitred ditch 200 yards in front of trench running diagonally towards Germans. It was found to be 5ft. deep and unwired. Patrol from No. 93 Trench reached German wire but encountered no enemy. 5 shells dropped round No. 82 Trench. (No casualties).

18th July 1915. HOUPLINES.
2nd Lt. Tantram and L.Cpl. Stagg reached German wire at 12 30 midday. They took a description of German wire and brought in samples. Height 3ft. 3 strands. Top one -3 ply barbed wire, 2nd- entanglements and 3rd- a trip wire. Enemy snipers active. Our machine gunners caused damage to enemy working party whose work was laid on by daylight and fired on by night. Several pigeons crossed the lines from Germans to Armentières. A relief apparently took place in the German trenches. (1 killed 3 wounded).

19th July 1915. HOUPLINES.
No enemy patrols encountered during night. Machine Guns in No. 83 silenced enemy Machine Gun. 6 00 am: Enemy shelled HOUPLINES, 100 shells, killing 1 civilian. They were trying to find our anti-aircraft guns which had seen enemy action earlier and then changed position. We loathe our Anti-Aircraft Guns though enemy aircraft was brought down.

20th July 1915. HOUPLINES.
Enemy rifle battery caused annoyance to No. 83 Trench during the night. Patrols reported a large working party of Enemy opposite No.81. Our machine Guns cleared Decker House of snipers at 2 00am who had been a nuisance on previous day. Our machine Guns fired on opening in enemy trench opposite No.80. Shrieks and Oaths were heard by 6th Northumberland Fusiliers which are said to prove that the M.Gun fire had the desired result. (1 Wounded).

21st July 1915. HOUPLINES.
A/65 Howitzer Battery shelled enemy working party 2 30 pm. 3 30pm: enemy replied with 5 Whiz Bangs which caused no damage. 7 30 pm: Battalion relieved

by 11th Middlesex. Battalion moved into 11th Middlesex billets in Armentières. H.Q. at 66 Rue de Quesnoy. Draft of 46 new and 4 old men arrived from England. Strength of Battalion now: – 1034 O.R.'s. (Other Ranks) and 28 Officers.

22nd to 27th July ARMENTIÈRES– In reserve & daily working parties.

22nd July 1915. ARMENTIÈRES.
9.15 pm. Working Party 180 men employed improving line under R.E. (Royal Engineers)

23rd July 1915. ARMENTIÈRES.
9.15pm. Working Parties: – 6 Officers. 310 men. 7.00 pm. Billets shelled. Shells used were old French 4.7 Shells from Lille. (3 men slightly wounded).

24th July 1915. ARMENTIÈRES.
5 Officers, 420 men employed as working parties. Billets shelled 7.00 pm. Working Party shelled at 3.30pm. (3 men wounded).

25th July 1915. ARMENTIÈRES.
Working Parties: – 7 Officers, 426 men. (1 slightly wounded).

26th July 1915. ARMENTIÈRES.
Working Parties: – 8 Officers, 382 men.

27th July 1915. ARMENTIÈRES.
6.30 pm. Battalion again took over original Trenches from 11th Middlesex. B Company shelled whilst going up Communication Trenches. Relief completed 7.45 pm. (1 Sergeant killed).

28th July to 2nd August. HOUPLINES: In the Trenches at Houplines

28th July 1915. HOUPLINES.
Enemy fairly quiet but sniping more active than previous occasion. Hostile aeroplanes active at dawn. Work of making parapets irregular was undertaken. The wire was inspected. (3 wounded).

29th July 1915. HOUPLINES.
5 00 am.: Enemy aeroplane came over HOUPLINES and our anti-aircraft guns came into action in village. 8.30 am. : 30x 10.5cm High Explosive Shells were fired at and around Battalion HQ. wounding 3 men in yard. During night from 28th to 29th enemy sniper was observed in long grass opposite No.83 Trench. 6.30 pm.: German working party was observed near 3 DECKER HOUSE. A/62 was notified and party shelled with Shrapnel. Enemy retaliated with 2 Field Gun Shells on our Trenches without result. (3 wounded). Our love for our anti-aircraft guns has not increased.

30th July 1915. HOUPLINES.
3.30 am. Mountain Guns, Trench Howitzers and Catapults from No. 79 Trench and machine guns from No.'s 78, 79, 80 & 81 Trenches opened fire on enemy parapet doing considerable damage. Enemy retaliated 8 00am with a few shells.

31st July 1915. HOUPLINES.
4.00 am.: Enemy fired 12 "Whiz Bangs" from Field Guns searching our Trenches along 300 yards of Front. 5.45 pm.: Enemy shelled No. 83 Trench. 6.30 pm -7 00pm.: Enemy shelled Le RUAGE with heavy shells. Snipers very active. Our Artillery demolished 4 HALLOTS FARM and shelled 3 DECKER FARM and other points. Heavy firing at enemy aeroplanes which were directing heavy gun fire and trying to locate our Batteries. (2 slightly wounded).

1st August 1915. HOUPLINES.
6.30 pm. While under the heavy shell fire of the 31/07/15, Privates H.G.Hatch and R.Wood showed great gallantry in attending to casualties of the 7th Royal Sussex Regt. The action of these men on being brought to the notice of the Brigadier General, elicited the following message:-

"The Brigadier General is much pleased to hear of the conduct of No.3923 Pte. H.G.Hatch and No. 1218 Pte. R Wood of the Bn. under your command on the 31st July and considers the action taken by them is highly creditable to themselves and in accordance with the best traditions of the Regt. to which they belong."

Patrols from each Trench were very busy; one party remaining out for 17 hours. Reports brought in "that Enemy working parties were utilizing Metal Posts for their wire entanglements". These working parties ceased work at 8 00 am. Much talking and whistling in Enemy Front Line. Enemy Artillery quiet.

2nd August 1915. HOUPLINES. Armentières.
6 00 am. Enemy exceptionally quiet. Bank Holiday. This fact communicated to us by the Germans opposite. Battalion relieved by the 11th Middlesex Regiment at 8 45 pm and marched to Billets of the 11th Middlesex Regt. at ARMENTIÈRES. Strength of Battalion:- 28 Officers, 1028 Other Ranks. (1 man slightly wounded).

3rd August to 8th August Armentières. In reserve & daily working parties

3rd August 1915. Armentières.
Working parties of 5 Officers and 230 men detailed for trench works under R.E.'s.

4th August 1915. Armentières.
10 Officers and 534 men employed as working parties under R.E.'s. 8 45 pm.: Capt. & Adjt. Hugh Lee Pattinson unfortunately killed by either a hostile sniper or a laid rifle while supervising. (1 Officer killed).

5th August 1915. Armentières.
Working Parties of 7 Officers and 320 men on Trench work. Funeral of Capt. & Adjt. H.L.Pattinson at Cite Bonjeau Cemetery. ARMENTIÈRES. 7.30 pm. The enemy

threw one High Explosive into "A" Company's Billet at RUE SOLFERINO killing 4 men and wounding 5. (4 Other ranks killed, 5 wounded).

6th August 1915. Armentières.
Working Parties found of 7 Officers and 322 Men. Trench Work.

7th August 1915. Armentières.
2 Officers and 72 men as Working Parties. Capt. M.E.Coxhead appointed Adjutant on 5th August 1915.

8th August 1915. Armentières-HOUPLINES.
10 00 am. Memorial Service for the late Capt. & Adjt. H.L. Pattinson. Bn. took over original Trenches at HOUPLINES from 11th Middlesex Regt. at 8 45 pm. Relief completed without mishap.

9th August to 14th August. HOUPLINES. In the Trenches at Houplines.

9th August 1915. HOUPLINES.
3.20 am.: The German Artillery was more active than usual, about 500 shells, 7.7 and 10.5 and minenweifer were thrown at Trench No.85 some of which fell round Trench No.84. Their guns also played on the R.E. screens erected on the RUE CARNOT. Very little damage was done considering the quantity of ammunition expended. A/62 retaliated with effect. Our patrols report enemy working in small parties at their parapets and wires. (3 Other Ranks wounded).

10th August 1915.HOUPLINES.
Enemy quiet. Patrols saw hostile working parties of nine men but failed to get within bombing distance. A few Whiz Bangs were exchanged. (1 Killed 1 Wounded).

11th August 1915. HOUPLINES.
Enemy exceptionally quiet. At 4.30 pm. A German aeroplane flew over our line and dropped 4 red smoke balls. 6 30 pm.: A British Aeroplane was seen to attack a hostile aeroplane which fell behind the German lines. 7. 50 pm.: A Bi-plane of ours was observed to bring down a German monoplane.

12th August 1915. HOUPLINES.
Though enemy snipers were active, the Germans were very quiet but during the day were generous with their Whiz Bangs. 9 00pm.: Lieutenant T. B. Jones and a patrol under him visited the enemy's wire entanglement and brought back cuttings; report of no hostile working parties- our own could be heard a considerable distance away. The enemy's entanglements have been vastly strengthened. (1 killed).

13th August 1915. HOUPLINES.
9.30 pm: A test SOS signal having given to our Artillery resulted in a shell lodging in enemy's Trenches, 58 seconds after. About 200 yds. in front of Trench No.82 the Germans had erected a large notice board 4ftx3ft on which was painted

WARSCHAU GEFALLEN and on its reverse side an Iron Cross. It was attached to a rod of twisted iron and wired to the ground. Our patrol brought the trophy to our trenches and it was put up with the Iron Cross towards the German Trenches. 9.30 am: At 9.30 am. Ten enemy Whiz Bangs fell harmlessly on PONT BALLOT ROAD and during the day several were thrown at HOUPLINES. No casualties.

14th August 1915. HOUPLINES.
Enemy quiet during the night. Hostile Artillery extravagant, practically no damage done though the amount of shells was large. 8 30 pm: Bn. relieved from the Trenches by 11th Middlesex Regt. at 8.30 pm. Battalion moved into Billets at ARMENTIÈRES. Satisfactorily completed about 11 00 pm. (2 wounded).

Sadler Account:

21. TRENCHES NEAR ARMENTIÈRES. "Warsaw has Fallen". Ten Small German Battleships Sunk.
Over this time the Germans would sometimes stand a large notice board up in a very dangerous part and would put different messages on it. One such message was "Warsaw has fallen", which was to be a memorable event at this stage of the War. For us it became a case that this German Board had to be taken. Next day they found their board standing on our Trench. A plucky Officer in my Platoon at this time and some hand-picked bombers saw to it that we soon captured the board after it had been put up. Just after the "Warsaw had fallen" event, a small victory happened at sea when our brave sailor boys sank ten small German warships. With having this good news read out to us in the Front Line Trenches, it was decided to get our own back on Old Fritz. That day, a nicely arranged Board was made and as luck would have it, it turned out to be a very misty night. The Officer and his party set out with this board and owing to the mist they were able to stand it up very near to the German barbed wire, the board was left for that night, the party returned, all work was stopped in front of our trenches and then we greeted Old Fritz with the sound of rapid fire and much shouting and rejoicing over the good news. Hopefully this gave the Germans a terrible fright.At daylight the next morning all eyes were fixed on the Board to see that nothing had happened to it. It was the coming night where the fun was set to hopefully really come off. As soon as dusk fell, the Bombing Party set off to lay and wait for Old Fritz to come and move the Board. After spending many hours lying in the grass, the board had to be brought back in with no luck, as the Germans, no doubt, knew that something awaited them. We also played a similar game with a Flag and lay in waiting but the Germans would have nothing to do with it.

22. TRENCHES NEAR ARMENTIÈRES. German Whiz Bangs.
Different sorts of shells were used at this part of the War, the first being the German "Whiz Bangs" which all infantry got to know so well. Not a large shell but very high velocity. As soon as the report of one of these is heard, the shell has reached its destination and burst. Because of that, it gave very little time to take cover and was a very uncomfortable shell to come in contact with when out in the open. The shell

is not so dangerous when anyone is in a trench but it was very much safer if one was in a dug trench and not a breastwork trench.

With the breastwork trench the shell was likely to penetrate through the parapet. This type of shell was used a great deal for the shelling of communication trenches and nearly always carried on in the way of enfilading purposes. By having this sort of gun in certain positions it was possible for the Germans to send shells straight to the bottom of the trench. This made it very dangerous for the infantry. This type of shell was used, very often, in the trenches that I am writing about in order for the Enemy to try and find our snipers.

23. TRENCHES NEAR ARMENTIÈRES. Our Sniper and German Trench Mortars.

Our snipers were positioned in an old house in the rear of our front line. Here snipers posts were made in the roof and our best snipers posted in them. I must say that it took the Germans sometime to find them; particularly one clever sniper who I got to know. Each night when it was too dark to do anymore sniping, this sniper used to come to the front line to stop for the night and my first words to him were generally "How many rounds have you fired today?" Sometimes he would answer "not many, only one or two rounds". Five rounds would generally last this man a week and, being in the roof of this old house, he was able to look right down in the German front and second lines. It was very seldom that the man which he fired at had time to think of the effect of their "Whiz Bangs". At last the Germans guessed that this old house was the only place that the bullets could be coming from; these having, no doubt, cost many German lives. When the Germans did start searching and found the old house it got rather a warm time from "Whiz Bang" shells. Small trench mortars were used by the Germans at this part of the line but, being very small and not reliable all of the time; they were not very dangerous. It was possible for us, at this time of the war in these trenches, to count anything from ten to twenty before an enemy trench mortar would explode. On hearing the gun fired in the German lines, all eyes were at once set looking towards the skies as it was possible to see the shells coming through the air. We then had time to go right or left in order to avoid them.

24. TRENCHES NEAR ARMENTIÈRES. Shelling the German Trenches at this time of the War.

I must say that both the British and German trench mortars eventually turned out to be a dreadful weapon of war for the infantry. I shall speak more about the larger trench mortars later. Along with these two weapons that I have just mentioned, there were also one or two rifle grenades but, with us being quite 300 yards from the Germans, they nearly always burst short in front of our trench. A few words about our own shells. As I have said we did not have enough shells at this time of the war to stop the German working parties. I do not mean to say, by that, that we never had guns behind us because we did; but from what I could see, they were always silent. One day, one of our artillery Officers came to our trench to have a look around and, up to this time, we had really experienced very little excitement as a result of the Artillery. We passed the remark to the Officer, "When are we going over to see what was in Fritz's line?" With that he said that we have not got the shells to make small attacks .The shells had to be kept in case the Germans opened a bombardment then we would have some shells to repay him with. But for all that, the Germans received some very hot times from us on some days.

Battalion War Diary:

15th August to 20th August. Armentières – In reserve & daily working parties.

15th August 1915. ARMENTIÈRES.
8 00 am: Thunderstorms and heavy rain. 4 00 pm: About 30 shells 7.7 were thrown into NOUVEL HOUPLINES.

16th August 1915. ARMENTIÈRES.
Instructions in Wire entanglements carried out. Working Parties of 6 Officers and 350 men attached to R.E. for trench work. More thunder and rain.

17th August 1915. ARMENTIÈRES.
Working parties of 5 Officers and 406 men supplied to RE for Trench work. Thunder and heavy rains.

18th August 1915. ARMENTIÈRES.
3 00 pm: 30 Incendiary Shells, 6 inch, fell in NOUVE HOUPLINES and several 7.7's. A factory and 2 or 3 small cottages caught fire. Working parties of 6 Officers and 296 men engaged on Trench work with RE.

19th August 1915. ARMENTIÈRES.
10 00 am: Several incendiary shells were thrown in HOUPLINES but very little damage done.

20th August 1915. ARMENTIÈRES. HOUPLINES
8 45pm. The Battalion took over original trenches, No's. 81-84, at HOUPLINES from 11th Middlesex Regt. at 8 45 pm. Relief completed by 11 00 pm. The 13th Bn. Royal Fusiliers were attached to us for instruction in Trench Duties in 24 hour reliefs.

21st to 27th August HOUPLINES. In the Trenches at Houplines.

21th August 1915. HOUPLINES
6 00 are: Enemy very quiet opposite Trenches No's. 81-84., there being no sound of hostile Transports nor of any machine guns or Snipers firing worth mentioning. Our patrol report that the enemy were not at work outside their parapets. Our rifle batteries and machine guns fired at intervals on roads used by the enemy. Our snipers are busy worrying Germans at work. On target, causing a cessation of work at some points. Orders arrive during the evening to make all preparations in case of a move to BATTLEFIELD REPORT CENTRE during the night. Everything prepared by 10 00 pm. but night passes quietly. Draft of 40 men arrive from the Base for the Battalion but we attach them for discipline to the 11th Middlesex Regt. pending our relief from

the Trenches.

22nd August 1915. HOUPLINES

1 00 am: Enemy again quiet. One of our patrols at 1 00 am encountered a hostile patrol opposite Trench No.83, bombed it and caused it to retire. Telephone wires laid to cellars in view of possible bombardment. Hostile machine guns active at dusk. A few enemy's Whiz bangs fell harmlessly on POINT BALLOT RD. But no damage was done. Lieutenant. Col. J.C.Robertson struck off strength. Returned to England 20/07/15. (1 other rank wounded).

23rd August 1915. HOUPLINES

Enemy quiet. Thick mist. Our patrols communicated the news of the German Naval loss to the enemy by means of notice board placed against their wire entanglements during the night.

24th August 1915. HOUPLINES

Another quiet day. We cleared a passage through the garden wall of No.22 RUE FAIDHERBE opposite our Headquarters thus opening up a quick means of communication to Brigade Battle Report Centre; suitable cellars were also located in view of possible bombardment.

25th August 1915. HOUPLINES

Enemy were quiet around our Trenches No's. 81-84, but their Artillery was fairly active, several shells being thrown at HOUPLINES. A new and complete circuit of D5 Signal wire has now been laid from Headquarters to Companies in Trenches- this line has been buried where necessary. (One civilian killed).

26th August 1915. HOUPLINES

Enemy quiet. Hostile Artillery threw the allotted amount of shells near us. We acquired the nose cap of one, which proved to be of American manufacture. 8 00 pm.: The Battalion was relieved from the Trenches by the 11th Middlesex Regt. at 8 00 pm. Original billets at Armentières were taken over by us. All satisfactorily completed at 11 00pm. (One killed).

27th August to 1st September ARMENTIÈRES In reserve & daily working parties.

27th August 1915.ARMENTIÈRES

Working Parties of 61 men supplied to RE's for Trench work. Several shells were thrown on ARMENTIÈRES, but little damage done.

28th August 1915. ARMENTIÈRES

Working Parties of 5 Officers and 480 men supplied to RE's for trench work. A list of efficiency of communication having been arranged, Headquarters proceeded to Battalion Battle Report Centre and opened up communication with Brigade Battle Report Centre- Result satisfactory.

29th August 1915. ARMENTIÈRES
6 Officers and 470 men as working parties were supplied to the R.E.'s for Trench Work.
A dozen shells fell on ARMENTIÈRES during the day but no damage was done.

30th August 1915. ARMENTIÈRES
Working Parties of 6 Officers and 460 men attached to R.E.'s for Trench Work. A
further test carried out proved the efficiency of new Field Telephonic communications.

31st August 1915. ARMENTIÈRES
Working Parties of 3 Officers and 278 men supplied to RE's for Trench Work.
ARMENTIÈRES shelled as usual.

1st September 1915. ARMENTIÈRES-HOUPLINES.
8 30 pm. Battalion took over original Trenches at HOUPLINES at 8 30pm. relieving
the 11th Middlesex Regiment. Relief safely completed at 10:30 pm.

Sadler account:

25. TRENCHES NEAR ARMENTIÈRES. My 1st Crime in the Army.
At different times we used to get visited by a Mounted Indian Battery which used
to blow the German Front Line about very much. After they had done their damage
they would leave this part for another and with this "trick" it used to make the
Germans think that we had a few guns capable of being fired. Whilst doing our turn,
or one turn at this part of the line, I succeeded in getting my first "Crime" in the Army.
My Crime Sheet was headed with a very good headline, this being, "Leaving my
Post without a pass and having Water Tins in my possession after they had been
called in". My actions I put down to a man trying to be a soldier but, in the Army, a
Charge like this, appeared to be more like authority trying to torment a good soldier.
My case was dismissed but here are a few words about my case. One morning,
my Platoon Sergeant owing to getting a very small supply of water for his Platoon
during what was a spell of very hot weather, asked me, in front of my Platoon
Officer, if I knew of any place where water was to be found. As I had noticed a
pump by the Old House just behind our Front Line; I replied, "Yes". A water can was
handed to me and I went off on the journey, filled the can and returned. That was
my first journey and it was quite successful. After tea the same day the Sergeant
asked me to get two cans and this time I was supplied with a man to help.

26. TRENCHES NEAR ARMENTIÈRES. My case dismissed.
Again the journey to the Pump went well but, whist we were returning, I was
stopped by my Company Sergeant Major at that time and asked what I was doing
with the water cans. I was told to attend Company Orders in the morning, which I
did. Company Orders that day were held at the Front Line.My "Crime" was read out
to me and I was then asked as to what I had to say. I answered that I had received
Orders from my Platoon Sergeant, which I had to obey. I was then asked where I got
the water from and, on giving my answer, the Company Sergeant Major then asked
if it was possible to do the journey under cover to which I replied "Yes", and that

part of the case was dismissed. With regard to the other part that is, Leaving My Post, this did not require much looking into as being one of the Company's Barbed Wirers I held no post at daytime. The comment was made at these Company Orders about men being brought up for Orders having to do so many hours in front of the Trench, I personally thought that this would have been a change to having the pleasure of doing two hours inside the Trench at that time of day. The "gallant" Company Sergeant who put me on Company orders later handed in the "Crown" and became a Transport Sergeant which meant not having to go into the Trenches and, later, this Officer was sent back to Blighty as a "Trench Worn" N.C.O.

Battalion War Diary:

2nd to 7th September HOUPLINES- In the Trenches at Houplines.

2nd September 1915. HOUPLINES.
Enemy quiet. A few shells were thrown in HOUPLINES by the Germans. (One man wounded).

3rd September 1915. HOUPLINES.
Enemy very quiet. A patrol of ours went over to the German wires and threw 6 bombs in their fire trench but only 4 shots were sent in reply. Usual quantity of shells were thrown in HOUPLINES by the enemy, no damage. Heavy rain all day.

4th September 1915. HOUPLINES.
Enemy quiet. Patrols were sent out at 9 00pm. and after cutting first line of German wire, they threw 10 bombs over enemy's parapet and caused much confusion but evoked no reply. At 11 00 am. Snipers from Trench No.83 fired on a hostile working party. The enemy immediately replied with 2 shells on our parapet. Hostile Artillery was very active many shells being thrown in HOUPLINES and ARMENTIÈRES; but our Artillery effectively replied at the ratio of 6 to 1. (No casualties). (Major Pope O.C.- 'A' Company left to take up duties as Brigade Major to the 6th Division).

5th September 1915. HOUPLINES.
During the night Hostile Machine Guns were very active. About 20 shells were thrown on HOUPLINES. No damage was done. (1 Other Rank killed).

6th September 1915. HOUPLINES.
Enemy very quiet. The few civilians still in HOUPLINES ordered to evacuate the town by the 7th inst.

7th September 1915. HOUPLINES – Armentières.
A bombing patrol was sent out from Trench No. 82at 9 00pm. and threw 10 bombs effectively in German Trench opposite – on throwing another 4 into their Trenches, the only reply evoked was "English Pigs". The Battalion was relieved from the Trenches at 7 00 pm. and proceeded to original billets at ARMENTIÈRES. Relief satisfactorily completed by 10 00 pm.

Sadler Account:

27. ARMENTIÈRES. Meals and Sleep.

When doing our turn out of the Trenches at this part of the British Front we were billeted in a School at Armentières which was a little change from the Trenches as we got our food cooked for us or, might I say, it was tried to be cooked. It was always the same old thing; Fresh meat put into cold water and boiled.

Getting tired of this; in the end, it was only wasted. We found that our little bit of frying was best when done in the Trenches but in the later part of the War, when the Cooks went away on Courses to learn how to cook, things got better. Whilst at this School it was far more comfortable when having a sleep and, if one was lucky, by lying on the floor with his "Great Coat" and a blanket, a soldier could manage to sleep very well.

But here as well as everywhere else there was much work to be done and little rest to be had. Our work was very much the same as when in the Trenches- Carrying Parties, Rifle Inspection and Kit Inspections etc. At this time there were no cleaning buttons and equipment but one had to shave and get the mud of his clothes.

Here he went on to relate the tragic loss of two brothers:

28. ARMENTIÈRES. Two Brothers killed.

There were several guard duties to be done. One Guard was stationed at the gate of the School and two more on the Bridges in the Town. On one occasion, the Guard Post positioned at the School Gate witnessed the loss of life of two brothers; one a Corporal, the other a Private. As they were both on different Guard duties, the Corporal at the School Gate and his brother, at one of the Bridges, planned to get together which they managed to achieve. It finished up with both of them being on the same Guard at the School where the guardroom was under the cover of a roof where the children played in peacetime.

All went well until about seven o'clock that night when over came a large German shell striking a little shed in the playground. This was not far from where I was standing and near the Main Gate, and it killed or wounded all of the Guard except a Sentry from the Guard who was doing his hour on duty outside of the gate.

This was the first Shell which we had witnessed doing such terrible damage and it was a very sad evening spent thinking about these two poor brothers killed by the same shell.

We soon got the wounded away with the aid of shutters from shop windows nearby.

Although close to where the shell struck the building, I only got a hit on the knee with a piece of flying brick and a small cut over the right eye but I was fit for work later that same night.

29. ARMENTIÈRES. Germans shelling the Town.

If the Town was shelled at any time, we had our cellars to go to, being supplied with a pick and shovel in case the falling bricks blocked the entrance up, but the cellars were only really needed on one occasion although we were thinking, one day, that we were in for a warm time.

When I was returning from a working party one afternoon, the Germans started shelling a certain part with inflammable shells catching a great number of houses on fire. If the houses had been empty it wouldn't have mattered so much but the civilians were still in the houses. It was a pitiful sight to see the women carrying little children in their arms and crying with fright but we soon managed to get them all in to places of safety.

This was the first time when I had walked down a Street with all the houses on fire. So great was the heat that I had to cover my face and hands up but one had to walk down the Street to get to the School.

We were allowed to go to view the town by getting a pass signed by the Company Officer which was no trouble at all if one could manage the time.

Shops were still in working order and it was a very interesting place and one was able to learn much French as the French girls made themselves very much at home with us.

So we spent three months in all of very little excitement, doing our last turn before leaving for the Loos Battle.

Battalion War Diary:

8th to 13th September ARMENTIÈRES – In reserve & daily working parties.

8th September 1915. ARMENTIÈRES.
Owing to lack of cellar accommodation, Headquarters were moved to No.68 Rue de Jesuits. HOUPLINES and ARMENTIÈRES were shelled by the enemy; comparatively little damage done.

9th September 1915. ARMENTIÈRES.
Working Parties of 4 Officers and 454 men supplied to RE's for Trench Work.

10th September 1915. ARMENTIÈRES.
Working Parties of 6 Officers and 406 men supplied to RE's for work in Trenches. ARMENTIÈRES was heavily shelled by the enemy but little damage was done. No casualties. Hostile aeroplanes have shown increased activity during the last two days.

11th September 1915. ARMENTIÈRES.
4 Officers and 313 men were attached to RE's for trench work. The enemy threw a few 5.9 shells in ARMENTIÈRES.

12th September 1915. ARMENTIÈRES.
Working Parties of 5 Officers and 418 men supplied to RE's for trench work. This morning one of our Biplanes shot down a German Albatross machine which was busy photographing our Trenches. The German Machine was trying to regain its own lines when it was fired at by a party of 50 K.R.R.'s (King's Royal Regiment) who were marching along the road. The German pilot and Observer were both shot dead and

the machine fell on the road near our Div. HQ's – this was scarcely damaged.

13th September 1915. ARMENTIÈRES.
The Battalion relieved the 11th Middlesex Regiment at HOUPLINES at 6 30 pm.
Relief satisfactorily completed at 8 45 pm.

14th to 19th September HOUPLINES – In the Trenches at Houplines.

14th September 1915. HOUPLINES.
Enemy very quiet. Nothing to Report. Good work in Trenches and at HQ's.

15th September 1915. HOUPLINES.
Enemy quiet. A few Whiz Bangs were thrown but little damage done. A German
prisoner was captured in our lines of Left Sector. This man gave us much valuable
information.

16th September 1915. HOUPLINES.
Enemy quiet. Patrols report no enemy working parties.

17th September 1915. HOUPLINES.
Enemy still quiet. Two bombing patrols reached German wire 150 yds. apart, opposite
Trench No.82. Each party threw 8 bombs in and around their parapet. Much scuttling
was heard but no response was elicited beyond that of a Sentry who fired 2 rounds high.

18th September 1915. HOUPLINES.
The enemy sent 6 shrapnel shells at the junction of Trenches No's. 80 & 81 without
causing any damage and 12 Whiz Bangs at No. 83. Same result. At 10 00pm. we fired
Rifle grenades effectively at German Fire Trench opposite Trench No. 83, otherwise
it was quiet on our Front.

19th September 1915. HOUPLINES.-Armentières
A hostile sniper in a tree was fired on. His rifle was seen to fall and no further movement
could be discerned. Although our Artillery was very active, the enemy did not reply
during the day. The Battalion was relieved in the trenches by the 11th Middlesex
Regt, at 7 00 pm and original Billets at ARMENTIÈRES taken over satisfactorily
by 9 00 pm.

20th to 24th September ARMENTIÈRES – In reserve & daily working parties.

20th September 1915. ARMENTIÈRES.
Programme of work arranged. Route March in for early morning of 5 to 6 miles. One
Company to undertake each morning. Working Parties at night.

21th September 1915. ARMENTIÈRES.
Enemy feebly reply to our Artillery. This fact was conspicuous owing to this being the
first hostile shelling for 3 days; no damage done.

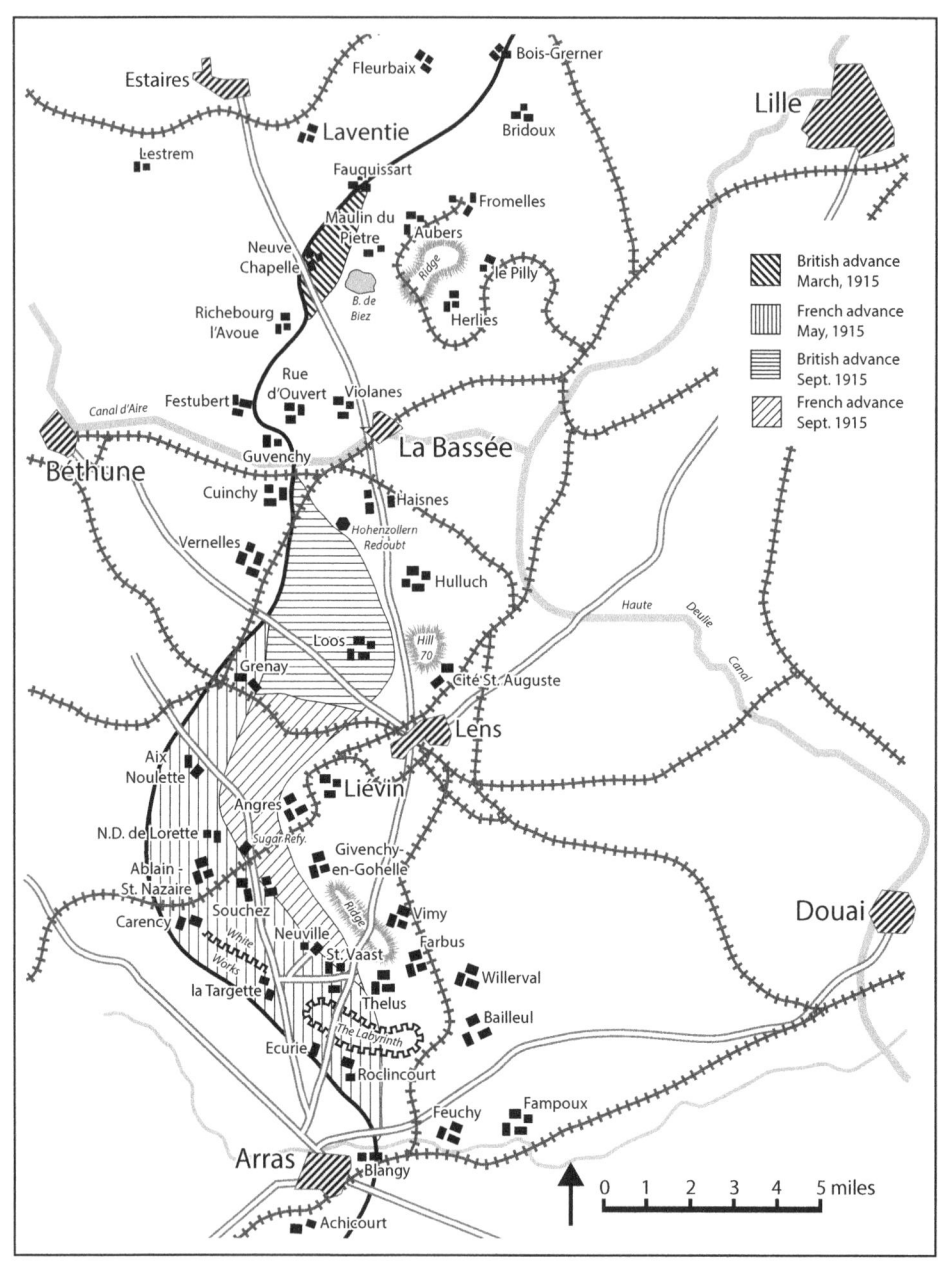

The Artois area of North East France, 1915-16. (George Anderson)

22th September 1915. ARMENTIÈRES.
Bomb throwing practice all day. All is quiet.

23th September 1915. ARMENTIÈRES.
Heavy Thunderstorm. Battalion employed in carting straw to Trenches.

24th September 1915. ARMENTIÈRES.
Tremendous bombardment further South. Continuous all day. General attack arranged by the French to take place 4 45am on 25th inst. Battalion standing to Arms in Billets- fully rationed.

To the south in Artois, the Battle of Loos (25 September-14 October) opened the following day ...

5

September and October 1915: The Battle of Loos

Now, less than four months after their arrival in France, 321 Private James Sadler and his comrades of 9th Royal Fusiliers prepared for their part in the ensuing Battle of Loos, part of the major Anglo-French offensive for 1915. The French intended to strike around Vimy and Champagne, whilst the BEF attacked at Loos and vicinity. The attack commenced on 25th September; the bombardment and ensuing infantry assault were accompanied by the first use of poison gas by the BEF. The 9th Royal Fusiliers received warning orders on 26th September; marching to Bailleul the following day as a preliminary to their first major battle. Part of 12th (Eastern) Division – a formation of "K1" or Kitchener's "First Hundred Thousand", they formed part of XI Corps.

The XI Corps (GOC Lieutenant General Richard Haking) was the sole reserve of General Sir Douglas Haig's First Army. Controversy would ensue following BEF C-and-C Sir John French's decision to retain Haking's Corps under his direct command during the offensive. The resultant muddle and tragedy subsequently led to Sir Douglas Haig superseding French in December 1915.

Battalion War Diary:

25th September 1915 ARMENTIÈRES.
4 45 am. Heavy Bombardment further South. Also our Artillery very active. Straw burned all along our parapet; proving successful. News arrives continuously all day. All news good except a setback for 2nd. Division. Few Shells thrown into ARMENTIÈRES and HOUPLINES.

26th September 1915 ARMENTIÈRES.
Received Orders. Battalion is moving into reserve at 1 00 pm. tomorrow. Several Shells thrown into ARMENTIÈRES and HOUPLINES. No casualties.

27th September 1915 ARMENTIÈRES–BAILLEUL.
At 1 00pm. The Battalion left their Billets at ARMENTIÈRESand marched to BAILLEUL arriving at 4 30pm. All were billeted in a very large School. (No one fell out).

Sadler Account:

30. ARMENTIÈRES. Leaving for Loos.
Two nights before we left Armentières, a large carrying party was "told off" for carrying large bundles of straw to the Front line. We could not make out why so

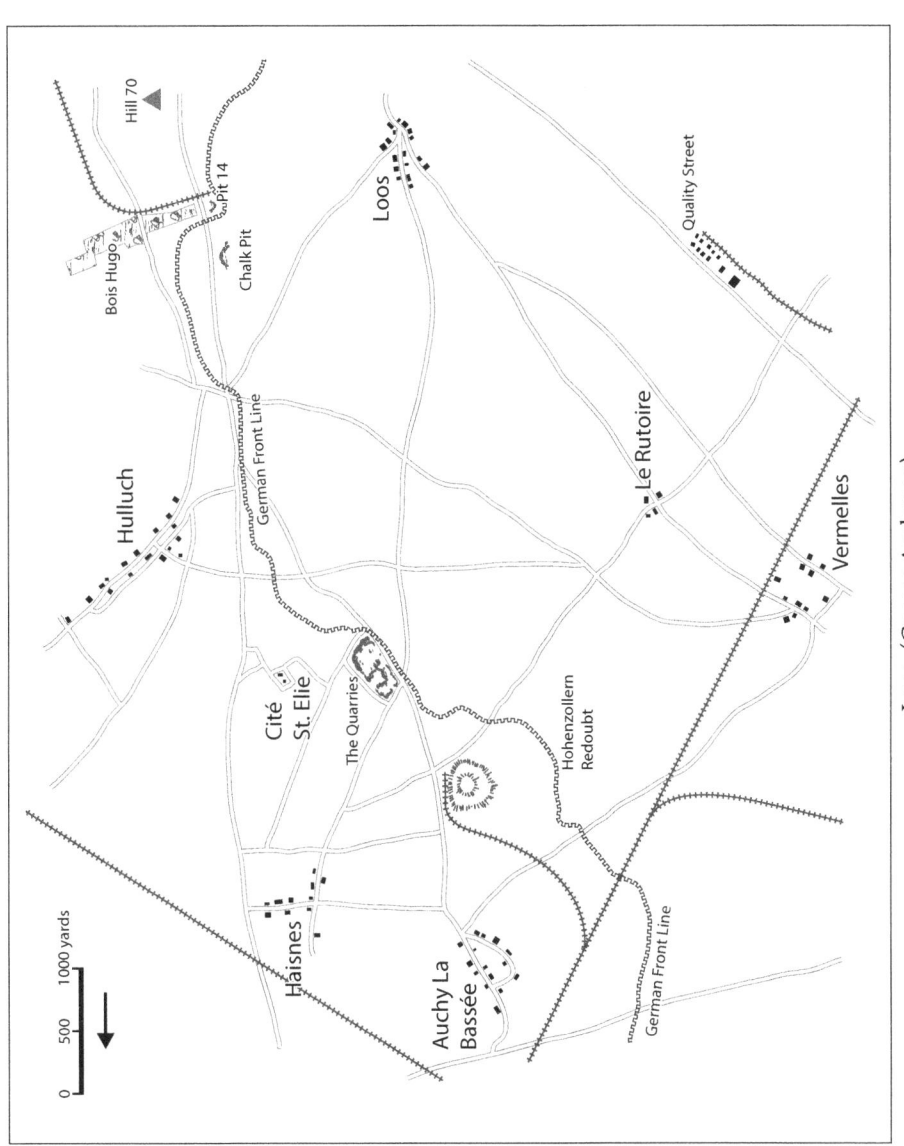

Loos. (George Anderson)

much straw was being taken to that place but it wasn't long before we heard what it was for. It was taken up for making a smoke screen to cover the fact that our Artillery were short of shells. The purpose of the smoke screen was that, at the time of the Great Battle starting, it was used to bluff the Germans into making them think that the Great Battle was actually taking place further along the line. This meaning that they would thin out their lines by sending reinforcements in the direction of the smoke created by the burning straw. On the morning of 25th Sept 1915, the day of the Great Battle, the straw was taken into No Man's Land and set on fire. As for ourselves, on the 27th Sept., "Standing To" at the School, in Bailleul, with full marching orders, we were ready to move at any moment.

Later in the day, details regarding the commencement of the Battle were read out to us and an hour or so afterwards, early on the 28th, we were on the road. With a train ride and a little marching we were soon to be on the scene.

31. LOOS BATTLEFIELD. A few words about the Battle.

At the outset of the Loos Battle, if only the first, second and third lines were taken from the Germans we were to consider the Battle was going all right. The starting of the Great Battle no doubt was a very great success and if it had been possible for us to have had plenty of reinforcements at the time, it would have been one of the most successful battles of the War. The greatest shock to the Germans was the outburst of the British Artillery as, before the Loos Battle, things were fairly quiet and never could the Germans have dreamt that we had managed to get together such a lot of guns in such a short time. What made it very hard for the British advancing troops was the great distance between our own line and the German front line as, at this time, there were no Creeping Barrages. When the time came for the men to start into battle, the Artillery was lifted from the German Front Line and, with the splendid deep dugouts which the Germans had, even though they had faced terrible days of the British Artillery fire, it was to have proved impossible for a shell to penetrate their splendid cover. As soon as our shellfire had lifted from their front line, the Germans knew that our "Brave Lads" were on the road. Up they came from their deep dugouts and our boys had nearly 1000 yards in front of them to go before they would meet a German. All the time that our very brave infantry were crossing the wide No- Man's Land, they had to put up with a curtain of bullets both from the Germans rifles and their Machine guns.

32. LOOS BATTLEFIELD. The Battle itself.

Before they reached the German trenches, including getting over the German barbed wire, many of our gallant lads had fallen. As to what I could see of the German barbed wire, it was put there thinking that no-one could ever get through it and it was far too strong for us to ever think about a small attack being a success. The wire was very different to ours. Instead of having spikes 4 to 5 inches apart, the spikes were on their wire and were so thick and very large that it was nearly impossible to cut it without wire cutters. Also to make it stronger there were many layers of a sort of tin plate wire with very large and sharp spikes and one could see that, as you took your place in the battle, the only way to cause the Germans a great loss of life was to get them out of their shelters and to do that it also had to

James's handwritten account of Action on the Loos Battlefield. September/October 1915.

cost us a very great loss of life. What a sight it was for the British Army; after getting through their very strong wire and having the "luck" to get into a German trench then to find such fine deep dugouts staring him in the face. I, myself, was one of the many that never dreamed such comfort could be made in such times as war.

33. LOOS BATTLEFIELD. Notes about the Battle.

Their dugouts had two entrances with 30 to 40 steps down into the ground. At the bottom of the steps came the dugout. Some of these places were very nicely furnished with furniture from the village of Loos and were also heated by the use of a French stove with a long pipe running up one of the entrances which acted as a chimney to let the smoke away. A grand supply of coal was readily available from the Coal pits of Loos.

Bells were fixed from the trench to the dugout to give warning if danger was about. I even noticed that they made special places for the sentries; a tunnel running from the trench under the ground to some little distance into No Man's Land all nicely boarded up. At the end of the tunnel was a square wooden frame running to the surface so that the sentry was able to sit, nice and comfortable, on a chair and with a long periscope could manage to see all that was going on without worrying about the British Artillery or any effect of the rain. So, one can see, by what I have written about the gallant lads that charged the first German lines at Loos, they had the full force of German Troops that were holding the German front line to face.

For all of our Artillery's shellfire, I did not consider that the effects of this killed many Germans.

Battalion War Diary:

28th September 1915. BAILLEUL.
7 30 am.: At 7 30 am., the Battalion marched to BAILLEUL Station where we entrained for CHOCQUES. A 5 mile march from there brought us to MONT BERMANCHON arriving there at 12 55 pm. where the Battalion was Billeted for the night. Orders arrive for us to march off at 9 30am in the morning.

29th September 1915. MONT BERMANCHON.
9 30 am: At 9 30 am the Battalion marched from Billets through BRUAY and FOURLEVEIUL to VERQUIGNEUL arriving there at 3 30 pm. A wet and trying journey of 13 miles. Roads in bad condition (1 man fell out). HQs established at MATHELIN WIEPOTTE VERQUIGNEUL. Strength of Battalion: 27 Officers. 1020 Other Ranks.

30th September 1915. VERQUIGNEUL.
The Battalion was ordered to relieve the Grenadier Guards in trenches at LE RUTOIRE. At 4 30pm. we moved off but, owing to the block on the roads and the extremely bad weather, progress was slow. We eventually arrived at the Trenches at 10 00 pm. and officially took over at 3 00 am. On our left our Artillery was active throughout the night.

Sadler Account:

34. LOOS BATTLEFIELD. On the road to the Battle.
My Regiment arrived at the battle some two days after it had started but I must say we had plenty to be going on with in the way of strengthening the lines. Also, in many places, the Germans were in the same lines as ourselves and had to be cleared out. By means of a communication trench running to the lines, the Germans were able to make some very strong points.At that time of day it was proper trench fighting. Bombs had to be used more so than a rifle and not the class of bombs as we were to have later in the War.

35. LOOS BATTLEFIELD. Our 1st Night.
We had started for the Battlefield, (Armentières to Bailleul), on the night of 27th Sept 1915.

Before we started out our Brigade Commander went to the front to find out about things. He returned with his head bandaged up, having got slightly wounded. It was on the 29th, that night we left to march to the trenches having a very long march before us, having several rests whilst getting towards two damaged villages,

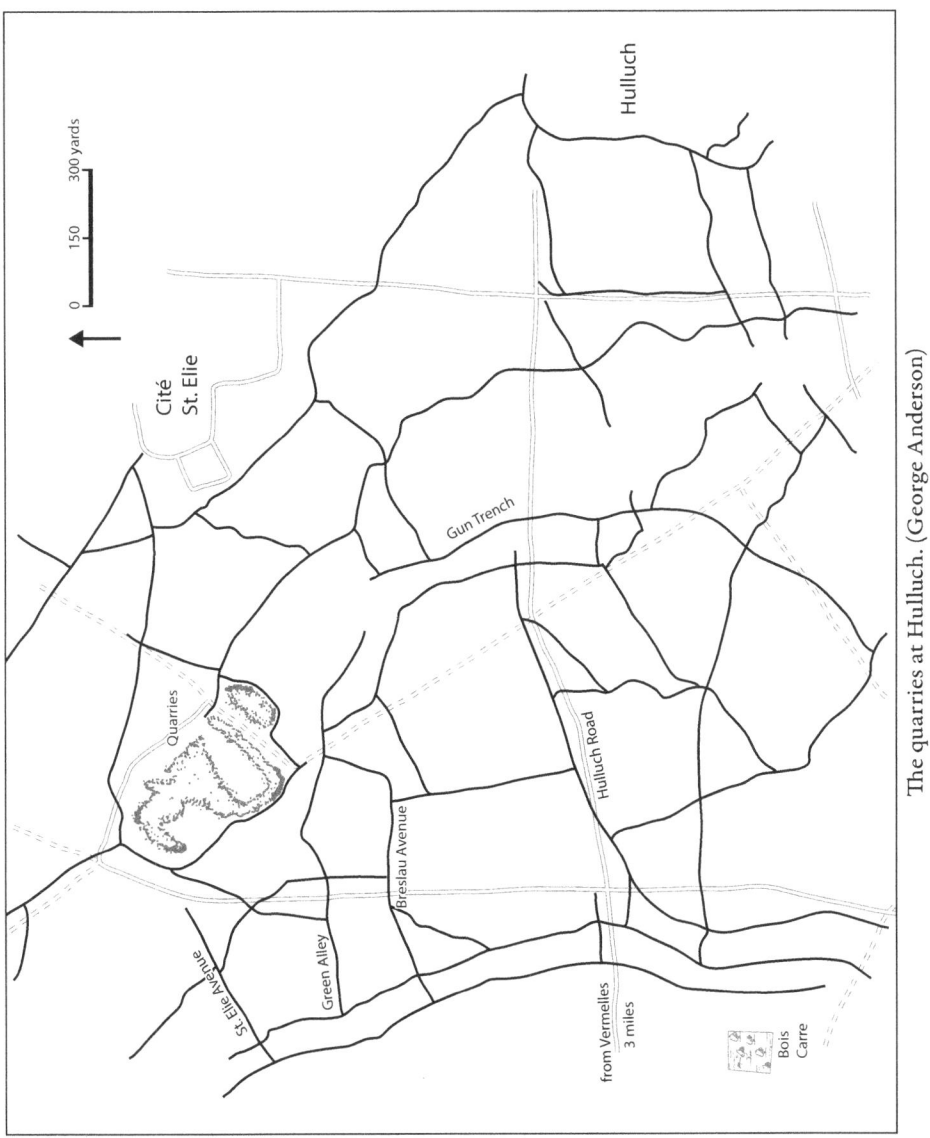

The quarries at Hulluch. (George Anderson)

(Bruay & Fourlevieul), and passing amongst the many field batteries. This involved marching by Platoon, with 100 yards between each, this owing to shellfire. It was a very trying time passing through the smashed villages with terrible reports from the Field gun and also the sparks flying from the guns making one wonder if it was the bursting of a German Shell or one of our guns firing. When passing through one of these villages, the Gunners that were off duty came up from their cellars to greet us, cheering us up by telling us that the Dardanelles had fallen into Allied hands. With that, we thought we must have been winning. On the 30th September, after leaving the villages in the rear and getting near the line we were met by a Guide sent from the Grenadier Guards to guide us to the Trenches. The Guide knew as much about the way as we did ourselves as I don't think the man had ever been over the ground before and a terrible night we spent following on from the long march which we had just completed. It was now beginning to rain hard and the ground was in such a state that it was becoming impossible to stand. This Guide dragged us nearly into the German front line; drawing many German bullets over to us. We lead back to the rear in single file with a little distance between each man. After standing up and falling down and leading on; due to the state of the ground, we managed to put up in a German trench for a short time. We began to think that this was to be our final "sleeping" place.

Battalion War Diary:

1st October 1915. LE RUTOIRE.
Great activity of Hostile Artillery, continuous shelling of our Trenches. A regrettable accident happened today. A Party of 10 men in a dug-out, while examining some German Grenades which had been left in our Trenches by the Enemy, accidentally exploded one. This explosion killed 4 men and wounded six others.

2nd October 1915. LE RUTOIRE.
On our Front the enemy were quiet but German Artillery were very active. Several 4.7 shells pitched on our Front Trenches and shrapnel shells were directed at LONE TREE and vicinity. Aeroplane activity. Covering party out at night to digging a Front Line Trench. One Officer wounded. Fierce strafe in direction of HULLUCH.

3rd October 1915. LE RUTOIRE.
Aeroplane activity excessive. Squadron of 8 French machines flew over towards LENS. Hostile Artillery still very active. A high explosive dropped in a dug-out occupied by a portion of our Machine Gun Section killing 3 and wounding 3 men and this put one of our Machine Guns out of Action. Working Parties carry on with forward Fire Trench. Strafe in direction of HULLUCH.

It was on 2nd October that the 12th (Eastern) Division suffered the loss of their GOC Major-General Frederick Wing. Sadler Account:

36. LOOS BATTLEFIELD. Making ourselves cover

Marching to this battle position with full marching order, including one blanket, we were starting to feel in need of another good rest. While in the trenches we took off our Packs etc. to rest our shoulders.

As it was we would only just get time to take everything off when the call would come along "Get everything together, we are going to move again". After several attempts like this, we at last managed to get to one stopping place which was in the third German line before the Battle had started. As we stood in our new position we had two of our Companys in front of us. These two Companys spent the night, 4th October, digging in the advance line on the left of Loos close by the large "Iron Tower", (Tower Bridge), and we were sent out to relieve them the next morning. Carrying on with this work for the next 24 hours, we managed to get a nice trench by that end of that time. Nothing very exciting happened during our twenty four hours but we were to spend a little time in collecting up a few wounded. Noticing several men waving to us from a position well in front of us; two Sergeants from my Company set out to fetch them in, having to cross another Company's front to do so. They were called in by this Company's Commanding Officer because they were passing his Company's front without having their rifles with them so they were required to give the job up to another Company; however the wounded fellows were brought in safe. These men had been lying out there for several days having had their wounds dressed by the Germans and had been given hot coffee by them. From what these poor wounded fellows said, the Germans were afraid to take them into their trenches because death might have awaited them.

37. LOOS BATTLEFIELD. Looking around.

That night we spent some of our time in burying a few of our dead and making the most of the gallant men. As things were very quiet this night it was impossible to find the German trench. It was a great distance off.

The next morning we got relieved by our two other Companys, which we had relieved twenty-four hours before. This morning turned out to be very misty and having nothing to smoke we set out searching the packs which were lying about and with this we found a few "fags" to get on with. I also can remember one man finding a pair of clippers for cutting hair, with which he soon started a barbers shop up with but the Germans soon made it very uncomfortable for us by giving us a large supply of heavy shells. These were a little larger than his 5-9 and we used to call "Coal Boxes" because so much black smoke which came from the shell on bursting.

I will now write my history of the Great Battle.

38. LOOS BATTLEFIELD. What to do when the Germans are coming.

That day finished up rather lively; myself being posted as a sentry at the entrance of one of the old German Communications trenches but, at night, I was taken off my post for a few hours to act as a companion to my Platoon Officer assisting in relieving troops in the advance trench. As things had quietened down a little, this was soon done and I took up my post again. Shortly after I had taken that position up again; an Officer came up to me and asked me where my Company Officer stayed. I told him "I didn't know" and I soon told him that "If they wanted us to know where they stayed they should tell us so that we would know". With this the Officer informed me that I was going to be brought up for Company Orders for insubordination but this never came off. This same Officer also asked me what I should do if I saw the Germans coming. I pointed to the Fires Step and said get up there and shoot. I also told him I wouldn't run about looking for an Officer when there was a Sergeant, posted, walking up and down the front to report things to. When daylight arrived next day and a sentry group was not needed to be on "Look Out" at the Communication trench; we left this place and moved a little distance to the right, this time being posted at a large Well which the Germans had constructed over this time for their water supply. It was a very up to date place and came in very useful for the supply of water to our Brigade.

39. LOOS BATTLEFIELD. Guarding a German well and getting wounded.

With the Germans having a good idea that this Well would be so useful to us, they, of course, set up a slow rate of shelling with "Whizz Bangs" and his deadly "shrapnel". Myself and the rest of the sentry group were posted at this Well with the instructions to only allow one man at a time to enter and fetch water because of this shelling. After standing a short time doing my hour on duty and talking to two of my fellow companions whose turns of duty followed after mine; all of a sudden a German shell burst on the back of the parapet. Having my back towards that direction, the explosion of the shell sent me two or three yards forward where I pitched on my head and knees with only a small piece of shell coming in contact with my head. This grazed my skull a little and I suffered a little from the effects of the fall. My other two chums soon got to work and bandaged my head. Meanwhile, the Germans also soon got to work with their Artillery, nearly making our trenches level in a short time.

40. LOOS BATTLEFIELD. Getting sniped with small shells.

Whilst waiting to be taken to the Dressing Station, one of our stretcher bearers and a great chum of mine said to me, "I will get your pack to take down to the dressing station when we are actually able to get away".

I passed the remark to him "There is no need to do that as I suppose I shall only have to go to see the doctor and then return again". With that, and leaving the pack behind, at last we managed to get to our Dressing Station. From there I was sent to Ado Ana Field Dressing Station, this time being supplied with a guide from the Royal Army Medical Corps. We were to receive a very terrible time before our journey ended. I had found out that the Germans were very fond of sniping at us with their rifles but, on this journey, I found out that bullets weren't enough for him. He had to snipe at us with his "Whiz Bangs" shells and so it was a case of going a yard or so and then lying down until the flying bits of shell had finished. This is how we had to carry on during the whole journey. At last we arrived at the Field Dressing Station and I stayed there a short time having my wound redressed. I left with many other wounded men, many being stretcher cases, these men being wheeled down by the use of a pair of wheels with the wheels then being returned to the dressing station once we had reached our destination.

41. LOOS BATTLEFIELD. – At the Clearing Station.

I stayed there some considerable time with our Field Batteries firing away like mad and the Germans returning a few shells in return, searching for these Batteries. Then a message arrived that the Red Cross cars were unable to come as far as this, so, after plenty of talking between the Royal Army Medical corps stretcher bearers as to who was going to carry this stretcher and who would carry this one, I said "Come on, get hold of that end of the stretcher and I'll get hold of this".

Seeing that I was a willing hand, despite the blow which I had taken to my head, they soon stopped talking and got on with the good work. At last we met the Red Cross Cars and were soon at the 63rd. Casualties Station. Here I spent a few hours sleeping on a stretcher and felt very much better when I awoke.

After passing the night resting, the next morning we "paraded". By that I mean, all of the walking cases, assembled for going further down the Line. Instead of me getting to go down the Line; because I was not wounded badly enough, I helped some of the men out on parade, including those that had been hit in the legs and who I considered should go before me. I received a very good job that night, being stationed at the gate of the Clearing Station, waiting for convoys of wounded to arrive.

42. LOOS BATTLEFIELD. Journey back to my Regiment.

When these Convoys arrived, my work started by carrying in the stretcher cases with the help of another man. We initially took the cases before the Doctor to get their wounds redressed. Following this, we had to take them to different rooms as we were told. After doing this in an all right fashion, I was getting more than fed up with it so the next day I said to the Doctor, "If you consider me fit to return to my Battalion, I will do so." With this he said "Alright", and I was soon off on my journey. After tea this day I finished up at my Divisional Headquarters and in doing so found where my Battalion was stationed. If only I had arrived half an hour earlier, I should have seen my Battalion pass by as they were relieved from front line duty just after I got wounded and had come back a little way to the rear for a rest. Anyhow I stayed the night at this Head Quarters at Sailly La Bourse; food being given to me by the staff there. The next morning I left and made my way towards Company Brigade Transport lines where again I was made comfortable, food again being given to me. Later this day I left with the Transport which at that time were taking the rations up to my Regiment. By doing this I managed to get to my own Transport lines, again being made very comfortable for a few hours by my Company Quarter Master Sergeant. Tea was supplied to me and also a packet of "fags" to smoke.

43. LOOS BATTLEFIELD. Back once more with my Battalion.

At Dusk that night I left with my Company Quarter Master Sergeant who was taking rations up to my Company. The Ration Limbers acted as a guide for me until my own company's Ration Party arrived for their rations. I had a fairly pleasant journey back to the Ration Dump as we only got delayed once owing to some barbed wire being laid across the road which caused the mules to get tangled up. Freeing them, we soon got on our journey again. At last we arrived at the Ration Dump and after putting the rations on the ground, the Ration Limbers returned to their transport lines once more; the Quarter Master staying to hand over the rations. This Dump was not altogether a comfortable place owing to so many stray bullets from the "Front". A stray bullet was capable of doing just as much damage as one that was fired straight at anyone. Anyhow we lay down together and waited for the Ration Parties to arrive. After spending some time lying down, I said to the Quartermaster, "I am going for a small walk round to see if I could find any parties". With this I started off and after a short time I heard voices. Some of the voices I knew so well. I shouted out "Who are you?" and received the answer back "Royal Fusiliers Ration Party". So once more I was back with my "old" chums again and I made my way back to the Trenches with this Party.

44. LOOS BATTLEFIELD. Burying the dead.

The day I arrived back, the first daylight attack had taken place, this attack being made by the use of Smoke Shells and Gas but from what I could see of things, it had turned out to be far from a success. Where we were holding the line, the Germans were quite ready to "greet" our lads, owing to the smoke not being thick enough The Division suffered very heavily. This day we spent in digging graves starting with the aid of large "Shell Holes". By this we were able to work in daylight and less under cover. These large shell holes were made into larger square holes and, whilst some of us were doing this, other men were working on digging out men and bodies from the Dugout that had been blown in by German Shells whilst the attack had been going on. The reason for digging the men out from the Dugout was to see if they were still alive and also for another important thing which was to get at the "Pay Books " from the dead so that they could be accounted for. This work was carried out as fast as possible until night arrived at which point a large party was selected to collect up the bodies hanging in the German Barbed Wire in the rear of our Trench. These men had not been killed in the daylight battle but whilst they had been involved in taking the Trench that we were now holding.

45. LOOS BATTLEFIELD. Getting shelled and moving later.

Work had been started collecting up our dead comrades when all of a sudden the Germans opened up their Artillery with low and deadly shrapnel, nearly catching the whole party of us. The Germans knew very well that he was likely to catch a larger party at night than he would in daylight. This being the case he was quite willing to let us work by day so as to get good "catch" at night. His Artillery fire got so great that the "good" work had to be given up.

Shortly after this, we had Orders to all get packed up, ready for moving. The reason I think for this moving was they were expecting the Trenches to go up in the air as we were to find that these Trenches had been mined. That night we left the Trenches and had a long drag to Vermelles were we were shown some shallow Trenches and told to make ourselves comfortable. This turned out to be a very unpleasant night. Just in front of our Trenches was stationed a Battery of Field Guns giving "Old Fritz" a very large supply of Iron rations and with this the Germans were returning some in exchange but with very much larger shells.

With the large flying pieces it was a night of always aiming to "keep low". We got through the night but the following morning we were supplied with two boxes of Bombs each.

Battalion War Diary:

4th October 1915. LE RUTOIRE.
Enemy quiet on our Front but Hostile Artillery Active. Good work done at night by our Battalion on making a communication Trench from our Front line to Fire Trench.

5th October 1915. LE RUTOIRE.
A fairly heavy bombardment of our Trenches by Enemy's Artillery took place this morning between 8 15 and 9 30am. and again at 10 30 to 11 30 am. Result: 2 men wounded and 2 dug-outs demolished. A large proportion of the German Shells were blind. The Battalion received Orders to move into Old British Trenches 500 yards behind German Line Trenches, being relieved by 8th Berkshire and London Scottish of the 1st Brigade. A dark misty night and relief was carried out with difficulty not being complete till 4 30 am. of 6th inst.

6th October 1915. LE RUTOIRE.
Thick mist at early dawn. During the day a few High Explosives and some shrapnel were thrown at our Trenches- two casualties.

7th October 1915. LE RUTOIRE. SAILLY LA BOURSE.
We received Orders to vacate these Trenches at 7 00 pm and proceeded to other old British trenches 3 to 4 miles back at SAILLY LA BOURSE, arriving there at 11 pm. Headquarters established.

8th October 1915. SAILLY LA BOURSE.
At midday, 6 High Explosives pitched in the neighbourhood of our trenches, possibly being aimed at the BETHUNE ROAD. At 4 00 pm. a heavy bombardment started and we subsequently heard that the Germans were attacking CHALK PIT in the vicinity of HULLUCH. We practically "stood to" for we were informed that, if reinforcements were needed, the 35th Brigade would be called upon and then, if further reinforcements were required, we should go.

Our whole casualties during this tour of Trenches were 14 men killed and 45 wounded. Strength of Battalion: – 29 Officers & 993 men. Number of sick and wounded at present in Hospital is 78, including 4 Officers.

9th October 1915. SAILLY LA BOURSE.
Misty morning. We learn that the attack of yesterday was directed on our Corps. Front and that the enemy had suffered very heavily. Battalion exercised. Small Route March of 2 hours. Bombing Practice.

10th October 1915. SAILLY LA BOURSE.
Quiet but French Artillery active. Receive orders to move on the 12th inst.

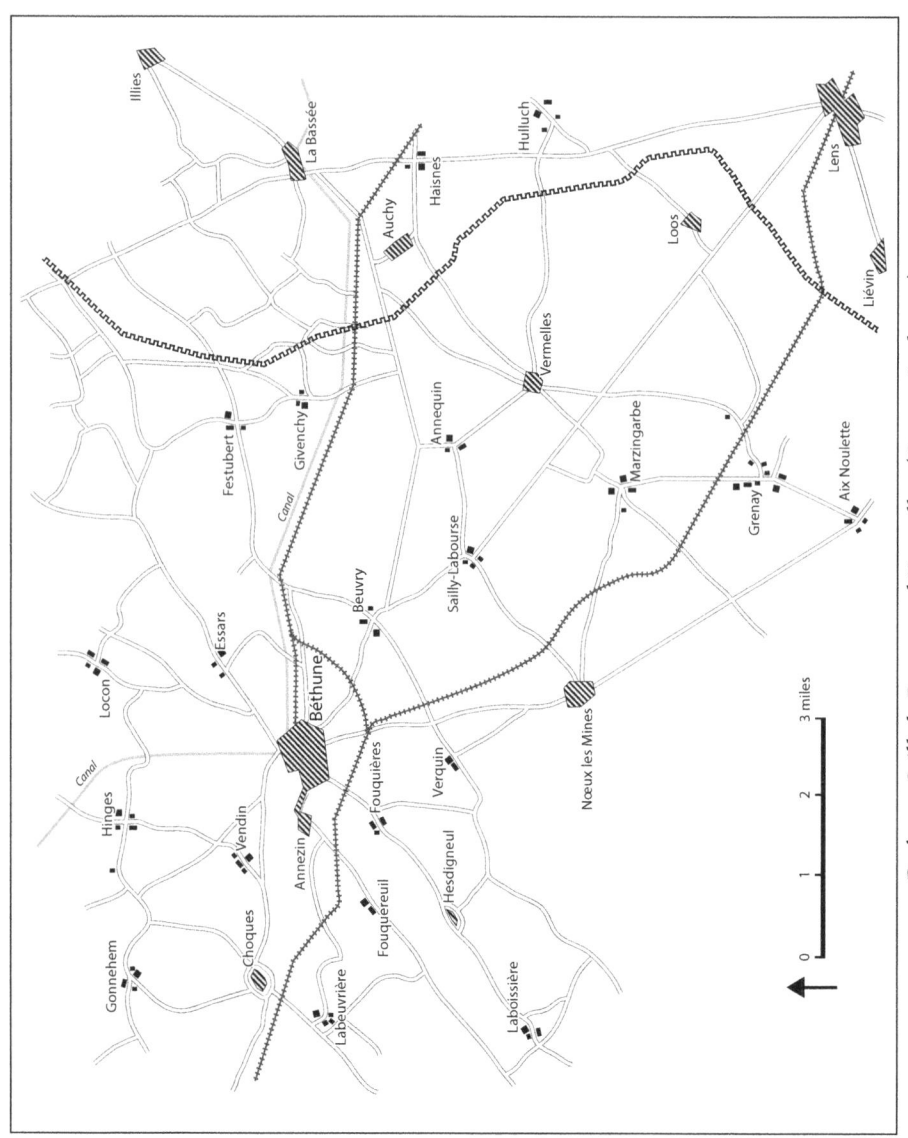

Bethune, Sailly la Bourse and Vermelles. (George Anderson)

11th October 1915. SAILLY LA BOURSE.
Company Officers reconnoitre Trenches. German aeroplane brought down just outside our HQ's at 9 15 am.

12th October 1915. SAILLY LA BOURSE. VERMELLES.
Bn. moves off at 2 00 pm. Congested road. Bn. HQ's underneath WATER TOWER building at VERMELLES at 3 15 pm. hear that Germans are attacking BIG WILLIE Trench in HOHENZOLLERN REDOUBT and we are warned that we may be needed at a moment's notice. At 6 15 pm. receive further details of tomorrow's planned attack. Bombardment from 12 00 to 2 00 pm. Gas 1 00 to 1 50 pm. Attack 2 00 pm. Covering and working parties engaged all night carrying Trench Mortars, Bombs etc.

Under orders to march to the Hulluch Road trenches near Vermelles, 9th Royal Fusiliers would soon see action again. The grim Loos struggle was moving on to what would become known as 'The Action of Hohenzollern Redoubt'.

6

October 1915: The Action of Hohenzollern Redoubt – Part 1

The Loos offensive had, in the estimation of the British high command, run its course by 13th October. It was during this period that 9th Royal Fusiliers were heavily engaged in 'The Action of Hohenzollern Redoubt' (13-19 October 1915). In effect, this was the operationally barren continuation of the great campaign which had commenced on 25th September. The redoubt, situated on a tactically important height, was bitterly contested throughout the offensive and, as we shall see, well into the first quarter of 1916. James's Battalion, in conjunction with the remaining units of 36th Brigade, were tasked with the capture of nearby Gun Trench and the southwest face of the notorious Hulluch Quarries.

Battalion War Diary:

13th October 1915 VERMELLES.
Whole Battalion out carrying and fusing bombs. Bombardment starts at 12 00 noon. Enemy retaliates but ineffectively. Bomb carrying continues till 5 00 pm. Bn. ordered to proceed to old German Line with all available troops. Very tiring march and hostile shelling was prevalent. One shell burst 10 yards in front of our column. Trenches blocked with wounded. Relieve 5th Berkshires in forward fire trench. Relief not completed till 8 30 am.

14th October 1915. VERMELLES (Hulluch Road Trenches).
Enemy shell us heavily during the day. Our guns reply vigorously. Bombing continues in front. Fairly quiet night.

15th October 1915. VERMELLES (Hulluch Road Trenches).
Fine but misty. Our bombers take over Sap. 54 from Berks. Bombers. Find an old shaft leading to QUARRIES but R.E.'s report it a dead end.

16th October 1915. VERMELLES (Hulluch Road Trenches).
Orders arrive for a "Stand To" at 5 00 am. Guards start a bombing attack. Receive orders to support 35th Brigade in a bombing attack on STONE ALLEY. A quiet night after much shelling on both sides.

17th October 1915. VERMELLES (Hulluch Road Trenches).
Hostile Artillery very active. Our artillery retaliates with effect.

Hohenzollern Craters. (George Anderson)

18th October 1915. VERMELLES (Hulluch Road Trenches).
"A" & "D" Companies to relieve BERKS. in fire trench on the 19th inst.. Officer in Command of ESSEX in charge of bombing attack due to start at 5 45 pm. 2nd Lieut W.W. Smith supports with 2 squads of bombers. We are responsible for Sap 54. backed up by Berks' squads. Shelling all day. Draft of 45 arrives. Apportioned, half to "B" Comp. and half to "C" Comp.. Bombing attack starts punctually, excellent supply of bombs and S.A.A., (small arms ammunition). Shelling very heavy. Hear from time to time all is going well but 2nd Lieut W.W Smith unfortunately killed. Essex CO wires objective gained and being consolidated. Receive a message from Guards "Well done neighbours, many thanks for splendid co-operation"

Sadler Account:

46. LOOS BATTLEFIELD. Winning the Hohenzollern Redoubt.

A great amount of the bombs that were used then were "Ball Bombs" about the size of a tennis ball with a fuse and when the weather was wet and damp it was then virtually impossible to get the fuse to light.

When this was the case it was a matter of trying to frighten Fritz by making a dead shot with one.

Later the same morning, 18th October, we set off back to the Trenches carrying our two boxes of bombs.

At night the "Brigade Bombers", who were the picked bombers from the four Battalions, were formed into a large party and the "Hohenzollern Redoubt" had to be won, the Guards having already tried to win it but without success. This night it was won, not by trying to bomb up the Redoubt and, in doing so, pushing the Germans out which had been tried several times. This night it was a case of rushing up each side of the "Redoubt" on the surface and bombing down on the Germans. Never have I before, or since, seen and heard such a terrible night of bombing. The bursting of the bombs was worse than the rattle made by many machine guns and the smoke from the bombs became so great that the alarm, "Gas", was given and helmets were worn for a short time near the place of the bombing. This night the Redoubt was ours and the night was one of much excitement. It was a job to know who was the owner of some of the Trenches, both the Germans and us holding them together at the same time. As this was the case so many bombing posts had to be held.

Battalion War Diary:

19th October 1915. VERMELLES (Hulluch Road Trenches).
"A" &" "D Companies relieve Berks. Fine but very misty. Move into Berks HQ's at 8 30 am. Hostile shelling starts at 7 30 am. We, with the Essex, hold the whole Brigade line. We get warning of a hostile counter attack. Rifle fire and shrapnel fire start at 5 30 pm. and at 5 50 pm. Essex CO report enemy attacking. 6 00 pm. Essex report enemy driven off. 6 15 pm. Essex CO reports that if he has gun fire on Quarry Trench he has situation well in hand. We find extra bombing parties for the Essex. 7 00 pm. All is quiet again. Attachment to 35th Brigade ceases.

20th October 1915. VERMELLES (Hulluch Road Trenches).
Fine. A good deal of shrapnel fire between 10 00 am and 11 30 am. Enemy again reported concentrating on the QUARRIES. Firing starts again at 2 30 pm. but very slight. Night quiet.

21st October 1915. VERMELLES (Hulluch Road Trenches).-FOURQUEREUIL.
Fine morning. Relieving Units of HLI (Highland Light Infantry) and KOSB due to relieve us at 2 00 pm. arrive though at 5 00pm. Battalion clear of Trenches at 7 30 pm. March to FOURQUEREUIL via VERMELLES, NOVELLES, SAILLY LA BOURSE, VERQUINEUL and VERQUIN. Battalion arrives 1 30 am. Billeted in canvas huts at FOURQUEREUIL.

Sadler Account:

47. LOOS BATTLEFIELD. German counter-attack.

The following day, 19th October, we took up our new position a little more to the left. This day turned out to be a very nerve trying day. Having just a little wire in front of our trench and with the Germans trying to win back the Hohenzollern Redoubt, they found it difficult to leave this small stretch of wire alone.

They kept sending over heavy shells to blow this wire to pieces. All this was happening a few yards in front of our trench. With these shells bursting, and at times nearly striking our trench, it was far from comfortable.

This slow rate of shelling was kept up until about 4 o'clock when things went very quiet again for a short time. At 6 o'clock on this same day, all of a sudden, the quietness broke into a terrible outburst of shelling and rifle fire. The German shrapnel came over in showers, bursting only a few yards above our heads. The shrapnel bullets were striking the ground in the rear of our trench. Then came the showers of rifle bullets and the Germans following it up. Despite all of this shrapnel and rifle fire their attack was to cost the Germans a terrible loss of life. Only three Germans had the "pleasure" of jumping in to our trench and they were not to live long enough to tell us what they had come for.

48. LOOS BATTLEFIELD. "Call that one a Dud".

This time our artillery were putting up a splendid barrage on the front German line to stop the German support troops from coming after us. Nothing could have passed through such a terrible line of bursting shells. After this attack, things again went very quiet except for a few heavy shells coming over at intervals.

This night, a man named Dudley made up one of our sentry group. Anyone could hear the report of the German gun as it was fired and could also hear the shell travelling through the air towards them. After hearing the report of the German gun, the shell seemed to say "Got you", "Got you" as it travelled towards us. When we heard the gun fired we shouted out to our sentry friend Dudley, "Another one coming "Dud". ("Dud" being the shortened form of his name). When the shell reached its destination and exploded with a terrible crash, Dudley was heard to remark "Call that one a Dud!" (Dudley was the sniper who I mentioned in the early part of this diary).

Battalion War Diary:

22nd October 1915. FOURQUEREUIL
Fine. Day spent in cleaning. Casualties during Tour – 1 Officer 24 men killed- 113 Men wounded.

23rd October 1915. FOURQUEREUIL
Strength of Battalion 28 Officers – 989 Other Ranks. New bombing parties arranged of 8 men per platoon practising 3 hours daily under Capt. J.P.S. Brown. Capt. D.E. Estill takes over command of "A" Company. General inspection at 11 30 am. General pleased and makes speech of thanks for our services.

24th October 1915. FOURQUEREUIL
2nd Lieutenant Cort arrives and is posted to "D" Company.

25th October 1915. FOURQUEREUIL-SAILLY LA BOURSE.
Battalion parades at 9 45 am and marches off to billet at SAILLY LA BOURSE. Billets limited hence very crowded.

26th October 1915. SAILLY LA BOURSE.
35th and 39th Brigade take over HOHENZOLLERN REDOUBT trenches.

27th October 1915. SAILLY LA BOURSE.
Various Officers pay visit to Trenches.

28th October 1915. SAILLY LA BOURSE.
Our Front in the new Trench line to be from GUILDFORD TRENCH just north of the Redoubt to the VERMELLES railway.

29th, 30th and 31st October 1915. SAILLY LA BOURSE.
Quiet. Bombing practice continues.

Sadler Account:

The next day, 21st October, we moved back to the support lines, not a great distance from the "Front Line". Here we spent some of our time doing "carrying parties". This time we were carrying some of our heavy Trench Mortars which I expect many may have seen pictures of in the daily papers.

49. LOOS BATTLEFIELD. Our 1st Trip with Heavy Trench Mortars.
These mortars we called "Plum Puddings" and weighed about 60lbs. And they were far from pleasant things to carry. They were carried in two different ways. Sometimes the "Plum Puddings" had the handle screwed on and sometimes the "Plum Puddings" were carried separately by being fixed into a wooden block and others of the party would carry the handles. When we saw these "creatures" for the first time we hardly dared to put them on the ground, wondering whether they

would burst or not. We soon found out they were quite harmless when they were knocked about, more harmless than when they were fired. They were fired with a very small gun, which was just large enough to allow the carrying handle to go down the muzzle. When they were fired one had to look out for the shell burst and also for the gun being sent up into the air along with the mortar itself.

The relative quiet experienced by James and his comrades at this time would prove short-lived.

7

November–December 1915: The Action of Hohenzollern Redoubt – Part 2

It was on 1st November 1915 that 9th Royal Fusiliers were re-deployed to the Hohenzollern Redoubt sector. The next fortnight would be a trying experience for all ranks.

Battalion War Diary:

1st November 1915. SAILLY LA BOURSE to HOHENZOLLERN REDOUBT.
Very wet. Take over from 6th R.W.Kents. Route and Order of march "D", "C", "A", "B" via FOSSE 9 along railway line up to RAILWAY ALLEY and hence to Front Line. 3 Company's in Firing Line and one in Support. Rain continues.

2nd November 1915. HOHENZOLLERN REDOUBT.
Rain all night. Trenches falling in everywhere. 2 feet of water in trenches in places. Projected attack by 11th Middlesex and 7th Sussex on LITTLE WILLIE considered impossible and abandoned owing to wet.

3rd November 1915. HOHENZOLLERN REDOUBT.
Rain all night. Good deal of firing by our own guns but not returned by the enemy. 11th Middlesex take over from GUILDFORD TRENCH to MUD TRENCH. Men's feet suffer heavily from the wet.

4th November 1915. HOHENZOLLERN REDOUBT.
Issue of gum boots arrive. Men endeavour to dry their feet and dry socks are sent for.

5th November 1915. HOHENZOLLERN REDOUBT.
Major WILLAN, 60th Rifles, appointed Brigade Major and visits us in the Trenches. Party of Germans come over to bomb "B" Coy. Party dispersed and two wounded brought in- one wearing an Iron Cross ribbon.

6th November 1915 HOHENZOLLERN REDOUBT.
Fine. Uneventful. Time spent daily in cleaning Trenches.

7th November 1915. HOHENZOLLERN REDOUBT.
Ditto. Corps. Commander General Gough visits Trenches.

8th November 1915. HOHENZOLLERN REDOUBT.
Fine.

Hohenzollern Redoubt Craters. (George Anderson)

9th November 1915. HOHENZOLLERN REDOUBT.
Fine. Trench Artillery activity. Rain at night and Trenches again fall in.

10th November 1915. HOHENZOLLERN REDOUBT.
Artillery active again. Are told that our billeting area will be ANNEQUIN.

11th November 1915. HOHENZOLLERN REDOUBT.
Aeroplane activity. Brig. General Borradaile superseded by Lt. Col. Boyd Moss. South Staffs.

12th November 1915. HOHENZOLLERN REDOUBT.
Officers of relieving Unit 1st KRR, (Kings Royal Regiment), visit us and new Brigadier.

13th November 1915 HOHENZOLLERN REDOUBT.
Quiet. Got Relief Orders.

Sadler Account:

50. LOOS BATTLEFIELD. Our new position. T –shaped Trenches.

This time in the Trenches we had a little to be content with. The weather started to get very unsettled and it started to rain very hard and continued to do so all night. The Trenches we took over this time were far different from the past. They were made in a way like a letter T and all connecting up to one trench in this way, TTTTTTT. I took a great fancy to this sort of Trench because, if the Germans attacked our lines and with many of their men most likely having been greatly cut up crossing No Man's Land; they would only be able to hold a few of the T shapes. This would give us a chance to throw bombs from the Trenches which we held and by doing this we would soon get him out. I shall say more about these T trenches later. At this part of the line we were very close to the Germans and were able to hear them talking and coughing at times. The Germans would throw one of their stick bombs which might hit the ground only a yard or so in front of us. With the rain and other sights, we spent a terrible night and we soon got wet through to our skins and could only sit down and stick it out. We did have the pleasure of thinking the Germans were just as badly off as us as they only had a roughly made trench and none of them were in deep dug-outs.

51. LOOS BATTLEFIELD. Bombardment and Rain.

However, before daylight, 2nd November, it was an insult to call our "holes", trenches. So much rain had caused the sides of the Trenches to fall in and when daylight arrived we were only just able to make cover for ourselves. This day all the men from our Company's Front, except two Sentry groups were sent back to the support line and this left only the Right Post and Left Post of the Company's front. Myself, I was one of the sentries on the Left Post and so had to remain at the Line. This day we had the pleasure, not only of putting up with the rain but also of having to put up with very much shellfire. The other men were withdrawn because of a three-day bombardment, which was going to start, commencing at

10 o'clock each day until 5 o'clock at night. This was to continue for the three days in this way. As the German Front Line was so close our own shells were likely to fall short and, this being so, there were only six of us left in our Front Line. When the bombardment started it was nearly impossible to hear each other speak with the noise of so many shells travelling through the air at the same time. We did not mind this as much as we did the falling short of some of our own shells which, at times, nearly blew us out of our trenches rather than the Germans out of theirs. Just to make it better (sic), the Germans started sending over his heavy "Coal Boxes" which nearly put a permanent end to our terrible times.

52. LOOS BATTLEFIELD. Another good job.

I shall never forget the impression on one man's face when one of the German's heavy shells burst only a few yards in front of us and fairly frightened us all. More so, this also affected a man who was also doing his hour on duty. He looked at me and said, "The Germans must know we are here, what about changing our position?" I began to think the same myself when, as a great surprise to us all, an Officer and a small party of men came to relieve us which we began to think was a real godsend. Anyhow, after a terrible struggle in the mud we arrived at the Support Trenches only to get another "good" job as soon as we arrived. Up came a Sergeant and said, "You, you and you for the Ration Party" along with the cheerful words "Come on, hurry up" Throwing our equipment and rifles down we had to go off for another good "swim" but we knew it was impossible to get any wetter than we were. Off we paddled through Communication Trenches, waist deep in water to fetch these rations. The Trenches had been so much damaged by the German shell fire making large heaps of mud under the water where, if one was not careful you might slip on one of these heaps and go right under the water. Different parts of these Trenches being covered over with hurdles to stop observation did not improve the trip.

53. LOOS BATTLEFIELD. Ration Party.

After a terrible struggle we arrived at the Ration Dump, thinking to myself that I would try to catch hold of a light load to carry back. This I did, but had it only for a short time before a chum of mine, one who had spent some terrible times with me at the Front Line, said "Change loads with me, Jim, as I shall never manage to get back with this load".

With his request I took pity on him and said "Alright", changing my light load with is heavier one. The load which he was struggling back with was a large box containing two gallon jars of rum. Anyhow, at last, we started again on our journey back. After getting so far back we came into contact with the covered part of the Trench and I said to the man in front, "Let us know when the party stops". At last the party stopped but the man in front of me forgot to let me know. I continued on in order to catch the Party up and it doesn't require much telling or imagination to recall what I said when I did catch them up. My right eye came in contact with the load being carried by the man in front of me nearly taking my eye out. After this I passed the word up to the Sergeant in front that I would like to stop for a few moments so that I could break open the box which I was carrying.

54. LOOS BATTLEFIELD. Ration Party.

Never had I been so taken aback in my life. I expected to find carrying handles on the jars. However this was not the case and I found out that, instead of making life easier for myself, I had made two loads for myself rather than one. I shall never forget my journey from that spot to the point where the rations had to be given up. I have heard people say that a good swear, at times, makes anyone feel better. I must say this was certainly the case with me during this particular night. I found that I had to jam one jar under each arm and then put my hands in my overcoat pocket. Having done this, when I slipped over on one of the heaps of mud under the water, I nearly got drowned. At last I managed to get back to where some of my Battalion were stationed, meeting up again with an NCO who I knew well. I dropped my jars of rum into the mud and had a few words with him. The remainder of the party were just in front of me, having a rest. If I had known then what I did the next day, I would have left them a jar. When it was time to make another start for home, I had a terrible struggle in getting my two jars out of the mud. The more I pulled; the mud seemed to pull harder in return. At the finish, not only did I have the two jars but plenty of mud as well.

55. LOOS BATTLEFIELD. Ration Party and drink.

I later found out that I was not the only one in some distress. Just in front of me there was a man struggling with a large bag of bread or, more accurately, a bag of bread and mud. He passed the remark to me that "I am not a slacker but if only I had my rifle here I would shoot myself. After losing ourselves and wandering around the same trenches two or three times, we, at last, managed to get back safely and I handed over my two jars but I did not receive a drink from them. We were told that we had to go back to the dump to fetch some boxes of emergency rations; these being needed for the coming attack which was going to take place when the three day bombardment had come to an end. Anyhow, after another most terrible struggle, we completed our second journey and I was dying for a drink of water. However, I had a job to think where I had left my equipment when I had been called up to the Ration Party. I knew I had to get a drink from somewhere so I set off to look for my water bottle, struggling through the mud and up the Trench to where I knew my equipment lay somewhere, but not knowing exactly where. There was not a living soul to be seen but, at last, I came across a set of equipment. I shook the bottle and, finding that it was half-filled with water, I set about trying to "draw" the cork, working very hard at this and despite not knowing if this set of equipment was my own. I had to give this up as it was impossible to draw the cork.

56. LOOS BATTLEFIELD. Trying to get a sleep.

After walking about for a short time I returned to the same set of equipment. Again I tried hard to withdraw the cork but again it was not to come out. I took a trip up the trench this time and came into contact with some moving objects and found out that this was one of our Sentry Posts with one of my comrades fast asleep. I looked at him and thought to myself that I would not wake this poor tired fellow up. I made my last journey up the Trenches and, at last, I found my own set of equipment. Now I felt that it was a case that, if the cork did not come out, I would resort to something quite drastic. However this time I succeeded and had what I considered was a very well-deserved drink. Having had this drink, though, did not finish my terrible time. The next thing was to try and get a little sleep. I had a blanket with me but this was just like a wet "house-cloth" which had only just been taken out from a pail of water.

Knowing that it was not going to be worth using the blanket to try and keep warm, I used it by putting it between the mud and myself. The next thing was to look for a resting-place. At last I found a hole which the Germans had cut out in the side of the Trench for some purpose. I needed it for putting my blanket in and very soon I was lying on it. I was more like a ball of mud than a living soul but still my troubles were to continue.

57. LOOS BATTLEFIELD. Unlucky for Rations.

Not needing much rocking to sleep, I was soon in "Dreamland". I had only been asleep a very short time when I was woken up all of a sudden by a terrible crash and splash. Thinking it was one of "Fritz's' Coal Boxes, I waited expecting another one to arrive. Having waited for a short time, I discovered that it wasn't the Germans trying to give us a sleepless night but only the sides of the Trenches falling in due to the rain. I very soon fell to sleep again not knowing, or caring, whether the Trench would fall in and bury me alive. This time I slept until I was called the following morning to collect my rations for the day. I might just as well have been left asleep as I was unlucky with regards to getting any rations. On just reaching the place where the rations were being served out, one of old "Fritz's" Coal Boxes came sailing over, striking about two or three yards to the rear of the Trench, knocking the Trench in on us and our rations. We were lucky to get out with only a good shaking.

58. LOOS BATTLEFIELD. Staying in a German Dugout.

Shortly after this we left this Trench for some more called "The Quarries". The planned attack, 2nd November, was unable to take place owing to the state of the ground and the weather. I must say that I was not sorry that "moving time" had arrived. Our new position was a place nicely ranged by the German Artillery. Here, one had to be very careful not to receive a German Coal Box all to one's self. However, at this position, we had the great pleasure of using one of the Germans deep dug outs for the first time. Although unfurnished, we made ourselves quite at home and we were able to have a fire. Although the Germans forgot to arrange a "French" stove for us, we were able to find one of our old "Biscuit Tins" which we knocked a number of holes in and this acted as our "Fire-Place" The next thing was to get some dry wood. We were rather lucky, as someone had arranged that a "Dump" should be made not far from our resting-place. We managed to collect wood from here and I must say that, whoever formed the "Dump" did us a very great kindness as they supplied us with plenty of nice new and dry Trench Boards. However we were not particular as to whether they were new or old, just so long as they would burn.

59. LOOS BATTLEFIELD. Getting closer to the Germans.

At these Trenches, the first supply of "Waders" or High-Boots were served out to us, (4th November), but the supply was not large enough for everybody to have a pair. Although I was unlucky at the start, I was soon able to get a pair because, at this time, we were losing half of our men with "waterlogged" feet.(Trench Foot). Our work whilst stationed here was consolidating a new "Front-Line" and we started this by working doing four hours on and eight hours off, night and day. We were able to sit around our fire when we were off duty. Our worst job was getting through the mud to the place where we started work. The mud, at times, was so thick that it was impossible to pull our "Waders" out of the mud. There were times when one of the "Waders" had to be left behind and one had to struggle "home" with only one on. Our consolidation work was carried out in a way as I have mentioned before; digging a straight trench running out to meet the German "Front Line". When it was considered that we were close enough we made a little T. By having a good number of these trenches being worked at the same time, the ends could then all be joined up to form a new Front Line. As we were working or sapping from inside the Trench and not working from the top downwards we were able to continue both night and day. It was rather risky work at times as the Germans were rather anxious to know what was going on and would crawl close enough to throw a hand grenade/bomb at us. One of our party would act as a Sentry and would keep a sharp look out and, as we were also well supplied with bombs, we were always ready for a sudden visit.

60. LOOS BATTLEFIELD. Making ourselves comfortable.

This work had to be carried out whether it was raining hard or not and very often we would get wet through to our skin. It became a case of letting our wet clothes take time to dry on us as we were unable to take them off, due to the fact that sudden attacks that were always liable. We used to manage to dry the outside with the aid of our little fire and very soon we found a way to make ourselves more comfortable underneath. Little did people at home, at this stage of the War, know how useful the newspapers were that they sent out to the Front for us to read. When we had finished reading them we used to put the newspapers between our skin and uniforms and this made us feel that little more comfortable. One day, whilst at our deep dug-out, we had the "pleasure" of feeling the sensation of a Heavy German shell bursting on the top of the Trench. It was a far from pleasant few minutes as the shock felt was very great. The candles were put out and it was some time before we could see across the dugout owing to the dry dust flying about. However the dugout was far too deep to be penetrated. One day, one of our men was feeling unwell and was going to see the doctor when, soon after he had started on his journey, he was stopped by a German shell. That trip to see the Doctor cost the poor fellow his life.

Battalion War Diary:

14th November 1915. HOHENZOLLERN REDOUBT to ANNEQUIN
Relieved by 1st KRR via QUARRY BOYAU, WATER BOYAU, INVERNESS

TRENCH, SCOTTISH TRENCH, and VERMELLES. Battalion arrives in ANNEQUIN at 4 45 pm. Billets- Fair. This had been our longest stay in the Trenches. Casualties very few but we suffered fairly heavily during the earlier part from chilled feet and lost 50 or 60 men.

Sadler Account:

61. LOOS BATTLEFIELD. Greeting our incoming comrades.
Finishing our turn at this part of the Line we left these Trenches for a little mining village just in the rear.

Whilst on the way out we were passed by the relieving troops who shouted out to us, "What's it like up there?" Our reply was that there was enough water about to be able to steam up the Trenches in a Dreadnought or Battleship. I thought that this was very cheerful news to be passing on to the in-coming Troops. The few days, which we spent at the mining village, were quite a change from the past month or so.

Although shelled at times by the German Artillery, one or two families of French people were still living there and we were always pleased to meet them. On arrival, the remainder of the first day was spent in us receiving real treats such as a good meal, a clean change of under-clothing, a new pair of trousers and getting the mud off of the remainder of our clothes. We also got a good telling off for cutting parts of our Great Coats off.

As our Great Coats tended to drag in the mud whilst in the Trenches, we, cut them off above the pockets and, by doing so, found that we did not have so much mud to carry around. We were told that we would have to pay a third of the cost of the coat but no more was heard about it. This night we had the pleasure to sleep in the empty miner's cottages which meant not having the sides of Trenches falling in on us. The next day was spent in resting and getting dried out. The day after we left this village for a little rest, this being our first rest since I had arrived in France.

Battalion War Diary:

15th November 1915. ANNEQUIN
Day spent cleaning up.

16th November 1915. ANNEQUIN to BETHUNE
March off at 9 am. "C","D", "B", "A" via BEUVRY to BETHUNE. Excellent billets there in RUE MICHELES.

17th November 1915. BETHUNE
Day spent in cleaning up. G.O.C. 12th Division visits us.

18th November 1915. BETHUNE to NORRENS FONTES.
One Officer and 2 O.R. to Bomb Course at ST.VENANT. March off "D","A","B","C" via DAIRE-CHOQUES-LILLERS-St HILAIRE COTTES to NORRENT FONTES where we take over billets from 40th PATHANS. Very good billets and

pretty village.

19th November 1915. NORRENS FONTES.
Programmes of work demanded. Battalion Baths. Battalion Bombing Ground, Reservation Room and Coffee Bar inaugurated.

20th November 1915. NORRENS FONTES.
Route March via. RUMBLY- LINGHEM. Frost.

21th November 1915. NORRENS FONTES.
1 Officer and 2 NCO's attached to Guards Div. 2 Officers to 12th Division School.

22th and 23rd November 1915. NORRENS FONTES.
Routine.

24th November 1915. NORRENS FONTES.
Route March

25th November 1915. NORRENS FONTES.
Leave allocation for Officers increased. 3 Officers and 4 O.R.'s granted leave.

26th November 1915. NORRENS FONTES.
Battalion Rifle Range inaugurated.

27th and 28th November 1915. NORRENS FONTES.
Routine.

29th November 1915. NORRENS FONTES.
Draft of 126 arrives. Divisional Football Contest inaugurated. Battalion Drawn against the 11th Middlesex.

30th November 1915. NORRENS FONTES.
Routine.

31th November 1915. NORRENS FONTES.
Warwicks Regiment Billeting party comes to take over.

1st December 1915. NORRENS FONTES.
Routine.

2nd December 1915. NORRENS FONTES.
Defeated 11th Middlesex 1-0 on time at football.

3rd December 1915. NORRENS FONTES.to MT. BERNENCHON
March off. "A","B"," C", and "D" via. HAM en ARTOIS–BUSNES–along LA BASSÉE Canal to Mt. BERNENCHON. 7th Sussex & 8th Royal Fusiliers to

HAISNES. 11th Middlesex to LES CHOQUAUX. Brigade H.Q.'s at BETHUNE.

4th December 1915. MT. BERNENCHON
Very wet. Country flooded all around.

5th December 1915 and 6th December 1915. MT. BERNENCHON
Routine. G.O.C Inspects Transport.

7th December 1915. MT. BERNENCHON
Special Duty in BETHUNE. Town raided for spies and deserters. Search unproductive.

8th December 1915. MT. BERNENCHON
CO to new Trench H.Q.'s to inspect troops near FESTUBERT.

9th December 1915 and 10th December 1915. MT. BERNENCHON
Routine. Very wet weather.

11th December 1915. MT. BERNENCHON
One Company takes our forward posts at RUE DE LEPINETTE & LE CAILLOUX from 11th Middlesex who take over from the 1st Middlesex, 33rd Division.

12th December 1915. MT. BERNENCHON to LE TOURET.
Remainder of Battalion marches via HAINES-LES CHOCQUAX to LE TOURET and takes over billets from Cameron Highlanders.

13th December 1915. LE TOURET.
Routine. Hot water baths arranged Regimentally.

14th December 1915. LE TOURET.
Routine. Officers in Charge of Coys. visit Trenches at FESTUBERT.

Sadler Account:

62. OUT ON REST. My first "stripe".
Whilst on this rest, the cleaning of buttons and equipment was undertaken and I also received my first "Stripe" which, at the time, was against my wishes. I was ordered to attend Company Orders one morning and was told that I was to become a Lance Corporal. I immediately said that this was against my wishes and that I was only out "here", like all the rest, to do "my bit". I said I could very well do this without taking a "stripe". However it was no good; I was told that I would have to take it. A few days after, before getting time to put the stripe up, I was given the duty of Orderly Corporal to get on with. When that was finished, I had to attend parades such as Rifle and Bombing Drill etc. then, all at once, we had orders to clean the Brass work on our equipment.

63. OUT ON REST. Trying to get rid of the Stripe.
Being a Lance Corporal, the requirement of cleaning of our equipment, when called for, was everything at that time. Myself and another Lance Corporal thought that, if we didn't trouble with shining the brass work up too much, it would be a very easy way to get rid of our "stripe". We had been told earlier, by our Captain, that it would prove hard to get a "stripe" and much harder to keep it. When we had finished our cleaning, we both had to attend Company Orders wearing our "properly" cleaned up equipment, ready for the Company Officer to inspect. My chum was called up before the Company Officer first. After his equipment was inspected he asked the Officer, straight out, if he could give up his stripe and the Officer agreed to this. Next came my turn. My equipment was inspected then I also put it to the Officer about giving up my "stripe". The reply which I got was that I was to keep my "stripe" for a few weeks longer owing to my role in the teaching of others how to put up a barbed wire entanglement. With this I was paid for my first "stripe" and put in charge of the Wiring Party. A short time after we left for the Trenches again.

Battalion War Diary:

15th December 1915 LE TOURET to FESTUBERT
Battalion take over Trenches from West Kent Regt. at FESTUBERT. Find Trenches waist deep with water. Hand pumping continues day and night. Weather wet.

16th December 1915. FESTUBERT
Enemy quiet. Heavy rain.

17th December 1915. FESTUBERT
Hostile Artillery Active – but no damage done. Vast improvement in condition of Trenches.

18th December 1915. FESTUBERT to LES CHOQUAUX
Battalion relieved by 7th EAST SURREY Regt., 37th Brigade, and proceeded to LES CHOQUAUX arriving there at 10 00 pm.

Days spent in these so-called "Islands" were vividly recalled by Lance Corporal Sadler:

64. TRIP TO FESTUBERT. Wondered if the Germans had made a mistake.
This time the Trenches were worked very differently to how they had been in the past. The Trenches were at Festubert and known by us at that time as "Glory Land". This had once been a lovely part but, owing to much shell-fire, only the "stems" of the lovely trees had been left standing which made it a very un-earthly looking place. This time we were holding what were called "Islands", these being areas of our Front Line which had stood much knocking about by shell fire. The Islands were pieces of land, here and there, surrounded by water. Once on these "Islands" it was impossible to move due to water and German snipers.

My Company had four posts to hold and my Platoon was picked, with myself being in charge, to hold No. 3 Post. Arriving at these Trenches, I was met by a

Guide to take me and my party of men to this Post. At last we arrived at what was another "far from pleasant looking" hole. Of course the first thing I asked of the NCO, who was in charge of Troops who were being relieved, was how far the Germans were off. "Shut up" he said, "They are only forty yards away". When the outgoing Troops had left, I could only think that this NCO was telling the truth. The Germans had started putting up some barbed wire round their Posts and, by the noise they were making, I wondered if they had made a mistake and were putting it up around our Post instead.

Close by, we could smell several good "German Cigars", until the German working party finally finished their work.

65. ON THE ISLANDS. Making ourselves comfortable.

We then started putting up a little shelter so as to make ourselves comfortable; the shelter being made up from waterproof sheets. The following night we were due to be relieved by fresh men and we were going to ask them for their waterproof sheets and leave them ours. However we found that there was no way that we needed to do that; our twenty-four hours finished up with us doing four days! Leaving again on 18th Dec, we also received Orders that we were not allowed to fire our rifles unless attacked. This was so as to not give the positions of our posts away. If, though, we had been allowed to fire there may have been one or two less Germans to trouble us. The Germans had some very fine snipers at this part and they killed two of our very fine snipers within two days. One of those killed being my old chum, Dudley. When anyone got wounded at these Islands it was impossible to get them away before night and under the cover of darkness. Because there were no Communications Trenches in this area, our rations had to be served out at night when we were able to get to the place where the rations were being served and whilst it was dark. It was a great pleasure to be able to go and fetch our Rations as this enabled us to have a stretch. In these places at the "Islands", it was impossible for one to stand upright. We had to virtually remain in a crouched position all day and there was not a square yard to turn around in. However there was plenty of mud and water to stand in.

66. ON THE ISLANDS. Having a fire.

We did take steps to make ourselves more comfortable. We found an old tin and knocked some more holes in it but we were not lucky enough, this time, to have a "Dump" alongside our Island so we burnt our hard Army biscuits which were part of our rations for the day. This gave us great delight by way of creating a little "sunshine" as we affectionately used to name the fire. All went well with our fire until one of the men put an extra supply of biscuits on it which caused a very large cloud of smoke. With the wind blowing towards the German Line it soon made Fritz think that we were sending over a cloud of Gas and, very soon, we received, in exchange, a few of his Whizz Bangs. I soon said to my chums that we had better keep low at the bottom of the Trench as, being that they were actually parts of our Breast Trenches; I could see that his "Whizz Bangs" were likely to come right through the front part of our Trench. However, after knocking a few sandbags out of place at each end of our Post, the Germans packed up with their shelling but we had a good idea that they now knew there was life in the old Trench.

67. ON THE ISLANDS. Nearly taken for a German.

On our last night at the "Islands", I nearly gave Fritz a visit. After walking to where the rations were served out and collecting ours, I was asked by the Sergeant to come back and take No.4 Post's rations over which I did. I set off on my journey and after getting entangled in much barbed wire; I made up my mind to try another route. In the end I lost my bearings and, for some time, cruised about in "No Man's Land". After a short time, I heard some clicking noises close by. Not knowing whether it was a British Trench or a German one, one can guess how I felt. I knew it was a case of having to say something or else a small shower of bullets would be coming at me. I soon said, "Are you Fusiliers?" and I soon felt relieved when a voice said, "Yes". When I reached the Post, all of the men were ready; only waiting to pull the trigger on their rifles. I will admit that I took jolly good care that I didn't lose my direction again after this. After doing our turn at this part, we left for the Le Bassee Front. It was now a few days off of Christmas 1915.We finished up at some huts, spending two days there, 23rd and 24th of Dec. 1915. Two of the Battalions from the Brigade had gone to the Trenches but we were doing our turn in Reserve and then relieving the other two Battalions on Xmas Day.

Battalion War Diary:

19th December 1915. LES CHOQUAUX
Routine. – Battalion scattered in Billets. Weather – Wet.

20th December 1915. LES CHOQUAUX
Route march to BETHUNE.

21st December 1915. LES CHOQUAUX
Routine.

22nd December 1915. LES CHOQUAUX to LES QUESNOY.
Battalion proceeded to LES QUESNOY. – Settled in Billets 7 00 pm.

23rd December 1915 and 24th December 1915. LES QUESNOY.
Routine.

25th December 1915. LES QUESNOY.to GIVENCHY
Battalion took over Trenches in GIVENCHY from 11th Middlesex Regt. A Shell exploded in the midst of a Platoon of "A" Company killing 5 men and wounding 6.

Sadler Account:

68. XMAS DAY 1915. And a terrible journey.

After spending two fairly comfortable days, Xmas Day arrived. We made the best of Xmas Day morning, as one might expect, thinking of our dear ones in

James's handwritten account of action near the Loos Battlefield: Xmas Day 1915.

Blighty. Dinnertime arrived. We received a small piece of Xmas Pudding also a tin of chocolate which was to be shared between so many of us; sitting down on the floor of the hut to enjoy it. Shortly after Dinner the order came to "Fall In", and we readied ourselves to march to the Trenches once more. We left by Platoons in Artillery formation, 100 yards between each Platoon. Owing to the shelling of the roads, I shall never forget the sights which we saw that afternoon. At 2.30, whilst marching up the La Bassee Canal, all of a sudden a large shell was heard travelling through the air. It struck the ground right in the centre of the Platoon to the rear of mine, blowing the poor fellows all over the place, many of them finishing up in the canal. Whilst collecting the wounded up, two more large shells came over which did not improve things. It was a terrible time, spent getting away the wounded, dead and those suffering from "Shell Shock". Out of that Platoon of men, only four were able to continue towards the Trenches and they were left out, suffering from the effects of shock.

69. TRENCHES AT GIVENCHY. Xmas night in the Trenches.

At last we arrived at the village of Givenchy; here we got served out with "waders" which we put on, leaving our boots in exchange. We walked on to the Support Trenches and in the afternoon, when we were within 100 yards or so from the Trenches, all of a sudden, overcame a shower of Wizz Bangs and it was lucky for us that we were not cut up by these. We soon made the cover of the Ditches running alongside the road and here we waited until things went quiet before we proceeded to the Trenches. Passing through the Trenches, knee deep in water, we finished up at newly made Breast Trenches, the type which had no backs to them. Here I was put in charge of another position. At these Trenches, the Regiment that we were relieving had lost several men, due to a mine going off under the Trench. So this is where I spent my Xmas Night. The night was very quiet. The following day we spent making it back to our Post. Again it was quiet, all except areas to the rear, which were shelled, with the Germans looking for our Batteries. Our guns had been rather active.

Thinking that Fritz was going to give us a "Xmas Box" in the form of an attack, this night we took a trip around to see who or what was on our left.

We did not find a living soul.

70. TRENCHES AND THE VILLAGE. Better off in the Trenches.
The Companies that should have been on our left were in a Trench but, they were in the rear, and to our left.

Due to this "trip"; my post could have been taken by the Germans without anyone being any the wiser.

There were so many disused Trenches about in this part that one could arrive on top of someone else before they were even noticed. Owing to the weather we were only in the Trenches for 48 hours and these soon passed. When our 48 hours were up we returned back to the village of Givenchy. This village was only a few hundred yards from the Front Line and was far from comfortable due to the Germans shelling it so much.

With them just over the Ridge and us on this side; they used to like sending over a few searching shells. All we could think about was that we most certainly didn't want one of them in our Billet. As there were a Company of men stationed in one billet, and that only an old barn, I was very glad when the time came to go back to the Trenches. We had plenty of dangerous working parties with shells dropping around our billet and it was a very nerve racking place. When one was in the Trenches, one had a much greater chance of his life being saved by being in a covered area. So after 48 hours in this village we were happier to return to the Trenches again. This time we were in Support Trenches and we had a fairly quiet time.

71. 2nd VISIT TO THE TRENCHES. Trenches instead of working parties.
Much Gas was being got ready for use on the Germans and whilst large carrying parties kept arriving with Gas Cylinders, nobody was allowed to walk about much which we didn't mind in the least. The second night, things were rather lively on our right. Rapid fire was heard but we only "Stood To" to "Stand Down" without anything happening. This position was the First Trenches where we had food cooked and sent up to us from our Cookers stationed in the village. It was a far from pleasant job for the men who were "told off" to fetch the food because of the roads being shelled with "Wizz Bangs". These caught one or two of our Ration Parties at different times. After 48 hours we left for Festubert, "The Glory Land",

near Givenchy once more, doing three days there. This time we were not on The Islands but were in Support Trenches. Myself, I was left out at the last minute to take charge of a Carrying Party which was to go up to the Royal Engineers G.S. wagons and help with unloading near the Front Line. After one night of this, I said to the Officer in Charge the following day that I would like spend the other two days in the Trenches if this was possible as, at this time of the War, I loved being with my chums.This Officer did his best for me and had a message sent up to the Company Officer in the Trenches. The message sent back was to say that I was to "Stay Out" where I was.

Battalion War Diary:

26th December 1915. GIVENCHY.
One of our patrols observed a working party- our Artillery successfully dispersed them. Enemy Artillery fairly active. It was noticed that preparatory to throwing bombs the enemy invariably blow a small horn.

27th December 1915. GIVENCHY
At 12 15 am. The Enemy made a Bombing demonstration against I Sap. They were easily driven off and did no damage. Otherwise it was all quiet on our front.

28th December 1915. GIVENCHY
At 11 00 am our Bombers used an electric catapult from K Sap and found this very effective. A hostile working party was observed driving stakes at DEADMANS TRENCH and CRATER.

29th December 1915. GIVENCHY
SCOTTISH TRENCH and GIVENCHY KEEP were shelled by the enemy but little or no damage done. Our Artillery retaliated with effect.

30th December 1915. GIVENCHY
Enemy Artillery Active but no damage done. At midnight several Trench Mortars were fired at K Sap and SCOTTISH TRENCH but their shooting was entirely ineffective.

31th December 1915. GIVENCHY
Battalion relieved from Trenches by 7th East Surrey Regt. and took over billets at ESSARS. Battalion arriving at 10:00pm. Casualties: 2 killed and 2 wounded.

So 1915 drew to a close. The recently promoted L. Cpl. Sadler was destined to remain "staying out" for the whole of 1916 and beyond.

8

January to February 1916
The early months – still in the
Loos Battlefield Area

The 9th Royal Fusiliers were relieved in the Givenchy sector by the 7th East Surreys on 31st December 1915. Brief stays in Essars and Le Touret respectively, were followed by a return to the Festubert sector on 8th January.
Battalion War Diary:

1st, 2nd and 3rd January 1916. ESSARS.
In Billets at ESSARS. Good billets and less scattered than LES CHOCQUAX. One Company at work in defences in GORRE WOOD. One Company and 1 Section on the defences around LOUNE. Weather wet and windy.

4th January 1916. ESSARS to LE TOURET.
Take over from 7th Norfolk's 35th Brigade at LE TOURET. Relief complete at 12 30 pm. All four Companies in billets- very compact but rather crowded. The Battalion finds two posts of 1 NCO and 3 men each at ROUTE A and TURNING FORK E.

5th, 6th and 7th January 1916. LE TOURET.
Work round billets and general improvements. Nightly working parties of from 150 to 200 men under supervision of the R.E.'s on such works as PIONEER ROAD. RESERVE TRENCH. Weather on the whole fine but windy.

8th January 1916. LE TOURET to FESTUBERT TRENCHES.
Relieve 11th Middlesex in trenches in evening. Relief commences at Drying Room FESTUBERT at 5 30 pm where trench boots are obtained. Companies relieve in the following order. Left Front ("A" Coy.), Right Front ("D" Coy), Support: RICHMOND TRENCH-"B" Coy., Reserve; ("C" Coy). Relief complete at 9 30 pm. Middlesex's lose one man during relief of RICHMOND TRENCH. Quiet night.

Sadler Account:

72. LOOS BATTLEFIELD. A warm part.
Leaving this part, (around LES CHOQUAUX to LES QUESNOY), we again went back to our "Old" part, The Loos Battlefield, spending from just after Xmas 1915 until six weeks before The Somme Battle, here, doing much work and seeing much action in Trenches named Kaiserin Trench, Hohenzollern Redoubt and Pilgrims Progress. These were not a great distance from the Giant Slagheap near Hulluch.

This was to be rather a "warm place" as, due to the view from the Giant Slag Heaps close by the Coal-fields near Hulluch, it made a splendid observation place for the Germans. They made it very hard for us as they were able to see what was going on for many miles behind our Lines. This resulted in us having the longest Communication Trench on any Front. Our main Communication Trench was called "Chapel Alley" and was two and a half miles long which was a real drag for anyone when taking over the Line or when getting relieved.

Due to the length of the Trench, we were unable to get cooked food sent up to us from our Cookers which at this time had just been brought up to The Front.

Battalion War Diary:

9th January 1916. FESTUBERT TRENCHES.
Very fine. Quiet day and no shelling. 2nd in Command and Adjt. visit front line trenches via RICHMOND TRENCH and back by PIONEER ROAD. The trenches are very much improved since the Battalion was last in the system from 15/12/15 – 18/12/15. Quiet night.

10th January 1916 FESTUBERT TRENCHES.
Fine and quiet. Warned of a demonstration by 2nd Division on our left.

11th January 1916 FESTUBERT TRENCHES.
Demonstration takes place at 7 00 am and there is a good deal of artillery fire. Colonel Carnegie – Central Force- attached for 3 days "focus" tour of instruction. A patrol from RICHMOND trench goes out in the evening and establishes connection with the 14th Royal Welsh Fusiliers on our left.

12th January 1916. FESTUBERT TRENCHES.
Very fine and slight frost. Much aeroplane activity. Rain in the evening.

13th January 1916. FESTUBERT TRENCHES.to ESSARS.
Colder. Sleet Showers. Attached Colonel returns. Reserves Company have been finding a daily working party of 120 men on extenuation and reconstruction of RESERVE Trench to the right. Relieved by 6th Battalion the Buffs 37th Brigade in the evening. Relief commences 5 30 pm. and all complete by 8 30 pm. Battalion has soup under regimental arrangements at LE TOURET on the way to ESSARS.

14th January 1916. ESSARS.
Battalion spends the day cleaning up and bathing at CANAL BANK baths.

15th January 1916. ESSARS.
Work on GOOREWOOD and LOISNE as before. Orders to move to MANQEVILLE on the morrow.

16th January 1916. ESSARS to MANQUIVILLE.
Move off to BETHUNE to proceed by train to LILLERS. Transport goes by road.

Train leaves BETHUNE 10 45 am – reaches LILLERS 11 15 am. 1.5 miles march to MANQUEVILLE where we occupy billets previously held by 22nd. Royal Fusiliers of the 33rd. Division. Very good billets but rather scattered. Told to expect an inspection by General JOFFRE on the 20th. inst.

17th January 1916. MANQUIVILLE.
Routine i.e. bathing- cleaning up men and repairing billets. Resulting work-Construction of range and Regimental Baths.

18th January 1916. MANQUIVILLE.
Routine- C.O.'s inspection parade in the afternoon.

19th January 1916. MANQUIVILLE.
Very Fine. Brigade inspection practice parade on ground just N. of LILLERS. Battalion ties with 8th Royal Fusiliers in Divisional football competition.

20th January 1916. MANQUIVILLE.
Morning spent in preparations for General JOFFRE's inspection in the afternoon. Inspection parade in position at 2 30 pm. C in C very late but inspection a great success. The Battalion receives congratulations from various sources for its turn out.

21st January 1916 MANQUIVILLE.
The first of four days of Battalion training- Sniping- Resulting- Reconnaissance by Junior Officers. Replay with 8th Royal Fusiliers in afternoon and beat them 2-love.

22nd January 1916. MANQUIVILLE.
Battalion route marches to BOIS DU REVEILLION and practice attack.

23rd January 1916. MANQUIVILLE.
Practice in the defence of a village organised by Officers and NCO's. Church Parade in the afternoon.

24th January 1916. MANQUIVILLE.
Ditto 22/1/16.

25th January 1916. MANQUIVILLE.
Brigade Route March. Order of March 7th Royal Sussex, 8th Royal Fusiliers, 9th Royal Fusiliers, 11th Middlesex. March to RELY and return by same route. Home 1.30 pm. Very fine.

26th January 1916. MANQUIVILLE.
Day spent preparing for Divisional Manoeuvres. Scheme and Orders arrive 7 00 pm. Manoeuvres cancelled indefinitely at 8 30 pm. Warning message at 11 30 pm to be ready to move at 2 hours' notice.

27th January 1916. MANQUIVILLE.
Routine. Range, bombing, baths etc. Dull.

28th January 1916. MANQUIVILLE.
Fine. 2 hours off. Beat R.E.'s in Divisional Football Cup by 1-love. 2 hours' notice again. Reports that Germans very unsettled. Artillery bombardment heard all day. Wind between E and N.E.

29th January 1916. MANQUIVILLE.
Coy. Training. Routine. Manoeuvres on again on the morrow.

30th January 1916. MANQUIVILLE to ENQUIN LES MINES.
Divisional Manoeuvres. Fine but misty. Parade 8.05 am. -"C"," D", Drums, "B"," A". Starting point 0.26.d. 9.7 at 8 20 am. 8th Royal Fusiliers, 7th Royal Sussex, 9th Royal Fusiliers, 11th Middlesex. Route as per Brigade Route march of 25/1/16. to ESTREE BLANCHE where Brigade halts for dinner for 2 hours. 35th Brigade are out in front from UPEN D'AMANT to CLARCQUES holding outpost line. At 2 15 pm. get Orders to move into billets at ENQUIN LES MINES. Best billeting area Battalion has been in in France. Receive Orders at 12 10 am for the morrows move.

31st January 1916. ENQUIN LES MINES to MANQUEVILLE.
March home again- all Divisions on one road. Order of March "A","B", Drums, "C","D". Starting point and time – ESTREEBLANCHE 10.24 am. 11th Middlesex, 9th Royal Fusiliers, 8th Royal Fusiliers, 8th Royal Fusiliers, 7th Royal Sussex. Back in MANQUEVILLE by 1.30 pm. End of Divisional manoeuvres.

1st February 1916. MANQUEVILLE.
Very fine- cold. Win the semi-final of Divisional Football Cup against 6th Btn. West Kent's. 1-love. Receive Orders to move by train on the morrow to the Trench area to take over from 33rd. Division.

2nd February 1916. MANQUEVILLE.
Move cancelled. Fine. Leave reopens for 5 Officers and Other Ranks. Battalion and Brigade- training.

3rd February 1916. MANQUEVILLE.
Routine. Fine- wind backing.

4th February 1916. MANQUEVILLE.
S.W. Gale. Receive Orders to take over from 37th Brigade at LA PIERRIERE on the morrow.

5th February 1916. MANQUEVILLE to LA PIERRIERE
Parade 9 50 am. "D", " B", Drums, "A", "C", Transport. In Billets by 11 30 am. Billets very scattered and dirty. Find a Range there.

6th February 1916. LA PIERRIERE
Wet. Routine and Company training.

7th February 1916. LA PIERRIERE
Final of Divisional Football Cup against 62nd Brigade R.F.A.,(Royal Field Artillery), at GONNEHEM. We win 13 to 1. The Major General presents medals for winning team. Team: – Goal: Sgt. HARRIS, Rt. Back: Sgt. FRAME, Left Back: Capt. COXHEAD, Rt. Half: Lt.Cpl. BATEMAN, Centre Half: Sgt. PEMBER, Left Half: Pte. EGAN, Outside Right: L.Cpl. JONES. Inside Rt.: C.S.M.NOAKES. Centre Forward: Pte. BADDELEY. Inside Left: L.Cpl. SHENTON. Outside Left: Pte. FITCHFORD. C.O. goes to hospital.

8th February 1916. LA PIERRIERE
Parade at 2 15 pm. For inspection by Major General and issue of medals and cards for conspicuous service and mention in despatches. No. 1171: Cpl. MANZIE.A.- DCM ribbon and red card for conspicuous bravery on August 1st at HOUPLINES. No. 252: Sgt. BRICKELL.G.–DCM ribbon and red card for conspicuous bravery on June 29th at DESPERRE FARM, PLOEGSTEERT. No. 11895: C.S.M. (Company Sergeant Major) COVINGTON. H and No. 5888: C.Q.M.(Company Quartermaster),Sgt. HOWSE.R green cards- mentioned in despatches for general efficiency. No.2430: PEVERILL. W mentioned in Despatches – green card. for conspicuous bravery on Oct. 8th at LE ROTOIRE.

9th February 1916. LA PIERRIERE
Fine. Battalion route march again through ST. VENANT and back.

10th February 1916. LA PIERRIERE
Fine. 2nd in Command and Company Commanders visit VERMELLES trenches.

11th February 1916. LA PIERRIERE to BETHUNE.
Cold and wet. Sleet. Parade 9 00 am. Order: "D"," B", Drums, "A", "C". March via BUSNES-BUSNETTES-LE HAMEL-CHOCQUES to billets in Orphanage at BETHUNE. 8th Royal Fusiliers to LA BOURSE, 7th Royal Sussex to SAILLY LA BOURSE, 11th Middlesex to SAILLY LA BOURSE. The Brigade is relieving "B" Dismounted Brigade of the Cavalry Division. All in billets by 1 00 pm. Brigade HQ at LA BOURSE.

12th February 1916. BETHUNE to VERMELLES. LANCASHIRE TRENCHES etc.
Early move by motor Lorries (20) at 7 30 am. Off Lorry at NOUVELLES LES VERMELLES and march by platoons at 200 yd. intervals via VERMELLES to reserve Trenches. H.Q.'s G.2.6.2.8.
   Brigade dispositions – 11th Middlesex: Front Line (Right). 7th Royal Sussex: Front Line (Left). 8th Royal Fusiliers: Support Battalion. 9th Royal Fusiliers: Reserve Battalion.
   Disposition of Battalion. "A" & "C" Coys. & HQs to LANCASHIRE Trench.

"B" Coy. to RAILWAY RESERVE TRENCH (8 platoons)-"D" Coy + 1 Platoon "B" in Cellars at BREWERY VERMELLES. Relief complete at 10 15 am. 33rd. Division on our left- 18th Royal Fusiliers. British Mine at HAIRPIN-midnight.

13th February 1916. VERMELLES. LANCASHIRE TRENCHES etc.
Showery. Quiet morning. Germans conduct an offensive (from 5 30 pm. to 6 30pm.) against 11th Middlesex. Heavy bombardment and explosion of two mines followed by small bombing attack which was easily repulsed. "C" Coy. (2 platoons with S.A.A. with bombs) ordered up to Middlesex at 8 00 pm. 8 30 pm. "A" Coy. Ordered up to support and clear Trenches (picks and shovels from CLARKES KEEP). "D" Coy. detonates bombs at CLARKES KEEP and sends up two small parties with sandbags. Middlesex casualties estimated at about 100 but afterwards proved to be about 80.

14th February 1916. VERMELLES. LANCASHIRE TRENCHES etc.
"A" Company returns in early morning. 50 men of "D" Company carry up Trench Mortar bombs. "B" Company ordered up at 4 30 pm.to work on communication and support Trenches behind 11th Middlesex. "A" Company relieved "C" Company at 6 30 pm. Disposition: 1 platoon to each Coy. of Middlesex.

15th February 1916. VERMELLES. LANCASHIRE TRENCHES etc.
Gale. Most of Battalion out on working parties. Quiet. Heavy rain at night.

16th February 1916. VERMELLES. LANCASHIRE TRENCHES etc.
Gale. "A","B","C" & "D" Coys. relieve "A","B","C", & "D" Coys. of 11th Middlesex respectively from right to left. Relief complete 10 15 am. Find Trenches very much knocked about and a lot of work to be done. Quiet night.

Inevitably, the return to the frontline brought with it a spell of bad weather and fear of German offensive mining beneath occupied breastwork defences.

9

January to March 1916: Further Action on the Loos Battlefield

From mid-February 1916 onwards, 9th Royal Fusiliers saw action within the dreaded Loos Salient, the final result of the inconclusive 1915 autumn offensive. The tour was far from routine, the Battalion experiencing steady losses whilst engaging in active trench warfare.

Sadler Account:

To help my [*James'*] readers to understand, I shall start by writing about "Kaiserin Trench" followed by "Hohenzollern Redoubt" and "Pilgrims Progress".

73. LOOS BATTLEFIELD. In Reserve Trenches.
This part of our time in the Trenches was worked by doing turns of 16 days. This started with 4 days in Brigade Reserve which was positioned in a village named "Sailly La Boise". From there it was a move to Battalion Reserve for four days and then on to for 4 days in the Support Trenches called Obbie, (O.B.I.), which stood for "Old British Line" as this was where the British Front Line stood before the Battle of Loos. The final 4 days to make up the 16 were spent in one of the Trenches. These were, as I have mentioned, "Kaiserin Trench", "Hohenzollern Redoubt", and "Pilgrims Progress". After doing a turn of 16 days, the troops would be withdrawn to Bethune for 6 days or so. These Trenches were the most nerve racking Trenches on the whole of the British Front; firstly because of so much mining and also because of the showers of Trench Mortars and Rifle Grenades which we were exposed to.In February 1916, we started working this part by commencing with 4 days in the Reserve Trenches.

The first night we made ourselves very comfortable in what shelters we could find and, being packed very tightly together, only made it warmer.This night passed very well and the next day we spent carrying our "Plum Pudding" Mortars to the Front doing two journeys in all. The "fun" started again that night. Towards 6 o'clock, the Germans opened out a very heavy bombardment, mainly on the Communication Trenches and, in doing so, cut off communication to the rear. The result was that it was impossible to send back messages.

74. THE LOOS BATTLEFIELD. Standing To and Standing By.
After the Germans had finished shelling, they made an attack on The "Hohenzollern Redoubt", coming over, this time, wearing our uniform. Owing to him shelling the Communications Trench and not the Front Line, they found plenty waiting for them. Only very few reached our line but they never returned. That night, 14th February,

we were called to the Front Line to "Stand To" in case of more attacks, "Standing To" at the entrance of the Redoubt. With the Trench Mortars we were carrying and many large flakes of snow falling, we spent a far from pleasant night. When morning arrived we "Stood Down" and shortly afterwards left for our Reserve Trenches. We spent the time resting until "Tea-time" when we received orders to depart for the Front Line and to "Stand To" for the night. The night passed without any excitement and instead of leaving to finish our 4 days in reserve, we moved along to the right and commenced our 4 days in the Front Line in the "Kaiserin Trenches". Kaiserin Trench was a trench dug fairly deep in the ground and not too wide at the top; this because of the use of so many rifle grenades and Trench Mortars, both heavy and small.

The Trench was also very close to the Germans and a noted part for mining activity.

75. THE LOOS BATTLEFIELD. Kaiserin Trench. Rifle and Grenade Mortars.

Whenever a moving object was seen by the Germans, overcame several Rifle Grenades. The Trenches were worked in much the same way as at Armentières but the Sentry groups at this trench were supplied with whistles so as to give warning to the others if Rifle grenades were being used. These sentries having to keep their ears open as well as their eyes. When a rifle grenade or Trench mortar was fired by the Germans, on hearing the report from the rifle or gun, the Sentry would at once blow the whistle. All eyes would start looking skywards, as it was possible to see the Trench Mortars or Rifle Grenades sailing through the air.

If the Sentry could pick it out coming across to our Trench, he would shout "Right" or "Left" to the position from which he stood facing the Germans. This would give the men a chance to get to the correct side and safety. For this game, the Sentry needed good eyesight and also did not have to mind having plenty of exercise when looking skywards and moving to the right or left. It was not advisable, at this Trench, for a Sentry to fire his rifle unless he was sure to hit his objective as, when the sparks were seen from his rifle at night-time, something was bound to follow in return by way of a rifle grenade. This would also occur when the last movement of the day took place.

76. THE LOOS BATTLEFIELD. Repaying the Germans.

We had no cover at all at this time so we "enjoyed" the Open-Air life. We were not even allowed to fix up our Waterproof sheets in order to keep the Trenches dry during wet weather. This was because the Trenches were so narrow and with so much running to the right and left having to be done, any overhead cover would have blocked the traffic. So it was one way or the other; good cover or none at all. Our orders were to fire back 5 rifle grenades to the Germans one. It wasn't a bad game sending them over but what we were liable to get in return was not. When sending over our five, we always needed a Sentry to be able to give us warning and to let us know what direction one was being returned from. This was so that we could fire the next five back towards that spot. I used to think that this was a proper "Fools Game" as one might guess the Germans had some good deep dugouts and, after firing his Rifle Grenade he was jolly well soon under cover. Hence I considered our five were only sent over for "fun" and, if the truth was known, we lost ten men to his one or, perhaps, none. At this part it was not quite so comfortable for us in the way of cooking as, at the first sign of smoke, "Fritz" knew there was life about and something unpleasant would soon follow.

77. THE LOOS BATTLEFIELD. Cooking and Sentries posted under our Trenches.

We used to manage the cooking by using a brazier and the coke or charcoal whichever was supplied. The brazier always had to be lit or set going before daylight so as not to let the Germans notice the smoke. Then we would use the charcoal with something over the top to keep the sparks from being seen during the daytime. We always managed to do our cooking but it was a case of having to wait your turn to get at the braziers as only one was supplied to each Platoon. As anyone can guess, from what I have already mentioned, we had a far from pleasant time but this does not include the "Mining activity". This was the worst of all, as a man never knew if, or when, the Trench he was in was liable to be blown up in the air.

When Mining we also required lookouts from the Royal Engineers who used to do their turn at being Sentries under the ground. Under our Trench was what was called a "Listening Trench" which enabled a Sentry from the Royal Engineers to hear when the Germans were boring towards our Trench.

The Royal Engineers Sentry, who may have been a Sapper or an Officer, would start his journey underground, wearing shoes so as not to make a noise. He would also be supplied with especially made instruments which were fixed to his ears so that it was possible to hear the slightest noise. If the Sentry was to have worn his heavy boots, and the Germans were to have heard him, our men would soon have to give up their work, as they would also have had a man listening in the same way as ourselves.

78. THE LOOS BATTLEFIELD. Mining and what it did for the Infantry.

If, at any time, any sounds were heard, the Order would be sent up to us above to stop walking about as it was a puzzle for the "miners" to hear, underground what was going on due to the noise we were making.

"Mining" turned out to be a terrible thing for the Infantry to do in the way of work. It required the carrying out of sandbags full of chalk. If "Mine Shafts" were started on our Front, it fell to us to carry away the chalk. We didn't mind carrying the chalk. It was when it was emptied from the sandbags that it caused the problems. As soon as the Germans noticed new chalk it was a case of "lookout", not because of his Rifle Grenades but because of his very heavy Trench Mortars. Some of his heavy Trench Mortars were nearly two foot long and a foot across. They were made of a thin casing of metal and filled with very high explosive TNT. When they exploded they were similar to a Munitions Factory going up and the draught caused by one these bursting could be felt some distance off. These Trench Mortars we called "Minnie Wathers" or "Mine Throwers".

79. THE LOOS BATTLEFIELD. Crater Snatching.

Mining also caused shelling and many raids as the Germans always liked to know what was about to happen.

However, the worst thing which fell to the Infantry as a result of mining was what was what we called "Crater" Snatching". When both "our people" and the Germans were mining close together it was always a case that, in the end, one of the two were bound to be heard. Whoever heard the sounds first, stopped work at once, laid his Mine and blocked the Tunnel. The mine would then be exploded and this would inevitably be strong enough to "blow in" any tunnels that were close by. Whichever side blew up his mine first, knew very well, he had cost the other side many valuable lives. This is what was called "Counter Mining". After the "Counter Mine" had gone up it was then the Infantry's turn to hold the "Crater", basically a hole caused by the exploding of the Mine. Sometimes we would have to wait until nightfall before digging a zigzag Trench towards the Crater. We had a terrible time at this "game", as the Germans would sweep the whole ground with machine gun fire but the "Crater" had to be ours. It often led to the loss of several good lives and we always had to be prepared to lie flat on the ground at the outburst of the machine guns.

One had to dig for his life and I hoped that I would never have to work so hard again.

17th February was a red letter day for 9th Royal Fusiliers, the Battalion diarist recounting the detonation and ensuing aftermath of a German mine:

17th February 1916. FRONT LINE ALEXANDER, BIG WILLIE, KAISERIN TRENCHES.

4 30 am. We hold Saps: 1 ("D" Coy.) 2&3 ("C" Coy.) 4&5 ("B" Coy), 6, 7 & 8 ("A" Coy). Look out posts: 5("D" Coy), 6("C" Coy), 7("B" Coy), 8("A" Coy). Trenches: from left to right, ALEXANDER TRENCH – BIGGER WILLIE – KAISERIN TRENCH.

At 4 20 am. Germans fire a Mine under Sap. No.4. It was followed by no bombardment and no attack.

A new block was immediately made (X) and a new sap started (Y).

Dimensions of Crater: 200 ft. across. 35 ft. deep. It is almost exactly half way between two front lines.

Casualties: 2 men dug out (shaken). 1 Killed and 3 injured by fall of Trench at and about point A.

Artillery conducts a bombardment on BILLS BLUFF. All saps and front line Trenches cleared by 12 30 pm. Bombardment commences 1 00 pm. T.M.'s. cooperate at 1 45 pm. Artillery lifts from Front to Support Front line at 2 00pm and returns again at 2 15 pm., object being to make the enemy expect an attack and bring up his reserves. Bombardment dies down 4 30 pm. Coy's back in line at 5 30 pm. A number of rifle grenades during the night otherwise quiet. 7th Norfolk – 55th Brigade on our right.

Sadler Account:

80. THE LOOS BATTLEFIELD Holding Craters or "Graveyards".

When the "Crater" had been reached by us, and a good Trench had been dug, then would come the holding of the lip of the "Crater". This we achieved by digging round the large hole. If the Germans were not doing the same on the other side of the "Crater" we would then be able to dig right around. This was known as holding both lips of the "Crater". When this was achieved, the Crater became a little less difficult to hold as it would be held by our "Bombers". The name which the Infantry gave to such a Crater was a "Graveyard" as, everything which the Germans had available to kill us with was concentrated on this spot. Hence we used to receive a very "lively" time. Why it was called a "Graveyard" was because the hole was already dug and sometimes it was simply a case of the Crater being a soldier's last resting-place. I quite believe that, in the end, we gained the upper hand in "Mining Activities". I have known twenty-one mines, both ours and German mines, to have gone up whilst doing a turn of sixteen days in this part.

This "Game" of Mining had a great effect on the nerves of many men, as, when a mine went up, it was a terrible sensation.

81. THE LOOS BATTLEFIELD. A mine exploding or going up.

The Trenches, if not blown up in the air, would rock as if an earthquake had happened.

It got on our nerves especially when we were lying asleep, as, all of a sudden, we would be woken up and jump in the air. What I noticed of the German mining was that they generally used to be short in judging distances underground and because of this their mines would generally explode in front of our Trench.

This was still very dangerous because of the flying earth etc. which always caused much work, if not resulting in us having to get involved with much digging; we, nevertheless, had to deal with the cleaning up of the Trench. All that could be noticed when a mine went up was a very large cloud of white smoke which could be seen for miles around. One would then wonder if he was on the ground or flying up towards the sky. Following this was the terrible roar of falling earth with the ground shaking. The effect was just like being on a rough sea.

82. THE LOOS BATTLEFIELD. Getting mines ready under the German Trenches.

Our mines were laid by special men of the Royal Engineers and the work had to be done without making a sound as even the very least sound was likely to cause the loss of many lives. They would generally bore a tunnel four-foot square, on the slant to start with. The Germans would, however, generally make shallower tunnels. Because of that, it meant our men were tunnelling deeper below the Germans. When our men got well down in the ground and into what was considered the "Danger Zone", the brave men really had to start working as quietly as possible. The sound of their boots had to be deadened and this was done by tying sandbags around the bottom of their boots; then came the working in the Tunnel. This was done by laying many sandbags on the floor of the tunnel to deaden the noise of the fallen chalk. The men generally worked by using a bayonet so the work could only be done slowly but surely. The chalk was taken to the surface with the aid of small trucks with rubber tyres and strips of board would be laid to act as lines to keep the little truck from slipping off. When the tunnel was getting close to the German Front

Craters formed by the blowing up of four mines on 2 March 1916 under German trenches in the Hohenzollern Redoubt by the 36th Brigade, 12th Division. The 8th and 9th Battalions, Royal Fusiliers attacked after the mines went up and the 7th Battalion, Royal Sussex with the 11th Battalion, Middlesex Regiment were in support. Copyright IWM Q 64053

Lines, a Sentry had to be posted in the rear of the Tunnel to listen for Germans trying to counter-mine. Finally, special air pumps would be required to pump fresh air down to the "Silent Heroes". We found that one way of giving the Germans a good taste of our mining activity was to send three mines up at a time.

83. THE LOOS BATTLEFIELD. Sending up three mines at once and shelling the Front Line.

When the three mines had been finished and made ready for action, all the Front Line troops would be withdrawn to places of safety such as down a disused mine shaft under the cover of fallen earth. A Sentry would be placed near the entrance of the disused mine shaft and then all of our artillery would have their guns concentrated on where the mines were going to go up. One could imagine Old Fritz was in for a very warm time. All of a sudden, the quietness would break into a terrible roar from the guns and the falling of earth. The sensation caused by the Mines was terrible. Deep dugouts were no good against this manner of warfare.Due to the Lines being so close to each other, when the German Front Lines were shelled by our Artillery, our Front Line troops were withdrawn, all except for two Sentry groups. The other Troops went back to the Support Lines in case of shells falling short. Hence, courtesy of our Artillery, the enemy would receive another "Good" time and even if the Artillery was not enough for him, then he would also get a good supply of our Trench Mortars, both heavy and small. After the bombardment was finished we would return to the Front Line again and take up our places once more.

And so the fighting continued, the Battalion diarist relating details of resultant troop deployments as deteriorating weather conditions until welcome relief on 21st February.

18th February 1916. FRONT LINE ALEXANDER, BIG WILLIE, KAISERIN TRENCHES.
Wet. Quiet day. Rifle grenades and T.M.'s troublesome at night- otherwise quiet.

19th February 1916. FRONT LINE ALEXANDER, BIG WILLIE, KAISERIN TRENCHES.
Two companies of 7th Royal Irish Rifles, 48th Brigade, attached to us for instruction-

a Company each to "B" & "C". Artillery supporting the 35th Brigade conduct a bombardment on Trenches opposite HAIRPIN. Germans bring down one of our aeroplanes flying low in the neighbourhood of GIVENCHY but behind our front line. Representatives of 6th Battalion, The Buffs, come round to see our Trenches. Hear Zeppelins or aeroplanes flying at night. New Sap from Sap No.4 reaches the Crater.

20th February 1916. FRONT LINE ALEXANDER, BIG WILLIE, KAISERIN TRENCHES.

Very fine. The wind almost nil but tendency to the East. Much aeroplane activity. Orders re: Gas helmets received. All men in the Front Line and Support Trenches are to wear smoke helmets rolled up whilst wind is in the East. At 4 30 pm. "C" Company reports Enemy manning parapet at POTSDAM Trench. Much Artillery activity on our Right and a mine is fired- presumably in the 35th Brigade area. Frost.

21st February 1916. FRONT LINE ALEXANDER, BIG WILLIE, KAISERIN TRENCHES to BETHUNE.

Wind N.E. The Brigade is relieved by 37th Brigade. The 6th Battalion, The Buffs, relieve us. Guides at BREWERY CORNER, VERMELLES at 9 00 am. Our Company's "D", "C", "B", "A" being relieved by their "B", "C", "D", "A" starting from right to left. They are all on their way up from VERMELLES by 10 00 am. Relief completed by 12 45 pm. Battalion marches by Company via VERMELLES-ANNEQUIN-FOSSEE No.2- SAILLY LA BOURSE-BEUVRY to TOBACCO FACTORY, BETHUNE. First Company arrives 3 00 pm. Battalion all in by 4 15 pm. We leave sounds of a very heavy bombardment behind us.

Total casualties during Tour: – 11 killed & 30 wounded. = 41men

8th RF., 9th RF, 11th Middlesex to BETHUNE. 7th Royal Sussex to VERQUINEUL.

Sadler Account:

84. THE LOOS BATTLEFIELD. Catching German working parties and in charge of work myself.

As soon as dusk arrived, many of our machine guns would be set on the German Front Lines from positions which were generally unused by Troops. If our machine guns were set in positions which were being used by our Troops then we would receive a very warm time in return. The Germans would knock our Trenches flat with his heavy Trench Mortars whilst searching for our machine guns.

As soon as it got dark enough, one would hear the Germans repairing their damaged lines, and then our machine guns would give him a full supply of bullets causing them to have a very uncomfortable time.

War around this part of the British Front was carried on to the extreme. Whilst at this Post, as a Lance Corporal, I was in charge of a small working party and also in charge of small "Wiring Parties", when needed. Whilst I was in charge of the working party, all we had to do was to keep the Trenches repaired. You can see, by what I have mentioned that we always had plenty to do as the Front Lines, at times, were much knocked about with Trench Mortars. Doing the work on the trenches, it was a case of doing three things at once; waiting to hear the report of the Grenade Rifle or Trench Mortars fired by the Germans whilst also trying to see the Trench Mortar sailing through the air and, at the same time, trying not to think about a Mine which could, at any moment, also go off under ones feet.

85. THE LOOS BATTLEFIELD. Living in a Trench Mortar Pit.

Whilst working as a Party, we made our "Home" in one of our Trench Mortar Pits. The class of the Trench Mortar which we had was not the same as in the later part of the War. Our small Trench Mortars used to be a tin filled with small pieces of iron, weighing fourteen and a half pounds and fitted with a fuse. They could be seen sailing over to Fritz's Line, both day and night. By day, the tin itself could be seen. At night-time it could be seen by the fuse. Nearly all Trench Mortars could be seen at some time but in the later part of the War, certain types could only be heard at night and they used to make plenty of noise when coming down towards the ground. This always used to make one wonder where it was going to burst and one was never sure if he was "going for a trip in the air" as one was liable to do when they burst. Whilst we made ourselves at home in this Trench Mortar pit, I could never make out why the men who used to fire these Trench Mortars were so frightened. They used to fire two or three and then leave. We had to clear out whilst this was done and return when they had finished; being expected not to take the slightest notice of what was going on.

86. THE LOOS BATTLEFIELD. Digging a Trench to a Crater.

One night when a Mine went up just in front of our Trench we were selected to dig the "Zig-Zag" Trench and I will never forget this. Seven of us in all were in the Party and this was to be the hardest bit of digging which I had done in my life. It was not altogether the digging; it was the constant sweeping of the ground by the enemy's machine gun bullets. Two of the seven men were killed as soon as we started and I was quite expecting to be hit at any moment. We managed to get into a little hole and then we didn't mind the bullets quite so much. After three or four hours working in relative safety, we got relieved and went back to our place of rest in the Trench Mortar pit where we were to spend a most uncomfortable night, having German Rifle Grenades bursting around us all night; yet still they did not drive us out. We guessed what old Fritz was searching for, the Trench Mortar Gun.

87. THE LOOS BATTLEFIELD. Getting followed by rifle grenades etc.

The next morning, wherever I went, I was followed by German Rifle Grenades. First, myself and a chum went to the end of a little Trench that was between our "Pit" and the Front Line, which was just around the corner. They were serving out the day's rations when all of a sudden we heard a Rifle Grenade. At once we started to look towards the sky to see if we could see it. Finally, I caught sight of it and was waiting to make sure which way to go; to the Right or Left? I didn't have the pleasure of managing to get very far at all as someone in a great hurry to get out of the way himself, all of a sudden, shot round the corner and sent me flying. The Trench Mortar came right into the Trench and burst on the Trench-Boards about two yards from my boots and, by suddenly lying down; I considered that I had had a rather narrow shave. On getting our rations, we set off for our "Home of Rest" and were just getting ready what was needed for breakfast when we heard another Rifle Grenade sailing down. We just had time to get out mighty quickly as the Grenade struck full on in our "Pit" and on some boxes of detonators, sending the whole lot skywards. This was my second narrow escape within five minutes. Not long after that we started work in a Communication Trench with another man joining us until they killed him. If we couldn't find any work to do in repairing Trenches we used to spend our time in making Snipers Posts and also, at these Trenches, we started making our first deep dug-out after the German style, assisted by any miners who we could collect together to help us. However, we never had the pleasure of having the comfort of them because they were not finished until after we had left.

88. THE LOOS BATTLEFIELD. Barbed wiring at the Kaiserin Trench.

I only had the pleasure of putting up one lot of barbed wire whilst stationed at this Trench; 175 yards of it in all. Wiring here was very dangerous because of the Germans being so close and the work was generally given to us to carry out on a very nice moonlit night. It wasn't only the noise that drew the Germans attention; it was also the moving about. Men working on wiring at this part were not actually sent out, they went out of their own choice and it took three of us, four nights to do the 175 yards, with one man being wounded on the fourth night. This is how the four nights were spent. The first night it was far from comfortable owing to German Sentries sniping at us but because we were putting in "Screw-Iron Stakes", we were able to keep on the move whilst the Sentry kept on shooting at the first place where we were noticed. We got a fair night's work done. The second night it was raining very hard but we got nearly all of the wire up. Owing to the rain, the German Sentry did not like to keep up his firing and also it was a very dark night. Every one of us got very much fed up with the work and the rain but we stuck to it as it was so quiet. The other two men kept saying to me, "We are going to give up as we are getting so wet" but although they kept grumbling, they didn't give up. They knew it had to be done. When I considered that plenty of work had been done for the night, I said to them, "Come on, we will give in now". I was sure they had had enough.

89. THE LOOS BATTLEFIELD. 3rd and 4th nights at wiring.

The third night we could not get started. I Went out with the party and told the men to stay where work was going to commence again, whilst I walked down the wire that had been finished to look for any more rolls of the barbed wire. Whilst doing this I heard a Trench Mortar coming close to me. I, at once, lay down to chance my luck. The Trench Mortar burst only a few yards away but, owing to me keeping still, I was unhurt. No doubt they had an idea that they had killed me. The next Mortar sent over was aimed at the other two men but before it arrived they were in the Trench. On getting down the Trench, and getting level with me, they called out to let me know they had been driven in and I soon joined them. That night, the Company Officer advised us not to go out again owing to it being moon-lit. We waited for the sky to become cloudy but it failed to do so and therefore no work was done that night. The fourth Night proved to be very excitable but the work had to be finished. Work started well but bombing started on our left and we were tormented by flying

James's handwritten account of action at the Hohenzollern Redoubt: Oct.1915-March 1916.

pieces. However, by keeping quiet, this turn passed off alright but whilst at work, another bombing "stint" started suddenly and one of the three men was wounded in the face, but not dangerously. We came in so that I could get another man to restart again. This time, my Platoon Officer came out to lend us a hand but not long after re-starting we were driven in by "Trench Mortars" and had to take cover. When it was quiet we restarted again and finished the 175 yards and were thanked for the good work done.

90. THE LOOS BATTLEFIELD. The Hohenzollern Redoubt.

"Hohenzollern Redoubt" was far from a pleasant place to stay and work. For one thing we were never sure when the Germans were going to pay a surprise visit and it was one of the most unearthly looking places that could be found.The earth around the "Redoubt" had been blown to a powder owing to so much shelling by both us and the Germans and it was impossible to dig a Trench. The "Trench" itself was made of sandbags filled with chalk from the Mine Shafts and was only just wide enough for two men to pass each other.

Running into this "Redoubt" were many underground tunnels which had been made by the Germans; no doubt, made for the purpose of blowing up their Trenches when we captured them. One can see why the Germans tried so hard to recapture it and why, despite all of their heavy loss of life, they were unable to do so. If we had let them hold the "Redoubt" whilst we had been in the Trenches, in the end many of us would undoubtedly have been reported as missing. With regard to the setting of Mines, Trench Mortars and Rifle Grenades it was very much like the "Kaiserin Trenches". The "Redoubt" was also very useful to us by way of protecting the Fronts of other Trenches on both sides. It was possible to enfilade the other fronts by shooting straight down the "Redoubt" and "No Man's Land", therefore causing rifle and machine gun fire from two directions.

91. THE LOOS BATTLEFIELD. Pilgrim's Progress Trench.

Pilgrim's Progress was by far the best Trench out of the three Front Line Trenches to hold. It was very close to the Germans and this could cause much fun on a dark night. On hearing a German working Party just in front of us, three of us would get together and we would then send up a "Verey" Light; straight towards where we heard the working going on. The result would be a very large Flare making it impossible for the Germans to get away without being seen. As soon as we saw them, we soon greeted them with a small shower of bullets making it very uncomfortable for them. However, as soon as we had finished this "Game", it was a case of changing our positions because the Germans would then start and search us out with their Rifle Grenades. However it would be too late as, by then, we would have moved lower down.

92. THE LOOS BATTLEFIELD. Wiring at Pilgrim's Progress.

One of the worst things, though, about this Trench was being infiltrated by German small shells. We could never be sure when one might burst at our feet. At times it was a case of getting behind the traverses of the Trench and waiting to luck. Putting up barbed wire here was done altogether differently to the way in which I have already mentioned. The wire was put on wooden frames which were made by the Royal Engineers and which would open and close. On a very dark night, the frames and wire would be taken out into the Front or into No Man's Land where it would be opened, stood up and pegged to the ground. If the frames were was not made firm into the ground, the next morning we would see it protecting the German Front instead of ours because they would come and take it. Mines and Trench Mortars were not used quite so much on this Front as they were on the other two but all three of these Fronts reminded one of the past "Battles of Loos" as sights from that Battle were still to be seen. We worked in the way I have mentioned right up until six weeks before the Battle of the Somme and this included us going into action on the morning of 2nd March, having to take the German Front Line and hold it.

Battalion War Diary:

22nd February 1916. BETHUNE.

Heavy Snow. Companies engaged all day cleaning up kit and with feet inspections.

23rd February 1916. BETHUNE.

C.O. returns from hospital. Snowing rather heavily. "D" Company caries out a practice trench attack in presence of Corps. Commander at Divisional School, FORQUIERE at 9 00am. 16 Bombers also carry out bombing practice at same School in presence of Corps. Commander. Baths allowed from 9 00am -6 00pm at ECOLE DE VAAST. Companies bathed as follows. "A" 9 00am-11 00am, "B" 11 00am-1 00pm, "HQ" 1 00pm -2 00pm, "C" 2 00pm-4 00pm, "D" 4 00pm-6 00pm.

Leave for 2 Officers and 17 men stopped as sailings from BOULOGNE suspended. Routine. Leave again opened 4 hours later.

24th February 1916. BETHUNE.
Routine. 2 Working Parties supplied. They were conveyed by Lorries to SAILLY LA BOURSE & NOVELLE X roads. 1st Party: 90 strong, 2nd Party: 30 strong. 40 men also supplied for cleaning mud at BETHUNE Station. Course for Vickers gun commenced. 24 men attending course under Brigade M.G. Officer. Leave stopped except in special cases until further notice. Very Cold – Snow. Enemy aeroplane seen over BETHUNE at 2 30 pm. Flying high in northerly direction. "A" Company detailed to report to Camp Commandant 1st Corps. at CHOCQUES for duty at CORPS. HQ.

25th February 1916. BETHUNE.
Routine. Weather Cold and Sunny. Company Route Marches. Instruction in Machine Guns continued.

26th February 1916. BETHUNE.
Routine.

27th February 1916. BETHUNE.
Service in Municipal Theatre, Bethune at 12 00noon. Visit of Lieutenant Ormesby Johnson who went into and advised on Company Accounts

28th February 1916. BETHUNE.
Weather fine and cold. Battalion Concert in 2nd. Divisional Recreation Room at 2 30 pm.

29th February 1916. BETHUNE to VERMELLES.
Fine. Parade 10 00 am. and marched to VERMELLES via. BEURVY, relieving the 6th Buffs in Right Reserve Trenches. Marched up at 200 yard intervals between platoons. "D" Company settled in OLD BRITISH LINE, "C" in LANCASHIRE TRENCHES, "B" in BREWERY, VERMELLES. Relief commenced 1 00pm.

Disposition of Brigade. 11th Middlesex. – Right front. 7th Royal Sussex.-Left front. 9th Royal Fusiliers. – Right reserve. 8th Royal Fusiliers -Left reserve.

1st March 1916. VERMELLES.
Fine. Things quiet. C.O. meets Brigadier and receives instructions with regard to attack on German Trenches on the 2nd inst.

2nd March 1916. VERMELLES.
At 5 45 pm. 4 mines were exploded at HOHENZOLLERN REDOUBT in front of

THE CHORD. Battalion in readiness to attack and hold THE CHORD & THE TRIANGLE from C 4. exclusive to BIG WILLIE. 50 men of "B" Company were lined up in the WEST FACE to lead attack under CAPT. HON. R.E.PHILLIPS. When the mines exploded part of the WEST FACE was blown in and 20 men were temporarily buried. The remainder rushed across, cut through wire or went over where earth thrown from the Crater covered the wire and seized THE CHORD from C 4 to the lip of CRATER A. There was a large number of enemy in Trench and many in dug outs. They were dazed but did not surrender so were killed. Three fierce grenade fights then began with enemy rushing up C4 and C3 and down from Northern End of THE CHORD. Enemy was, with some difficulty, held until Craters No.1, No.2 and A were seized and temporary stops established and grenade supply facilitated. Later THE CHORD was heavily shelled and practically obliterated but was cleared up to C 3 and held by us.

"C" Company under MAJOR N.B. ELLIOTT-COOPER rushed Craters C1, C2 and A and then seized German crater in TRIANGLE. The grenade attack on right lost direction and a fresh attack, hastily organised and led by No. 1970 Sgt. CRONYN, rushed down SE face of TRIANGLE and into BIG WILLIE killing a few enemy met with and rolling or throwing grenades down all dug outs which were crowded with men who would have surrendered. Unfortunately Sgt. CRONYN's party was not large enough to take prisoners. This party was eventually held up by an enemy grenade party and a fight ensued for a considerable time until the CRATER in TRIANGLE was roughly defensible and the three trenches from it parquetted and stopped. It was decided to hold this instead of going further forward as it commanded the whole TRIANGLE. Telephonic communication with both Companies was quickly established and work of consolidation of ground gained, communication trenches and establishment of forward dumps of ammunition and grenades went on during the whole night. Wiring was possible from 11 00 pm. and a considerable amount was put out in front of Crater A.Total number of Casualties during attack: – KILLED: 1 Officer, 14 O.R. WOUNDED: 4 Officers, 141 O.R.

Sadler Account:

93. THE LOOS BATTLEFIELD. Our attack for three craters.

On commencement of the Battle, and with the concentration of our Artillery and the explosion of four mines it turned out to be a very terrible time for the Germans as they tried to hold both "Lips" of the craters created by the four mines but I think it proved a far more terrible time for us in trying to hold these afterwards. One of the Mines was the largest the Germans had ever had to deal with up to this time of the War. On our commencement of the Battle, so great was our gunfire and the effect of the Mines, that we did not receive even a single rifle shot from the Germans whilst we were taking the Position. We did get several men put out of action by falling earth etc. but, talk about holding "Hell", when it came to later in the day. When the Germans got their Artillery under way, supported by the heaviest Trench Mortars that had ever been invented up to that time of day, and also with German Troops trying their hardest to bomb us out, I think that, at the finish, we possibly received the most uncomfortable time and this led to some great losses on our part. We

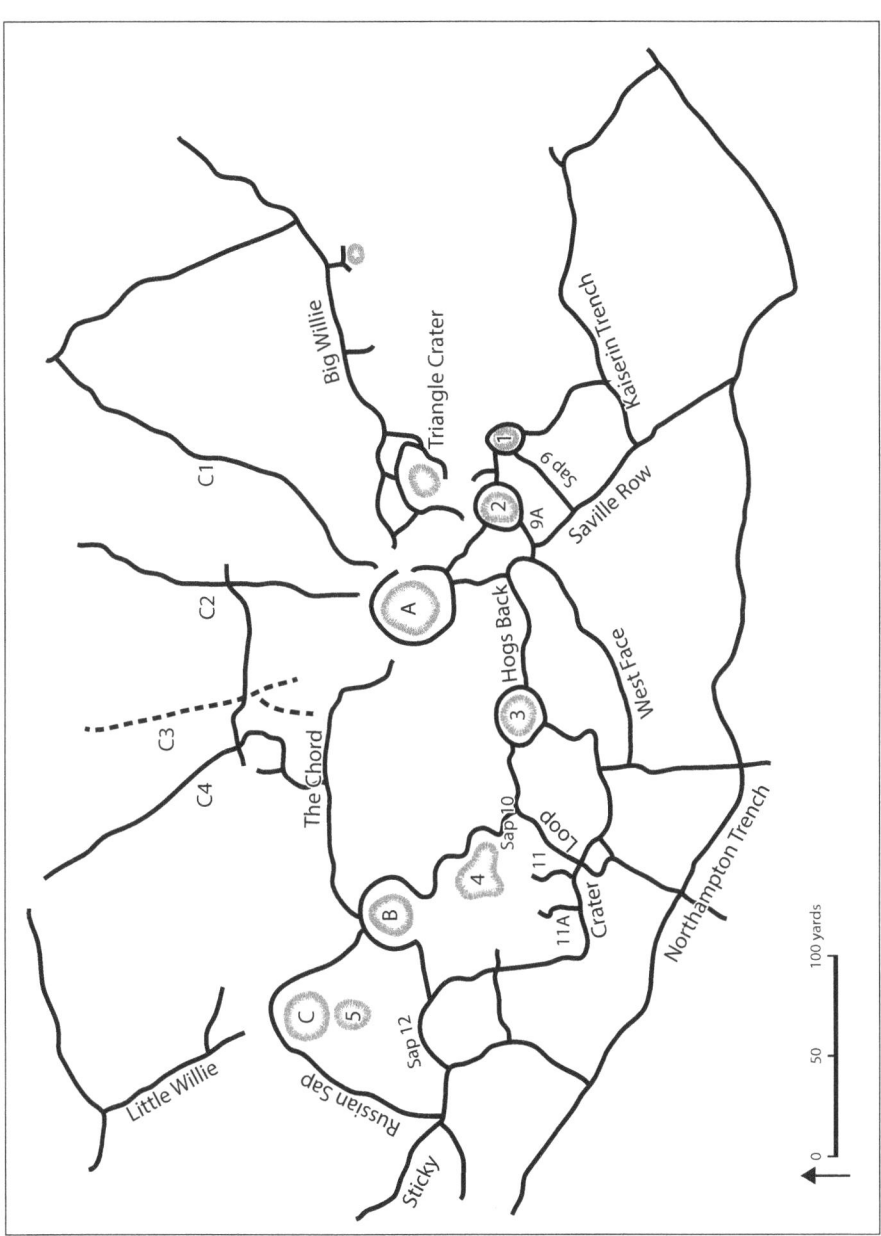

Sketch from the 9th Royal Fusiliers War Diaries showing map of craters formed by mining at Hohenzollern Redoubt. (George Anderson)

found out this Battle had been given the name of "Crater Snatching". The holding of these Craters, however, resulted in us quite rightly calling them "Graveyards". A day of so after the Battle we were relieved and carried on with our usual Trench holding whilst another of the Brigades from our Division took to holding the "Graveyards" which we had won. This Brigade held both "Lips" until the 18th March, when it became their turn to be attacked.

Battalion War Diary:

3rd March 1916. VERMELLES.
At 5 30 am. "D" Company relieved "B" Company. Relief complete by 6 30 am. At 3 00pm. the 11th Middlesex relieved the Battalion and took over all ground gained. We moved back into reserve Trenches. We heard that the Germans were attacking the Middlesex at 6 00 pm.

4th March 1916. VERMELLES.
Battalion spent all day carrying grenades up to Front Line. Weather: cold and wet. Heavy shelling on and off all day. Orders for relief received.

5th March 1916. VERMELLES to BETHUNE.
Battalion relieved at 3 00 pm. by 6th QUEENS. Companies proceeded independently to billets at Tobacco Factory BETHUNE. Battalion settled in billets at 7 00 pm.

6th March 1916. BETHUNE.
The day spent in cleaning- The Corps. Commander visited Battalion HQ this afternoon and congratulated the Battalion on the excellent work performed during recent operations and wished to have conveyed, to all ranks, his appreciation and admiration for the way in which it carried out a most gallant attack. Attached will be found copies of congratulatory messages received by the Battalion for work carried on during the recent attack of 2rd & 3rd March. (Marked A).

A.
Congratulatory Messages sent to 9th (S) Battalion Royal Fusiliers for work carried out during their occupation of the Trenches 20/2/16 to 5/3/16.

Message from Corps Commander (Gen. GOUGH). "BM 703 3/3/16 AAA
"The Corps Commander sends his congratulations to the Battalions in particular who have been fighting".

Message from GOC 12th Division (Major Gen. SCOTT). "BM 707 3/3/16 AAA
"Well done Thirty Sixth Brigade all ranks and congratulations 8th and 9th Fusiliers also for their excellent work"

Letter from Lt. Col. GRANT DSO – GSOI. 12th Division.
My Dear Gubbins:-
I am sorry I have missed you. Very best congratulations on your magnificent

performance. I fancy the Bavarians will long remember their day with the 9th Fusiliers.
Yours sincerely
(Sd.) Charles Grant.

Letter from Brig. Gen. BOYD MOSS 36th Support Bde. March 6th
Dear Gubbins,
I am sorry I have not had the time to write to you before to congratulate you on the
splendid behaviour of your battalion on March 2nd. The success of the attack was due
to the excellent organisation and training of the Battalion and to the great gallantry
and keenness of the Officers, NCO's and men.
Yours Very sincerely.
(Sd.) "L. Boyd Moss"

The Battalion's diary continues ...

7th March 1916. BETHUNE.
Weather Cold. Sunny. Three large working parties supplied for work at CLARKS
KEEP, VERMELLES. Remainder of Battalion- Training.

8th March 1916. BETHUNE.
The Corps. Commander (Lt. General Sir H. D.W.P.GOUGH. CB) addressed the
Battalion at Tobacco Factory, BETHUNE at 10 00 am this morning. Attached
will be found extracts from his speech, (Marked B). He was accompanied by Major
General SCOTT CB. DSO. Commanding 12th Division. The Battalion bathed in
baths at ECOLE St. VAAST.

B.
**Excerpt from Speech of Lt. General Sir H. D.W. P. GOUGH KCB. Commanding
1st Army Corps. delivered to the 9th Battalion Royal Fusiliers at TOBACCO
FACTORY, BETHUNE on 8th March 1916.**
"I wish to thank all ranks for their gallant conduct and splendid services rendered
during the attack on March 2nd ... I want you all to realise that I am not thanking
you for any personal service to myself but for your services rendered to our England,
Our Empire and cause and the Land of Our Fathers. I thank you because you are all
inbred with the Spirit of English Soldiers who always have been great soldiers."
"I conclude by thanking everyone for doing their duty for King and Country and
for keeping the tradition of a grand old Corps."

Settled into their Bethune billets, the 9th Royal Fusiliers would soon be on the
move again:

9th March 1916. BETHUNE.
The Divisional Commander visited our Billets this morning and conversed with
some of the men who took part in the recent attack. Grenadier training carried out in
morning. In afternoon a Battalion Concert took place in the 2nd. Divisional Concert
Hall, RUE D'AIRE, BETHUNE. A large number of aeroplanes, – probably 20-were

seen about 10 30 am. flying in a North Easterly direction. Weather still cold, snow still hanging around.

10th March 1916. BETHUNE.
Snow in morning. Company route march in morning. Training of Grenadiers continued- Orders for move next day to NOVELLES received. Colonel goes on leave to England.

11th March 1916. BETHUNE to NOVELLES .
Parade at 10 00 am. Order of March: – Drums, HQ, "A"," B","C","D" proceeding to NOVELLES. Arriving NOVELLES in relief of 11th Middlesex Regiment at 12 00noon. Middlesex take over our front line Trenches opposite QUARRIES. Companies billeted in Huts and Stables-all in by 12 30. Day very quiet, sounds of bombing attack during the night.

12th March 1916. NOVELLES
Fine and warmer. Bombing practice by all Companies in the morning. Three German aeroplanes flew over but were chased off. Rest of day quiet.

13th March 1916. NOVELLES
Commanding Officer and Company Commanders go to Trenches to reconnoitre. Battalion takes over extra bit of line from 15th Division. Decided to make disposition as follows- "B" & "A" Companies, taking over from 11th Middlesex and "C" & "D" Companies from the Cameron Highlanders (15th Division). Above Officers away reconsidering Front – 8 00 am to 3 30 pm. Surprising weather & thunderstorm at night. Six new officers arrived and posted to their Companies.

14th March 1916. NOVELLES to QUARRIES SECTOR.
Parade by Battalion at 7 20 am in following order: – "D", "C", HQ, "A","B" with 200 yard interval between Platoons. Relieve 11th Middlesex and Cameron Highlanders. Relief completed by 11 00am. Very fine day. Quiet Trenches. Various working parties and cleaning and renovating of Trenches. Quiet night. A few shells dropped in STAFFORD LANE. No damage.

15th March 1916. QUARRIES SECTOR.
Fine Warm. A certain number of hostile rifle grenades and aerial torpedoes on our right between 9 00am and 10 00 am. We retaliated. Exceptionally quite day. At 9 00pm, a mine was blown up by us on the right of our line. Enemy scared and man's his parapet and fires rapid rounds. Beyond this, all quiet during the night.

16th March 1916. QUARRIES SECTOR.
Fine weather. Things very quiet. Enemy shelled Communication Trenches for an hour. Rest of the day and night passed without incident.

17th March 1916. QUARRIES SECTOR.
Relieved by 11th Middlesex. Relief completed by 11 30 am. We take over Support

Trenches as follows: "A" and "D" Companies to O.B.1 with FOSSE WAY as dividing Line; "B" Company to CURLY CRESCENT; "C" Company,- 1 Platoon to O.B.4, 3 Platoons in O.B.5. Dug outs few but very fair. During relief "C" Company were bombarded and the other Companies were much worried by Rifle Grenades but no casualties occurred during relief. Weather turned colder but quiet night.

18th March 1916. QUARRIES SECTOR.

Fine. Quiet up to 5 00pm. General Boyd-Moss came round the Trenches. Enemy started a bombardment on the HOHENZOLLERN REDOUBT at 5 00pm. Heaviest bombardment we have seen or heard so far. They used apparently all their heavy Howitzers and Minnewaffer. Enemy also used Lachrymatory, (Tear Gas), shells in VERMELLES which necessitated wearing of smoke helmets. One such shell fell near "B" Company. It was afterwards discovered that enemy had attacked the HOHENZOLLERN and captured Band C Craters, No.4 also taken but recaptured by us. Our guns retaliated heavily. There was very little rifle fire and at 7 15 pm the show died down.

Sadler Account:

94. THE LOOS BATTLEFIELD. German attack.

On the 19th March, I was due to be starting my first leave back to England. However, at Dinnertime on the 18th of March, it became clear that the Germans were going to try and clear our Troops out of their Front Lines at the Hohenzollern Redoubt, and this, at all costs. In the afternoon they started the most terrible bombardment which I had ever witnessed up to that time. Shells were coming from all directions, from miles on our right and on our left, and they were all bursting on that one spot. Nothing in the world could have lived under such terrible shellfire and the smoke from the bursting shells was choking. After keeping this bombardment up for a few hours, over came the Germans in order to ensure that they held their Front Line once more, which they were to have the pleasure of achieving. At the finish of the day we were holding one side of the Craters and the Germans the other, so the craters were of no use to either side. At the time when this took place, we were stationed in the Trenches which I have mentioned earlier, O.B.I, our Support Line, and not a great distance off from where the attack took place. In these Trenches and Lines, one could make himself fairly comfortable, when time allowed, as there were several shelters and also one or two of our deep dugouts. Of course the use of deep dugouts had nothing to do with us as I suppose the Front Line Troops were not considered to be entitled to use them and the Machine Gunners and Officers thought they were more deserving of them, rather than us.

95. THE LOOS BATTLEFIELD. In Reserve Trenches. O.B.I.

Whilst I was at this Line, I had the pleasure of being able to wear my first steel helmet whilst in the Trenches. There only being a few of these about then, they were left by each Regiment as "Trench Stores" when any changeover of troops took place. What, though, proved to cause us the worst trouble, whilst at this Line, were the Germans heavy shells. Being only a little distance away from our Front

Line, he was able to shell us without worrying about any of the shells falling short. One had to be very careful about possibly getting a heavy shell all to himself or, at least, one of the many flying pieces. Once in this Trench, and when leaving for the Front Line, I took my Steel Helmet off and was saying to the man collecting them up, "Here you are", when a large piece of a shell dropped right on top of my head and slightly cut my head open. After being ordered, at the time, by my Platoon Sergeant to go and have it seen to owing to the bleeding, I gave the Regimental Dressing Station another visit and, having had it seen to, I carried on again with the "Good Work".

96. THE LOOS BATTLEFIELD. Starting my 1st leave; but recalled.
It was from this Line that I left for my first "Leave to England" on the 19th March 1916; only to finish up once again back at this Trench. On the 19th, I left the Trenches bound for England and after a long walk, arrived at our "Transport Lines". It was here that, after meeting up with several more men who were leaving for Blighty; we got together and started to give our clothes a "holiday" by way of cleaning them up and also cleaning our boots. Having done this we set of for a nearby village and here we were greeted with the long stay that resulted with us returning back to the Trenches. Whilst at the Village we were paid, ready for starting off home and were lying down, waiting for the Transport to take us to the nearest Railhead, this being at Boulogne, when, after waiting two hours, the message was received was that "All Leave to England was cancelled", and we were ordered back to the Trenches; myself finishing back in O.B.I.. I returned to the Trenches feeling very little different from when I had started off to go on leave.

97. THE LOOS BATTLEFIELD. Trip to Pilgrims Progress.
After spending one night in O.B.I.; on the 20th, we again set off to do our turn in the Front Line, finishing up at "Pilgrims Progress" where many excitable things started happening. I was beginning to wonder if I would ever have the luck to see "Dear Old Blighty" again. Not long after we had taken over the Front Line, a very funny occurrence happened, one which I shall not forget for some time. A small German Shell came sailing down the Trench. Before this shell ended its journey, it had caught one side of the Trench, making a very deep groove in that side of the Trench. Then it had crossed over the Trench and did the same on the other side of the Trench. After doing this it, finished up at our feet and we stood there wondering what was going to happen next. As luck would have it, it turned out to be a "dud" and we finished up giving the shell, or part of it, as a "keepsake", to an Officer who was near the spot where this took place. This was only one thing that stared me in the face whilst my mind was set to thinking again about my anticipated return to "Dear Old Blighty". Not long after this, the Germans started shelling the "Hulluch Road" which ran through our Trenches into No Man's Land. The Germans were shelling it with their heavy Shells which we called "Coal Boxes"; sending them over at the rate of one every two minutes and, as we knew where to look for the shell when it was about to strike the ground, we were able to see the shells hitting the road. All that we had to think about was what might happen if one of the shells fell short and made its "resting-place" in our Trench; we knew that this would put a

finish to any or all of our thoughts of "Blighty". This shelling was kept up until nearly dark but what for, I could never say. Whilst here, I was drinking some tea out of a tin mug when a piece of flying shell from one of these heavy shells actually struck the mug which I was drinking from.

After the shelling had finished and darkness fell, we received orders to keep a very sharp lookout owing to the shelling which had taken place. They wondered if the Germans were going to attack this night. For myself, I only wished for it to remain as it was and for them to stay where they were. Thankfully, this turned out to be the case.

Battalion War Diary:

19th March 1916. QUARRIES SECTOR.
Very fine. Day quiet. Working parties supplied to Battalion in Front Line. In evening at 10 30 pm. we blew up mine at HAIRPIN. There was little or no demonstration following this.

20th March 1916. QUARRIES SECTOR.
Fine weather. We relieve the 11th Middlesex in Front Line. Relief complete by 10 00 am. Whole sector quiet. From 5 00 pm to 6 00pm. Enemy worried us with rifle grenades and aerial torpedoes. Quiet night and much work done.

21st March 1916. QUARRIES SECTOR.
Fine and quiet. Trouble with rifle grenades again but this stopped on calling upon artillery for retaliation. Three parties were sent out to do wiring. One did good work. Other two had to retire owing to enemy searchlight. The night was quiet. Lt. Cpl. TAYLOR, 6th STAFFS Regiment. attached for instruction.

22nd March 1916. QUARRIES SECTOR.
Raining. Wind Easterly. Enemy starts firing with 5.9's on Support Line at 12 15 pm. and carry on at the rate of one a minute until 3 15 pm. and then ceases. A good deal of damage was done to S.F.T. and DUDLEY STREET. The night was quiet. 2 Officers of General CADORNA'S Staff. stayed half an hour, shown round VERMELLES.

23rd March 1916. QUARRIES SECTOR to VERMELLES.
Relieved by 11th Middlesex. Relief completed by 11 00 am. During Relief, enemy shelled O.B.I. in DUDLEY STREET with a high velocity gun. Number of casualties during last part in Trenches: – 1 Officer killed, 1 Officer wounded, 2 OR's killed and 31 wounded. Battalion moves to reserve and occupy billets as follows. H.Q.- Brewery, VERMELLES; "A" and "D" Companies- Cellars, VERMELLES, "B" and "C" Companies- in huts at NOVELLES. Ration parties and carrying parties supplied nightly whilst Battalion is in Reserve. Colonel returns from leave. Weather-colder.

Sadler Account:

98. THE LOOS BATTLEFIELD. 2nd and successful attempt to go on leave.

After doing our four days, we left for the cellars at Vermelles, another far from comfortable sort of place.

The village was very much knocked about and, at intervals, very much shelled by the Germans. After settling down in our Cellar and having a rest after our very long drag from the Front Line, I had only rested for a very short time when an Orderly came to tell me to pack everything up and parade at the Orderly Room, at once, in readiness to return to England. I did not take long in doing this and I soon started on my journey. This time I did not trouble about cleaning up, only having time to have a wash and a shave before it was parading time for the Boat. My clothes were covered with chalk from the Trenches but this did not worry me so long as it didn't appear to matter to anyone else. After getting to London and leaving my Comrades, I started on my journey on the Underground tube. Looking around the carriage, and with every seat full, I thought what a sight my clothes must have looked against those of the other troops, who, I could tell, had not come from the same place on the battlefield as myself.

99. THE LOOS BATLEFIELD. A return home and a welcome visitor.

On the train a young lady kindly offered to give up her seat to me but I politely refused saying that it was against my wish as I felt, in my condition, far more comfortable standing up than sitting. At this time of the War it appeared that no one could ever be too kind towards a "Tommy". Spending the night near London, I arrived home in Swanage the next night and spent a very happy time until it was time to return; this being after only 10 days. On my return journey, whilst waiting at the Station, I was asked by someone, a friend; whether it was right that men "From the Front" were in a hurry to return. Not knowing whether this man thought my past twelve months had been spent as a holiday and that I was home for these few days for fun; I said to my, more welcome, friends, "What Regiment, on God's earth, does the man who told you that belong to?" I thought to myself it was certainly not someone from the Infantry or from the Front Line Troops.

I also thought to myself that I should be very lucky, from, what I had seen already, if I was going to be able to see another leave in 12 months' time from then. The past twelve months had been bad enough. However on my return to France, I was about to start a much worse time. Anyhow, I was to get over it.

His leave at an end, L. Cpl. Sadler embarked for France to re-join his comrades.

10

March–June 1916: The return to France and the time leading up to The Battle of the Somme

T he war would not remain "on hold" whilst Lance Corporal Sadler spent a well-earned rest in Blighty. Meanwhile, the Battalion diarist recorded events occurring during his absence:

24th March 1916. VERMELLES
Four inches of snow on ground and snowing continues till 2 00pm. Weather then clears and it is fine. More snow at night. All men of Battalion out at night ration carrying, bomb carrying and knife rest carrying. During the night the Germans fired two mines and occupied both craters. Lt. Col. TAYLOR attached to us, returns to England.

25th March 1916. VERMELLES
Fine and frosty. Orders received that we were moving to BETHUNE the next day but these were subsequently cancelled. "C" Company sent up to reinforce the 11th Middlesex Regiment at 2 30 pm. They stayed in O.B.1 for the night. It was anticipated that the Germans might attack but the night passed off without incident. All of the Battalion again out on working parties.

26th March 1916. VERMELLES
Fine. Hail showers with bright intervals. "C" Company returns from O.G.1, their place is taken by "B" Company. "B" Company leave at 2 30 pm. to reinforce 11th Middlesex. Arrive at 4 00 pm. "B" Company receive certain Orders to reinforce Middlesex in certain eventualities. Two raids were made by Middlesex. At 11 15 pm. the raid took place and failed. Company take over new dispositions – Middlesex again attack at 4 20 am but takes the form of another raid. A look into the Crater was successfully obtained. It was not necessary for the men of "B" Company to be engaged in these raids. Other Company's men were out in the evening on fatigue parties.

27th March 1916. VERMELLES to BETHUNE
"B" Company return from helping Middlesex at 9 00am. Battalion moves to BETHUNE and is relieved by 7th East Surreys at 1 o'clock. Relief completed by 1 30 pm. Companies proceeded independently to BETHUNE and whole Battalion is billeted in TOBACCO Factory. All in billets there by 4 00pm. Battalion HQ's situated at 121 RUE DE LILLE, BETHUNE.

28th March 1916. BETHUNE
Fine and windy. Battalion engaged in cleaning up etc. Time quiet.

29th March 1916. BETHUNE
Battalions allocated to Battalion at ECOLE DES JEUNE FILLES. All men bathed.
Fitting of clothing etc. Quiet.

30th March 1916. BETHUNE to SAILLY LA BOURSE.
Battalion moves to SAILLY LA BOURSE and takes over billets occupied by 11th
Middlesex who take over billets lately occupied by us. Parade at 10 00am and march
off to SAILLY LA BOURSE in the following order. HQ, "A", "D", Drums, "C", "B".
Weather fine and we arrived at SAILLY LA BOURSE without incident at 11 00am-
All in billets by 12 noon. Leave party goes off. Rest of the day spent in cleaning up,
reorganising etc.

31st March 1916. SAILLY LA BOURSE.
Weather fine and warm. All Companies carry out Company Training, specialist
training carried out. A number of enemy aeroplanes were chased off. In evening
Major General A. B. Scott CB, DSO. Divisional Commander attended a Concert in
Divisional Cinema Hall at 6 00pm and presented Medals to the Battalion Football
Team which was successful in winning the recent Divisional Tournament.

Official information received that the following decorations have been awarded
for work carried out on March 2nd. D.S.O.: Lt. S. GUBBINS, Major N.B. ELLIOTT
COOPER – Military Cross: Capt. The Hon. R.E.PHILLIPS – Military Cross: Lt.
E.W.T. BECK- Military Cross: D.C.M.: No. 1970 Sgt. E.M.CRONYN, No.8338
L.Cpl. A.LOWREY, No. 398 Pte. A. McINTOSH.

1st April 1916. SAILLY LA BOURSE.
Companies at disposal of Company Commanders for field training. Draft of 99 OR's
arrived. Visibility Good.

2nd April 1916. SAILLY LA BOURSE.
Divisional Service in the DIVISIONAL Concert Hall.

Sadler account:

On my return, after spending another night near London, I soon left for France
again; meeting my Battalion at Sailly La Bourse. We spent the night there then
proceeded back to the Trenches the following night.

This reunion was followed by return to the much-contested Hohenzollern
Redoubt sector:

3rd April 1916. HOHENZOLLERN SECTOR. Right Battn. Right-Subsector
Relieved 7th NORFOLKS; 35th Brigade, in the Trenches HOHENZOLLERN
SECTOR. Brigade Station. Right Construction. Battalion H.Q.:- GORDON

Men of 9th Royal Fusiliers wish to thank GENERAL GOUGH very much for his kind wishes and congratulations".

17th April 1916. HOHENZOLLERN SECTOR-BETHUNE.
At 8 50 am enemy exploded a mine opposite SAVILLE ROW. The Crater is South of No.1 Crater and appears almost to touch the German Front Line. Damage was evidently done to the enemy wire and to some of his loophole plates. After the explosion, our Trenches opposite the Crater were shelled with Field Guns, light howitzers, but no damage was done. The Battalion was relieved by the 6th BUFFS. and Platoons proceeded to SAILLY LA BOURSE via FOSSE where the Battalion joined up and were met by the Drums and proceeded to BETHUNE and took up Billets in the ORPHANAGE. Relief complete 1 30pm. Arrived BETHUNE around 4 00pm. H.Q.'s 151 Rue de Lille, BETHUNE.

18th April 1916. BETHUNE.
Day spent in reorganisation and cleaning up under Company Arrangements. Divisional Concert at OLD THEATRE, PLAS RUE DE PAUMES.

19th April 1916. BETHUNE.
Companies at disposal of Company Commanders for training. Bath at disposal of Battalion ECOLE DES JEUNNE FILLES from 8 30am.

20th April 1916. BETHUNE to SAILLY LA BOURSE.
Battalion relieve 11th Middlesex in Billets at SAILLY LA BOURSE. Relief complete by 12 noon. C.O.'s billeted at house of the Mayor. Draft of 73 arrived.

21th April 1916. SAILLY LA BOURSE.
GOOD FRIDAY. Beautiful Day. Companies at the disposal of Company Commanders. Commanding Officer inspected the Draft and deemed quality "Good". Voluntary Service in Divisional Recreational Room at 6 00pm.

22nd April 1916. QUARRIES SECTOR. Right sub-section.
Left SAILLY LA BOURSE at 8 00am and relieved 7th NORFOLKS in the Trenches. "D" Coy.: -GUN TRENCH, "C" Coy.:- HILL, GUN, SUPPORT and NEW RESERVE TRENCH. (PUTTY TRENCH.), "A" Coy.: -LOOKOUT CRESCENT, NEW GUN SUPPORT ,QUARRY BAY,GRIMWOOD TRENCH. "B" COY:- BROOKWOOD TRENCH. QUARRY BAY and O.G.1. Enemy very quiet. A few minewaffers in GUN and SUPPORT TR. During the afternoon our Artillery retaliated. Two new Officers joined Battalion. 2nd Lt. EVANS and 2nd. Lt. BASTABLE.

23rd April 1916. QUARRIES SECTOR. Right sub-section.
Quiet Day and night until our Artillery fired a salvo at 10 00 pm. Enemy retaliated with Artillery, missing us and one Company in CHAPEL ALLEY. Whizz bang fell on BRETSAU AVENUE. Our Artillery retaliated promptly and everything became normal. At 10 00pm there was a TEST GAS ALARM which was satisfactory as far

as our men were concerned. About 8 30 pm, No. 12791 Lt.Cpl. J.E.GIBSON was returning to HILL 1 TRENCH from a Patrol with Pte. HOLLINGSWORTH from NEWPORT SAP when he came across a German man in front of parapet of the Fire Trenches near its junction with HILL 1. He ordered him to put up his hands and took him prisoner. He appeared to be lying or crouching under the parapet. On approach the German called out "Mercy, English, do not kill me". He was unarmed and no more men could be found at the spot. Prisoner dispatched to Brigade H.Q. at 9 35pm.

24th April 1916. QUARRIES SECTOR. Right sub-section. (SUPPORT BATTN.).
The Battalion was relieved in the Trenches by 11th Middlesex Regt. Relief complete by noon. "B" Coy.- CURLY CRESCENT, "C" Coy.- OB 4&5, "D" Coy.- OB1 South of FOSSE WAY, "A" Coy.- OB1 and FOSSE WAY.

25th April 1916. QUARRIES SECTOR. Right sub-section. (SUPPORT BATTN.).
Everything quiet C.O. and Adj. of 8th SEAFORTH HIGHLANDERS visited the Trenches.

26th April 1916. QUARRIES SECTOR. Right sub-section. (SUPPORT BATTN.).- BETHUNE.
The Battalion was relieved by 8th SEAFORTH HIGHLANDERS. Relief complete by 2 30pm. Platoons proceeded to SAILLY LA BOURSE at intervals of 200 yds. via ANNEQUAS, FOSSE. At SAILLY LA BOURSE, the Battalion joined up and marched to BETHUNE, Drums in the centre, and billeted for the night in the TOBACCO FACTORY.

Sadler Account:

100. THE LOOS BATTLEFIELD (Cont.) Relief, On Reserve and Rest.
At last we got relieved by another French Division with ourselves going back to the Tobacco Factory in Bethune where we were "Standing To" at the Factory. We remained in the position of "Standing To" until dinner time but the same day, 27thApril, we left to start our rest and training in the Company's Rest Area, at a little village called LaPugnoy. Here a very enjoyable time was spent doing only a few working parties from here and going to the Trenches in Motor Buses when the work had to be done. We spent some time here making Cable Trenches and from here we were able to witness, at a distance, the retaking of Vimy Ridge, an area which we could see by watching the all coloured star-lights. The Germans had, again, won the Ridge but were to lose it later at The Battle of Arras.

Battalion War Diary:

27th April 1916. BETHUNE to LAPUGNOY.
At 1 20 pm, the Battalion proceeded to Corps. Reserve Area's at LA PUGNOY arriving about 4 00pm. H.Q. Billeted at "The Chateau" LA PUGNOY. Billets scattered.

28th April 1916. LAPUGNOY.
Companies at disposal of Coy. Commander for re-organisation, cleaning and rest.

29th April 1916. LAPUGNOY.
Companies at disposal of Coy. Commander for re-organisation. Half holiday. Men allowed to roam in woods.

30th April 1916. LAPUGNOY.
Divine Services. Men allowed to roam in the woods from 2 00pm to 5 00pm. Beautiful weather.

1st and 2nd May 1916. LAPUGNOY
Platoons training. "A" Company -Sandpit Range in morning. "B" Company in the afternoon.

3rd May 1916. LAPUGNOY
"D" Company to French Range. 8 00am – 12 noon. Brigade Route March. Starting Point: – Road Junction D.26. c. 8.1. Order of March: 8th Royal Fusiliers, 11th Middlesex Regiment, 7th Royal Sussex Regiment, 9th Royal Fusiliers . Route: LABUISSIERE- Road Junction E.25.d.4.9 to-Road Junction D.24.d.6.1- FOUQUEREUIL CROSSROADS E.7.c.7.4 to LABEUVRIERE to BILLETS. Returned 2 00pm. Very Good March.

4th May 1916. LAPUGNOY
Platoon training. The 37th Infantry Brigade held their sports in the CHATEAU GROUNDS- LOZINGHEW. Open event to all Units of Division. 400 yds. won by No. 1000. Cpl. Flood, "B" Company, 9th Royal Fusiliers. and third place No. 12441 Pte. Evans-"D" Company, 9th Royal Fusiliers.

5th May 1916. LAPUGNOY
Platoon Training. "B" Company to Sandpit Range in the morning. "C" Company in the afternoon. At 2 00pm in Divisional Canteen, LAPUGNOY- Bayonet Fighting lecture by Major Campbell. 50 Officers and NCO's from each Battalion present. Finals of 12th Division Boxing Tournament. The Heavyweight contest was won by Pte. King, (Lewis Gun Detachment), 9th Royal Fusiliers. Reward-10 days special leave given by Brigade.

6th May 1916. LAPUGNOY
Platoon Training. "D" Company- French Range in the afternoon.

7th May 1916. LAPUGNOY
Battalion Church Parade at 11 o'clock in Woods behind Crucifix- D.15.a. with 7th Royal Sussex Regiment. The Bayonet fighting Competition between Units of the 36th Infantry Brigade resulted in a win for the 9th Royal Fusiliers.

8th May 1916. LA PUGNOY

Commencement of Company Training. "A" Company to Sandpit Range in morning. "B" Company in afternoon. A Cinema Show was held in the Divisional Canteen at 5 30pm.

9th May 1916. LAPUGNOY

Company Training. "D" Company to Sandpit Range in morning. "A" Company in the afternoon.

10th May 1916. LAPUGNOY

Company Training in the morning. "C" Company to French Range in the morning. In the afternoon, sports were held in Football Ground behind 18th Casualty Clearing Station at 2 00pm and finishing at 6 00pm. The Matron of the 18th C.C.S. presented the prizes. The Officers staff made the Battalion very welcome and the Sports were a great success.

11th May 1916. LAPUGNOY

Company Training.

12th May 1916. LAPUGNOY

"A" and "C" Companies – Route March under Major N.B. Elliott-Cooper. "B" Company to Sandpit Range in morning, "D" Company, in the afternoon. Capt. G. Cazalet; Capt. The Hon. R. E. Phillips; Capt. J.P. Brown and Capt. M.E. Coxhead commence 2 days on Bayonet Fighting Course.

13th May 1916. LAPUGNOY

Company Training. "C" Company to French Range 2 00-6 00pm.

14th May 1916. LAPUGNOY

Church parade cancelled owing to rain. Capt. E.W.T. Beck and one N.C.O. per Company proceeded to CHATEAU LE REVEILLON for Course at Divisional Anti-Gas School.

15th May 1916. LAPUGNOY

Company Training.

16th May 1916. LAPUGNOY

Battalion Tactical Exercise in LE MOREQUET WOODS. 11th Middlesex Sports Open Event of one mile won by Corporal Wright, "A" Company, 9th Royal Fusiliers. Second: L. Cpl. Phillips, "C" Company, 9th Royal Fusiliers.

17th May 1916. LA PUGNOY

Company Training. "B" Company to French Rifle Range 8 00- 12 00noon. "D" Company -Attack practice.

18th May 1916. LAPUGNOY
Brigade Tactical Exercise in BOIS DES DAMES WOODS. Company Training. "A" Company to Rifle Range, 8 00-12 30 pm. "B" Company- Attack practice.

19th May 1916. LAPUGNOY
Gymkhana Sports held in grounds behind 18th Casualty Clearing Station. Very interesting as everything went off "A1". The Matron of 18th C.C.S. presented the prizes.

20th May 1916. LAPUGNOY
Route March. Route- AUCHEL-LOZINGHEM-A'LOUAGNE-BILLETS. In the afternoon, Brigade Sports took place at MARLEWS LES MINES starting at 2 00pm. The following events were taken by 9th Battalion Royal Fusiliers:-
    ½ mile: – 1st:Cpl. Wright, 9th R.F., 2nd: Lt.Cpl. Phillips, 9th R.F.
    220 yds. – 1st:Pte. Evans, 9th R.F.
    Alarm Race: – Pte. Fisher, Cpl. Kennedy, Pte. Loftus – all 9th R.F.
    Officers Mile Race: – 1st:7th Royal Sussex, 2nd:Lt. A.E. Winton 9th R.F.
    NCO's Race:-1st:Sgt. Harris 9th R.F., 2nd:7th Royal Sussex, 3rd:11th Middlesex
    ¼ mile: – 1st: Pte. Evans 9th R.F., 2nd: 7th Royal Sussex, 3rd: 11th Middlesex.
    3 mile Race: – 1st:Capt.Wright,9th R.F.,2nd :7th Royal Sussex,3rd:36th
        M.G. Section.
    Warrant Officers Race: – 1st:C.S.M More, Gym Instructor, C.S.M.
        Callaghan 9th R.F.
    Tug of War: – 9th Royal Fusiliers.
    ¼ mile Open to all in the Divisions: – 1st:Lt.Cpl. Phillips 9th R.F., 2nd:Sgt.
        Harris 9th R.F.
The Battalion won 407 Francs in prizes; also 7 "Leave" prizes.

21st May 1916. LAPUGNOY
Battalion Church Parade at 10 30 am in Woods behind Crucifix D.15.c. with 7th Royal Sussex Regt.

22nd May 1916. LAPUGNOY to SERNY and FLETCHINELLE.
Battalion moved to 1st Army manoeuvre Area. March of 14 ¼ miles. "A" and "B" Companies billeted in FLETCHINELLE. Head Quarters, "C" and "D" detachment billeted in SERNY. Settled in Billets by 6 30pm.

23rd May 1916. SERNY and FLETCHINELLE
Battalion Tactical Exercise- Defence of a position.

24th May 1916. SERNY and FLETCHINELLE
Battalion Tactical Exercise- Attack.

25th May 1916. SERNY and FLETCHINELLE
Battalion Tactical Exercise- Advance Guard. Corps. Commander General Sir Chas Morris K.C.B., saw Battalions at work.

26th May 1916. SERNY and FLETCHINELLE
Battalion Tactical Exercise – Outposts.

27th May 1916. SERNY and FLETCHINELLE to RAIMBERT
500 men digging Trenches SW of ENGUINGATTE under Capt. G. L. Cazalet. Remainder of Battalion to Tactical Exercises under Capt. M. E. Coxhead. Concert at "B" Company's Billet at 7 00pm. During the Concert, wire received at 8 45pm Order for Brigade to move. Battalion paraded at 9 45pm and marched to RAIMBERT arriving there at 3 30am- 28/5/1916.

28th May 1916. RAIMBERT
Company Commander visited the Trenches and made a reconnoitre of the VILLAGE LINE occupied by 1st and 12th Divisions.

29th May 1916. RAIMBERT to LAPUGNOY
Battalion paraded at 6 20am and marched to LAPUGNOY taking over same billets as occupied previously. Route: – AUCHEL- LOZINGHEM- MARLES LES MINES- BILLETS. Arrived at LAPUGNOY 8 30am. Seconds in Command of Companies visited the Trenches and made reconnaissance of Rear Line occupied by 23rd. Division.

30th May 1916. LAPUGNOY
Companies at disposal of Company Commanders. One Officer per Company visited Trenches, Line held by 1st Division.

31st May 1916. LAPUGNOY
Companies at disposal of Company Commanders.

1st June 1916. LAPUGNOY.
Companies were at disposal of their Commanders for bathing, bayonet fighting, dummy bomb throwing and gas helmet drill in the morning and for lectures in the afternoon.

2nd June 1916. LAPUGNOY
8 30am- At 8 30am, "B" and "C" Companies practised an attack through LE MAREQUET WOOD particular attention being paid to the system under which the first line of Scouts and the LEWIS GUNS advanced as laid down by the Division.
    10 30am.- At 10 30 am. "A" and "D" Companies carried out the same practice, also in conjunction with the LEWIS GUNS. In both cases the enemy was represented by the Signallers with flags. 6 00pm.:- The Second in Command, (Major N.B. Elliot-Cooper), held a class of instruction for newly joined subaltern Officers.

3rd June 1916. LAPUGNOY
7 00am. – Physical Training. 8 30 – 12 30 pm. "A" Company fired on the French Range near LAPUGNOY.
    9 00am. to 12 noon "B","C" and "D" Companies practised bayonet fighting,

bomb throwing, musketry and gas helmet drill. Snipers of all Companies fired on SANDPIT RANGE during these times. 3 30pm.:- Lecture to subalterns by Second in Command on Trench Warfare.

4th June 1916. LAPUGNOY

11 00am.:- Battalion Church Parade with 7th Royal Sussex.

5th June 1916. LAPUGNOY

8 30am.:- Battalion Tactical Exercise in BOIS DES DAMES WOOD. 6 00pm:-. Working Party, 4 Officers and 200 men under CAPT. E.W.T.BECK burying cable at PHILOSOPHE. 7 00pm.:- Open Air Concert in grounds of BURNT CHATEAU.

6th June 1916. LAPUGNOY

7 00am.: – Physical Training. 9 00am to 12 noon.- Companies at disposal of Officers in Charge of Companies for Bayonet fighting, Bomb Throwing, Musketry and Drill. Snipers of all Companies firing on SANDPIT RANGE for periods of ½ hour starting with Company "A". 3 00-5 00 pm.:- Lecture.

7th June 1916. LAPUGNOY.

9 00am.:- Working Party of 4 Officers and 100 men under Lt. E.H.SHOTT filling in Trenches at GONNEHEM. 8 30 am.:- Battalion attack in LE MAREQUET WOOD. 6 00pm:- Free Cinema entertainment at the Divisional Canteen.

Battalion training continued about LaPugnoy until the middle of June, after which transit to Amiens and vicinity followed:

8th June 1916. LAPUGNOY to NOYELLES and ANNEQUIN.

8 00am. Battalion proceeded to NOYELLES and ANNEQUIN and took over the billets of 7th NORFOLK REGT. "A" & "B" Companies to ANNEQUIN. CAPT. The Hon. R.E.PHILLIPS- Officer in Charge of Detachment. Lewis Gun Detachment to VERQUIN. Head-Quarters, "C" and "D" Companies to NOYELLES. TRANSPORT & Q.M. STORES to VERQUIN. Battalion to work under 15th Division. BRIGADE H.Q. in VERQUIN E.sq.c.5.4.

9th June 1916. NOYELLES and ANNEQUIN.

9 00am to 2.30 pm. Detachment at ANNEQUIN. Working party of 25 men under 91st Company Royal Engineers work on deep dugout at VILLAGE LINE. 7 00pm. Working party at ANNEQUIN cleaning, cleaning and relaying Trench Boards in HULLUCH ALLEY under 9th Gordon Highlanders. "C" & "D" Companies- 3 Officers and 100 men from each Company working on Railway to OB 4 & 5 under 9th Gordon Highlanders. Lewis Gun Detachment returns to VERQUIN.

10th June 1916. NOYELLES and ANNEQUIN.

Work continued as on 9th.

11th June 1916. NOYELLES and ANNEQUIN.
Work continued as on 9th. Church Parade for men not out working previous night. "C" & "D" Companies to CHATEAU NOYELLES at 12 noon. ANNEQUIN 3 30 pm. Draft of 11 arrived. Inspected by C.O. Quality: "Good".

12th June 1916. NOYELLES and ANNEQUIN.
Work continued as on 9th. "C" Company proceeded to SAILLY LA BOURSE taking over billets vacated by 9th BLACK WATCH.

13th June 1916. NOYELLES and ANNEQUIN to VERQUIN.
Battalion proceeded to VERQUIN passing SAILLY LA BOURSE at 1 00 pm. Settled in billets by 2 30 pm.

14th June 1916. VERQUIN.
7 00 am. Physical training. 9 00am to 12 00 pm noon: At disposal of Company Commander for Bayonet Fighting, Bomb Throwing, Musketry and Drill. 2 00pm to 3 00pm. Lecture. Detachment "C" and "D" bathed.

15th June 1916. VERQUIN.
8 30 am to 10 30am "A" & "D" Companies –Attack Practice on field near MINX FOSSE. 10 30 to 12 30 pm: – At disposal of Company Commander – 8 30am to 10 30: "B" & "C" Companies at disposal of Company Commander. 10 30 to 12 30pm:- Attack Practice near MINX FOSSE. 2 00 to 3 00 pm.: Lecture. Lewis Gun Detachment, Pioneers, Q.M's and "C"& "D" bathed in morning. "A" & "B" Companies bathed in afternoon.

16th June 1916. VERQUIN to VIGNACOURT.
4 30am- Transport & Lewis Gun Detachment proceeded to FOUQUERUIL STATION and entrained. 5 15 am.:- Battalion proceeded to FOUQUERUIL STATION entraining at 8 00am. Departure of Trains at 9 00am. Arrived at AMIENS 6 00 pm and from there marched to VIGNACOURT and FLESSELES arriving in billets 4 30 am on 19/06/1916.

Sadler Account:

101. THE BATTLE OF THE SOMME. JULY 1st 1916. Our journey towards the Somme Battlefield.
Whilst in our Rest/Reserve Area, a position was found similar to what it was anticipated that the Germans would be taking at the starting of the Battle, but not necessarily as it was to be on the First Day.(1st July).

After spending several mornings in undergoing training as to nature of the Trenches that we had to take, our "Rest" neared its end and we were all looking forward for great events at the commencement of The "Great" Battle. We thought to ourselves that, if this one turned out to be a great success, it would end the War.

Not long after, on the 16th June, we marched to the Railhead and took the train for Amiens.

After a very long journey we arrived in the evening and the main thing what took our eyes were the great amount of our Heavy Guns which being taken off of the Trucks, artillery guns such as Lucky Jim etc.

9th Royal Fusiliers' participation in the on-going Picardy push on the Somme Battlefields was barely two weeks away.

11

The Battle of the Somme, June and July 1916 – Arrival in the Area, More Preparation, Attack at Ovillers

The Battle of the Somme, 1 July–18 November 1916, has been analysed by a plethora of historians over the years. The following section is intended to recount the personal experiences of L. Cpl. Sadler rather than chronicle the long-drawn out campaign from military perspective. From 18 June, the 9th Royal Fusiliers, having undergone a period of divisional training, were encamped near Amiens awaiting orders to enter the fray and take part in the immediate aftermath of the infamous opening day of the battle during which British Fourth Army sustained some 57,000 casualties killed, wounded and missing.

Sadler Account:

102. THE BATTLE OF THE SOMME. Getting bread and marching towards the front line.

Not spending much time at the Station in Amiens, we left to do a very long march. Large numbers of French people turned out to see us and our Band as we marched through the City and we received quite a grand reception. Leaving the City behind us, we marched for several hours and then received an hours rest.

Tea was supplied and this freshened us up a little. We again "Fell In" and marched for several hours more until we were dead tired but, at last, we arrived at our stopping place, Vignacourt, and received a well-earned rest. Here we started living on Iron Rations and continued to do so for some time. Same old diet day after day, "Bully Beef and Biscuits". The Baker Shop in the village had rather a busy time in supplying troops with Bread, the Troops lining up waiting for it to be taken, "all hot", out of the ovens. On the First of July, the day of the starting of the Great Battle, we left this village to march towards the Line and then to stop until our turn arrived. Another good march lay ahead, one which I shall never forget. After marching for several hours we came to a stopping place under some trees and out of sight of German aircraft. Whilst resting here we had dinner supplied and received news of the day's fighting and we watched the battery of shells ahead.

103. THE BATTLE OF THE SOMME. Tired out.

After a rest we "Fell In" again and marched towards the Battlefield. At that time of day each Platoon had a bombing section which was charged with carrying a Bomb Bag containing 12 Mills Bombs and which was handed round to men to carry in turn. This task never served to improve matters. We marched all the afternoon until the then Commanding Officer said to us "Only a few hundred yards to go".

James's handwritten account of action leading up to the 1st Battle on the Somme. June 1916.

A messenger cycled up on a motor cycle and gave our Commanding Officer a "Paper". We at once guessed something was up and so on we had to go, passing by the Outskirts of Albert and on to the Trenches. When we got to the Communication Trenches, the Germans were using their "Tear" shells for the first time and, in our tired condition and with the "Tear" Shells, it was more than a puzzle and very difficult to keep awake. On-going up the Trenches, the order kept being sent back "Lost connection", either in front of us or in the rear. When one sat down, one fell fast asleep and then got woken up when the time came to move on again.

Shortly after that something would happen, we would stop and, again, one would fall asleep. This is how we managed at last to reach the Front Line, still being shelled with those lovely "Tear" Shells until daybreak when we could see, or tell, the area where a part of the Battle had been fought.

Battalion war diary:

17th June 1916. VIGNACOURT.
8 30 am Commanding Officer, Adjutant and Company Commanders reconnoitered ground at ALBERT. Party conveyed by us. 10 00 am. to 12 00 noon -Companies at disposal of Company Commanders.

18th June 1916. VIGNACOURT.
10 30 am. Battalion Church Parade.

19th June 1916. VIGNACOURT.
8 30 am. C.O.'s and Second in Commands took Junior Officers in map reading around VIGNACOURT. Capt. G.P.S. BROWN took Battalion for Route March.

20th June 1916. VIGNACOURT.
8 30 am. Battalion practiced attack at FORET near VIGNACOURT. 6 00 am – Q.M. and T.Q. reconnoitered road to Trenches.

21th June 1916. VIGNACOURT.
8 30 am Battalion practiced attack at FORET near VIGNACOURT.

22th June 1916. VIGNACOURT.
8 00am. Brigade Field Day at MONTVILLERS. Practice Attack on Trenches by 8th Royal Fusiliers and 7th Royal Sussex and on village of FREMONT by Battalion. Dinners eaten on Field.

23rd June 1916. VIGNACOURT.
8 30 am. Battalion practiced attack at FORET near VIGNACOURT.

24th June 1916. VIGNACOURT.
8 00am. As on 22/06/1916 except that Battalion attacked with 11th Middlesex. Trenches taken and other Battalions took village.

25th June 1916. VIGNACOURT.
10 30 am. Battalion Church Parade.

26th June 1916. VIGNACOURT.
8 30 am Battalion practiced attack at FORET near VIGNACOURT. 6 30 pm. Concert for W.O.'s of 35th and 36th Brigades.

27th June 1916. VIGNACOURT to FLESSELLES.
6 00 to 8 00 pm. Battalion Parade for March to FLESSELLES, 4 miles distant. Badly checked and arrived 8 30 pm. Bivouacked for the night.

28th June 1916. FLESSELLES.
Very Wet. Sent by Brigade to billet in the village with 11th Middlesex's in the evening.

29th June 1916. FLESSELLES.
Inspection by Companies in the morning. 2 30 pm.:- Battalion paraded for the C.O. to give out "Honours Cards", (sent by G.O.C. XII Division), to 7 NCOs and men for Distinguished Conduct. 6 00 pm. -Divisional Band played in Main Square.

30th June 1916. FLESSELLES to FRECHENCOURT.
Inspections and gas Helmet Drill by Companies in morning. 12 30 pm.: – Lecture by M.O. to all Officers on "Veins and Arteries". 7 15 pm.:- Battalion marched to FRECHENCOURT (Distance of 10 ½ miles.)

Sadler Account:

104. THE BATTLE OF THE SOMME. A few words about the Battle.
Before I continue in fuller detail, I would like to say a few words about the Battle. This Battle, by what I saw of it, was the most terrible Battle I ever witnessed and it was here where the "New" Army took its great part. The men of Kitchener's Army who faced the Enemy on the first day, 1st July, were mostly smart young men between 20 and 30, including many married men but none of these were in my Battalion. Myself; I was in three "Battles" of The Somme. These started from the German Front Line, near Albert, where my first Battle took place, through to the Transloy Ridges, this side of Bapaume. The three Battles I shall mention later. The Battles on The Somme were far different from those which were to take place afterwards. They were of the "Old" style, similar to the Loos Battle etc., and the ground that was won was won at the terrible cost of young men's lives. Never could one witness more terrible sights of War. During these Battles on the Somme, it was just like a young man going forward and charging a stone wall; falling down dead and then being followed by another doing the same thing and then followed on by many more.I walked over the Somme Battlefield and some terrible sights took my eyes. I thought to myself, what is a man's life? Alive one minute, dead the next; not having had so much chance of his life as a mouse or rat.

105. THE BATTLE OF THE SOMME A Few words about the Battle.
You will see, as I start writing about it, what it cost us to win even a little bit of Trench. This Battle was carried on by way of "nibbling" little bits of ground at a time and this under the most terrible bombardment that ever could be used in War. With the "nibbling" a bit here one day and a bit more, somewhere else, the next; it was a case of both sides concentrating all their artillery fire on whichever spot was being attacked or taken at any particular time. This could lead to the most terrible shellfire imaginable. With the German Army being so well supplied with plenty of their machine guns, they were able to cut human life down just like cutting grass. What were once lovely little villages when they were taken by us were, later, only heaps of stones and, if anything, the cellars in which the Germans were prepared to cling to their last, were only made stronger by the stones and bricks which fell in on top of their places of shelter. When these, so called, villages had been won by us, the "roads" badly needed repairing owing to the terrible shellfire. Stones, bricks, wood etc. were taken from the village to carry out the repairs. After a month or so, and after giving the grass time to grow, all that could be seen of the village was a green or clean patch. Owing to so much concentration of shellfire, it was nearly impossible to walk on ground that had not been touched by this and it made it a very unearthly looking place, this due to the chalk that had been blown to the surface by the shells. All that could be seen of what were once lovely woods was

now the stumps which remained and these were only about two or three feet high. The trees which had fallen were taken and used for some purpose or another.

Battalion War Diary:

1st July 1916. FRENCHENCOURT.
Arrived here about 12 midnight and billeted. 7 30 am:. Marched to BAIXIEUX WOOD. Arrived at 9 00 am. and bivouacked. 6 30 pm. Battalion marched off, at half an hour's notice, to billets at MILLENCOURT but was stopped on route and ordered to Trenches.

2nd July 1916. THE "NAB"
4 30 am. Took over Trenches from all that was left of 70th Brigade, (8th Division), who had just attacked, (objective OVILLERS), and had been almost wiped out by Machine Gun fire. Fairly quiet day as far as we were concerned but our bombardment continues. Holding Brigade Front without support.

3rd July 1916. THE "NAB"
2 00am. – Intense bombardment of Enemy's Trenches on right till 3 15 am. 3 00 am. – Made smoke barrage on our entire Battalion Front till 3 20 am. 3 15 am. – 35th and 37th Brigade attacked on right. Held up by M.G. fire and shrapnel and forced to retire to their own line again. Enemy retaliated but did not do much damage with shells. Heavy curtain of Tear Shells sent over, affecting Bn. H.Q. and "C" and "D" Companies. Goggles brought into use. Platoon of "D" Company had heavy casualties being caught by shell in Trenches when carrying. Artillery quieter as morning wore on. Quiet afternoon. 9 00pm. – 11th Middlesex came up in support.

4th July 1916. THE "NAB"
Enemy bombarded our Trenches: 10 00am to 11 00 am and 3 00pm to 4 00pm. Some damage done and direct hit on a dug out of "C" Company. – 12 Casualties. 5 00pm.: 11th Middlesex took position in our Firing Line. With both Battalions in Trench-Trench very crowded. 10 30 pm.: heavy shelling on both sides on our left. Some shells came into AUTHVILLE WOOD but did not affect us.

5th July 1916. THE "NAB" to ALBERT.
Quiet morning. Some heavy bombardments on our left during the day. 10 00pm-Relieved by R.W.K. Regiment, (37th Division), and marched to ALBERT. Got into billets around 3 00am.

6th July 1916. ALBERT – TRENCHES IN FRONT OF OVILLERS.
7 00am -The C.O. and all Companies Commanders ordered to take over Trenches in front of OVILLERS. Arrived in the Trenches about 5 30 pm. Battalion received Orders to attack OVILLERS tomorrow morning. The attack is to be made by the 36th Brigade- 9th Royal Fusiliers on Left, 7th Royal Sussex- Centre, 8th Royal Fusiliers – Right and 11th Middlesex – Reserve. The position is a very strong one and has been attacked without success by very large forces of the French, by the 8th Division and

Ovillers battlefield today.

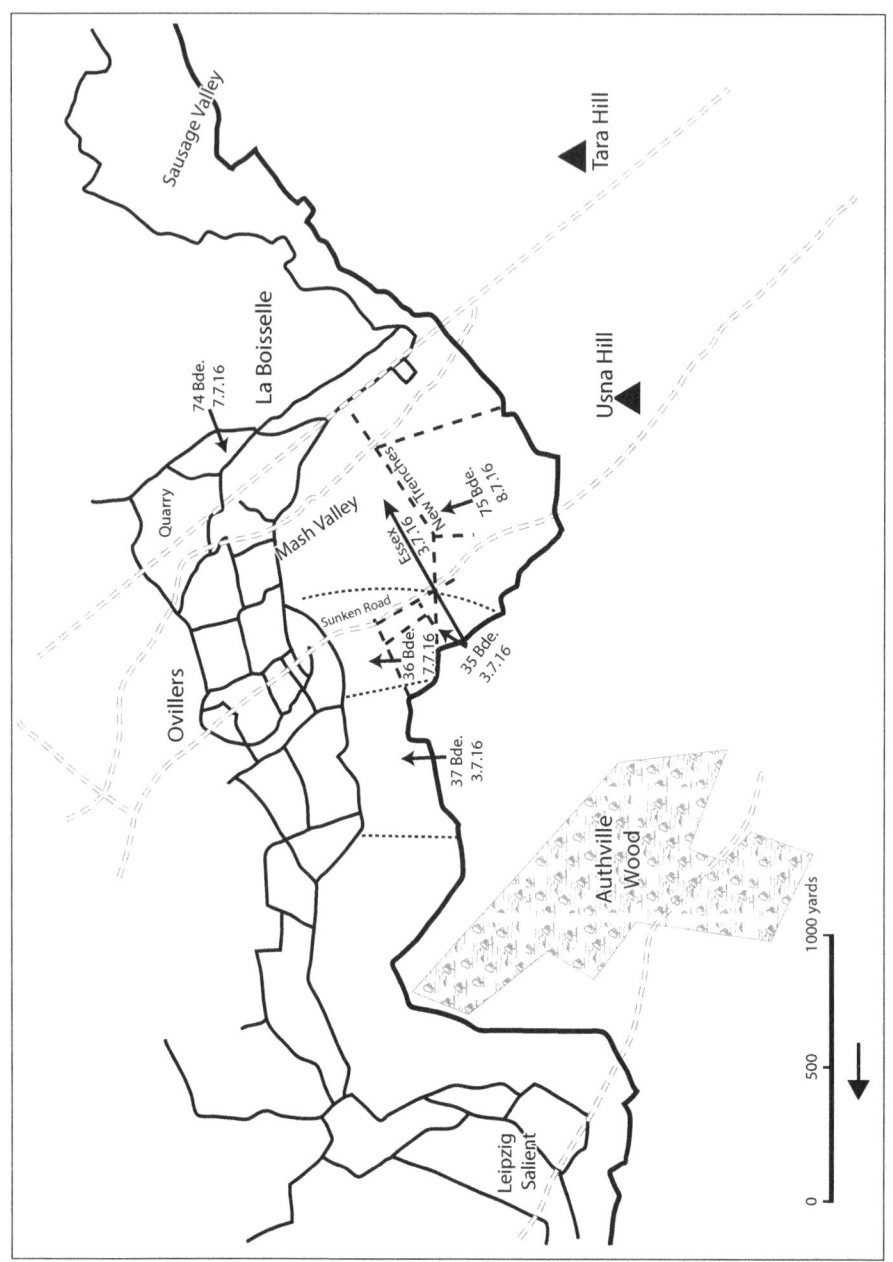

Ovillers, 3rd to 7th July 1916. (George Anderson)

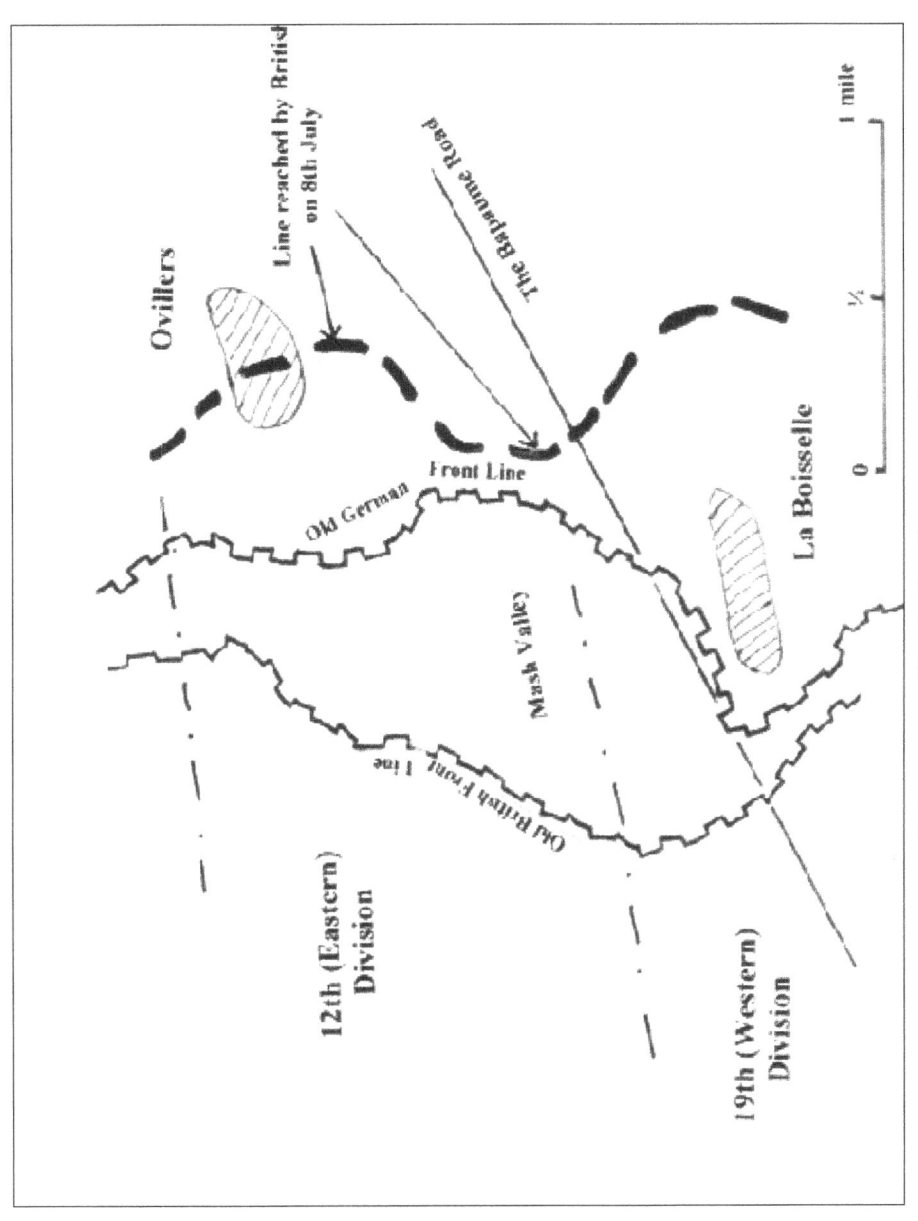

Map of advance at Ovillers by the 9th R.F. on 7 July 1916.

by the 35th and 37th Brigades. The night was spent by us in continuous preparation. Collecting of bombs etc.

7th July 1916. OVILLERS.

4 30am Our bombardment commenced and became intense at 5 30am at which time the Companies took up their positions in the Front Line ready for the assault. "A" on Left. "D" on the Right were to form the 1st Line and to be followed immediately by "B" and "C" Companies respectively. The Enemy retaliated almost as soon as our bombardment commenced and our Trenches were heavily shelled by guns of big caliber. There were no dug-outs available and our casualties were very heavy. "C" Company suffered most heavily being reduced to about 40. It was then decided that "C" Company should go over with "D". At 8 30 am: the time fixed for the attack. "A" and "D" and the remainder of "C" left our Trenches. 8 30 am: "A" Company were decimated by M.G. Fire and the same fate met 2 Platoons of "B" which followed. The remaining Platoons of "B" Company were ordered to remain in the Trench as it was seen to be useless to send them across at the same place. "D" and "C" on the Left were more successful and although greatly weakened managed to reach the German Trenches which they carried by assault. The Enemy's Fire and Support Trenches were captured and consolidated. Two M.G.s were put out of action and 50 prisoners were captured. Continuous bombing attacks were beaten off with loss to the Enemy. About 5 30 pm the remaining Platoon of "B" Company managed to get across and brought with them a large supply of Bombs. It was raining heavily through the day.

Sadler Account:

106. THE BATTLE OF THE SOMME. Our first sight of the Battle and getting in the wounded.

I shall follow on now from where I started to write about this Battle. On arriving at the Front line to start our part in the "Great Battle", the only men I saw were two or three Pioneers who had taken part in the first day of the Battle. When daylight arrived, we then saw just what the start of the Battle had cost us at this part of the Line. With the Germans still holding their Front Line, looking into No Man's Land; many of our wounded were to be seen there most of whom had already spent one day and night lying in No Man's land.

In the afternoon it was a case of trying to see if the Germans would allow us to start "getting -in" these poor fellows. Many of us got on top of the Trench expecting, every minute, that the Germans would fire a fatal bullet at us. Taking with us what stretchers we could find and also taking with us many of our waterproof sheets to act as stretchers; the Germans, seeing what we were doing, never fired a shot at us. We carried this out a great number of times until after midnight by which time over 200 "Stretcher Cases" had passed through our Dressing Station.

107. THE BATTLE OF THE SOMME. Smoke Candles

Getting towards two o'clock in the morning, 3rd July, we received Orders that we were to make a smoke barrage. The smoke candles had arrived early in the morning, being brought by a Carrying Party. When this Party arrived in the morning,

I was called upon to run to my Platoon Sergeant, at that time, to report that Smoke Candles had arrived and asking to know where they were to be put. On receiving this Order, I quickly went down the Trench to report it to the Sergeant. Whilst stood at the door of the Sergeant's Shelter, a small shell burst at the other end penetrating through the dug-out and slightly wounding several men. Anyhow with plenty of help being handy, we set off to see about the Smoke Candles. We found that we hadn't a great number of Smoke Candles to take over but we had a good job in knocking in the end of the Trench; this in order to put out a Smoke Screen which had already been started by accident. A German shell had burst in the centre of the party, killing and wounding many of the party and the Shell had caused many of the Smoke Candles to catch fire.

108. THE BATTLE OF THE SOMME. Making a smoke screen whilst an attack is taking place.

These Candles were the cause of much excitement at this early hour of the morning. Whilst we were making our Smoke Screen to bluff the Germans, another one of our Brigades from the Division were going to make another attempt to take the Trenches around Ovillers. This was the first attempt by my Division but it was the second attempt in all. We were supplied with so many candles and a box of matches and we were put out in small groups to await for "Starting Off" time. Just before daylight we received Orders to light up and all our guns were set into working order. Another terrible bombardment started once more. We were to be re-paid for our little bit of smoke by the Germans. Their bombardment was not with "Coal Boxes" but with another type of German Shell which the Infantry know so well and were called "Five-Nines". We received a good supply of these until daylight when the Germans could see for himself that no more Troops were coming after him. Shortly after this, a man jumped into our Trench, the man being from the Brigade that had gone into Action. I received Orders to take this man along the Trench to his Battalion's Front and hand him over to one of his Officers. This man was being taken as a coward as it had been thought that, instead of following his Company, he had crawled into our Front Line instead. This was quite wrong. On reaching this man's part of the Front Line I found that, by the looks of things, this man, along with a very few more of his companions, was very lucky to be alive. The Germans had counter-attacked in large numbers and driven them out and back. This had been the 2nd attack of the Battle and had proved unsuccessful. This all took place on the 3rd of July and, although unsuccessful in gaining ground; due to this attack, much news of the well-fortified positions of the Germans was discovered. This information concerned their Ground Cover, Deep Dugouts, and Tunnels leading from one Line to another and such like.

109. THE BATTLE OF THE SOMME. Ourselves preparing for Battle.

Later on 5th July, we left for a small Woods just in the rear of the Line called "Blighty Woods"; these Woods getting their name because of many stray bullets and pieces of shells flying around at times.

We did not stay there long enough to get many "Blightys". After we had been there an hour or so, we again received Orders to get packed up, ready to move again. This move happened after a short time and this time we finished up at an old Tram Yard in Albert where, after a feed, we soon laid down and had a sleep, as if we were in feather beds. We did this between the pools of water, not knowing when we were likely to get the next piece of sleep during this night. On getting called, next morning, we were supplied with breakfast and also two "Mills Bombs". This time, on leaving, we left our Packs behind, having to wear "Battle Order" when we started to march away. Before dinnertime we left to take over some reserve Trenches and then prepare for action. After being greeted with one or two short and sharp bursts from the German Artillery we reached the Trenches. Before we left for this place and, because of what we had been "handed" to carry, it began to make us think, "What is a Soldier for"?

110. THE BATTLE OF THE SOMME. Getting ready for Battle.
Not long after getting in the Trenches, a very large party was called forward to carry the bombs which were starting on their journey. The few men that were left including all Section Commanders, myself being one of these at this time, were ordered to make a large number of wooden pegs, enough to supply all the men in their Sections with four each. These pegs were to be used so as to peg a waterproof sheet over the entrances of German Deep Dugouts. This was to be done so as to make it impossible for the Germans to throw bombs up at us. When this was done, all Section Commanders were called to Company "Headquarters" to hear all the news for the coming battle. Myself, I was put in charge of the "Barricaders" and had the names of ten good men given to me to take charge of. Then I was shown a lot of maps with Trenches marked on them and where I had to put up the Barricades.

111. THE BATTLE OF THE SOMME. Myself in charge of Barricades.
Myself and my ten men were told that we should carry a pick and shovel, and also where to put up a Barricade in the German Front Line. A Barricade, made by filling in the Trench, was needed when both sides were holding the same Trench so as to stop sudden attacks from the Enemy The barricading was commenced by knocking in the sides of the Trench first, this whilst being supplied with a covering party of "Bombers" in order to keep the Germans busy. After this the Barricades were built up. The Germans were bound to come over the top of the Barricade if they attacked and, when the Barricade is finished, a Lewis Gun or Machine Gun was set so as to stop anyone walking over the top. I must say it is far different doing the real thing, than it is writing about it. Later we were called to tell us when the Battle was going to start.

The Battle was going to commence the next morning at 8 30 am, 7th July, when all the Artillery was going to be concentrated on this position and would bombard the German Trenches for four hours before the start.

This would also be supported by our heavy Trench Mortars, including the "Flying Pig", which I will talk about later. Towards night, the large Bombing Party arrived back with their large supply of bombs and later Section Commanders were called, one by one, to bring their Sections forward to get their supply of bombs.

THE BATTLE OF THE SOMME.
CROSSING "NO MANS LAND."   113

...from the Germans Rifle & Machine Gun. It was impossible
to cross from trench to trench. Without getting under
cover & shooting at the Germans Which we could see
ahead With our Rifles. With this although "slow & sure. We
were able to count for as many Germans as all our
hell fire, No one can think What a mans feeling was like
Seeing the Sights from the other Battles Which had taken
place on this ground. Also seeing his own Comrades falling
in dozens And after one had fired a few rounds at
the Germans ahead. When getting up to advance again
Perhaps being the only moving object seen at that time
every German would point his Rifle at that moving
object, and fire a round. And the Bullets would fly
by ones head in "Hundreds" And "all one" could think to himself, was, I shall get one" through" the head shortly. The
closer one got to the Germans The safer he was. Because
he began to get the "wind up" And his Rifle Fire was
not so steady. But his bullets "still" would come at anyone.
When I got within Sixty yards from the German front
line. There was hardly a living Soul to be seen. And
I was right out on the left of the attack by myself
Knowing it wasn't any good to charge the German line on
my own. And by now The Germans were putting up a

James's handwritten account of Action at Ovillers during
the Battle on the Somme: 7th July 1916.

112. THE BATTLE OF THE SOMME. What is a soldier for?

On taking my "Barricaders Section" forward, we were supplied with another twenty bombs each; this making the Grand Total of 22 for each of us. At this Battle every man was also carrying two sandbags tied to the straps of his equipment for consolidating new positions. By using our un-filled sandbags we managed to carry our 20 bombs, leaving the other two in our pockets. By putting ten bombs in each bag and tying them together we were able to swing them over our shoulders in order to carry them. By this time the Germans had started making things rather lively with his very high explosive shrapnel. So at this time as we were ready, my section had to carry a pick and shovel each, 22 bombs, 4 wooden pegs and also two candles and a box of matches for dug-out searching. Besides this lot, each man also had his own rifle to carry.

Never have I before, or since, carried so much whilst going into action. However, it was now a case of this position being taken; this time at all cost and the anxious time now was waiting for the battle to commence.

On the starting of the bombardment we left the Trench to take our positions in the Front Line; myself and my "Party" taking our positions on the Left Flank of the Attack. At Four o'clock the bombardment started and, as we left for the Line, the Germans opened out a terrible rate of shellfire on all of our Communication Trenches. Shells were bursting only a few yards from us on both sides of the trenches.

113. THE BATTLE OF THE SOMME. A terrible German Bombardment.

After a time that I will never forget, we managed to get to the Front Line and into our positions ready for starting. Then the Germans lifted the shellfire from the Communication Trenches and concentrated it all on our Front Line. With more than 3 hours of it to stand before going into battle, the German shell fire was more than terrible. In fact so much shellfire was being played on our Line that the Front Line appeared to rock just like being in a small boat on a choppy sea. It got so bad that stakes from the barbed wire in front of our Line were flying into the air along with human beings. Men, being taken and lifted clean out of the Trench and sent hundreds of yards into the sky. Never could one, whether in Wartime or not, witness such a terrible sight. So thick were the shells and so great were our losses that the message kept coming along the Line "Send back and tell our Artillery to put more range on their guns". One can see that we thought we were getting both of the two sides of concentrated shellfire. We were getting cut up so much. At last we got the Order to "Fall Back" into a Communication Trench and await Starting Time. This was done but very little was to be gained by it. We were just longing for the time to come when we would go one way or the other.

114. THE BATTLE OF THE SOMME. Getting knocked over and starting into battle.

By now we were getting greeted, as usual, with plenty of rain. At last the Orders were passed down the Trench, "Five Minutes to go. Return to the Front Line and take up positions". "Ready for Over the Top".

On returning to the Front Line a German shell burst on the top of the Trench sending, high into the air, many sandbags etc. One sandbag returning from its "Trip" caught my equipment and sent me flying to the ground and into the mud. Finding it now impossible to move, owing to my load and the mud, I said to a chum of mine, "Lend me your hand". He did so immediately and I was then able to proceed. Whilst tracking up the Trench, I was greeted with a few welcome words from my Sergeant who remarked, "Been trying to disguise yourself as a sandbag!?"; this owing to my being covered, head to toe, with mud. After leaving him in the rear, the Order was passed along, "Over the Top!" Not seeing many ladders handy, I said to a passing chum, "Come on, give me a leg up" which he did. I was very lucky not to have been knocked back into the Trench again by a German bullet. Our bombardment had now lifted from the German Front Line and the Germans had come up from their deep dugouts to greet us. Crossing No Man's land was to prove a very trying "game".

115. THE BATTLE OF THE SOMME. Crossing No Man's Land.

Due to the amounts of bullets from both the German rifles and machine guns, it was impossible to cross from Trench to Trench without getting under cover and shooting, with our rifles, at any of the Germans who we could see ahead of us. Although this was slow and sure, we were, I think, able to account for as many Germans as all of our shell fire had managed. No one can imagine just what a man's feelings were like, seeing the sights from previous battles which had taken place on this ground earlier and also seeing his own Comrades falling by the dozen.

After one had fired a few rounds at the Germans ahead, and then getting up to advance again, perhaps you would be the only moving object to be seen at that time and then every German would point his rifle towards you and fire a round. The bullets would fly by one's head in hundreds and all one started to think to himself was, "I shall get one through the head shortly". The closer one got to the Germans, the safer you became because they began to get the wind up and their rifle fire was not so steady but, nevertheless, his bullets would still come at you anyway. When I got within sixty yards from the German Front Line, there was hardly a living soul to be seen and I was right out on the Left of the attack and by myself. I knew it wasn't any good trying to charge the German Line on my own and by now the German Artillery was putting up a barrage just in front of their Front Line.

116. THE BATTLE OF THE SOMME. Getting into the German Front Line.
Looking to my right, I could see a few more men still left and, using the smoke from the Germans bursting shells, I was able to cross to my right and join up with my comrades there. We were held up by machine gun fire, about 40 yards in front us, from a plucky German who was still working his gun. A Sergeant from another Company got a "Bomb" ready for throwing and, being a prize thrower, he got up quickly and sent the "Bomb" flying at this plucky German. Luckily this sent both Gun and German flying. With that we got up and struggled over the German Barbed Wire. A bullet fired from the left caught the edge of my left leg but, knowing that it was not wise to stop to see to it, I rushed into the German Front Line with the others. If the Germans had only known how few of us had succeeded in getting into their Line, they would have had little trouble in driving us out again but instead they made for cover, once more, down in their deep dugouts. The German Front Line Troops expected a counter attack from their "Second Line" to take place and drive us out so that they, the German Front Line Troops, could come up once more. But the few of us that were left were out to win a "Position" so that our comrades who had fallen could be collected up.

117. THE BATTLE OF THE SOMME. Searching the Line and looking for a place for a Barricade.
We found the German Front Line looking something like a sunken road, judged by the great amount of shellfire it had withstood. My first words, made to the man that was closest to me, on getting in to the German Trench was to get the bags of bombs off of my shoulders as they had caught up in my equipment and were choking me. After that, a few of us went along the Trench to the right and a few went to the left. At each dugout entrance we pegged our waterproof sheets over the doorways. After doing this to several dugouts we would leave a man on Sentry duty. The Germans could not make it out, having their doorways blocked up, and they didn't like to come up to see what was going on as they were not sure what awaited them.

On going a good way up the Trench we met a German Strong Point and we had to stop. This is where my Barricade had to be made but, before starting on that, men had to be found to lend a hand and men were very hard to find. There wasn't an Officer or an N.C.O. of my Company to be found; only one or two men could be found. Anyhow, I had to try my luck and at last I came in contact with an Officer from the 7th Royal Sussex Regiment of my Brigade who had taken part in this Battle.

118. THE BATTLE OF THE SOMME. Looking for men to help with the Barricade.

When I asked this Officer if he could let me have a few of his men for putting up a Barricade on the Left Flank, he wanted to know how many. I asked for as many as could be spared and I finished up with three.

We set off to do the task as it wasn't any good worrying about having cover from a party of "Bombers" as had been planned. Getting to the place where the work had to be started we soon found out it was impossible to fill in the Trench owing to it being so wide. What we planned then was to get as much barbed wire and Stakes as were possible and put up a barbed wire fence instead. We did this and had to make this do, knowing it was good enough to stop a surprise attack. After this job was finished we then had to make two "Bomb Stores"; one at this end of the Trench and one at the other end of our Front. Having done this we then collected up as many bombs as possible including both our own and the German "Stick bombs" or "Hand Grenades". A Sentry Group was now posted to keep a sharp lookout. On leaving this part, I took a walk down the Trench and, whilst on the road down the Trench, a small German Shell, or one of their hand grenades, struck the side of the Trench and nearly blew my head off and this left me dazed for a short time.

119. THE BATTLE OF THE SOMME. Searching German Deep-Dug Outs.

Getting over this, I continued my journey down the Trench until I was stopped by the Officer that I had asked to borrow men from.He was standing by a German Dugout when he said to me, "Come on, we will search this dugout. Light up your candle and we will go down together". I began to wonder what was going to happen as we started our journey down the staircase. Never the less it had to be done. We both started off, down below, to see what was there when we were greeted with voices from the Germans shouting out "Comrades". It was impossible for them to start a fight because they were short of men so they made their way up the stairs towards the daylight. There were four of them but I didn't really care how many it was. All I wanted to know was how many remained as I was about to proceed to the bottom of the Dugout.

I made sure that the Germans knew where I was going and, with my fingers pointing towards the bottom of the Dugout, I said, "Any more down there?" One of the Germans held up one finger, meaning, I guessed, one more below. I soon made them to understand that I wanted them to call him up which they did. He had only stayed below collecting up rubbish to take with him. We handed over our Prisoners to someone to look after whilst we finished our search; looking for Tunnels that may have run into this dugout from other Lines.

120. THE BATTLE OF THE SOMME. A German Helmet.

After seeing to this and finding everything correct, we started looking around the Dugout to see if we could find anything of any value. I spotted seven German

Helmets hung up in covers and these took my attention for a short time. When a few more men entered the Dugout, I said to them, "Want a German Helmet?

The answer I received was "Yes!" so I handed them all out, except one. That one I kept for myself.

I got one of the men to undo my haversack straps, put the straps through the Chinstrap on the helmet and do the straps up again. The helmet never crossed my mind again for some time. My only thought was that, if I did have the luck to get out of this alright, it would mean that my chums and I could have a little pleasure with it and so it was. A Royal Engineer later offered me Forty Francs for it after the Battle. I let him have it as it was no good to me in that I had to carry it around and also plenty more could be had. They were the very best helmets that could be had; "Prussian Guards". Another very unusual occurrence took place here, which was very seldom seen in battle. One of the men, on entering the dugout, picked up one of the Germans packs, opened it and found it contained a clean change of washing. This man took off all of his clothes and changed his underclothes for this clean set and then got dressed and ready for action again!

121. THE BATTLE OF THE SOMME. Having a feed and needing a drink.

Shortly afterwards, the Commanding Officer of The 7th Royal Sussex entered the dugout and complained that he was hungry and could do with something to eat and wanted to know if there was anything about that was suitable to eat. After looking around to see what there was, he decided to have his feed which he appeared to enjoy very much whilst I acted as "Waiter". I could not make it out as to why this Commanding Officer kept bringing up the name, Sadler. After a while, I asked the Officer who I had searched the dugout with what his name was only to find that his name was the same as mine! A short time after this, I left this dugout as Commanding Officer Sadler had decided to make it his Head-Quarters. On arriving at the "surface", I felt very dry. I had water in my water bottle but was not sure where this had gone to and, therefore, when I was going to get my next drink. I asked one of the men if he knew where there was any water, fit to drink. "Yes", he said, "Down the next dugout you will find plenty of Perrier Water in bottles and the dugout is quite safe". He had himself only just come from there so, at once, I started off towards this dug-out to try my luck.

122. THE BATTLE OF THE SOMME. German Counter Attack.

Reaching the Dugout, I found the bottles, soon picked one up and knocking the top off, started drinking.

I then had one of the greatest surprises of my life from which I was, I guess, lucky to get out alive.

Just as I started drinking, someone rushed by the dugout entrances, shouting down, "Look out the Germans are on us!" With that; down went the bottle and up the stairs I went. I could never tell anyone how many steps I took at a time in order to reach the top quickly but I got to the top to find the Germans nearly on top of us and with bombs bursting all around. To make things even better, there was a man in front of me running with his rifle and bayonet fixed and he managed to get caught up in some hurdle work in the Trench and in doing so made a Barricade, with us on

Derelict German Trenches at Ovillers, looking towards Albert. July 1916. Copyright IWM.

the wrong side. After a struggle we got over this and got to within throwing distance from the Germans. We met up with a few more men including three Officers, two of them being officers from other Companies in my Battalion and the third being my, "Old Friend", Commanding Officer Sadler of the 7th Sussex. Also there was the Sergeant who threw the Bomb which had knocked their machine gunner out of action when we first entered the German Line. With these plucky Officers, and just the two or three us, we had the means of saving another "Big Battle". Many of the men were making a start to retreat when one of these gallant Officers shouted, "If you run back without Orders, I will shoot you as you go".

123. THE BATTLE OF THE SOMME. Sniping at the Germans.

These few words, which I shall never forget, were the means, as I have just said, of saving us being involved in another "Great Battle". To take this position had cost us a terrible loss of life, and, if it was lost in this attack, it would have cost still more. After we started bombing back at the Germans and thereby checking them, I was used to look over "the top" with my rifle set, ready to snipe at all the Germans I could see and also to cover the bombing party so as to keep the Germans at a certain range. Whilst doing this, I noticed that the Germans were jumping from "Shell Hole" to "Shell Hole", looking like a lot of rabbits and I called for more help. The answer I received from many was "We are all done!" "Done or not", I said, "Clean your rifles and load them up to me".

The "cleaning" was done using the empty sandbags which we had carried the Bombs in and it was necessary as, owing to the mud, many of the rifles were clogged to the extent that it was impossible to pull the "Bolt" back. After firing a further ten rounds, these cleaned rifles were handed to me and another two more men joined me to carry on with the sniping.

124. THE BATTLE OF THE SOMME. Using each other's Bombs

This was the finest day I ever saw in France for getting our own back on the Germans. The Germans were charging at us with their belts covered with hanging Hand Grenades and didn't even seem to think of using their rifles as they prepared their Hand Grenades for throwing. As they stood up quickly to throw a grenade into our "Checking" party, one could fire his rifle at them and cause him drop the grenade so that, even if our bullet did not kill him, the bursting of the grenade would. This attack went on for a very long time until we had run out of our Bombs and the Germans had run out of theirs. After this it was a case of throwing whatever could be found at each other! In the dugout, which Commanding Officer Sadler of The Royal Sussex and myself had searched a few hours before, we found a large supply of German Hand Grenades and also several German rifles; rifles from which one was able to fire twenty-five rounds without reloading; the rifle being served with a twenty-five round magazine. This was the first time that I had ever had the "pleasure" of seeing such a thing as this being used in the War. Before this Battle ended, we had the pleasure of firing these, their own special rifles, back at them and their Hand Grenades that we had found in this dugout were brought to the surface and used against them. As every one of us had been instructed in how to use all German bombs; this again saved us from losing our position. As I have already mentioned, after putting up the Barricades earlier in the day when we entered the Trench, we had made a bomb store and had collected up a lot of our bombs. The Germans were now holding this part of the Trench and they were, therefore, able to get at this supply of our bombs which they could use against us. This was to be the only time, during the War, that I ever saw an attack kept going by using each other's weapons of war.

125. THE BATTLE OF THE SOMME. In charge of the "Checking Point".

At last things quietened down with the Germans "winning" 100 yards of Trench from us, something which I will write about later. It was now a case of holding on to what we had as we had run short of everything and it was going to be impossible to get reinforcements to us until after dark. It paid us to keep quiet until reinforcements arrived, carrying with them a fresh supply of bombs. This took place later that night.

After things quietened down, I was put in charge of the Checking Point, being supplied with three more men of the Royal Sussex Regiment, and three good men they were. It was here we had to stay and, at intervals, throw over a German Hand Grenade to let them know that there was still life about. We kept this up till it was nearly dark but very sadly I lost one of my three men with a German bullet through the head. Our Checking Point was about six yards from the Dugout where Commanding Officer Sadler of the 7th Royal Sussex Regiment had made as his Head-Quarters. It made no difference to him how close the Germans were, he never moved his Head-Quarters.

126. THE BATTLE OF THE SOMME. Reinforcements arrive.

I stayed in charge of this Post for several hours until; at last, the Post was relieved by other men which enabled us to get a rest. After this we walked around to see what was happening and I found that we were holding three German Lines. At once, I could guess what the Germans were after. Their intention was to drive us out of what had been their Front Line so that they could take the other two lines prisoners. I also discovered that we were on top of the Hill and were able to see for miles down the other side. The Germans didn't seem to like the idea of us being able to see what was happening, on the other side. It was possible to see, from our newly won position, the smoke from the German Guns when they were being fired. This led to us having a very quiet night as the Germans decided to move their guns into new positions.

As soon as it got dark that night, reinforcements from other Brigades of the Division arrived in hundreds. Also our own Battalion from the Brigade, which had been in support to us, arrived carrying two boxes of Bombs each and even the Division's "Pioneers" Battalion arrived to dig a communication Trench back to our own lines; the Lines which we had started from when going into this Battle. All the newly won positions, at that time, had to be joined up so that it was possible to get "To and Fro" under cover. Wires were laid back to the Rear including wires to our Artillery, this so that we could get support from our Artillery at a moment's notice. Now everything was again prepared for any more sudden attacks.

127. THE BATTLE OF THE SOMME. Having a feed and a smoke.

That night I was so tired that I had a little sleep; even with all the activity of the reinforcements passing up and down the Trench and stepping on my feet. I would only just wake up before I would soon fall asleep again. In these Trenches, we found our "Iron Rations" very acceptable as no other rations arrived for us.

In the end we were pleased enough to eat little pieces of biscuits that had been carrying in our haversacks for ages and which had been soaked with "Rifle Oil" from the can which we carried our haversack. Since the beginning of our Action on the 7th July, we hadn't even a "Fag" to smoke, and we had used what German cigars we had managed to find. It was a case of smoking all the "Fag-Ends" that we could find and even then, in the end, we collected the dust which had shaken out of the "Fag-Ends" into our pockets.

A "smoke", whilst holding a Position such as we were doing, was considered to be worth a Pound, (£,) in anyone's money; capable of putting fresh life back into anyone in a moment. I feel sure that the British "Tommies" could not thank the people at home, enough, for sending out cigarettes to them at that time of the War.

128. THE BATTLE OF THE SOMME. Great surprise and Bombing raid.

The next morning, as soon as daylight arrived, I received another great surprise. Two Officers of my own Company had arrived along with a Bombing Sergeant and three or four men. I had lost contact with these men, the morning before, when the Battle was taking place. All I have got to say is that it's a good job we didn't all "loose our connections" or else we wouldn't have had the pleasure of enjoying all the "fun" that had taken place in the last twenty-four hours. Anyway, with the Bombing Sergeant arriving back, this was to result in the Germans getting a warm time with regard to us winning back the 100 yards of lost Trench which we had lost on the previous morning. The Captain of my Company, who was one of the two Officers, passed the remark to me that I looked nearly all done in. I didn't know how I looked; but I knew how I felt.

He said to me to go to one of the deep dug-outs and get a rest. My reply to him was that they were already filled by the reinforcements that had arrived that night. However, talking about getting a rest, things, in a very short time, got very lively again. The Bombing Sergeant who had arrived back wanted to get a large Bombing Party together to push the Germans out of the bit of the Trench they had won from us in their Counter-Attack.

129. THE BATTLE OF THE SOMME. Forming a Bombing Party and getting Germans to surrender.

He got his party together by walking down the Trench, coming into contact with many of the new reinforcements. When he said to the men, "What are you, a Bomber or not?" many of the men, knowing that some dirty work was about to commence, said, at once, "No, I am not a bomber". Hearing this, the Bombing Sergeant would say, "Alright, you will do as a bayonet man". This is far more dangerous than taking the place as a Bomber as, after the Bomber had thrown his bomb, the bayonet man had to go forward to see that all is clear. Doing this then allowed the Bomber to go forward to throw his bombs a longer distance up the Trench. By doing this, the Bombing Sergeant soon got a party as large as was required and, with a jolly good supply of bombs, they made it hell for the Germans in a very short time. The first German prisoner that was captured had one of his arms nearly hanging off. This had been caused by a large piece of a flying bomb. This German's arm was carefully dressed and bandaged up and, knowing that the German would never again be any good for fighting, he was sent back to try and get the other Germans to surrender. However, this man brought us no luck. He never returned, nor did any other of the Germans surrender.It was a choice of three things for them, Surrender, Die or get out of the way of the Bombs. Many of the Germans preferred the second, which was to Die or Fight to the Death.

130. THE BATTLE OF THE SOMME. Winning our lost part of the Trench back.

With a very hard struggle, the Germans were driven back to wherever we had put up the barricade the morning before. In doing this we could tell our "luck" by finding the number of Germans who lay dead.

We found some who had been killed by the effects of the Bombing which had taken place on this day and we also found many who had died from the same effects and the sniping from the day before. Shortly after this attack we received a much warmer reception, this time from the German Artillery; the Germans using just about every type of shell which it was possible to use. We had very little cover owing to the Trenches being blown about so much and also the Trenches were filled so full with the reinforcements. We again suffered very heavy losses. Then the

Germans made another bombing attack to cut off our Front Line, once more, but they were unable to do this as we now had plenty of men. It was a case of both sides fighting it out to a finish.

131. THE BATTLE OF THE SOMME. Bombardment and sights.
Soon, the Order was passed along the line for everyone to "Stand To" which was done as soon as the message arrived. Owing to the state of the Trenches, it was only a case of running up the side of the Trench or Sunken Road. The Germans must have seen the flashes of our bayonets and had an idea that we were going for them again. All of a sudden, a great outburst of German Artillery started once more. When the heavy shells were bursting right in the centre of our so called "Trenches", it was a case of lying where one was and awaiting his "luck"; life or death. Never could one have gone through a worse Battle than this one and never have I seen such a sight as these Trenches were in. When we left the Front Line, later this day, we had won the Trenches around Ovillers it was true but we had paid a heavy price for it in blood. The Germans had set many of their Hand Grenades in the mud. By just unscrewing the cap, leaving the string and button out, and leaving it lying in the Trench, just covered with mud, anyone who stepped on was liable to set it off; this, owing to the fuse being cut in such a way as to detonate it. One time during this Action, I noticed two Stretcher Bearers from the Essex Regiment going down the Trench carrying a very badly wounded man on a stretcher when one of them trod on one of these Grenades which exploded and killed two of them and badly wounded the third.

132. THE BATTLE OF THE SOMME. A Lost brother.
There is another thing which I can recall happening on the day before we got relieved. Two brothers were together when the Battle started; both serving in the Royal Sussex Regiment. When one of these brothers missed the other, he went out, behind our newly won line, to look for his missing brother. After searching for a long time he managed to find him, badly wounded in both legs and he had been lying out there for 30 hours. He set off to the nearest Dressing Station in order to get a stretcher to carry his wounded brother on and also looked to get permission for another man to help him with the task. After getting the stretcher, he arrived back at the Trench and laid the Stretcher against the side of the Trench before going down a dug-out to see about something. When he arrived at the surface again, he found his stretcher missing. I was walking down the Trench when I met this man who was in a very upset state and I asked him what the matter was. Here, I am re-telling what he told me. Once more he set off to the Dressing Station to fetch another stretcher and arriving back; this time he did not leave the stretcher lying about. The next time I saw him, I was grateful that he was with his brother on the stretcher, passing down the Trench. After a few words with him they then set of for the nearest Dressing Station.

133. THE BATTLE OF THE SOMME. Getting relieved.
After this attack, we had to "number" around the Trenches which I had never seen done before or since. This was done to find out how many men we had left in

each Regiment. My Regiment came along the Trench and found me. I had to say my Regiment and the next number following the one which was sent along to me and then I passed this information down the Trench. My number at the time was nine. About five o'clock this night we were relieved by a Manchester Regiment and I was not at all sorry to leave the Trench. However, the Germans didn't intend for us to leave it without giving us a few shells to send us on our way. They shelled the Communication Trench all the way along and sent over the last shell just as we stepped on to the roads, not far from "Crucifix Corner". Here we were met by our Cooks who served us with the first drop of hot tea which we had tasted for three days and also something to eat. With regards to what we had eaten in the last three days; we had eaten anything which we had found it was possible to eat as I have mentioned before. After we had finished our welcome feed and had a short rest, we started the crawl back towards Albert. I cannot say we marched towards Albert because there wasn't a man left who could march. It was a case of getting there best way we could. What few men came out alive were dead tired and beat to the world.

134. THE BATTLE OF THE SOMME. Company's Roll Call.

After a terrible struggle, and in single file, we managed to arrive at Albert, one by one, and we were shown some fairly comfortable wire beds and, after having some more food and drink supplied to us, we made use of these beds. We only had to lie down before we fell asleep. Here we were allowed to sleep until late into the following morning when breakfast was served out to us and then we fell in for a Roll Call. My Company, which included everyone, numbered just eighteen. Later in the morning we left for a village named Bus le Artois, this being a two day march away. We stayed one night at a village on the road. Also we had a long rest whilst doing the first day's march and had Dinner supplied on the roadside. Here the stretcher-bearers bandaged up my left leg which had been hit whilst I was getting over the German barbed wire for the first time. I hadn't had much time to think about it before. Towards tea-time we arrived at the village of Senlis to stay the night. Here I cleaned up my German Helmet and was, as I had said earlier, given Forty Francs for it by a Royal Engineer and with what few of us who were left, we managed to have a little enjoyment on this.

Resting the night, we started off the following morning for the village, Bus le Artois.

So ended L.Cpl. Sadler's participation in the first phase (Battle of Albert 1–13 July 1916) of the continuing Somme offensive. For a short while, 9th Royal Fusiliers – soon to be reinforced by drafts from Great Britain –would be spared front line service. Meantime, the Battalion would undergo further training before returning to action.

12

The Somme Battlefield, July and August 1916: After the Ovillers Action, on to Pozières

Away from the Somme trenches for the time being, the manpower-depleted 9th Royal Fusiliers was brought up to strength with drafts from Great Britain. Provided with further active service instruction, preparation of these men for battle was both necessary and important. After the period of rest and recuperation the Battalion went into action near Poziéres in early August.

Battalion War Diary:

8th July 1916. OVILLERS-ALBERT
In the morning we bombed along the Trench on our left flank and gained about 90 yards. We handed this area to a reinforcement of the 9th Essex, (35th Brigade,) which had arrived. During the day the Enemy shelled us and we lost rather heavily. 7 00pm: – Trench taken over by 2nd Battalion Manchester Regiment. The Battalion was met by the cookers at CRUCIFIX CORNER where they had tea. Arrived at Billets in ALBERT about 11 30pm.

9th July 1916. ALBERT to SENLIS.
10 00 am: Battalion paraded to march to SENLIS. Had dinner on the way and reached billets around 4 00pm.

10th July 1916. SENLIS to FORCEVILLE
Battalion paraded at 9 45 am marched to FORCEVILLE via. HEDAVILLE arrived 11 30 am.

11th July 1916. FORCEVILLE to BUS LES ARTOIS
7 58am. Battalion paraded to march to BUS LES ARTOIS via ACHEUX -arrived midday. General SCOTT (12th Division) inspected the men as they marched past. The Division's Band played the Regimental March Past at one point on the road.

12th July 1916. BUS LES ARTOIS
Companies at disposal of Company Commander for Kit Inspection, Equipping, etc. General Scott paid a visit to the men in their Billets.

13th July 1916. BUS LES ARTOIS
Company at disposal of Company Commanders for Bombing, Bayonet Fighting and

Physical Training.

14th July 1916.BUS LES ARTOIS
9 00 – 12 00 noon Companies at disposal of Company Commanders for Bombing and
Bayonet fighting. The Battalion, with the exception of H.Q., L.G's, Drums, Padres
etc., paraded. "A" & "C" Coy's paraded: No.1. "B" &" "D Coy's paraded: No.2. The
two Companies are to be attached to the 7th Royal Sussex; the "Composite Battalion"
to be in reserve to the 48th Division.

15th July 1916. BUS LES ARTOIS
A draft of 292 men arrived at BELLE EGLISE at 4 00a.m. 8 20 a.m.: Drums played
draft into billet, the men had breakfast. 11 15 am.: Draft paraded and were inspected
by Brigade General Boyd-Moss who gave them a very inspiring speech. The men were
attached to their various Coys. and marched to their billets. 6 00pm: A concert given
by the Divisional Concert Band was held in the Y.M.C.A. at BUS.

16th July 1916. BUS LES ARTOIS.
9 15 am.: Bn. Paraded for Divine Service. The Parade was held in a clearing in the wood
beyond 8th R.F. Huts-all units of the Brigade attended. 5 25 pm. The 2 Companies
attached to the 7th Royal Sussex, (14/7.16), returned to BUS.

17th July 1916. BUS LES ARTOIS.
9.12am.: Bombing practice, bayonet fighting, drill etc. General Scott visited the
Coys in their training groups. 2 00-3 00pm Lectures. Draft of 167 men from BELLE
EGLISE, arrived here at 7 00pm. 7 00pm: Marched to transport ground where they
were inspected by the C.O. and posted to their various Coys.

18th July 1916. BUS LES ARTOIS
9 00am. Bombing practice, bayonet fighting, drill etc. 2 00–4 00pm: Lectures.
2.20pm General Scott (12th Division) inspected the men of both drafts. All the
recent drafts to the Brigade attended.

19th July 1916. BUS LES ARTOIS
12.20pm. Parade as per yesterday. A draft of 50 men arrived from the 7th Royal Sussex.
These also included some men of this Battalion who had been down at the base.

Sadler Account:

135. THE BATTLE OF THE SOMME. Taking the 2nd Stripe.
After a long march we reached our destination at, Bus Les Artois, towards tea-time.
Having spent the evening resting, we received Orders to attend Company Orders
on the following morning. Here, The Company Officer informed me that I was to
be made a Full Corporal and paid for the two "stripes" straight away. My comment
to the Captain was that it was not my wish to take the two stripes until I had had
my leg seen to and, with that he passed the remark, "Do not leave the Company
unless you are obliged to do so. There will be so many new men arriving later and

the few "old hands" who are left and "understand the game" will be needed". With that, I left to attend our Field Dressing Station where I had the wound cleaned and dressed and I also had an injection in my chest and was told to attend for daily "treatment". I then returned to carry on with the "good work" once more. We all spent this day resting. On the 14th, we left to "Stand To" as Reserve in the rear of a certain part of the Front and ended up spending four days there in all. My Battalion was formed into a small Company and with three Regiments, including members of the 7th Royal Sussex; we managed to be about a Battalion in strength. We had little to do during these four days so we spent a very enjoyable time. Finishing our four days in Reserve, we return to the Village of Bus les Artois once more. Here being greeted by several hundred fresh men, reinforcements for the Battalion, straight from England.

136. THE BATTLE OF THE SOMME. Having a sharp move towards the trenches again.

The next day we were again made up and ready for action. The morning was spent in training the new men.

After Parades had finished, in the short time to spare before Dinner, a Sergeant who was a new comrade of mine and myself, spent the time with a family in a French house, having a drink of coffee. Then, on the 20th July, we received the Order to get the men to pack everything up and have "Full Marching Order", ready to move at a moment's notice. This was done. After Dinner, we received Orders to parade ready for marching off. We were soon to leave for the Trenches and, once more passing through Mailly-Maillet, we arrived at some Trenches in an area called the "Nab", just to the left of where we had last been in Battle. This was a "breaking-in" period for the new men. There were very few Shells and Trench Mortars around and we formed working parties and managed to get through the next four days.

Battalion War Diary:

20th July 1916. MAILLY–MAILLET

8.15 am: C.O. HALL, Company Commander, proceeded to H.Q. 11th Infantry Brigade at MAILLY-MAILLET to reconnoiter the line of that Brigade which 36th Brigade is to take over this afternoon.11.20am.: Received orders from Brigade for Battalions to take same trenches from 1st East Lancashire Regiment. "A" Coy paraded and marched to MAILLY-MAILLET, the other Coys following at 5 minute intervals. Coy. guides met the Battalion at the railway crossing Q.1.d Reference Map 57 D.N.E. "D" Coy took over ELLES SQUARE from 1st Somerset Regiment. "B" and "C" Coys took over from the same two Coy's. of 1st East Lancashire. "A" Coy were in support in WHITE CITY . The relief was completed by 6 00pm. At 6.30pm. Transport came up as far as WHITE CITY where rations were dumped. On the way back they were shelled, Transport Officer and 9 others wounded. 2 horses killed. The night passed quietly except for some shelling by hostile trench mortars on the same front line.

21st July 1916. MAILLY-MAILLET.

Weather fine and bright. Enemy were very active with 5.9 shells and Whizz Bangs N.

of and including WHITE CITY. Shelling was most noticeable at 1 00 pm and 9.45pm. Coys. were kept very busy on clearing trenches, making fire steps and building up parapets. CHATHAM TRENCH and MAXIM blown in by Rum-jars between 10 00 pm and 11.30pm. 6.30pm.:- Transport arrived. WHITE CITY- had been shelled on the way up, 6 casualties reported. An Officers patrol went out from FRONT LINE about the point Q.4.6.7.9. to reconnoiter the REDAN. No trace of the enemy was seen but the disused trenches are, in many places, flattened.

22nd July 1916. MAILLY-MAILLET.
3.45 am.:- A party of about 15 Germans were seen working on their front line parapet opposite MAXIM TRENCH. On fire being opened on them, they immediately scuttled into their trench. ROMAN ROAD drained from 6th AVENUE to MOUNTJOY TRENCH. New wire was put out in front of our firing line between MAXIM and DOG ST. Old wire strengthened and gaps blocked. MAXIM TRENCH flattened in 3 places by enemy trench mortars. The day was fairly quiet – usual shelling by 5.9 shells of WHITE CITY. 6 00pm.:- Trench mortars fell in CHATHAM TRENCH blocking the trench in 2 or 3 places. "B" Coy worked hard trying to keep the trench cleared.

The shelling was kept up all through the night, several casualties occurred.

23rd July 1916. MAILLY-MAILLET
11.30 am.:- 11th Middlesex Officers came up to reconnoitre the line – they will relieve us tomorrow. The 12th Divisional Artillery officers visited H.Q. in WHITE CITY. They had taken over from the 4th Div. Artillery about 6 00pm yesterday. About 2.30pm we had a message from the Brigade asking us to send 2 guides to Brigade H.Q. to meet Officers of another Brigade who were coming up to reconnoiter the line. 5.30pm.:- Coy. Commander of 13th Royal Welsh Fusiliers arrived at 5.30pm and told us they were taking over the trenches from the Battalion tomorrow. They intended holding the line by having their Coys. up in front line from WATLING ST. to EGG ST and some back in the given points (N.9. WHITE CITY). Work of clearing the trenches continued – one could walk round the whole system without getting ones back at all wet or dirtied.

24th July 1916, MAILLY-MAILLET
1 00am – 2 00am.: Enemy shelled front line trenches with trench mortars continuously through the night. CHATHAM TRENCH and MAXIM were blown in, in several places. "B" Coy had several casualties. Artillery retaliated also with a 60 lb. trench mortar which was in our lines. "A" Coy put out 80 feet of barbed wire in front of fire trench from WATLING STREET to MAXIM.

Coy Guides paraded at H.Q and were marched down to MAILLY STATION under Capt. COXHEAD where they were to meet 13th R.W. Fusiliers and guide them up to the trenches. Capt. COXHEAD, with billeting party, proceeded to BOIS du WARNIMONT where the Battalion was to billet. 1 00pm.: The first platoon of the relieving Battalion arrived at WHITE CITY. 4 00pm: Enemy opened up a very heavy bombardment on our communication trenches – some of "C" Coys. platoon was hit. 4 men wounded and 1 killed. 6 00pm. Relief completed. 8.45pm. Battalion reported present in billets at BOIS du WARNIMONT.

25th July 1916. MAILLY-MAILLET to BUS LES ARTOIS/HEDAVILLE.
7 00am. Reveille. Coys. at disposal of Company Commander for inspection, cleaning up etc. At 10 00am. Message from Brigade warning Battalion to be prepared to move at 3 00 pm. 5.30 pm:-. Battalion paraded at 5.30pm moved off at 6.05 pm. Marched through BERTRANCOURT, FORCEVILLE to HEDAVILLE where we bivouacked for the night. Arrived about 9 00pm.

Sadler Account:

137. THE BATTLE OF THE SOMME. Being asked to change Companies.

At these Trenches, my plucky Platoon Officer asked me if I would like to change Companies and come and join him to take charge of the wiring and repairing of Trenches. He had now been promoted to the rank of Captain and was being left out of the latest Battle in order to take charge of a Company if the situation arose where another Company's Officer were killed. When this did happen it was a case that he took over "C" Company whilst, myself, I was to remain in "A" Company. Despite his request for me to follow him to "C" Company, I eventually decided that this was not what I really wished for. I remained where I was, in "A" Company, where I was well versed in, and had taken part in plenty of the "game" of putting up barbed wire etc. for a long time now. I was, though, beginning to wish that someone would, very soon, come along and take the job away from me. As regards to the Officer who made the request, it would have been impossible to have found a better soldier to take charge of a Company of men. He was an Officer, so different from many others, a man that you could put your trust in and feel quite safe when he was with you. I intend to make more mention of this Officer as I go on.

138. THE BATTLE OF THE SOMME. Awarded the Military and on the way to the Front Line once more.

Leaving these Trenches we finished up in the Albert defence [line]. Here we spent a short time in training our new men in the ways of Bombing etc. After spending three or four days here, the Battalion was ordered to Parade in loose dress and, just before Dinnertime, the four Companies paraded and formed a Square. My name, a Stretcher Bearers and also the Bombing Sergeant's name were called and we had to go to the centre of the Square where we were told that the three of us had been awarded the Military Medal for the good work which we had done in the last Great Battle. The medal was awarded to me for sniping, good work done and Gallantry shown in the "Field" on July 7th at the assault and capture of Ovillers. We were told that we were able to wear the ribbon as soon as it was supplied. After the Parade was dismissed, many men and Officers came over to congratulate me on my reward as, at that time of the War, there were but very few Military Medals that had been awarded; so few in fact that we didn't even know the colours of the ribbon.

Battalion War Diary:

26th July 1916. HEDAUVILLE.

9 00am. Coys. paraded for bombing and physical training. Remained in the same bivouac for the night.

27th July 1916. HEDAUVILLE to BOUZINCOURT to ALBERT.

9.10am.: Battalion paraded and marched to BOUZINCOURT where we arrived about 10.30am. Bivouacked in a field just outside the village with the 8th Battalion Royal Fusiliers. At 4.00 pm. The 36th Infantry Brigade got orders to take over trenches from 143rd Infantry Brigade. 11th Middlesex to relieve 8th Royal Warwicks. in front line from Pozières section to X.3.C 7.9. Map 57 D.S.E. The present front line is from about R.34.C 2.1 to X.3.b.2.8. 7th Royal Sussex to relieve 6th Royal Warwicks in LA BOISELLE. 8th Royal Fusiliers to relieve 5th Royal Warwicks in TARA-USNA line. Our Battalion was to be in reserve in bivouacs W.23.d 1.3. 4 00 pm.:- Left BOUZINCOURT and marched to bivouac where we arrived at 5.30pm. On the way we were held up by Australian artillery who were moving in to ALBERT. The day was warm and bright.

28th July 1916. ALBERT.

9 00am.: Coys paraded for bombing, arms drill etc. Several carrying parties detailed. Men bathed in the ponds close to the bivouac.

29th July 1916. ALBERT

Got orders to move into Intermediate line W.21.d. "A" Coy marched off at 10 am. "B", "C", and "D" following at 10 minute intervals between Coys. 11 00am:. Battalion arrived at Intermediate line (H.Q.s W.21.d.4.4 sheet 57.D.S.E.). Very hot day. Enemy dropped a few shells into ALBERT during the day.

30th July 1916. ALBERT

There was very heavy bombardment during the night in the direction of Pozières. Coys. spent the morning bombing and clearing trenches with bombs. 12 00noon. Battalion paraded for C.O. to give out that the following N.C.O.'s had been awarded the Military Medal.

No. 1344 Sergeant S.TURNBULL; No, 2186 Sergeant J. LOMAS; No. 256 Corporal J.J. CURLING; No. 321 Lance Corporal J.SADLER; No. 14325 Private J.WRIGHT; No. 1210 Private H. LINDOP; No. 10199 Private S.J. SPALDING; No. 1549 F.ELLIS; No. 133 Private F. O'DOHERTY.

Sadler Account:

Nothing very exciting happened whilst we were at the Albert Defence. The Germans kept up a fair rate of shelling on Albert Station which, very much, made the dust fly but, by this time, I had got quite used to such things. As long as they were not close enough to hit me, I took very little notice of them. It wasn't very long, though, before two more sandbags were handed to us along with two Bombs. It was quite three weeks since the last Battle and we were now at full-strength once more and "Ready for Action".

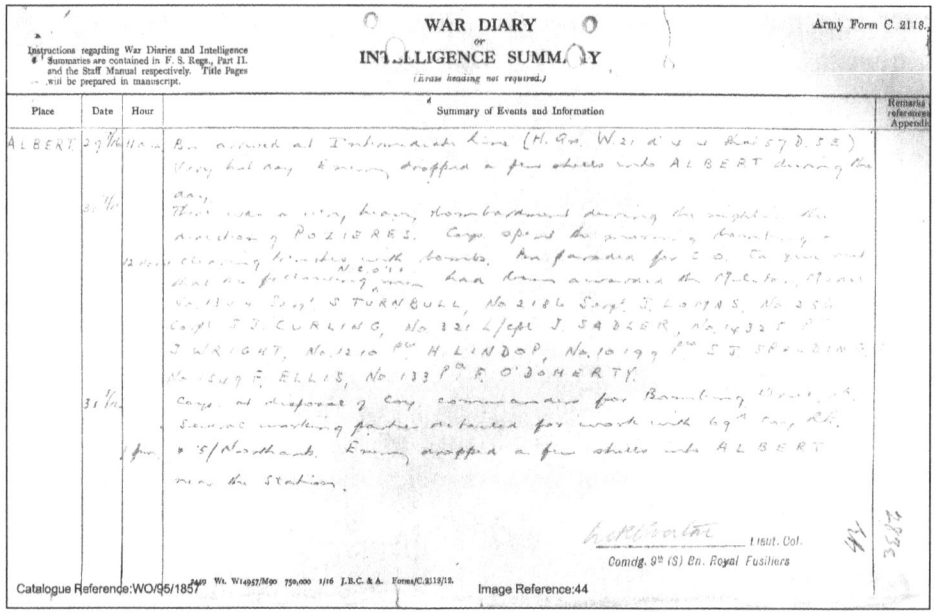

9th Royal Fusiliers. War Diary records James Sadler M.M.

Battalion War Diary:

31st July 1916. ALBERT.
Coys at disposal of Coy. Commanders for bombing, drill etc. Several working parties detailed for work with 69th Coy. R.E.'s and 5th Northants. 1 00 pm.:- Enemy dropped a few shells into ALBERT near the station.

1st August 1916. ALBERT DEFENCES.
Officers reconnoitre Trenches N.W. of Pozières. Working Parties of 275 men. Companies at disposal of Company Commanders for bombing, etc.

2nd August 1916. ALBERT DEFENCES.
Routine- Heavy Bombardment Pozières during the night.

3rd August 1916. ALBERT DEFENCES.
Routine. 36th & 37th Brigades assault. Entirely successful and the whole of 4th Avenue is captured- 1 Officer and 93 O.R.'s German prisoners taken. 8th Royal Fusiliers were the most successful.

4th August 1916. ALBERT DEFENCES and 3rd and 4th AVENUES.
Uneventful morning but got ordered to take over Trenches with a view to attacking RATION Trench in combination with 7th Royal Sussex and 8th Royal Fusiliers. Leave ALBERT DEFENCES at 8 00pm and take over 4TH. AVENUE and 3RD. AVENUE. Relief complete at 6 30pm.

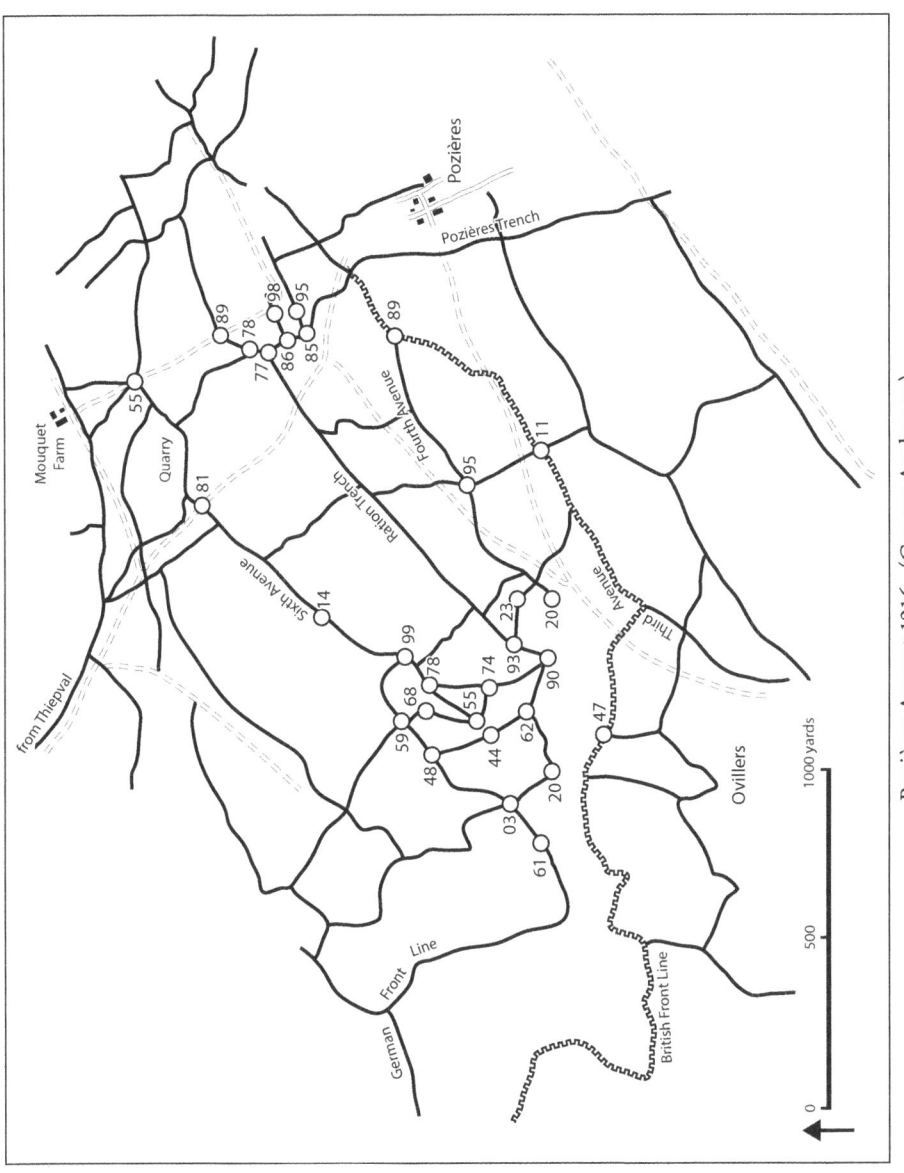

Pozières August 1916. (George Anderson)

36th Infantry Brigade Order:No.121 received. The Order was received at 8 17pm and the Attack due to start at 9 15pm.

9 15 pm: – "A" on right, "C" in centre and "D" on left go over the top. "B" Company take over 4th AVENUE. 9 35 pm.:- 3 Prisoners give themselves up to "B" Company. 10 00 pm.:- Message received, "A" and "C" Companies have gained their objective but have gained no touch with right or left. 10 45 pm.:- "A" Company send 9 Prisoners and report All's Well. No Report of "D" Company. 11 10 pm.:- Message from O in C, 8th. R.F. stating that their Bombing Officer is in touch with our "Left". No touch with Sussex's.

5th August 1916. 3rd and 4th AVENUES.

1 30 am.:- Rumour that there are some enemy between 4th AVENUE and RATION TRENCH. This partially confirmed by a report from the Pioneer Battalion, detailed to dig a Communications Trench across. They stated that they were fired on from somewhere between the lines. 4 30 am.:- Platoon of "B" Company and some stray men of "D" Company sent up to reinforce. "D" Company has been held up half way in an unknown Trench.

2 00-5 00am.:- Enemy Bombardment Heavy. 5 00-8 00 am: – Quiet. 8 30 am.:- O in C. "A" Company reports his bombing step to be at R.33.d.46. in RATION TRENCH.

5 00 pm.:- Orders received by Brigade to strafe Germans in between the lines. 6 00-700 pm:- Germans who had been surrounded for 20 hours gave themselves up. Rest of the Day is quiet.

6th August 1916. RATION TRENCH.

12 30am-4 00am.:- Heavy bombardment of our lines. Germans attack our block in RATION TRENCH with Flammerwerfer and succeed in driving us back a short way but we regain all but 40 yards and our Block is established at R.33.d.4.5. (See Appendix 1 for account of attack).[1]

Sadler Account:

On the 3rd of August we had Orders to Parade about 6 o'clock in the evening and then proceed to the Trenches and this is where the "New Men" got a terrible "Breaking In" with shell fire.

We marched up the main Road at hundred yard intervals until the Communication Trenches were reached by the Platoons. Whether we were seen by the Germans, I could not say but, as soon as we entered the Communication Trenches, it was like Hell once more.

139. THE BATTLE OF THE SOMME. Getting ready for battle.

The Germans were shelling the Trenches for all they were worth causing us to get very many wounded and as the Trenches were fairly narrow, and with us having to make our way pass the wounded, it was far from comfortable for the wounded

---

1   Appendix 1 can be found at the end of this Chapter.

but it could not be helped. After a terrible journey we succeeded in reaching the so-called Front Line, this being a newly dug Trench on top of a ridge and very quiet in the way of shelling. We found the Germans were too close to us to be able to shell our line which I didn't mind at all. One or two Sentry Posts were posted and the remainder took things easy, even taking their haversacks off in order to rest their backs. At this time we had no idea of when we might be going into Battle but it wasn't long after that when we received the Order for every man to get dressed, wearing Battle Orders, as we were going into Action at dusk. Shortly after this, all N.C.O.'s were called to receive Orders of Battle and I was quite interested in these. We were told that there was going to be no bombardment before starting but that when we mounted the Trench ready for the starting time, given as 9 15, we were going to have a terrible bombardment of small shells, including shrapnel, played on the German Front Line. This would last for as so long as we were walking across "No Man's Land" and, if the shelling of the German Front Line, hadn't finished, we had to lie down and wait and then all us were to "spring" into the Trench all at once.

140. THE BATTLE OF THE SOMME. After the Germans again.

Three of our Four Companies were going into Action and one was being used in support of us. My own Company was the right hand Company of the attack and, myself; I was taking centre position of the Company as my Platoon was in the centre. Everything, at this time, was so nice and quiet at this Line. The Germans were still shelling the back areas; little knew what was waiting for him. At last the Order was passed along for everyone to get out of the trench and to lie still on the top so that we could all move forward at once. This was done with the time to start being given by the outburst of our Artillery. The quietness was broken at last with the terrible roar of our shells going through the air, all bursting on what was supposed to be the German Front Line. As it was, we found a newly dug German Trench on our side of this Front Line and, as luck would have it, this Trench was very shallow and some of the Germans had flocked along to where it was deep; those who didn't think of doing that soon got mixed up with us. Because of the Order of Dress the Germans were wearing, it was a great puzzle to be able to tell exactly who was who. It was also a case of who started this Battle first as they had clearly been waiting to come after us and had dug this shallow Trench to act as a starting point for their attack.

141. THE BATTLE OF THE SOMME. Reaching our objective

As I said, it was a great puzzle to be able to tell just who was who at this Attack. With the darkness and the Battle Order which the Germans were wearing they looked just the same as us.

The only difference was that they were wearing their Overcoats whilst we were wearing our haversacks.

In the darkness, anyone "new to the Game" would not have known the difference.

With the Germans moving along to where their newly dug Trench was most likely to give them the best cover, this gave us a clear passage to their "Second Line", without having a shot fired at us.

Site of Pozières, August 1916. Copyright IWM (Q4078).

By the time we got there, our Bombardment had lifted into what was now our "new" No Man's Land.

From here, we noticed that the Germans had got mixed up with us due to them "moving on" instead of stopping in this Line. They soon got help on their journey with a large shower of bullets.

Getting to this Line, we only had four men wounded and this was due to one of our shells bursting short.

When we got into the Line we had to be careful not to get into the way of one of our shells which were still being aimed into this Line. Whatever battle one goes into, there are always one or two Gunners who send their shells short or do not lengthen their Range in time.

When we had been in the "New Objective" a short time, we were ordered to spread ourselves along the Trench, to the right and left, which was duly done.

142. THE BATTLE OF THE SOMME. Making a Barricade.

In fact we went along so far to the left that we came into contact with other Battalions that had gone into Battle the day before. Between them and us there should have been two of our Companies who had started into battle with us but, where the Germans had flocked to the deep part of their Trench, and, because our shelling wasn't touching that Line, it meant that these two other Companies had met with hand to hand fighting and had, therefore, been held up. We, ourselves, had, in fact, taken what three Companies should have taken and we also held it until they had got over their struggle. The men who had gone along the Trench, to the right, did not get very far before they met a German Strong-Point and the Germans showed fight by bombing very hard. It was here where I was to finish up myself, being supplied with a few good men and called upon to put up a Barricade. When we started building the barricade, we had a party of bombers to cover us whilst we were at work but, nevertheless, it was a far from comfortable job owing to the German bombs bursting rather close at times. At this Attack we found that the Germans were using "Egg" bombs which they could throw twice as far as our "Mills" bombs. Anyhow we had to work very hard filling this Trench in. It was towards morning, when we had very nearly finished our task, and when myself and one of my men were right on the end of the Barricade, that, all of a sudden, the men cried, "Look Out, the Germans are coming". I looked up to see a German Party following their Trench along to the far end of our Barricade.

143. THE BATTLE OF THE SOMME. Stopping a small German raid and an Officer's remark.

My chum quickly made his way towards the Trench and I soon followed him.

On getting into the trench, I soon called out to what few men I could see in our Trench, or close at hand, to come and get ready to fire their rifles.

We kept quiet until the approaching Germans got close enough for us to see what we were firing at and then we greeted them with a shower of bullets and those that got away, soon rushed for cover in their Trench, the other side of the Barricade. This took place just about half an hour before the correct time to "Stand To" but, owing to us opening fire; everyone in the Trench was ordered to "Stand To" early. I received a visit from a very welcome friend when an Officer came up to me and asked me what we had been firing at. I told him we had seen a German Bombing Party coming towards us and, when they were close enough to see they were Germans, we had soon opened fire and scattered them. This very gallant Officer made the remark to me, "You don't want to get the wind up and fire at just anything". This Officer was one of the two who I had met the day after the last Battle. I do not know if he had had more of the War than I had.

144. THE BATTLE OF THE SOMME. Liquid Fire Attack.

Because I had stopped that small attack, I was told, by this Officer, to go and show the men where to put the large supply of Bombs which a Platoon from our Support Company had brought forward to us; this, because I was now an "old-hand" at the job. One may guess that, whilst making a Barricade, the men who were doing it have their eyes looking around them all the time. By doing this they are soon getting used to the new ground won. So I was sent to see about these bombs and because all the men in my Company were new to the Action, they, of course, looked to their front, not taking much notice of the right hand flank where the Barricade had been made. All of a sudden this flank was attacked again and, this time, no one saw them coming. It was just very lucky that everyone was on "Stand To" from the last attack. However, instead of it turning out to be a German Bombing Party, it turned out to be a party of Germans using their "Flammerwerfer" or Liquid Fire. This time I didn't get the "wind-up" although many others did and many suffered because

Pozières battlefield today.

of it. As we were all ready for Action, including having an extra Platoon of men and plenty of bombs, we soon got the situation in hand without losing a yard of Trench.

145. THE BATTLE OF THE SOMME. Getting surrounded and sniping.

When daylight arrived we found out that we were surrounded by Germans. The Germans had got out of their Trench, well on the right of the Barricade, and had, again, manned the trench which we had left in the Rear the night before the day of our attack. We found this out by getting men hit from the Rear although it did not seem to worry us much. We had some fine shots at them, at close quarters, as repayment for their shots on our men. I shall never forget the then Sergeant Major of my Company and myself having such a day of shooting. It was just as if we were shooting game birds. The Germans, at times, would get up and cross over to another part. When we saw them we would call out for them to surrender and drop their rifles. If this wasn't done, they would be most liable to go on and surrender to death. We both enjoyed ourselves until we thought our time had come. Something dropped by our feet and the Sergeant Major ran one way and I rapidly went the other way. We waited for this thing to explode. After waiting for some little time, nothing happened and I walked to see what it was and found it was nothing dangerous, unless we had been directly hit by it. It was one of our empty shells, the contents of which had blown out and the empty shell had been blown back and pitched at our feet.

146. THE BATTLE OF THE SOMME. A large number of Germans surrender.

We managed, at last, to capture a German officer and our Officers got this man to get up on the side of the Trench in order to try and get all of the other Germans to surrender. Instead of getting them to surrender he got a bullet, from the other direction, right through the head, killing him outright.

Anyway, for us, it was a case of getting them to surrender or else making it a very uncomfortable time for them. We received Orders that everybody would have to "Stand To" at 4 o'clock in the afternoon and then we were going to sweep that Trench with Rifle Grenades. About half past three that afternoon, some of the Germans made signs that they would like to surrender so my former Platoon Officer, now Company Officer of "C" Company, got all of the Lewis' Guns set on the Germans in case anything happened whilst he, himself, walked out to bring them in. By doing this he was able to get 115 Germans to surrender. These all got into our Trench in single file holding their hands up in the air. This surrender taking place saved us making the rifle grenade attack half an hour later.

147. THE BATTLE OF THE SOMME. Finding news from a captured German.

This same day we watched an attack take place well on our Left. It was a grand sight to watch the men keeping in one straight line going up the side of the Ridge. It was, though, a far from grand sight to watch them when they got to the top and in full view of the Germans. Then the machine gun and rifle fire started and this soon thinned out the Line. For all this, their objective was won but the Germans made up their minds that, at night, little if any reinforcement would be able to reach them. They did this by keeping up a grand Barrage from dark until daylight when they were able to see, once more, our attacking troops for themselves. Also on this day, which we were spending trying to make life very uncomfortable for the Germans, a young Officer in my Company found out, from a German prisoner, what a certain "Star" light meant when it was fired. This was a signal given by one Green Star branching into two a short time after it had been fired. To the Germans this was a signal indicating that their shells were falling short.

What the prisoner told us was quite correct as we tried it for ourselves later. These different coloured "Starlights" could be found in all newly captured German positions, along with a pistol to fire them.

148. THE BATTLE OF THE SOMME. Second Liquid Fire Attack.

Whilst we had been in this Trench, it had, up until now, been impossible for the Germans to shell us because the German troops were, themselves, also everywhere. However, on the following morning, Sunday 6th August; the Germans played their next attack with Liquid Fire from the same position as before. This time we were lucky that we hadn't been driven out of our Trench. They got over the Barricade and started walking down the Trench clearing their way with their "Liquid Fire". If it hadn't been for the smoke caused by the Liquid Fire, they might well have achieved what they had intended to do. With so much smoke about we were able to get out on the Flank or side of our Trench and wait for them and, whilst they played their Liquid Fire to the front, we bounced in on them from the side and, with bombs and rifle-fire; we soon got rid of them and captured their "lovely" weapon of War. That morning, we received a very warm time with regards to the red flames, smoke and the roar of the Liquid Fire and the bursting of shells. I do not think I ever saw a more dreadful sight of War itself. I thought to myself that if Hell is worse than this then I certainly have no wish to go there.

149.THE BATTLE OF THE SOMME. Liquid Fire. Using German Verey Lights.

After the third attack with "Liquid Fire", Stokes Trench Mortars were brought to the Front and these were set on the far end of the Barricade. With Stokes Trench Mortars, it was possible to have a large number of shells in the air even before the first one had touched the ground and exploded. This Trench Mortar consisted of very high explosives and made a terrible report on bursting. With the Germans taking notice of where the shells were being ranged at that point, they thought it very advisable to keep quiet. Later that same day, towards dusk, the Germans sent over very large shells which exploded on striking the ground, only a few yards in front of our Trench. We began to wonder, yet again, if we were in for another "Warm" time.

Of course, by now we had a German "Verey Light" pistol and many of his coloured lights, the sort of which we had always been on the lookout for. After having found out earlier, from the German prisoner, the information regarding what various flares meant, one Officer used the information and tried his luck by sending up one of the green lights. By doing this we found the German prisoner had been quite correct in what he had told us. Many more shells were sent over but, after the Green Light had gone up and branched into "stars", the range was, at once, lengthened on the German guns and the shells passed over us and went well to the rear. This meant that we had nothing whatever to fear from the shells and they caused us no damage.

Sunday night passed very quietly.

The following morning, towards midday, we got relieved with only a few "Whiz Bangs" to greet us as we left the Front Line. We soon managed to get going down the Communication Trenches where one or two of our men fainted with the heat as there was very little water to be found. Also, we passed the in-coming Troops and wished them well.

Battalion War Diary:

7th August 1916. RATION TRENCH

Continual Bombardment of our Lines. Relieved in the afternoon by the 35th Brigade. The Suffolk Regiment.

The following Officers casualties were sustained during the Attack on RATION TRENCH and the German counter attack. Killed :- Capt. H.M. GREEN; 2nd Lt. Ingram STEVENS; 2nd. Lt. F.W.LUPTON; 2nd Lt. C.C.HEAVER; 2nd Lt. G.E.BUNGEY. Wounded :- Lt. KNOTT E.H.; Capt. G.L. CAZALET (at duty); 2nd Lt. PILGRIM, 2nd Lt. T.L.CALWELL; 2nd Lt. G.G.R FOX; Capt. P.THORTON R.A.M.C.; 2nd. Lt. E.L.FIFOOT. 281 other Ranks killed wounded or missing.

Total Prisoners to Brigade. 2 Officers, 1 Officer (wounded) and 135 Other Ranks. Battalion all in BOUZINCOURT by 7 30 pm.

8th August 1916. BOUZINCOURT.

Reorganisation. Capt. RUSSELL appointed to Command and pay of "D" Company.

9th August 1916. BOUZINCOURT to VARENNES.

Move to VARENNES where Battalion goes into Huts.

Warning Order that 36th Brigade will be inspected by his Majesty the King on the morrow. Practice Parade in the afternoon.

Appendix 1

Report on Flammenwerfer Attack 6/8/16.

At dawn on the morning of the 6th, a sudden burst of flame appeared over our barricade and along the track in the rear of it for some 25 yards. The flames came from various directions. The method of employment seems to have been for one man to creep forward with a hose while a second man pumped up pressure in a tank to supply it with liquid. The men using the Flammenwerfer were clad in what looked like shiny black oilskins. No. of jets used is doubtful but was probably about 8. The attack was supported by about 40 bombers who used the smoke as a screen. The attack was checked and finally beaten off by extending some 20 men in the open on each side of the track, supported by 2 Lewis Guns. Bombs were also thrown as the ground was so broken that rifle fire could seldom reach the enemy in the shell holes. Flames were of short duration- thick smoke hung about for some considerable time. Towards the end of the encounter we obtained superiority of fire and were able to dig in 30-40 yards of trench in daylight and this formed an efficient barricade; after which the covering party on the flanks was withdrawn.

(Signed by) G.L.Cazalet Capt. O.in C. "A" Coy. 9th Royal Fusiliers. Dated :8/9/16.

The Somme Battlefield, August and September 1916: On from Pozières, Rest and in Reserve at Agny

C orporal James Sadler and his comrades found themselves out of the front line again. It was a chance for a small rest. He recalls the time, after leaving of the Ration Trench area, near Pozières.

150. THE SOMME BATTLEFIELD. Relieved from the Front Line. Being inspected by the King. (9th August 1916).
At last we arrived at Bouzincourt, not a great distance from Albert, where we spent two days resting, waiting, in Reserve, ready to be called up again if required. As we were not called for, two fairly comfortable days were spent here.

The next day we left for our old village, Bus les Artois, and, whilst on our way to this village, we lined the road, not far from Albert, to be inspected by the King as he was on his way to view the Somme Battlefield.

This inspection was carried out in a very simple way and, as the King walked up the road, each Company presented arms in turn. When the King had passed, the order was given to "Slope Arms" and very shortly we were on our way again towards the village.

On this day, when the King inspected the men, it was the first time, whilst I had been serving in France, that I had the pleasure of having my boots cleaned for me. Men were "told off" to walk round whilst we stood in position and were instructed to clean our boots.

As the King passed by me, I heard him remark to his Staff as to how well the men looked.

The Battalion Diaries are brief when describing the inspection:

10th August 1916. VARENNES.
Inspection takes place on road from SENLIS to V.5.3.9 in Order: 8th Royal Fusiliers; 9th Royal Fusiliers; 7th Royal Sussex; 11th Middlesex from South to North. Formation: One rank on either side of the road facing inwards.

No: 321 Corporal James Sadler M.M. continues with his recollections:-

151. FROM THE SOMME TO ARRAS. A new part of the Front. Meeting G.O.C. 12th Division. On Reserve in Agny.

The following day we left to take over a new part of the Front for a short time. This was quite a change for a few of us longer serving and older men.

We were to take our part in the Line, near Arras, not very far from a little village named Agny.

There was much marching and movement required in order to get the 9th Royal Fusiliers, and the other troops which made up the 36th Division, into the Trenches at Agny. But the advantage to them was that they were away from a major part of The Somme Battlefield and, although still involved with Trench duties, life was to be somewhat quieter.

The Battalion's diary recorded those movements over the next few days:-

11th August 1916. VARENNES.
Remainder of Brigade moves to VARENNES. Routine- Bombing practice etc. Congratulatory messages received from Commander in Chief on success in operations N. of Pozières.

12th August 1916. VARENNES to PUCHEVILLIERS
9 00am.:- Brigades march 7 miles to PUCHVILLIERS via. LEALVILLIERS & TOUTENCOURT, arriving at 12 30 pm. Very hot for marching but only one man falls out.

The following awards are awarded for Gallantry during the attack and capture of OVILLERS.

Capt. E.W.T. BECK- D.S.O.; 2nd Lt. T.L. CALWELL -Military Cross; No.6271 Sgt. HAMMOND- D.C.M.; No. 2183 Cpl. STAGG -Military Medal.

A letter also received from Divisional Commander conveying appreciation of the work done by "A" Company in the capturing and defence of RATION TRENCH (4.8.16 to 7.8.16).

13th August 1916. PUCHEVILLIERS.
Church Parade.

14th August 1916. PUCHEVILLIERS.
Bombing, Drill and Musketry etc.

Corporal James Sadler recalls the time spent in Puchevilliers with some affection:

We spent four days at this village, carrying on with a few hours of work, daily, but I must say it was a good rest. The village was only a short distance behind the Front Line but was very seldom shelled.

From what I could see, this part of the Line was used as a Rest Camp for both the Germans and ourselves. Used, that is, as a Rest Camp for tired men from the Somme Battlefield.

However the Battalion, including Corporal Sadler, was soon to be on the move again as they made their way towards Agny.

The Battalion Diaries give the details:

15th August 1916. PUCHEVILLIERS to SARTON/ VAUCHELLES.
7 00 am.:- 7th R. Sussex, 8th R.F. and Brigade HQ moved to SARTON. 11th Middx. and ourselves moved to VAUCHELLES.

Bn. Moved off at 7 00 am and arrived 9 00 am. Bn. In huts. Heavy rain all afternoon. Seven Brigade cards given out for gallantry shown on 4th and 5th of August.

16th August 1916. VAUCHELLES to BEAUDRICOURT.
5 30 am:- Bn. Paraded & marched to BEAUDRICOURT via MARIEUX, SARTON, ORVILLE, HALLOY, LUCHEUX – a distance of 13¾ miles. Arrived 12 30 pm.

17th August 1916. BEAUDRICOURT to GIVENCHY LE NOBLE.
6 15 am: – Bn. Moves off via SUS S' LEDGER, GRANDROULECOURT, LINGEREUIL to GIVENCHY LE NOBLE. "D" and "C" Companies and HQ's are billeted in the Chateau; "A" and "B" Companies at VILLERS-SIRESIMON.

18th August 1916. GIVENCHY LE NOBLE.
Bombing, Drill and Musketry etc.

The Battalion was to reach Agny on the 20th August.

19th August 1916. GIVENCHY LE NOBLE to SIMENCOURT.
5 30 pm.:- C.O. and Company Commanders report at Brigade HQ's 32nd. Infantry Brigade and reconnoitre the trenches around AGNY. Battalion parades and marches via MANIN, AVESNES to SIMENCOURT. Arrive about 10 00 pm.

20th August 1916. SIMENCOURT to AGNY.
7 45 pm: – Bn. marches off to AGNY to take over from 9th West Yorks. via BERNEVILLE, WARLUS, DAINEVILLE & ACHICOURT. Platoon Guides meet Bn. at Railway Bridge outside DAINEVILLE and conducted them to AGNY.

Corporal Sadler recalled time briefly spent in Simencourt:

Before taking over this new part, we spent a night and part of the next day at Simencourt.

At this village, I had the great pleasure of shaking hands with the G.O.C. (General Officer in Command) of the 12th Division, Major General A. B. Scott, for the first time and being congratulated on my good work done in the Field.

He then continued with his, and the Battalion's, journey towards Agny:

This day, towards dusk, motor buses drove up to take us as far as possible towards the Line.

After a nice ride and a long march, we finished up at Agny to start our first turn in "Reserve". Myself, now as an Acting Orderly Sergeant had to "tell off" working parties and see that they paraded on time.

We were to spend five days in the village before it became our turn to take our first turn up in the Front Line and, again, one wouldn't have thought there was a War on. When we arrived, not a shot was fired by us or the Germans.

At this point, I lost my "job" of putting up barbed wire but managed to get hold of another job, quite as good; this was the taking out of Patrols and escorting the Patrols who were assisting the Officer in Charge.

The Battalion's Diaries record of those five or so days support James's view of the relative peace and quiet of the sector:

21st August 1916. AGNY.
Very comfortable billets. "A" & "D" Companies are in AGNY LIBRARY and "B" & "C" in SUNKEN ROAD. Very quiet.

22nd August 1916. AGNY.
Two working parties of 100 men each under the 67th Field Company R.E.'s supplied. Good news from Pozières.

23rd August 1916. AGNY.
Usual working parties under R.E.'s. Very quiet.

24th August 1916. AGNY.
Fine. Heavy bombardment going on down South.

25th August 1916. AGNY.
11th Middlesex's. 2nd. in Command comes round to Bn. HQ's to take over. Heavy bombardment in South continues. Usual working parties.

26th August 1916. AGNY.
Relieve 11th Middx. In the line, "B", "C" & "D" Companies in Front Line. "A "Company in reserve. Relief completed by 12 noon. Except for a Meinwerfer firing on "B" Coys. Trenches, everything very quiet.

However, at this stage, No. G 321. Corporal James Sadler, "A" Company, did encounter a disagreeable so-called "duty" which enabled him to give his opinion on particular officers he had served with:

152. THE FRONT LINE NEAR ARRAS. Own view of Officers. (Regular and New).
One night, whilst at these Trenches, I was called to the "Company Office" Dug-out and was told by a "so-called" Officer to go out on a pitch black night and see how much wire was around a German Sap Head -a Saphead being a Trench running out into No Man's Land.

Both sides dug this type of Trench and used them so as to give warning of any sudden attacks.

This Officer wished for me to tell him as too how much wire would be required if it was wound up on rolls.

The German Saphead was only 70 yards from one of our Sapheads and, after I had listened to what the Officer had got to say, I had my say.

"Give me your glasses, in daylight,", I said to him "and I will be able to tell you more by that means than from what I am able to see by going out tonight".

Anyway, it was an Order so the job had to be carried out. When dark arrived, a comrade and myself put on our Patrol Suits, these being made from a sort of canvas which enabled one to crawl about in the grass without getting wet. However, whilst we were still in the Trench and just about to start on our journey, we were called back and stopped from going further due to it being so dark and the rain setting in.

I would like to have had the pleasure of taking this "so called" Officer out on such a trip.

I would have taken him to shake hands with "Old Fritz".

If he had never had a fright before, he certainly would have had one that night.

It is not for me to necessarily talk about people above my Rank but, after we had taken part in several Battles, we had lost all of our Regular Officers. They were the type of Officer who understood men and knew how to treat them. It was now a case that, having lost this class of Officer in previous Action, we now appeared to have to put up with anything.

I can only say, from what I saw of some of the newer Officers, if they had been required to undertake a Drill of a Platoon of men, something which was their duty as they had to be able to get their men under control; then the majority of them would have been lost.

153. REFLECTIONS ON THE SOMME. N.C.O.'s and their role in the War.

Myself, by what I was to see of The Great War, was a war run by N.C.O.'s and it mattered little, even if the man was only a Lance Corporal; other men were only too willing to follow him if he treated them as men and had a good nerve.

It requires a N.C. O. that would stick with his men until death, if required, and under any sort of shellfire. It would surprise many if they only knew what a great comfort it is to any soldier to have a good N.C.O., capable of cheering his men up.

At the moment, when going into Action, and death maybe staring them in the face, the first thing a man would, more than likely ask is "Which N.C.O. is in charge?"

If the N.C.O. was the right sort of man, a man who they respected, then they would care for nothing and be pleased.

If, however, it was an N.C.O who did not have their confidence it could turn out to be the other way about and then the men could be very unwilling to co-operate.

At times like these it was not a case of thinking of money or sense, all that was required was nerve.

I do not wish for my readers to think that I am writing this because I was an N.C.O. myself. I feel sure I have made it clear it was not necessarily my wish to rise in the Ranks, but it was case of having to do so.

Please do not think that I am writing this in favour of all N.C.O.'s as, from what I have seen at The Front, if I were to have been classed with some of the N.C.O.'s I have observed, then I would have been only too willing to give my rank up.

In this terrible War it wasn't just a case of shouting and bullying on the Parade Square or trying to see how many men could be mustered for Company Orders. I personally would have fought to the last, both on Company Orders and Commanding Officers Orders, in order to free a man from a "crime".

154. REFLECTIONS ON THE SOMME. The role of N.C.O.'s (continued).

I have taken my place as a witness at a Field General's Court martial in a situation where the accused man had been charged with falling asleep at his Post. This was so small a "crime" that it should have been able to have been dealt with by simply using Company Orders.

By not being afraid of the look of an Officer and by telling the truth, I have been able to free a man who could have suffered heavy punishment for practically nothing.

If at any time I had made up my mind to carry a thing forward, and it was required by my Rank, then it had to be done.

I quite understood when I signed up to fight at the start of the War; it was only a case of fighting and not one of making a fortune.

It was clear to me that I had to be straightforward and do my duty and I am pleased to think my comrades noticed my straight-forwardness.

I was, eventually, stretchered away from the Battlefield, something which I shall talk about later, and the last few words of some of my comrades who were able to see me being taken away, were to the effect that they were losing a very best friend.

In answer to their concern, I wished them the best of luck and told them to "Cheer Up".

I do not want anyone to think that I haven't met some of the very best of Officers, as I am proud to say that I was later to receive letters of thanks and letters from them which bring back many memories of times spent together in the War.

I have received letters from the Commanding Officer of my Battalion, Lieut.-Colonel G.C.R. Overton, who was also my Platoon Officer at an earlier stage and, in mentioning that Officer, I would say that it is unlikely that there was ever a more gallant Officer to have served in France.

155. REFLECTIONS ON THE SOMME. Being a Platoon Sergeant.

When I, later, reached the rank of Sergeant, I was, very shortly afterwards, handed a Platoon of men to look after and made Platoon Sergeant.

In a very short time I got to know each man, very used to each of them, and thought the world of them all.

When in Action at one of the later Great Battles, I, once, received an offer to "Stay Out-On Details" for a change.

I told my Company Officer that it was, in no way, my wish to "Stay Out" and that I would take my place in the Battle along with my comrades; knowing the men had got used to me.

I knew that, if I was missing, the men might soon lose faith in their task.

It was the man they had got used to being with who they needed to lead them into battle. They did not need a person who they only saw at certain times, they

Major General F.D.V. Wing CB, CMG,
GOC 12th Division, March–October 1915.
Killed in Action at the Battle of Loos.

Captain G.L. Cazalet DSO, CO
'A' Company, 9th Royal Fusiliers
throughout the Somme campaign.

Major General H.W. Higginson,
CB, DSO, GOC 12th Eastern
Division. April–November 1918.

Major M. E. Coxhead CO 9th Royal
Fusiliers June 1916–May 1917.

Commanding Officers under whom James Sadler M.M. served.

needed a man who they knew had experience and who had played his full part in
several battles.

   With this knowledge that they had an experienced leader; the men would then
often be prepared to fight to their last.

Whilst Corporal James Sadler has taken time out to reflect on the nature and qualities
of those chosen to play the role of a leader of men as they went into Battle; the 9th Royal
Fusiliers were to continue with their commitments in the Agny area and the Trenches.

Battalion War Diary:

27th August 1916. AGNY.
Very quiet. "D" Coy. sent out a patrol of 1 N.C.O. and 8 men during the night and they report a Bosch wiring party of 20 men.

28th August 1916. AGNY.
Very quiet. The following N.C.O.'s and men of the Battalion were awarded the Military Medal for Gallantry during the attack and capture of RATION TRENCH on 4th and 5th August:-
    No. 15934 Pte. J. YOUNG; No. 705 Sergt. A. McQUEEN; No. 533 Sgt. C. QUINELL; No. 255 Pte.(L.Cpl.) C. CROSS; No.1080 Cpl. R. BROOKFIELD (attached 37th T.M.B.); No. 10898 Pte. L.ROUSE; No. 10156 Pte. H.HARRIMAN; No. 3749 Cpl. F.R.YOUNG (attached 36th T.M.B.).

29th August 1916. AGNY.
Enemy slightly more active today. "B" Coy. were bombed a lot with RUM JARS. (German mortar bombs in the shape of a Rum Jar). Very heavy thunder storm about 7 00 pm.

30th August 1916. AGNY.
Very wet. Heavy bombardment going on all day down South. "B" Coy troubled again with "Rum Jars".

31st August 1916. AGNY.
Weather fine. Some aerial torpedoes fell into "D" Coy. Line wounding six men. Got orders that 11th Middx. would relieve us tomorrow.

Sadler account:

154. TRENCHES AT AGNY. Trenches at Agny . Food.
I will now continue with the Trenches at Agny.

It is not now my intention to say much about Trench Life as I have mentioned that earlier. What I will do, is write about just one or two things which were different from earlier.

We worked in these Trenches at Agny for a short time in a similar fashion to the Trenches at Armentières.

So many days in and so many out and it was only to be for a few weeks as we were soon to be back on The Somme Battlefield.

Once again, the Division which we were to relieve had been on the Somme doing their turn and, when they had been cut up, they arrived back and we had to take their place.

Whilst serving at this quiet part of the Line we were able to have the Company Cookhouse stationed in a Sunken Road only a few hundred yards off. This meant that we had no cooking to do ourselves and that, when the food arrived at the Trenches, it was always hot which we quite enjoyed.

155. TRENCHES AT AGNY. Keeping clean. "Flying Pigs" and firing them.

Whilst doing our few weeks at this part and our turns in the Front Line, washing and shaving every morning came to be important. This was carried out whether or not it was possible to get hot water.

I have seen hundreds wash and shave in the hot tea that was part of their breakfast.

Sometimes the remark was also to be heard that, if water or tea was not available, then make use of rifle oil.

Would anyone ever think of such a remark being made, other than in Wartime?

For Troops in the Front Line remarks such as this made one feel very miserable. Furthermore, it wasn't the outside appearance that we were concerned with; it was the under-clothing that we wanted clean in order to feel comfortable.

The Germans were not the only Enemy that we had to fight in the Trenches; we also had to live with the terrible torture from rats and vermin.

With regard to the on-going hostilities, James continued...

156. TRENCHES AT AGNY. "Flying Pigs" and firing them.

Before my Division had been on this Front for very long, we set about the task of tormenting "Old Fritz".

As the 12th Division was a Division known for making things lively, we were given what was known as a "Flying Pig" in each section at the Front.

A "Flying Pig" was a sort of Trench Mortar, very heavy and very large. It was capable of making the Germans feel very uncomfortable, even in their deep dugouts.

The gun used for firing it was fixed at the bottom of a pit which was connected to a very deep dugout. This dugout was also used for the shelter of the men when on and off duty.

The reason why the gun was fixed in a deep pit was because the shell itself was so large that it proved impossible to keep it out of sight of the Germans when it was fired. The Pit holding the gun was built on a slant so that it was impossible for an enemy shell to strike the bottom.

It proved only possible for the German's shells to strike and burst on the side of the pit walls, so keeping the Gun safe.

The spot from which a "Flying Pig" was fired was very soon searched out by the German Guns and heavy Trench Mortars.

157. TRENCHES AT AGNY Firing and transporting "Flying Pigs".

The German Front line Troops were often drawn to their Support Lines from where they could see the large "Flying Pig" shell sailing high into the air up until a time when it became impossible to see it for a short time. Then, all of a sudden, one could see it hurtling downwards towards the earth for all it was worth.

When it landed it would penetrate itself very deep into the ground and even if it did not smash the deep German Dugouts, I'll bet that no Germans came out alive if it burst within a few yards as it would make a hole or crater quite 12 feet deep and the same distance across.

I noticed it was always the responsibility of the Infantry in carrying these large

"Flying Pig" creatures, to the guns in order to fire them.

One day the battalion had the pleasure of supplying a large working party to carry a large amount of these shells to the Trenches.

Whilst we were on the road, the Germans started shelling just to the rear when one man stopped and passed the remark to a comrade, just behind him, "Look where that shell burst". The response was, "That shell has nothing to do with us, these things are all we have got to worry about and as soon as we can get them to where they have to be fired, so much the better".

158. TRENCHES AT AGNY. Playing cards. Making Fires, Buying Food.

When we were stationed in the village of Agny we managed, on one or two occasions, to organise a Whist Drive between ourselves; giving so many Francs as First, Second and Third prizes.

Many of the men took part in these, as I think card playing became one of the most popular of ways to pass the weary hours away.

I have seen cards being played in the Front Line with it taking a shell bursting, very close by, before the game was called to a halt.

I shall never forget a game of cards at Armentières.

I was sitting close by a game of cards, reading a little bit of news about Swanage, when a very large shell came sailing over which could have only just missed our roof.

I began to think to myself that, this was going be the last bit of news I would ever read of Home, Sweet Home.

It was, I think, the only time I saw men stop playing, lie flat on the ground and await their luck.

The shell finished up in the front garden, making a very large hole but it did not explode. The "Card Players" then started their game once more as if nothing had happened, the shell being put down as only being a stray one.

Another thing which used to make our life a little more enjoyable whilst in the Village at Agny was when we used to get a sandbag and go round and collect up all the little pieces of coal, coke and ashes. With these, and a tin, we were then able to start a warming fire.

We were unable to buy anything in the village itself but passes could be had from the Company Officer which enabled anyone, who so wished, to go on a "trip" to seek out a village where goods could be bought.

This meant that we used to be able to buy different things to eat such as Quakers Oats, condensed milk and tinned fruit, all of which made quite a change for us.

As Corporal Sadler has noted, Trench life at Agny followed a routine of so many days in the Trenches followed by a spell away from the Front Line.

And, so at the beginning of September, the 9th Royal Fusiliers were relieved at Agny and took over a less active sector near Dainville.

The Battalion's Diaries note this as follows:

1st September 1916. Trenches at AGNY to DAINVILLE.

9 00am.:- Bn. Relieved by 11th Middx. Relief reported complete at 10 45 am.

Companies proceeded via. GRANTHAM STREET to DAINVILLE where Bn. is billeted. Settled in billets by 12 30 pm.

2nd September 1916. DAINVILLE.
8 30 am.:- Coys. At disposal of Company Commanders for cleaning up and inspections. About eight 77mm shells burst close to C.O.'s billet. One falling in the garden. Rest of the day very quiet.

3rd September 1916. DAINVILLE.
9 30 am.:- Parade Service for Presbyterians etc. in Y.M.C.A. Hut. Voluntary Services for Church of England.

4th September 1916. DAINVILLE.
Very wet. Coys. paraded for Bombing, Musketry and Smoke Helmet Drill. The following honours awarded by the G.O.C. in Chief under authority granted by H.M The King:-

2nd. Lt. E.L. FIFOOT- D.S.O.; Capt. P.THORNTON (R.A.M.C.)- M.C.; C.S.M. BRESLAIN (36th M.G. Battery) – D.C.M.; Pte. T.CROW ("A". Coy.) – D.C.M.

The above honours were awarded for gallantry during the attack on RATION TRENCH (Pozières), 4th August 1916. 4 30 pm.:- Some very exciting bombing took place at one of "C" Coys. billets.

5th September 1916. DAINVILLE.
Pte. J.M.SPITTLE ("D" Coy.) awarded the Military Medal for great gallantry during the attack on RATION TRENCH.

6th September 1916. DAINVILLE.
Capt. G.L.CAZALET awarded the D.S.O for gallantry during the attack on RATION TRENCH. 4th Aug 1916.

6 00 pm.:- The Divisional Concert Party gave a performance at the Y.M.C.A. Hut, DAINVILLE. The show was a very clever one and was greatly appreciated.

7th September 1916. DAINVILLE to THE TRENCHES AT AGNY.
9 00 am:- Battalion relieved the 11th Middx, in G Sector. "A" Coy. moved off first with 2 minute intervals between platoons. "C","D" & "B" followed with same intervals. "D" Coy. on right of the Sector, "C" Coy. in the Centre and "A" Coy. on the right with "B" Coy in reserve. Relief completed 11 30 am.

8th September 1916. THE TRENCHES AT AGNY.
Our patrols were very active last night. Sap D was reconnoitred and found to be strongly wired. A Patrol under 2nd.Lt. BULL was discovered by the Enemy and was very heavily bombed and fired on. All three of the patrol were wounded but returned to same lines.

9 00 am:- A few 77 mm shells fell in between Support Reserve Lines.

9th September 1916. THE TRENCHES AT AGNY.
Very quiet. Our patrols active again last night. About 6 00 pm the Enemy shelled our front line with "Whizz Bangs" – no damage done.

10th September 1916. THE TRENCHES AT AGNY.
Very quiet day. Work in Support Line carried on with. Our Artillery did some wire cutting.

11th September 1916. THE TRENCHES AT AGNY.
Three German working parties were discovered about 1 00 am by a patrol. Our Lewis Guns dispersed them. The approximate positions were M 14.d.1.05, SUNKEN ROAD by Sap F & M14.c.15.1 (Map Sheet 51b S.W.)

12th September 1916. THE TRENCHES AT AGNY.
Had Orders that Bn. would be relieved by 11th Middx, tomorrow. Officers Valises brought up and stacked in AGNY. Very quiet day.

13th September 1916. THE TRENCHES AT AGNY – AGNY.
10 00 am.:- First platoons of Middx. arrive – relief complete at 12 30 pm. The Bn. then moved to AGNY. "B" & "C" Coys. in SUNKEN ROAD. "A" & "D" Coys. to AGNY DEFENCES. 6 30 pm:- Our Artillery shelled the Bosch Lines and Wire.

14th September 1916. AGNY.
Very quiet. Working Parties supplied to R.E.'s (300 Strong). 8 30 am: – Heavy M.G. fire heard, apparently a raid was taking place on our left. 12 30 am: – A few shells fell into AGNY causing no damage.

15th September 1916. AGNY.
Very quiet day. About 6 shells fell just outside AGNY at 12 45 am. Working parties supplied to R.E.'s (310 Strong).

16th September 1916. AGNY.
Very quiet day. All available men in the Battalion in working parties under the R.E.'s.

17th September 1916. AGNY.
Very quiet. A few shells fell into DAINVILLE about 11 00 am. A raid was carried out at 8 45 pm by the 37th Brigade. Military Medals awarded to Sgt. BARLOW W.M.; Sgt. COOPER C.M.; Lt.Cpl HEYDON F.L.; Lt.Cpl. TAYLOR G.F.; C.S.M. WALKER J.J.; Pte. PRESSINTON F. and Pte. W.H.WALKER. All available men in Battalion on working parties under R.E.'s.

18th September 1916. TRENCHES AT AGNY.
Very quiet until 9 00 pm when our Artillery was heard. Also bombing. A raid was carried out on a Bosch Sap by the Middx. At 8 45 pm. received orders that we would relieve the Middx. in the Line on the 19th. inst.

As Corporal Sadler is now to note, there was allowance made in this area, for men to spend time on leave a fair distance away from the Front lines and the bombing and hence they were able to relax.

He was to find that, following this, on his return to join up with his Battalion, there was a far less comfortable time waiting. It was to be back to the Somme Battlefields.

Sadler account:

159. TRENCHES AT AGNY A rest trip to Boulogne. Back to the Somme Battlefield. Tanks enter the War.

About the middle of September 1916, I was given the pleasure of going to Boulogne for six days "change and rest". This turned out to be a grand holiday as there were no restrictions whatsoever.

We were allowed to go into the city as we pleased by getting a pass.

However we found out it was best to take trips on our own, these without a pass, as no one seemed any the wiser what time we returned.

If we had a Pass written out, it had to be handed in at the Guardroom at the time stated and that didn't always suit our plans.

Over that time, we only had one parade. That was a rifle inspection, the morning before returning to the Front when our six days of enjoyment was coming to an end.

I arrived back to my Battalion to have some more "good" news. We were leaving for the Somme Battlefield once more.

Our general rest, and somewhat easier time in Agny, was also coming to an end.

In Corporal James Sadler's absence in Boulogne, the 9th Royal Fusiliers maintained their presence in the Trenches at Agny as the Battalion Diaries recall. It was quiet most of the time, but not always so.

By the 26th September, the Battalion and the 36th Division were to be preparing, not only to welcome Cpl. Sadler and his comrades back, but, as noted, to embark on another spell on the Somme Battlefield.

Battalion War Diary:

19th September 1916. TRENCHES AT AGNY.

1st Platoon moved off from SUNKEN ROAD into Trenches at 10 00 am. The relief was completed at 11 30 am. "B" Coy. on right; "C" Coy in centre; "A" Coy. on Left; "D" Coy. in reserve. Our Artillery put over a few shells on the Bosch Line, otherwise very quiet. All three Companies out on patrol at night to find starting point for raiding.

20th September 1916. TRENCHES AT AGNY.

Very quiet day. One of our medium TMB's put a shell onto G 6, badly damaging the fire-bay. A few fish tailed shells came over on or left Coy. front and some rifle grenades on the right Coy. front- no damaged caused. "C" Coy sent out a raiding party of 1 Officer and 10 men with a covering party of 1 Officer and 10 men to raid Enemy Sap X. They started at 9 30 pm and found the Bosch wire 45ft. deep with shell holes full of balls of barbed wire. After 4 hours steadily cutting through the wire they still had 15 ft. to get through and they returned to our trenches as it was becoming too light for further work. The night had been most favourable up until then- extremely dark with a light drizzle of rain. They discovered that the Sap was occupied- a horn being blown in the enemy trench and footsteps heard as soon as the wire cutting commenced at 10 00 pm. The 8th Battalion also attempted a raid with a negative result. The object of these raids was to take a prisoner or prisoners for identification purposes. Much Artillery preparation.

21st September 1916. TRENCHES AT AGNY
Very Quiet Day. All Companies hard at work on the improvement of trench drainage: resettment of C.T.'s, (Communication Trenches) and Fire Trenches occasioned by the wet weather. The improvement of the newly opened up sections in the front line also proceeded with. A Patrol went out at night; 1 Officer, 8 men and part of an R.E. detachment, with their guns, to a point where the raiding party on the night of 20th Sept. had cut the enemy wire. They found it untouched. Also saw no enemy working parties at all. They also found a place in the enemy wire on the south side of Sap Y at about Map 25.03 where wire appeared fairly weak and a good spot through which to raid the Sap.

The Colonel went on leave in the morning, Major Coxhead resuming command of the Battalion.

22nd September 1916. TRENCHES AT AGNY
Quite day. G.O.C. came round at 11 am. with news that Division could be relieved on the 26th inst. and the Battalion relieved in the trenches on the 30th inst. At 8 15 pm. a raiding party of 1 Officer, 1 Sgt, and 12 men with a covering party of 1 officer, 1 Lt.Gen. and 10 men left the 1st Bay E of the SUNKEN ROAD G.8, at 8 15pm and 8 20pm respectively, with enemy Sap X as their objective. The enemy line was reached at 10 00 pm. The point at which the Sap was to be entered, Map 20.04, was reached at 12 midnight. Whilst going across, the party was fired on several times by snipers from the right flank and by the M.G. from the base of the Sap which was being raided. A line was found through the wire and the Officer made his way along into the Sap which he found disused though it seemed to have recently been a good trench. The grass was growing over the sides and there was no resetting. It was 8 ft. deep and blocked every 2 yards by thick masses of concertina barbed wire. After being in the Sap 5 mins. a Trench Mortar opened up on the right and 6 rounds rapidly fell very near the Party. Verey lights were being sent up from the back of the Sap the whole time. Much talking was heard and the party returned at 1 30am. The covering Party was in attendance at Map Sect d 5.20. In their opinion the Trench Mortar was firing at Sap X from a position 50 yds. East of the base of the Sap in the front line. Heard that Division would be relieved on the night of 26/27th September.

23rd September 1916. TRENCHES AT AGNY
Very quiet day on the whole. Our medium T.M.'s fired on enemy front line during the afternoon-practically no retaliation from enemy. An artillery strafe took place on the left of the Battalion's front in the evening. New Saps on our front connected today- all

Companies working on them. All leave cancelled and this week's party recalled.

24th September 1916. TRENCHES AT AGNY to DAINVILLE.

Battalion relieved by the Middlesex- commencing at 9 00am. Relief completed 11 20 am. Battalion went back to DAINVILLE taking over there from the Sussex in Billets. Orders received re: Relief by the 42nd Infantry Bde, 14th Division, on the 26th inst.

25th September 1916. DAINVILLE

Day spent in cleaning up, inspections and resting- also bathing. Quartermaster & Hon. Lieutenant G.T.SHELLEY awarded the Military Cross.

26th September 1916. DAINVILLE to SIMONCOURT.

A Gas Alert on from 12 35 am (night) to 11 30 am. At 12 30 pm a very intense bombardment heard in the South which lasted until 2 00 pm. Battalion relieved by the 9th Rifle Brigade commencing 9 00 pm. Relief complete 9 55 pm. Battalion marched by WARLUS-BERNEVILLE to SIMONCOURT and went into billets there for the night. Transport etc. re-joined the Battalion from BERNEVILLE.

36th Brigade, including the 9th Royal Fusiliers and the recently re-joined Corporal James Sadler, prepared for a return to the front line; it was to be the Somme battlefield again.

14

The Somme Battlefield, September–October 1916: From Agny and back into Action at Transloy Ridges in October

Late September 1916, the 36th Brigade, including 9th Royal Fusiliers, returned to participate in the latter operations of the Somme offensive:

Battalion War Diary:

27th September 1916. SIMONCOURT to NEUVILLETTE.
Transport left SIMONCOURT at 6 00 am. and marched to NEUVILLETTE. Battalion left SIMONCOURT at 10 00am. marching to the Bde. Rendezvous at WANQUETIN where Lorries were boarded and moved off at 11 00am. BOUQUEMAISON reached at 1 45 pm. Battalion marched from there to billets at NEUVILLETTE.

28th September 1916. NEUVILLETTE.
Routine. Clearing Up. Inspections etc. at NEUVILLETTE. Transport left there at 7 50 am. and proceeded with Brigade transport to TALMAS.

29th September 1916. NEUVILLETTE.
Battalion paraded at 8 00 am. Marching to BOUQUEMAISON where French motor buses were boarded under French Military Control and the Brigade was conveyed to a point about 2 miles SW of ALBERT on the ALBERT-AMIENS road. The route was DOULLENZ-BEAUVAL-TALMAS-VILLIERSBOURGE-RAINEVILLE-QUERRIEU. From the point of disembarkation from the Busses the Batn. marched to Bivouacs at POMMIER REDOUBT. Route BERNAUCOURT-MEAULTE-FRICOURT-MAMETZ. Bivouacs reached at 12 midnight.

30th September 1916. NEUVILLETTE to POMMIER REDOUBT.
Routine. Cleaning Up. Inspections and cleaning up of Camp. The C.O.,(Commanding Officer), reconnoitred line to be taken over.

Sadler account:

159. TRENCHES AT AGNY (Continued). Back to the Somme Battlefield. Tanks on the Battlefield.
The next morning I received the Order to go billeting for the Company, finding places for the men to rest after their long day's drag back to the Somme.

After three or four days marching we had succeeded in reaching a Support Line,(Pommier Redoubt), not a great distance from Flers where we soon found out there had been some dirty work taking place around the village, or what was left of it.

We saw the first tanks which had been used in the War and several lay there, "out of action", having had direct hits from German shells.

We were soon to find out that this part was far different from the "rest camp" area around Agny which we had just left and we could not get this out of our minds.

Our "Trenches" here were just a hole here and there; the remainder had been levelled by German shellfire.

Battalion War Diary:

1st October 1916. POMMIER REDOUBT.
Routine and cleaning up of Camp. Orders received for the Relief of 21st. Division in the front line by the 12th. Division. The 123rd. Brigade relieved by the 36th. Brigade. The Battalion moved off from Camp at 4 30 pm and marched to the Trenches West of GUEUDECOURT by MONTABAUN-LONGUEVAL-DELVILLE WOOD-FLERS. Battalion relieved the 23rd. Middx. in the line, the relief being completed at 11 15 pm.

"C" and "B" Coys.:- FRONT LINE in GIRO SUPPORT Trench and advanced Strong Points.

"A" and "D" Coys.:- SUPPORT LINE in GIRO TRENCH.

One German prisoner brought in by "C" Coy. at 3 00 am. Heavy shelling during night on our Front Support Trenches causing a few casualties.

2nd October 1916. POMMIER REDOUBT to TRENCHES WEST of GUEUDECOURT.
Heavy shelling by the Enemy all day long, particularly from 2 00pm – 4 00pm when a heavy barrage was put up on the whole of our Front Line causing much damage to our Trenches and a number of casualties were sustained. A large number of "Blind" shells fell into GIRO TRENCH. "C"Coy. sent out a patrol in front who found nothing of any importance to report. Much work was done in linking up the strong points in front and also linking up the Right & Left Coys. Also work was done on a new Communication Trench to the Front Line and the fire trenches were deepened all being shallow and in a shocking condition from the bad weather and heavy shelling. 2nd Lt.'s CLARK and BACKLEY wounded.

3rd October 1916. TRENCHES WEST of GUEUDECOURT.
Heavy hostile shelling of our Trenches. More or less continuous throughout the day. Work on the damaged trenches rendered extremely difficult by the very bad weather and shelling. 2nd Lt. BARBER killed and 2nd Lt. COPP wounded. A fair number of casualties among O.R., (Other Ranks), being sustained.

Batt. relieved by 11th Battn Middx. At 11 00pm. Went back to Reserve Trenches S.E. of FLERS. These were in a very bad condition, the men mostly sleeping and resting in Shell Holes on top. 7th. Sussex and 11th. Middx. in Front Line and 8th.

R.F. in Support.

4th October 1916. TRENCHES WEST of GUEUDECOURT.
Day spent by men making shelters for themselves from the weather in the trenches. Carrying Parties supplied to carry up water, stores and bombs to the Middx. Bn. from the Bde. Dump. Enemy shelled FLERS a good deal, also the LONGUEVAL-FLERS RD. behind the Reserve Trenches. No casualties caused.

Sadler Account:

160. THE SOMME BATTLEFIELD. Digging Trenches. Shelled by the Germans.
As soon as we arrived we were, of course, set to work digging out the Trench. The Germans had a grand way of making this Trench digging very uncomfortable; this by sending over his shells in a triangle fashion all the way along the Trench. By doing this they were bound to get a direct hit in the bottom of the Trench at different times. When they packed this little game up, they started shelling in the rear of our Trench. One of my comrades passed a remark to me about the shelling. I said it was all right as the shelling was well in the rear. Immediately, on my saying this, the next one nearly burst in our Trench leading my comrade to say, "You'll do better to shut up". Again, just after this the shelling had seemed to have died away for a short while; I commented, "How quiet it had become". No sooner had I said this when, all of a sudden, once again, the German's shells started coming over; this time in large numbers. Following this, I began to think it would pay me just to keep my mouth shut, keep still and keep smiling. That night I passed a few hours under a sheet of tin which had been put across the Trench by the Germans when off duty. Things went well this night although there were shells bursting all around.

161. THE SOMME BATTLEFIELD. Sentry Posts, a narrow escape and a life lost.
The following night, just as it was getting dark, a chum said to me, "We will move our quarters tonight".

I said, "I don't see what we have to move for" but, after a lot of persuading, I finally decided to change position to few yards away. I suppose that it was destined for my chum to have known what danger lay in that spot on that very night. We had only two Sentry Posts in support. This being as the Front Line was only about 50 yards or so in front of us and that night these Trenches were nearly blown flat.

The Sergeant of the Platoon stayed at the other end of the Trench and had a Sentry Post near him. We had another Post near us so there was no need to walk up and down the Trench. We always tried to stay near our Sentry Post and looked to cheer up the man who was on Duty. When it came to my hour to do my turn at Trench Duty, I always planned to spend a short time with each Sentry by getting up on the Fire Step and looking over the top whilst having a chat with him in order to cheer ourselves up. As we only had one Sentry Post here, that meant me spending my hour with him. On this particular night I was talking to the Sentry who was just a few yards away from our old Shelter Post. A large Party, who had been to collect water, had just passed by when; overcame a large Shell which burst right on our old shelter sending the sheet of tin and all that was close by, high into the air. When this, my shelter from the previous night, arrived back down on the ground, it pinned me down at the bottom of the Trench. After a struggle, I managed to free myself and then heard a voice saying, "No! No!" I shouted to the Sentry, "Are you alright?" as it was impossible for me to see him for the smoke from the Shell. When he said, "Yes, I think I am", I found that, like myself, he was only a little shaken up. Seeing he was alright, I made for the Shelter to see if the Water Party had passed it safely. When I got there it was far too dark to see anything so I felt around with my hand to see what I could find. At last I came across a steel helmet, with that, I knew something must have happened nearby.

I struck a match to try and make it easier to see and also to see what I could find. This resulted in me receiving a very "warm" time from the enemy's "Whizz Bangs". In spite of this and despite all the shells flying around, I made up my mind to find the owner of the steel helmet. After a short and terrible time I found what were the remains of the owner. He had stayed a minute or so longer, under the Shelter to have a rest and this particular shell had burst by his side.

161. THE SOMME BATTLEFIELD. Reflections on the loss of life.

I have often thought on about one or two things that I have seen and which have happened whilst this War has been on. Unless a man's time has come, he will get over anything and that was the case with myself.

Men have said to me, "You don't seem to worry about anything" and I have replied "Not really. If I am to catch it, I will catch it alright, without worrying about it". I once attended a Church Parade just before the starting of the Somme Battle with the text for the Service being taken from the Officer who sacrificed his life by laying on a bomb and who, by doing so, had saved the lives of many of his Comrades. This Officer was awarded the Victoria Cross which I expect many can remember. I have often thought to myself, on hearing so much about "self-sacrifice" at different times, that the best type of situations when many may be called upon to make their personal sacrifice, happen as a result of events which are short and sweet. This was not, however, to be the case in the class of War which this one had turned out to be. I have seen many brave men face nearly three years of this War; then have been called to give their lives up. I have also discovered, by playing a part in this terrible War, that life is very sweet whilst it lasts, no matter what terrible conditions one may be called upon to put up with.

162. THE SOMME BATTLEFIELD. Making Tea in the Trenches.

Whilst doing this turn in these so-called Trenches, I had another great surprise in the discovery of a new way in which one could make tea. One night when it was pitch black, a Lance Corporal said to me "What about making a cup of tea?" to which I replied "What's the good of talking of making tea?" At that particular time I was thinking about the matches which I had lit, not that long before, and which nearly cost me my life. Nevertheless, he said "I'll go and make some". I wanted to know how it was going to be made. He said that he had got some small pieces of candles and that he would soon be able to find and tear off a few rags to go round the candles. I began to think that it would probably take a week for the tea to be served; but I was altogether wrong. It wasn't long though before he came back and handed me a canteen containing hot tea which, I must say, was a really fine little drop of tea and went down really well. It is one which I will long remember, especially being served in such an unearthly place and the fact that we hadn't had the pleasure of something warm to drink for some time. After it was found this "trick" or method worked the once, it was a case of getting a supply of candles before going into the Trenches and, by this means, it was possible to get ourselves a nice drink of tea; even though we were almost close enough to shake hands with Old Fritz. We could manage this without him having the slightest idea as to what was taking place as tea, made in this way, resulted in not even the slightest amount of smoke.

This was a little different from the method which we had of making tea during our previous Battle action. There, we stood two tins of Bully Beef up on end and rested the Canteen on these. Then small pieces of wood were placed between the tins and the fire started. The fire was then kept going by a supply of small pieces of wood whilst we sat close by and anxiously waited for the tea. After waiting some time, all we generally got in the end was a thin coating of shreds of Bully Beef which happened when those making the tea had forgotten to knock a hole in the tins before starting the fire! With the heat of the fire, the tins burst, upset what little water we had and put a very sudden end to our "perfect" cup of tea.

163. THE SOMME BATTLEFIELD. " On Reserve" and Changing Trenches.

After we finished our forty-eight hours, between 1st and 3rd October, in these Trenches, we left for some Reserve Trenches to start another 48 hours in reserve. It was terrible journey before these Trenches were reached; this owing to the German shelling of the Sunken Roads which we had to travel along.

We had to put up with heavy storms every now and then. There were also many very deep shell holes.

Some of the shell holes which I noticed on the Somme Battlefield were very often only a yard or so across at the top but many feet deep. It was quite possible for anyone to fall down one of these shell holes and to not be missed for some time. Changing Trenches on the Somme Battlefields was enough to make a man cry as, at times, it was impossible to stay on ones feet. After a terrible drag we finished up in some more Trenches near Flers or, near the heap of stones which were once part of Flers.

164. THE SOMME BATTLEFIELD. German Shelling. Injured by a piece of shell.

On getting shown into the Trenches we soon made a point of getting very close together in order to keep warm and we managed to get ourselves some sleep. We slept like logs after several sleepless nights.

The next day we spent in carrying bombs to the Front between the "Whiz Bangs" and flying pieces of shell.

We were now in Trenches between several batteries of Field Guns and our 60 pounders. The large flying pieces of shells were from the shells which the Germans were sending over to find our Batteries. From what I could see of things, the Germans were making it very uncomfortable for our Gunners who were giving "Old Fritz" a very large supply of "Iron Rations" despite all the shells which were

The Transloy Ridges today.

bursting around them.

The German Shells were also making it extremely uncomfortable for the poor old Mules who were very busy employed in supplying the Guns with shells, carrying six 18 pounder shells in belts strapped around their bodies. As for the German's "Whizz Bangs", they would strike the ground only a yard or so from the Mules but did not get to do much damage as these shells were going so deep into the mud that it was virtually impossible for the pieces of shell, on exploding, to find their way out through the mud. One of the German shells struck one of our G.S. Wagons filled with shells and this caused a terrible explosion sending black smoke skywards. As the wind was blowing towards the German Line this resulted in the large black cloud of smoke moving over towards "Old Fritz" like a cloud of gas. Because of this, the Germans could see that they had saved themselves from receiving a few of our shells, as our Gunners were unable to see sufficiently well enough to send any of them over in their direction. At this point, whilst I was standing talking to my Platoon Officer, I had a very narrow escape from having my head cut off by a large piece of flying shell. The very large piece of shell passed by my shoulder and neck and finished up sticking in the side of the Trench.

The Officer said that it was a very close shave and would have been more than a "Blighty" if it had caught me. Yes, I began to think to myself. It would have been a "dead homer".

164. THE SOMME BATTLEFIELD. Rainwater. Losing three comrades. Road Conditions.

There was no need to run short of water whilst we were doing our turn here as we only had to slip over the top and dip our canteens into the water lying in the Shell Holes.

By doing this we were able to get a very large supply but later this activity was stopped as some of the Shell Holes were those being created by Gas Shells and the water was, in no way, fit to drink.

Gas shells were used on us, as a unit, for the first time at the Somme Battle and, up to this time, we didn't know whether it was a shell hole which had been created by a Gas Shell or a High explosive shell.

I don't think many of us really cared as long as we were able to get water to make a drink of tea with. It was impossible to think of having any of our Cooks up in The Line with us at this part. Our own rations were brought to us strapped to the mule's backs and then we had a party of men, going to and fro, bringing the rations from the mules to us. At times this had to be carried out under terrible shellfire. The same day which I am writing about, I witnessed a terrible sight. One of the Germans shells pitched right under a stretcher being carried by two R.A.S.M.C. stretcher-bearers who were carrying a badly wounded man. All three got blown to pieces. The worst thing about it was these two stretcher bearers had carried the man about two miles over the most terrible roads and, after having made it all that distance with the poor wounded fellow, all three were killed. Some of the sights which lay on the road between Longville and Flers were a disgrace to the passing Troops. To think that after being willing to give their lives for King and Country they would be left to lie about in such a manner. If it had been dead horses or mules, the Infantry would have been called upon to go and bury them. The less I say about this, the better I shall be pleased.

Moving from the reserve trenches on 5 October, 9th Royal Fusiliers marched forward to play its part in the Battle of the Transloy Ridges.

15

The Somme Battlefield, October 1916: The Battle of the Transloy Ridges

F rom the 5th October, the battalion diarist noted the attack build-up for what would be a disastrous day for 9th Royal Fusiliers.

Battalion War Diary:

5th October 1916. TRENCHES WEST of GUEUDECOURT
News that continuation of the Offensive was postponed for 48 hrs. received. Was originally to have taken place today. The C.O. returned from leave. Occasional shelling of FLERS and the main Rd. behind during the day. 2nd Lt. COULSON in charge of Bde. Dump detachment was wounded (shell shock)-buried in dug out. Battn. relieved 11th Mdx. in front line commencing at 6 00pm – relief being complete at midnight, Heavy shelling by both Hostile and our own Artillery. 2nd. Lt. CARMICHAEL wounded on the way up to take over his platoon trench.
"A" & "D" in FRONT LINE – GIRO SUPPORT & ADVANCED TRENCH.
"C" & "B" in SUPPORT- GIRO TRENCH.
A fair number of casualties sustained during the night. 8th R.F. Battn. on our left. 37th Bde. on our Right. 7th Sussex Regt, in Support. 11th Middx. went back to Brigade Reserve.

6th October 1916. TRENCHES WEST OF GUEUDECOURT
Hostile Shelling very heavy all day on Front and Support Trenches and our Sunken Road also FLERS. Casualties sustained not quite so heavy as usual. 2nd.Lt. BIRD – Wounded. At 11 30am and 12 45 pm two hostile aeroplanes came over our lines, flying very low about 200 ft. up. M.G.'s opened fire and sent them back. Orders received for tomorrows resumed offensive. 2nd. Lt EDWARDS went down with shell shock. Systematic bombardment of enemy line by our artillery began at 7 15pm and continued up to ZERO.

7th October 1916. TRENCHES WEST OF GUEUDECOURT
ZERO at 1 45 pm. 8th R.F. and 9th R.F.'s attacking. 7th Sussex in Support. 11th Middx. in Reserve. 37th Bgde. attacking on our right. 35th Bgde. in Bde. Reserve.
"A", "B" & "D" Companies took up their position in the Advanced Trench in front of GIRO SUPPORT overnight with "C" Coy. in the GIRO SUPPORT TRENCH as the supporting Company. "D"-Right Coy, "B"-Centre Coy, "A"- Left Coy. Coy's went over in two lines and also the supporting Coy. which rushed over from GIRO SUPPORT to the Advanced Trench immediately the attacking Coy. went forward.
Contrary to expectations, very heavy M.Gun fire was encountered immediately

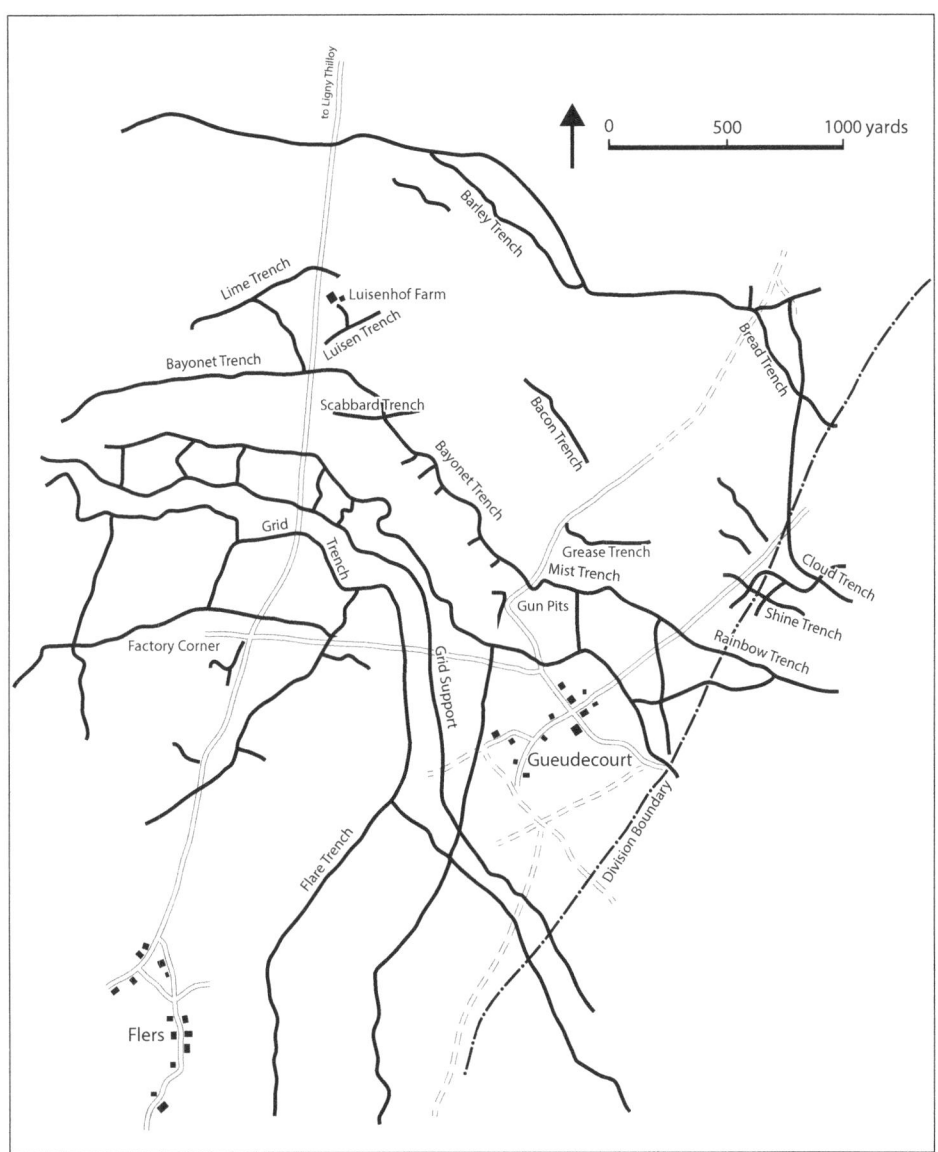

Geudecourt Trenches on the Transloy Ridges. (George Anderson)

the first line reached the top of the ridge; also very heavy shelling. The three front Coy's. and 2 platoons of the supporting Company were practically decimated by the fire. "B" Coy. apparently swung out to the right to get into touch with "A" Coy. and were enfiladed by 2 M.G.'s The first objective was not reached by any Company. Enemy were observed to take in some of our wounded of "B" & "D" Coys.

A body of Germans also commenced to advance on our left but were driven back by our M.G. fire which was immediately opened up on them. Some stragglers crawled back at dusk and we continued to hold our original front line with these men and the remaining platoons of "C" Company. The artillery barrage had been a creeping one and apparently had missed the first German Trench which was nearer than it had appeared. Our barrage remained for some time behind our second objective until it was known that the attack had failed. A similar result accrued from the attack on the left and right.

Up to the time of going over the top our casualties had been Officers -8; Other Ranks- 109 and 20 sick so the Battn. was rather weak. On going-over in the Attack the losses were:-

	Officers	O.Ranks
Killed	4	21
Wounded	1	131
Missing	4	161
Total	9	313

In a personal note to the Commanding Officer the G. in C. of 36th Inf. Bde. was to say, "Will you please thank all ranks of our Battn. for the magnificent Gallantry they displayed yesterday. They advanced very steadily under a very heavy fire which only the best troops would have faced. Although unfortunately unsuccessful, your gallant conduct has added to the fine reputation which you have already won for yourselves".

The Battn. was relieved by the 11th Middx. (2 Companies), the other 2 Coys. of the 11th Middx. relieving the 8th R.F. on the Left. The 7th Sussex moved up in Support.

Sadler Account:

165. THE SOMME BATTLEFIELD. Preparing for October 7th 1916.

The next day, we received Orders for our coming battle which was to take place on the 7th October 1916, this being an attack taking place all along the Front. The first attack we had to do was with a creeping barrage. The Barrage was to start by shelling the German Front Lines for four minutes before we started into "Action". After we had taken the German Front Line we were to wait for four minutes whilst the barrage crept ahead and, by that time, the Company in support of us would come over to that Line whilst we followed up the Barrage for about 2000 yards. We were then to dig ourselves in 250 yards this side of a German Trench and that was to be done in daylight. This attack did not take my fancy. One young and plucky Officer of my Company, the one who had earlier succeeded in getting the news off of the German prisoner, passed the remark to me that this was going to be quite a simple task and a "walk-over".

I confess that I didn't think this so as, up to this time, I had had plenty of free fights with "Old Fritz" and I had begun to learn that, whatever bombardment took place, he always seemed ready to greet us on our crossing "No Man's Land". I had discovered that "Fritz" didn't allow anyone to walk about between the Trenches, in daylight, without giving them a very warm reception.

166. THE SOMME BATTLEFIELD. Bayonet Trench. A wounded colleague. Oct 5th. to 7th. Journey to the Front Line.

The answer which I was to give to this Officer was that we should soon find out whether it will be a simple task or not was when we started crossing "No Man's Land". This plucky Officer was wounded, this day, by a flying piece of shell striking his arm. He went to our Dressing Station, got it dressed and returned. It wasn't his wish to leave. All he wanted to do was to go after the Germans but that was not to be. Two days later he was wounded again in the same arm and on this occasion, fairly badly. Against his wish, this time, he had to leave the Line. On the day when he was wounded for the first time, he did me a very great favour by giving me a pair of his boots; my own being no good because one of the soles had fallen off of mine. Using his boots I found it became much more comfortable, again, getting about in the mud. At dusk, 5th October, we started for the Trenches, having in the meantime, been supplied with our usual two Bombs and rations for two days. This was to be the start of our "Walk to Berlin" which we were to find all about on 7th October. At dark, this night, we started our journey once more to the Front Line Trenches but we didn't reach them without falling down a few dozen times in the mud. We also had the pleasure, on our travels, of being greeted with a fair supply of German Shells as well as our own.

167. THE SOMME BATTLEFIELD. Bayonet Trench. German Shelling. Positioning in the Trench.

There have been times when a few German Shells, bursting in the rear of a working Party, have resulted in some of the very "tired" men, who were causing a lot of waiting around, to soon catch up with those who were not so tired. Sometimes a shell bursting in the rear would make a man forget they were tired. Soon they would move to the head of the Party instead of hanging around in the rear. One can see that shells, at times, might put new life into a soldier. Mostly though, from what I have seen in the past, shells were really designed to take anyone's life away and I have a good idea that this really was what they were made for!

Anyhow we managed to get to the so called Trenches which were similar to our last, a little bit of Trench here and there and a grand supply of German "Whizz Bangs" coming from certain parts. These "Whizz Bangs" were able to make the dust fly from the bottom of the Trench. It was a case of not standing about too long at these Trenches unless you could find a turn in the Trench where you knew Old Fritz had not yet infiltrated.

There were several German deep dugouts that had been started but never finished and, as I was put in charge of my Platoon, owing to three N.C.O.'s going away, slightly shell shocked, I was told that I was able to take one of these "started" dugouts if I wished. Such a position was far from my wishes because, I knew, for anyone coming out of the doorway of the dugout, they were likely to catch a "Whizz Bang" all to himself.

I preferred to get to where a bend had been made in the Trench and then dig a hole in the side of the Trench, similar to what the Germans called a "Funk Hole". It was this which a comrade and myself started to make by using our Trenching Tools. After working very hard, one of us would say to the other "Let's chuck it in". But, No, the job had been started and it had to be finished. After working like rabbits it was finished, by daybreak the following morning.

168. THE SOMME BATTLEFIELD. Bayonet Trench. Tea making and sleeping.

From our "Funk Hole, it was possible , by walking a few yards to the right and left, to watch all my men up to about a 100 yards away and this was without walking out from one of these dugouts and running the risk of catching all the shells which were being sent over. When our work came to an end, the next thing was a drink of tea, if possible; so we both sent off along the Trench to find a piece of dry wood as, unfortunately, we hadn't had the recent pleasure of going into town to buy candles. At last my chum found a large piece of timber which had been used by the Germans for timbering up their deep dugouts and which we were to use for the making our cup of tea, or "char", as it was known in the Army. We soon got to work with the small chain saw as supplied to a Platoon and we got this piece of wood cut into pieces like match stems, then our fire was started and our tea was soon made.

We were able to have our "light refreshments" in comfort even with "Whizz Bangs", like fast Express Trains, passing outside our "Worm Hole". When we had finished our much needed "feast"; next came a sleep.

After a look around we returned to our "home", the "Funk Hole", and nestled close together and were very soon in Dreamland, little thinking, whilst asleep, that there was a war on. A German shell would have had to burst very close by or even on top of me to have woken me up. When I awoke I was told that the Officer who was in charge of my Company had called to see me and that, as I was fast asleep, he decided that he would not have me woken up.

169. THE SOMME BATTLEFIELD. Bayonet Trench. Shell Shocked. Digging in No Man's Land.

What the Officer had come to see me about was if I felt like sticking with it and going in to battle because nearly all the N.C.O.'s were going away shell-shocked. He wondered if I was catching the "complaint".

I will confess that I was beginning to feel a little shocked, taking my experience of the War on the whole, but I made up my mind, not to give way. With this brave Officer, who was in charge of the Company at this time, I felt that I would have been prepared to follow him until death. It was this Officer who, as I recalled earlier, gave the Command that he would shoot any man that went back without his Orders and he was a man quite willing to give his life for his men; something which, sadly he was to do when the Battle commenced. But we had much to do before the Battle started. At dark that night, I was ordered to take my men out into "No Man's

Land" to dig a Trench between the Shell holes and also a Trench to act as the starting point for the coming Battle. This was so as to bluff the Germans when they opened out their barrage on the starting of our bombardment. The undertaking of digging this Trench was well fixed in my head and that was all that we did this night. The Trench was really only for our own benefit and I considered it was a good plan; knowing how well taped the German Artillery always was on our Front Line. The men and myself were always quite willing to have the pleasure of missing the German Shells. We all left the Trench with a good heart to start a good night's work especially as it was for our benefit.

170. THE SOMME BATTLEFIELD. Bayonet Trench. Trench Digging in No Man's Land. A disagreement.

On getting out into what must be, as I have already said, the dreariest place on earth that is in "No Man's Land"; the ground was something like a very rough sea. Not moving but rough and lying still. So much shellfire had taken place on this piece of ground that the shell holes met each other. Anyway, we were soon shown where to commence our work and the work was started in great haste; the reason for this being in order to get cover from flying pieces of shells and the shells which were bursting nearby. These shells were being sent over by the Germans in an attempt to hit our "Old" Front Line but they were dropping short. After we had worked like niggers for an hour we were told we had started in the wrong place and that we were to leave the work which we had already done and move along to the left. So we were then to move on from the position of our first start at the "good work" which, supposedly, we were doing for our own benefit.

At last, though, we got stuck into the work in the right position and, after a few hours hard work we got down several feet deep and began to feel fairly comfortable despite a shower of "Whiz Bangs" being sent over.

Then, if I'm hanged or not, if an Officer from another Company, and whose men should also have been out there doing their own Trench, didn't come and tell me to collect my men together as he was going to show me where we were to commence work on another Trench; this I felt being for his own men's benefit.

With this I began to get – – – – – wild and said to him that, Officer or not, "I had been told by my Company Officer, that what work we were to be doing that night was only for our own Company's benefit ,not necessarily for others".

171. THE SOMME BATTLEFIELD. Bayonet Trench. Trench Digging in No Man's Land. Advantages gained.

The reply which I received back from this Officer was, "Do you want me to put you on Orders?", a very nice thing to be said to a soldier out in "No Man's Land"! Well, such were my feelings, at hearing this that I began to think I would chance my luck. This Officer and myself were going into Action later that day and I knew it was most probably to be a case of life or death for both of us. With this I decided to stick out, hard and fast, for my tired men. So I answered this Officer by saying, "I don't care a damn what you do".

Anyway, after a while, we decided that we would go and give them an hours help. We started but the men were so tired that they were falling down and going fast asleep. It was a shame to expect these men, in wartime or not, to do their own share of work and then be expected to do other peoples as well. It was only by bad management that this other Company were not out there, doing their task, at the same time as us. We were holding the Front Line but, instead of holding that Line we had found ourselves out in "No Man's Land" where we were quite prepared, at any moment, to meet "Old Fritz". We would have been saving him a long journey by meeting him in here in No Man's land instead of our old Front Line. I must say that this newly dug Trench was to be the saving of many lives. It was impossible for us to be noticed by the Germans because of the ground being blown about so much. We had the pleasure of hearing "Old Fritz's" Shells passing over our head and bursting near the empty Trench which we had left in the rear.

172. THE SOMME BATTLEFIELD. Bayonet Trench. Rations. Drinking "Petrol".

The next thing that needed to be done was to serve out some rations that had arrived and this was quite a job owing to the newly dug Trench being so narrow. It was impossible to pass each other so these rations had to be cut up and passed from man to man until they reached the man they were intended for. When waiting to go into battle it is good enough to approach the Action without too much to eat. As long as one can get a drink of water, when needed, then you usually felt quite content. However, water was one thing which we could not get at this Trench. All that we managed to get was one Petrol Tin full of water and that was like drinking petrol itself. Mind you, at this stage, that made no difference to us as anything was good enough to refresh us. We had no water in our Water Bottles because we were depending on a Water Carrying Party to arrive but, that was not to be our luck as they failed to do so. We finished up by drinking two or three tins of Ideal Milk which was sent up with the rations to go with the tea, if and when tea could be made.

173. THE SOMME BATTLEFIELD. Bayonet Trench. Getting ready for Battle.
The Artillery's Range

Breakfast time arrived and no Orders had been received about what time the battle was going to start ;so we had nothing to do but to sit and think of the coming battle and that is quite as bad, if not worse, than actually going into battle. This was felt more by a few of us old "hands" who were getting proper battle worn by this stage. For all that, though, it was a case of trying to keep cheerful whilst awaiting one's luck. While we were waiting for Orders, my mind was kept busy by thinking about the Trench that had to be dug 250yards this side of the 2nd German Line, and this, if the Battle Plan was to be followed , was to be done in broad daylight. I tried hard to knock it into my men to take cover in shell holes and then dig towards each other. By doing this they would make some sort of trench. Then when darkness fell it would be possible to get on top and do the finishing off touch. However, for all my talking, that was not to be needed for reasons which one will see later. At 2 o'clock am. this day, 7th October, we received Orders that the battle was starting at 2-30 am. In between these two times, one could scarcely believe that so many guns were going to be spitting forth so much fire all at once. In this half-hour, though, hardly a shell was fired by us or the Germans. There is an old saying of ours that there was always "Quietness before Mischief". Anyone, from the sound that was to come from our Artillery fire, would have thought that an easy task lay ahead of us. We could see the 1st German Line not a great distance in front of us but, between us and their first line was not only a wilderness but also a very steep bank on which there was some new barbed wire which looked as if it had been put out that night. Our Artillery did not seem half as good as I had noticed in the earlier Actions of the Somme Battle. They certainly sent over some very heavy shells which, at times, frightened us more than the Germans. One of our Officers had taken on the duties of Observation Officer for the battle and I passed the remark to him that I didn't care much for the range of our Artillery on the German Front Line. Our shells were falling very short and in doing so were not worrying the Germans so much as it was my comrades and myself.

174. THE SOMME BATTLEFIELD. Bayonet Trench. The Artillery's Role.

What was really wanted, and what there should have been, was one of the Artillery's Observations Officers up and along with us in the Front Line instead of being perched up in a position, towards the rear, on a high ridge. One did have to ask, what good was giving the job to one of our Infantry Officers? I can only suppose that, if one of our Officers complained about the shells falling short that very little notice would have been taken of him. I thought it a great pity that some of these people with, what we considered such good jobs in the Artillery ranks, didn't attempt to carry out their duties out in, what we considered, the most efficient and proper manner. Why, we started to think, should the Infantry be pushed to the Front in such an unearthly wilderness; expected to do their best and perhaps die without a murmur? However, this was something which we were often "pleased" to do but on the condition that all operations were carried out in the right manner and as long as things were made as easy as they possibly could be for us.

175. THE SOMME BATTLEFIELD. Bayonet Trench. October 7th. 1916. Battle Commences. "Over the Top" and Advancing at great loss of life.

When the time reached twenty five minutes past two, the Order was passed along the Line "5 minutes to go".

A minute or so after this, our Artillery broke the quietness of the past half-hour; opening up a terrible bombardment on the German Front Line. They kept this up for four minutes, before the time came for us to face life or death carrying out our duty which we believed was for our loved ones at Home. The Germans were by now shelling our Old Front Line for all they were worth but, up to that point, we were in a position of safety. The next Order was "Over the Top" and I shall never forget what this Order was to cost us by way of loss of life. As soon as we mounted the front, one of the most terrible Machine Gun Barrages I have ever heard, or witnessed, started. It appeared that every German, in their Front Line, was in possession of a machine gun with which they were able to cut human life down, just like they were cutting grass. The rattle from the guns was terrible and how it was that some of us were lucky enough to pass through it all, goodness only knows. If ever faith was to be believed in, it was shown in this battle. With bullets flying past each one of us by the hundreds; we were still able to go on until the high bank, which I had mentioned earlier, was reached. Here, I was to see the worst cutting up of men I had ever seen or will ever be liable to see. Every German machine gun was set on this ridge and, at this fatal moment, men were to die like flies being caught by the cold. Nevertheless, a very few of us were able to go ahead until we reached a point just a yard or so from the German barbed wire. At this stage, we could go no further until reinforcements could be supplied. We made as much use of what little cover we could find and were to endure a most terrible and anxious time. The slightest move was to mean a bullet through the head. Even the gallant lads who had fallen so far during the Attack, and who had given their lives, were "tested" by bullets from the Germans as they sought to ensure that no life remained. Yet, even with all the loss of life that there had been so far, more men were going to have to try their luck and face death as they came over to support us. I watched a Platoon from the Support Company try to reach us in order to lend a helping hand. Here, again, I watched one of the most terrible sights ever that one could ever be called upon to witness. So many bullets were hitting the men and one could also watch the little pieces of turf flying into the air as the Germans bullets struck the ground.

176. THE SOMME BATTLEFIELD. Bayonet Trench. October 7th 1916. The loss of life. Trying to kill Germans.

Within twenty yards from the starting point of this Platoon, not a man was standing. Every one of them had paid the price in blood. With this Platoon now being unable to get to us, it was impossible for us to get help so all that it remained for us to do, was to lie perfectly still until dark when, if not sniped by the Germans, we should hopefully be lucky enough to return to our starting place and get cover once more. It wasn't only, though, the snipers that made it such a terrible time for us, there were also the large shells which were bursting a few yards from us and which, at times, were to nearly send us way up into the air from behind our cover. I shall never forget just how hard I tried to kill two Germans who were running about in No Man's Land not far to my left. They were running between my dead comrades, no doubt to see what they might find for keepsakes.

In the end though, it was to cost both of them their lives. Unfortunately, not by my doing as I should have felt greatly honoured to have killed them. I tried my very hardest. I tried, with my bayonet fixed to my rifle, to get a shot at them but as soon as a likely moment arrived, a bullet was to just miss my head. Not satisfied with this, it then came into my head to try and fire at them with the bayonet off of my rifle just to see if I could manage to get a shot in without making any show. I struggled for some considerable time but I could not "unfix" my bayonet because it had nearly rusted on to the rifle as it had been on there for such a time. I experienced some very anxious moments until I eventually succeeded and was, at last, able to try a shot but without success. After this I called across to one of my men who was not too far from me, asking him to try his luck. After a very short time he succeeded in, as one might say, putting both of the Germans, "to sleep".

177. THE SOMME BATTLEFIELD. Bayonet Trench. October 7th 1916. Surrender? Noting Directions and getting back to our Starting Trenches.

Not long after this we had an "offer" from a German Officer who, by waving his hand, was warning us and inviting us to give ourselves up if we so wished. I don't think he succeeded in getting a large amount of prisoners. He may, perhaps, have got one or two after dark due to finding some of our men who forgot to take their bearings or direction when it was daylight. The main thing which passed through my mind whilst it was still daylight was to make sure that I took notice of the right direction to take when dusk arrived. By doing this I was also able to show men, who were wandering around, lost, in No Man's Land, the correct way and who, otherwise, might well have finished up by walking into the German Line. The few hours spent in this dreary place were beginning to seem like many months and I was longing for darkness to set in.

When it did arrive, I managed to have a good look round and found a few of my comrades. One or two of them were slightly wounded and there were another three who were untouched. The remainder appeared seemed to be lying at "eternal rest". At last, together, we were able to reach the Trench which we had started the Battle from in the early afternoon. Out of three Companies of men, only a dozen or so had succeeded in getting back. The strength of the Support Company, which had only managed to send the one Platoon to our aid, was only 30 or 40 men strong. Owing to the shell fire which they had got caught up whilst getting to, and holding, this Advanced Line, they had found it impossible to get further. I returned, being only one of two full rank N.C.O.'s left in all of our four Companies. Myself, I was the only N.C.O. remaining of the three Companies who had actually gone "Over the Top" into action. Only one Sergeant could be found and he belonged to the Support Company. With regards to men out of my own Company, I could only find two who had started into Action and two stretcher-bearers. That, then, left just five of us. The two men and myself, lent the stretcher-bearers a hand to get away any of the wounded that we could find and I think we succeeded in getting every man away.

178. THE SOMME BATTLEFIELD. October 7th 1916. Bayonet Trench. Counting the Cost. The number of survivors. Being relieved.

The Germans gave us a very quiet time which we took advantage of and spent the time in searching No Man's Land. After this was finished we spent what a very dreary time improving our Trench in order to make ourselves safe and comfortable just in case it fell to us to hold the position for any length of time. Most of us felt far from like working. I felt nearly dead due to the smoke and various different substances which had been created by bursting shells and which had got inside me. It was a case of working for a short time then lying down, being sick, getting up again and carrying on in that way until midnight; just occasionally having the pleasure of seeing another living soul.

Just after midnight we had a very great and most welcome surprise. Another Battalion came to relieve us and what a pleasure that was for the few who were left, as we were then able to think of going back to the rear. I think that there were about 30 of us from my Battalion who had gone out from the Trench altogether.

I started to think, I will look round to see if I can find any of my comrades but there was not one to be found.

The men who I had met up with earlier in the day had already gone out of the Line before me.

And so it was, on 8th October, that L.Cpl. Sadler and the remnants of 9th Royal Fusiliers marched away from the carnage at Bayonet Trench; their participation in the Battle of the Transloy Ridges was at an end.

16

The Somme Battlefield October–December 1916: From the Transloy Ridges to the Reserves Lines and the Lead-up to Christmas

Welcome relief for 9th Royal Fusiliers was followed by placement in the reserve to refit and absorb drafts in the immediate aftermath of the barren and costly assault on Bayonet Trench.

Battalion War Diary:

8th October 1916. FLERS.
Relief complete at 3 30pm. Battn. moved back to Bgde. reserve trenches SW of FLERS. Day spent in resting the men who remained. The Battn. relieved by two Coys. of the 5th Berkshires at 11 00pm. Battn. marched back through LONGUEVAL-DELVILLE WOOD to the RESERVE Bgde. Camp at NE Corner of BERNAFAY WOOD. Valises and Cookers already there with hot soup and rum for the men. Camp consists of several tents & bivouacs & dugouts (numerous). Shared the Camp with the 8th Battn. Royal Fusiliers.

9th October 1916. BERNAFAY WOOD.
Routine day spent in inspections, clearing up and resting the men.

10th October 1916. BERNAFAY WOOD.
Routine. 100 men supplied to 5th Northants (Pioneers) for carrying shells from Dump at DELVILLE WOOD to COCOA ALLEY (communication trench) from 8 00am to Mid-day, all available men brought up from Transport, (at POMMIERS REDOUBT), for this purpose.

11th October 1916. BERNAFAY WOOD.
Routine. Inspections & Physical Drill parades, Party of 100 men sent to 35th Infantry Bgde. for carrying Stores up to the line. Whilst on road by DELVILLE WOOD the party was held up by congestion of traffic and a shell burst on the column killing 4 and wounding 6 Other Ranks. No further casualties were sustained.

12th October 1916. BERNAFAY WOOD.
Battn. under ½ hours' notice to move if required. The 4th Army Offensive continued, the 88th Bde. being attached to the 12th Division and operating on the right of the

35th Bde. Attack held up in the same place as on the 7th inst. The Reserve was not called upon and the ½ hour notice was cancelled at 9 20pm.

13th October 1916. BERNAFAY WOOD.
Routine. Inspections and Physical Drill Parades. Great Artillery activity heard at 6 15pm- died down at 6 45 pm probably a hostile counter attack.

14th October 1916. BERNAFAY WOOD.
Routine. Inspection & Physical Drill Parades.

15th October 1916. BERNAFAY WOOD.
Routine. Armourer Sgt. Inspected all rifles of the Battn. Voluntary Services held for all denominations. A carrying party of 2 Officers, 4 NCO's and 90 men supplied to the R.E.'s for the 35th Bgde. in the line at 6 30pm- No casualties sustained.

16th October 1916. BERNAFAY WOOD CAMP.
Routine. Two parties of 1 NCO and 10 men each supplied to 178th Tunnelling Coy. R.E.'s at 1 00pm and 9 00pm respectively. First party sustained 6 casualties (all wounded) whilst going up the Trenches near GUEDECOURT. Also a party of 1 Officer 2 NCO's and 50 men supplied to carry for the 35th Inf. Bgde. at 7 00pm- No casualties.

17th October 1916. BERNAFAY WOOD CAMP
Routine. ADM's 12th Division visited the Camp at 3 00pm. Divisional Band played in the Camp during the afternoon. Draft of 29 men arrived at transport in the evening- 10 00pm.

18th October 1916. BERNAFAY WOOD CAMP
Offensive resumed at 3 40am- 35th Bgde. with 88th Bde. (attached to 12th Division,) Sussex, (attached to 35th Bgde.) in support. Battn. under ½ hrs. notice . Camp shelled at 7 00am to 7 45 am. Several bivouacs knocked in. Three parties of 10 men and an NCO each provided to 178th Tunnelling Coy. R.E.'s at 5 00am, 1 00pm and 9 00pm. One fatigue party of an NCO and 10 men engaged on burying dead horses and clearing obstructions on LONGUEVAL- FLERS ROAD from 8 00am to 12 noon. First news of attack received at noon- about 20 prisoners taken. Right Bgde. took and held all their objectives. One carrying party of 50 men under an Officer supplied to 35th Infantry Bde. At 5 30pm. Returned at 6 00am- 19th inst. One man missing from the party. Battn. relieved from being under ½ hrs., notice at 9 00pm.

Sadler Account:

179. THE SOMME BATTLEFIELD. Reserve Trenches at Flers. A Terrible Journey. Roll Call and Reflections.
That night, 8th October, we finished up, after a terrible struggle, at the Reserve Trenches around Flers. This was the worst journey I ever had in getting relieved from the Trenches. If anyone can understand what mud, rain and shelling is like

at its worst, then that is what we had to put up with. On getting to the Trenches around Flers we all mixed together and made a little tea then we were then able to lay our weary bones down and fall to sleep. Next morning, after we had made our breakfast, we fell in for a "Roll Call". Every man that belonged to my Company had to parade, this including the Head Quarters Ration Party that we had left out in order that they could get our rations up to us. With everyone that could be found, my Company mustered 14 in all. "B" Company was 12 and the other two Companys were very little stronger. Myself, as a Corporal, was the only Full Rank N.C.O. left out of the three Companys who went into Action and there was only one Sergeant left in the Battalion and he was in the Support Company which hadn't been "called for" to take part in the Attack.This battle was the greatest "Cutting Up" that we as a Battalion ever received in the War and the only battle where we had failed to win our objective. I understood that we had drawn the German rifle and machine gun fire and, by doing so, that we had enabled the troops on our Flanks to meet with great success but we had paid dearly for it. We were later to be told that we had been very unlucky in attacking the German Line just as the Germans were relieving and, because of that, we had heavy odds against us as we had not only the Germans who were holding the Line to face but we also had to face the incoming Troops.

180.LONGUEVAL Flers to Longueval. "Standing To". Living Quarters. Bombs from the sky.

Soon we were to leave for Longueval, heading to Bernafay Woods, not great distance from Delville Woods and spent forty-eight hours in reserve. At both of these places, where we were "standing to", we were still liable to be called upon if needed. The Battalion was formed into a small Company with the help of a few extra men as details who had been sent up to join us and who had not been involved in the battle. We were living in what cover we could find, or make, such as little tents or large holes dug in the ground which we covered over the top with sailcloth and we also used little huts which we made from boxes which came from the Field Guns. These boxes had contained four, eighteen pounder shells and they also came in very handy for making fires. It was also around this time that aeroplanes started bombing the back areas and all the fires had to be put out when ordered. Here it was that I received my first insight of bombing from the sky. I wondered what was going on when I first heard the bombs coming down but I took little notice of them because I hadn't, to this time, seen what damage could be done by the bombs.We spent over a week at this place doing working parties. I heard many men grumbling, towards the later part of the War, over working parties, when the work which was being served out could not be finished in or around four hours.

However, when one started a working party at this place and at this time, a man was very lucky if he finished in 24 hours. At most times he was also extremely lucky if he got back at all as nearly every part of the area was searched with German shells. These roads were "searched" by the German heavy guns and 9.2's which they were able to station on the road, this making it very easy to supply them with shells. This made it very dangerous to the Ammunition Company R.A.S.C., taking up the shells by motor transport and owing to the roads getting shelled so much, it also made it very dangerous for us.

181. LONGUEVAL. Working Parties. Myself as an Orderly Sergeant. NCO's.

We were called upon for anything, burying dead horses and doing work under the Royal Engineers, forming carrying parties and making deep dugouts. We did this in shifts of 8 hours, starting from the time we reached the place where the work had to be done. It also took us about 2 hours to get there and the same on returning. Worst of all was being given the job of taking rations up to advanced positions as our troops pushed the Germans back. Whilst we were doing our turn at "Standing To", until our Division was relieved, I took on the position of Orderly Sergeant for the newly formed Company and we also had a few N.C.O.'s sent up to us from the rear to help in the "good" work. Owing to having several working parties being caught by German shellfire and badly knocked about; after a short time, these N.C.O.'s were stopped from taking charge of working parties and the organising and leading of these working parties was to fall on the one or two who had been lucky enough to get through the recent battle. I was to consider this as very unfair on us battle-worn N.C.O.'s and I felt that the Commanding Officer of the Battalion, at that time, a man who had also been lucky enough to get through the three battles in which we had played our part since the starting of the first Battle of the Somme, would have thought this to be the case as well. I decided that having considered the un-fairness of this, it was to be my wish to go before the Commanding Officer and ask to give up my rank. Not one of these N.C.O.'s had been out there so long as myself and yet they were being excused the task of taking charge of working parties and all that went with this.

182. LONGUEVAL. Working Parties. Duties and worn out soldiers.

There were in fact, in the Company, only three or four of us left who had been through all of the three battles on the Somme. As regards to the situation with N.C.O.'s, I think I was the only one left. Yet still I was being asked, not only to continue doing Orderly Sergeant, but also expected to take charge of working parties; this owing to there being this shortage of N.C.O.'s as well. I offered my services for the first working party because no other N.C.O. could be found and the working party which the men and I were going to relieve had seven men wounded out of ten. I had to parade ten men at 4 o'clock to start for Longueval in order to report to a Royal Engineers Officer, with no stretcher bearers being provided. We were extremely lucky in having no one in the Party wounded. On arriving at the smashed up village, our work commenced by loading, onto a General Service Wagon , forty sets of timbering which were required for the sides and roofs of deep dugouts. I can safely say that whoever took their part in this working party will never forget it.

I cannot say how many times we had to reload the wagon before we reached our destination. The men themselves were begging and praying of me to allow them to be allowed to walk the wagon up through a Communication Trench which as it happened was a greater distance than our planned route. Owing to their nerves being shattered, through being war weary, they were very much afraid that every minute would be their last as a result of a shell bursting on the road. Nevertheless,

I had to give the order that, as long we were able to keep the wagon on the road, this was the route which we were to follow it and they obeyed the Order. With the roads that we were travelling being covered with large shell holes, the sets of timber kept shaking off and, at various different times on our journey, the wagon had to be unloaded in order to get the load organised again. It then had to be reloaded before we could re-start our journey again. After a terrible journey we finally reached our destination and here the wagon had to be unloaded.

183. LONGUEVAL. Working Parties

Having unloaded, we received orders to take cover in an old trench and wait for the Guide who was to show us to the place where we were to commence our work. Whilst we were waiting, much heavy shelling took place with the result that it was some considerable time before the Guide could reach us. When he did finally arrive we were each told to catch hold of so much timber and then to follow him. At last we reached the place of work and here we started and did our eight hours of work, emptying sandbags of chalk from the dugout.

The working party of ten men who we had gone to relieve had started for "home" and had managed to get their wounded men away. These men had been wounded by bombs which had been lying around. At daylight, after doing our eight hours, we also started, to try and find our way "home". This was just at the time when the Germans were fond of shelling the back areas, searching for massing troops etc.

Not one of us had the slightest idea of our way back but, after wandering about for considerable time, and as luck would have it, we managed to take the right direction. At the sort of place where we had been working, there were no men stationed along the route to show which different directions we might take so it really was just a case of trying ones luck. Anyway we managed to arrive "home" at 8 o'clock in the morning.

This working party had only taken us 16 hours.

184. LONGUEVAL. Further Duties. Ration carrying parties with mules.

After this particular working party, I gave up the role of being an Orderly Sergeant and was allowed to spend some time resting but I was allowed only very little time for that "complaint". Being in charge of what few men were left in my Company, I was constantly being called upon for this and that. About the same time, one night, myself and the only Sergeant who had been left after the Battle, were ordered to go on Parade at a certain place. This time, with an Officer in charge, we were to be part of a large carrying party with the task of carrying up rations to an advanced Brigade which had been attached to our Division. About 5 o'clock or so we started on our journey; split up into three parties with a distance being left between each party because of the shellfire. When we reached the village of Longueval we took to the communication Trench which led us to where we had to report the Brigade Head Quarters. We set down near the Headquarters for a rest and waited for a Guide to show us where we had to go and also who was to tell us what we had to do. It was not, altogether, a comfortable rest owing to the shellfire, but when it was dark enough, we were taken by our guide to where some mules were waiting for us.

We were spilt into smaller parties with a certain number of men being instructed to go with each mule. When our "jolly" journey was about to begin, the "Rations" were strapped on the mules back. They were to carry them as far as possible and then we were taking them to the advanced positions. This time, unlike on our previous "adventure", we were not called to stop so many times and there was no need to unload and load again. The only trouble was that there were so many trenches running across the ground that, at times, when the mules required a change of direction, they took to trench life by deciding to fall into these dis-used trenches.

185. LONGUEVAL. Ration parties with mules. Being Shelled.

When they fell into a trench, they generally managed to fall so that their legs were pointing skywards whilst their bodies remained stuck at the bottom of the trench. When they decided to play this little "game", we had to unload them and act as the mules ourselves but, eventually, we were able to get the rations to the ration dump which was in a sunken road not far from Longueval. From here, using parties of twelve men, we started delivering the rations to the Front Line Troops with each group of twelve men, doing several turns.

We were to carry on doing this until about 2 o'clock in the morning.

Just at the point when we were going to start heading back "home", one of the Quarter Masters, attached to one of the advanced companies, found 12 cans of water had been left behind which also needed to be taken to the Front. This was to further delay our journey towards "home". When the Officer asked for volunteers, and in spite of all the men being tired out; eleven men stepped forward to undertake the journey with myself taking charge. We all fully understood what water meant to the Front Line Troops. The rest of our working party sat down in the Communications Trench and awaited our return. The journey went very comfortably. That was until we reached our destination. Having put all of the cans of water down, and whilst we were collecting together to start on our return, a very large German Shell was heard coming towards us. From the terrible sound it was making; it was coming down towards the ground and towards us. We all started to wonder if our time was up. I am sorry to say that it was for many of the men in the area but this was not to include any of my men.

186. LONGUEVAL. Ration carrying Party. Attacked with Tear Gas Shells.

Where the water had been dumped which was in another sunken road; that road was completely packed with men and it was due to fact that there were so many men on this road this that none of my party were killed.

The shell burst only a few yards from us but the great number of men who were stationed there, acted as a "living" shield for us.

Stretcher-Bearers were soon on the scene and the wounded were carried away and the terrible cries from the injured men, who were in much pain, began to die down. I got my men into a Trench and counted them to see that they were all present and then we started back to join the remainder of the Party. We joined them just at the time another attack was taking place on the Front Line and on the Communications Trench which we had just passed down. Both were getting very much knocked about by German Shellfire. That night was the first time that I had noticed the different sounds between "Tear" shells and High Explosive shells as they were coming through the air. When I heard a whistling sound coming towards our party, I expected to hear a terrible crash as if it were coming from the bursting of a Trench mortar but, instead of that, it was to be a real job to hear the shell burst at all. Shortly afterwards, though, it became nearly impossible to keep our eyes open. We were soon to leave these "Tear" shells behind us though as we made towards "home". On this journey back we were greeted with some very heavy showers of rain at frequent intervals with the result that we were to lose our way on the road on one or two occasions. We finally managed to arrive "home" at about 8 30, wet through to the skin with the rain. This carrying party had taken us just about as long as the working party from the night before. I had never had the "pleasure" of doing working parties such as this, either before or since. When I heard men grumbling in the latter part of the War about having to do a four hour working party, I used to think, and not only think, but also tell them that they really didn't know just what a working party was.

187. LONGUEVAL A change of clothes. Leaving the Somme Battlefield.

The next morning I was feeling rather lucky. Some new uniform had been sent up to the Company Quarter Master Sergeant and as I was wet through and covered with mud, I was handed a brand new change of clothing. After changing out of my old uniform and putting on these clean clothes, I was soon to be found lying down and having a little sleep. However, I was only asleep for a few minutes before I was woken up with the Order that we were leaving this place at 10 o'clock. With this came the packing up of everything up ready for the move. We were delighted to think that the end of our "perfect" visit to the Somme Battlefield was coming to an end. On leaving and marching a short distance, we were greeted by meeting our Fife and Drum Band and fell out for a short rest before marching in the rear of the Band. The Drummers came and greeted what few of us "old hands" were left and they were delighted to meet us. On "falling in" we then marched away to the music of the Fife and Drums; but our minds were wandering back to our fallen comrades. Gone but never to be forgotten.

189. BACK TO AGNY 1916. Return to the Agny Area.

Spending a few nights here and there we soon arrived back to our old Rest Camp on the Agny Front Line, near Arras. Here we were reinforced by a very few men and held the Line very thinly. At Agny, we carried on in much the same way as I have described earlier and were at this part of the Front until a week or so before Xmas 1916. Then we left for a village in the rear of the Line at Houvigneul to wait for a few more reinforcements who joined us shortly after our arrival.

Battalion War Diary:

10th November 1916 AGNY TRENCHES.
Had similar working parties supplied to-day by 7th Sussex. The top of GAME ST. was drained and cleared and work was also done in GEM ST. and GEORGE ST. A Unit was put out at night by all Companies in the Front Line. Sniping was active opposite

G1-G2 and a German working Party near the top of Sap. D was dispersed by our Lewis Gun Fire. During the night there was considerable hostile activity in which numerous lights were used. Five Green lights appeared more than once. At 11 00pm whistling was distinctly heard from the vicinity of Sap D. "God save the King" and "Marseilles" were distinctly heard.

11th November 1916 AGNY.
Work still being done on cleaning and reclaiming the Trenches. Wire being put out at night in front of the firing line. The enemy appeared to be working hard in his Saps opposite. It was reported that during the night aeroplanes were heard over the German Lines and that enemy machine guns fired using "tracer" bullets.

12th November 1916 AGNY.
Front and Support lines re-vetted and trench boards laid. GAME ST. and GEORGE ST. cleared. Paraded and traverses in RESERVE LINE re-vetted, trench boards laid. Enemy still busy opposite. Work on Saps "D" and "E" continued. An enemy wiring party, observed near Sap "E", was dispersed by our Lewis Gun fire. An Officers Patrol went out to examine enemy wire near Sap 13. It was about 30" deep but appeared to have been well cut by our T.M. fire. A Sentry was heard at head of Sap Enemy M.G.'s fired on our wiring parties near Sap G.3.a. Only one slight casualty caused. An evening Patrol was observed examining our wire to left of Sap G.4.a. They were fired on and ran away.

As 1916 moved to its close, the Battalion were to spend their last spell in the Agny Trenches between the 13th and 16th December which the Battalion Diarist records as "Very Quiet".

On 16 December, the 12th (Eastern) Division received Orders that they were to move back from the Front Line Area as they were to be involved in six weeks of Divisional Training.

On 17 December the 36th Brigade bade the trenches at Agny farewell and spent the major part of two days marching via Magnicourt to Houvinguel where they were to be billeted, a distance of some 15miles.

Sadler account:

189. (Continued) FROM AGNY TO HOUVINGUEL – XMAS 1916.
This year we spent a very Happy Xmas with our new comrades with each man aiming to give as much as they could in addition to what was supplied by the Army. We had the School in the Village loaned out for us to use for the occasion.

Xmas passed merry and bright, a little different to the year before. Christmas morning started with a Church Parade. After this Parade and a short interval, dinner was prepared. The First Course: – Veal, Beef and Ham, a little of each, also Potatoes and Cabbage. This was served out on plates to everyone which was quite a change and was well enjoyed. 2nd Course: – Sweets, Figs and Jellies, Xmas Pudding and Custard and also a large supply of Oranges and Chocolates and plenty to smoke and drink. As these things were not to be had in England at this time, I think we did exceedingly well. Myself, I spent nearly a week in buying the stock for the occasion and hiring the plates from the small town of Frevent. Also the glasses for us to be drinking out of which were hired from the village in which the Dinner took place.

190. XMAS DAY 1916. HOUVINGEUL Christmas Day Concert.

This day was one that will be remembered by all. Tea this day was served at the School. After tea we had a concert amongst ourselves, this bringing the day to a happy end. Further reinforcements, arrived in early January; these were men who came from Ireland, Roughriders and Sharp Shooters Cavalry; men that had enlisted shortly after the outbreak of war and who had been very lucky in staying in Ireland for that time. They turned out to be good men in every way. The Battalion was again at full strength and ready for Action.

As 1917 dawned, the 9th Royal Fusiliers, now restored to its full complement of men, anticipated six weeks of divisional training away from the front line.

17

January 1917: the Arras sector. A New Year but more assault preparations

S tationed near Arras, 9th Royal Fusiliers experienced no action during January. This training, as the Battalion Diary briefly notes, included route marches, platoon and company drill, parades, lectures and physical training. Regular church parades, concert parties and football matches were also the order of the day.

Sadler Account:

190. 1916–1917 HOUVINGEUL (cont.). Preparing for the Battle of Arras.

After doing our turn at cleaning and repair work at Houvigneul throughout January 1917, we left for "Barbed Wire Square", Arras, spending eight days doing working parties and, between the working parties, getting the pleasure of looking round the City of Arras. The City itself was very close to the Germans and the Germans had also had the pleasure of spending a short time in Arras before being driven back by the French. The main buildings in the City had been very much damaged by shellfire.

191. ARRAS 1917. A cold start to the New Year.

The few weeks after Xmas had been spent in training our new men and getting ready for the Arras Battle but it was very cold and a job to keep warm at night, sleeping rough in an old barn. In the morning it was nearly impossible to cut our small ration of bread because it had frozen so hard during the night. Washing and shaving early in the morning was far from pleasant. Much cleaning of rifles also took place. We also spent a short time in making the ground level so as to lay a railway line for the coming battle. Owing to there being so much frost it was like chipping concrete. The work which a man could complete in a week would, at other times, normally been done in an hour.

192. ARRAS 1917. Reflections on the City and buildings in Arras.

The City of Arras, itself, was very close to the Germans and the Germans had also had the pleasure of spending a short time in Arras before being driven back by the French. The main buildings in the City had been very much damaged by shellfire. The Town Hall, Hotel de Ville, and Belfry and buildings nearby were but a heap of stones; the largest heap of stones I had ever seen in France. The Hotel de Ville had been treated in a different way. This had been burnt out by inflammable shells leaving the high walls standing and the wood around what were once the windows were nothing but charred remains. The high walls came in very handy by way of protecting the cellars which were used by the Troops. Many of the large

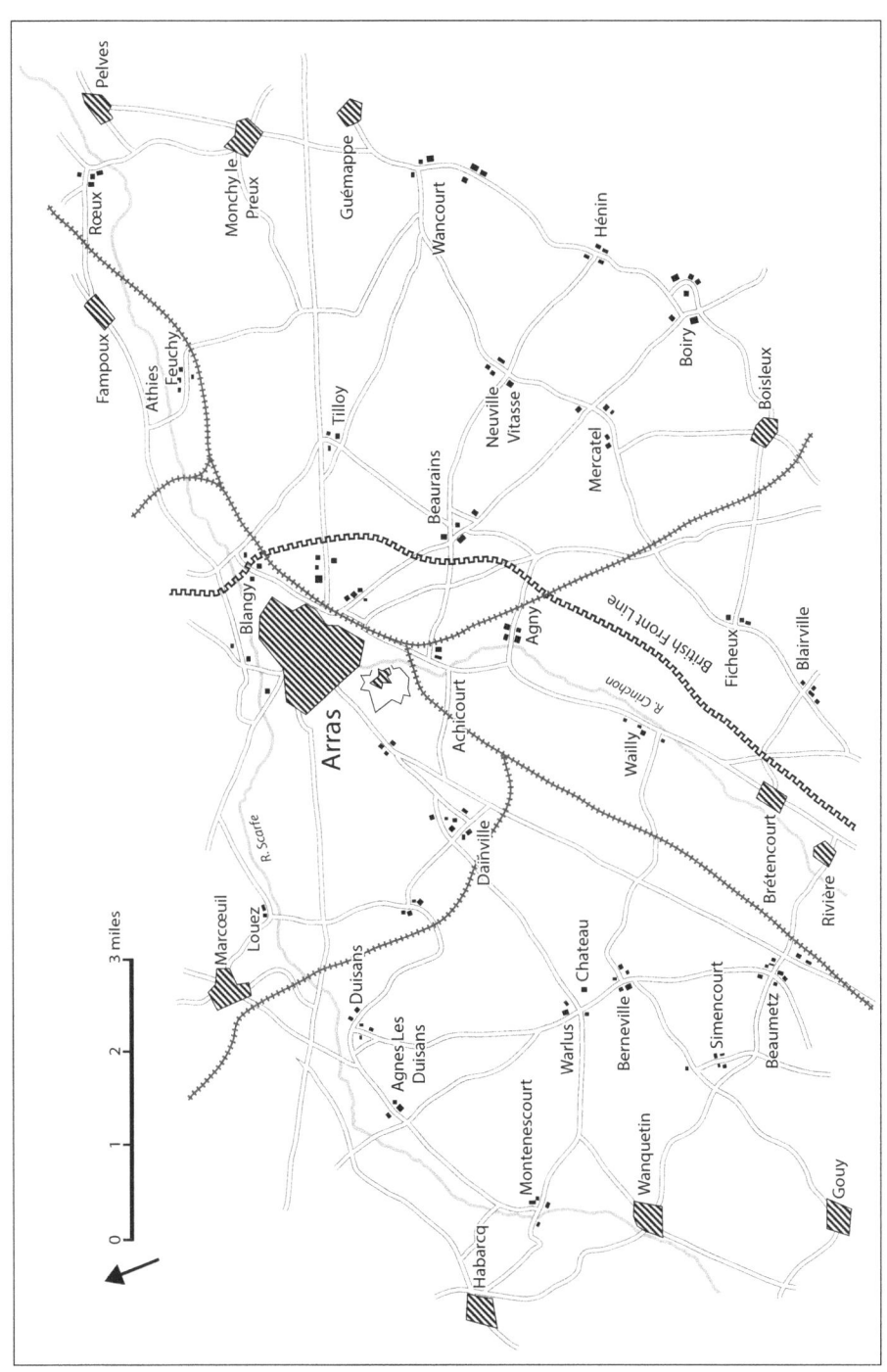

The Arras Front 1917. (George Anderson)

3 miles

Pelves

Monchy le Preux

Guémappe

Wancourt

Hénin

Rœux

Fampoux

Feuchy

Athies

Tilloy

Neuville Vitasse

Boiry

Boisleux

Beaurains

Mercatel

Blangy

Arras

Achicourt

Agny

British Front Line

R. Cinchon

Ficheux

Blairville

Wailly

Brétencourt

Rivière

Dainville

R. Scarfe

Marcœuil

Louez

Duisans

Chateau

Simencourt

Beaumetz

Agnes Les Duisans

Warlus

Berneville

Montenescourt

Wanquetin

Gouy

Habarcq

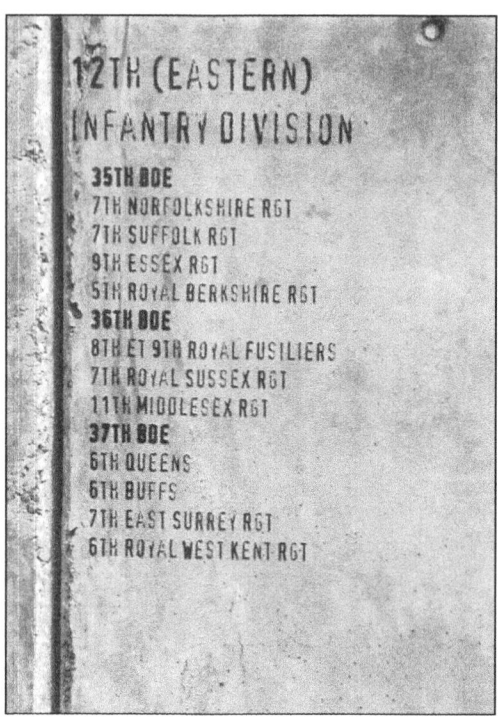

12th Division Memorial, Wellington Barracks/Caves Arras
from which the Division attacked on 9th April 1917.

Hotels made been turned into heaps of stone. All the buildings which stood higher than the ordinary houses of Arras were smashed by shellfire because the Germans were able to see them very well from the High Ridge positioned behind their Front Line and all the buildings had been subjected to very heavy bombardment. This Ridge was of great use to the Germans for ranging purposes of their Artillery. Also, around the outskirts of the City, more damage had been done. We were stationed in the Cellars of what was named by the British as "Barbed Wire Square". Much damage had been done here by shellfire but the Cellars were very strong due to the high buildings. The more shells that the Germans sent over and which struck the building itself, only made our cellars stronger as the fallen stones, masonry and chalk only fell on the roof of our cellars and by that made the roof much thicker. In the front of the doorways, leading to these cellars, were walls built by us to stop the German Shells from giving us a "visit" by coming straight down the doorway. It was very dangerous for troops to stand about in small parties.

193. ARRAS.1917 – Troop movements in the City.
During daylight the Troops were not allowed to walk about unless on Duty and then they had to keep close into the wall of the houses so as not to be seen by the German airmen. However, even with all such orders as these, one would still see such things as rifle inspection being carried out just outside the cellar doorway and in full view of everyone and everything. This was to be the cause of, and result in,

the loss of many lives.

On one occasion I was at this Arras Building for my Company when a Platoon of men stationed in this Square were having a rifle inspection outside when overcame a large shell which fell amongst the men, killing or wounding nearly everyone. It was a great pity that the ones, who were responsible for and allowed such carrying on, during the wartime, had not been sent home, and out of our way. Although Orders were to be seen as warning men of danger, this sort of thing was allowed to happen and I do wonder if the German Troops were ordered to do such foolish things. At these cellars, I noticed that the stone steps which led down to the cellars had been boarded over in a way such as to be able to allow horses to walk down and hence the cellars also acted as stables. No doubt the Germans also did this as I noticed a number of German Uniforms which had been left. These Cellars turned out to be very comfortable places for Troops owing to the great amount of wood which could be found close at hand and which made lovely fires. The heat in the Cellars at times was very great but it was nice and comfortable especially during and just after such cold weather.

Battalion War Diary:

7th to 9th February 1917 ARRAS.
Bn. in Support Coys. in GRANDE PLACE. Provide working parties.

10th February 1917 ARRAS.
Two working parties provided.

11th February 1917 ARRAS.
Starting at 6 15 pm "A" Coy. relieved the front of the 111th MIDDLESEX holding I Sub-Sector and "C" Coy relieved part of the 8th R.F. from INFANTRY ROAD to IBEX LANE-IVY STREET inclusive.

12th February 1917 ARRAS.
One Company of the 10th Royal Welsh Fusiliers relieved "B" Coy in the ST. SAUVEUR'S DEFENCES. "B" Coy moved to the Reserve Line. "D" Company in the CEMETRY DEFENCES were not relieved.

13th to 14th February 1917 ARRAS.
Things fairly quiet. A few trench mortars fell in the front of Ret. Company. One casualty from a rifle grenade in the Left Coy. while wiring.

15th February 1917 ARRAS.
Relieved in the morning by the 7th Bn. Royal Sussex Reg. Relief complete by 9 30 am. Bn. moved to the Div. Reserve in ARRAS. All Coys. billeted in l' Ecole des Jeunes Fillen. Rue GAMBETTA.

16th to 18th February 1917 ARRAS.
Whole Battn. engaged in finding the following working parties:- 151 for New Zealand

Tunnelling Coy.; 28 for 70th Coy. R.E.'s.; 100 for 987th Coy. R.E.'s.; 270 for the R172 Dump.

Sadler Account:

194. ARRAS 1917- Preparation for Battle. Underground Tunnels.

Our eight days, at the beginning of February, were spent in giving a helping hand for the great coming of the Battle of Arras, which was due to take place on Easter Monday morning April 9th 1917. As well as giving a helping hand, we were also getting used to this part of the Front because, as a Battalion, we were to play our part in the Great Battle; however, very much more had to be done before that date. Here, in Arras, because of the high ridge behind the Germans Front Line, it was possible for them to see all that was going on above ground and on the surface. It would come a complete surprise to all of the people back home in England to see just what was done under ground for our benefit. At this stage, I will attempt to tell how everything was done, under cover, with the aid of the city's Cellars. Underground communications Trenches and the connecting of deep dugouts in the Support Line were built to act as the main starting point of the Battle.

As far as our working parties were concerned, firstly, we were working in carrying away sandbags of chalk from the underground Communication Trenches which were being worked by the New Zealander Troops; these were special men employed for trenching and, I must say, were first class hands at their work. They worked like niggers for quite twelve months to get the job finished in time.

The underground tunnels were made in such a way so as to enable the largest man to walk upright in comfort and they were made wide enough to be able to lay "lines" down in order that small trucks could be used for running bombs and Trench Mortars to the Front Line. These underground Trenches were supplied with fresh air by, every now and then, running down a tunnel from the Communication Trench above ground and, by doing this; it meant that we were well able to carry away the sandbags from the tunnels without the Germans seeing what was going on. Whenever "new" chalk was seen by the Germans it was always a case of "look out" but the Germans here were never to know that we were making some deep dugouts for our comfort.

195. THE BATTLE OF ARRAS. 1917 Underground Tunnels. Extending the Cellars.   A Trip to the Front Line.

When these tunnels were finally completed they ran right up to the German Front Line, electric lights were laid on supplying the tunnel with a first class light and, most importantly, we were now able to get to the Front Line under cover. Whilst all this was being carried, our own Royal Engineers were digging deep dugouts in the support line which were about 70 yards to the rear of the Front Line. We were now also called upon to empty sandbags of chalk for them and when the deep dugouts were completed, they were all connected up to each other by tunnels and also connected up to the underground communication Trenches.

When these two tasks had been completed, we were able to "mass" Troops right at the Front Line and under cover. Following on from this our next task was to be connecting all the Cellars by knocking holes from one to another. We were now able to walk round certain parts of Arras entirely under cover. After our eight days at this kind of work came to an end we went up to hold part of the Front Line for four days at the point where we were due to be starting from on the 9th of April. This was the first trip to the Trenches for our new comrades and it was a good "breaking in" for them as things were fairly quiet.

196. THE BATTLE OF ARRAS. The Front Line. Sentry watch in tunnels under the Germans.

In these Trenches we worked the same way as anywhere else but here we had to have Sentry Posts, posted underground to keep a sharp lookout in order to make sure that the Germans did not dig into our underground Communication Trenches. This lookout was done by using candles supplied by the Royal Engineers and a barricade was built using sand bags under and level with our own Front Line. A "Post Hole" was made so that the Sentry could see ahead. The candles were placed in the far end of the tunnel and always kept burning. The end of the tunnel was under the German Front Line. Walking up the tunnel to change the candles one could notice, in places, the bottom of the German barbed wire stakes sticking through the roof of the tunnel. We could tell when danger was ahead by using the candles. The Sentry would look through the "Post Hole" made in the barricade and, looking ahead, could see the candle burning.

If the atmosphere was still, the candle would burn still. If the atmosphere was disturbed, the candle would flicker. If the Sentry noticed the candle flickering it was a case of "look out" but here the Sentry groups were supplied with a certain sort of bomb. If the Germans did manage to dig their way into our tunnel, the Sentry had to light the fuse of one of these bombs and run after the Germans. When he had driven the Germans back as far as possible, he had to throw his bomb ahead. This bomb would then burst and was usually quite strong enough, on bursting, to blow the tunnel in with the Germans on one side and the Sentry on the other.

This sort of Sentry Post was alright for those who liked excitement but nothing of any great importance happened whilst we were doing our turn.

Battalion War Diary:

19th February 1917 ARRAS.
Bn. relieved 11th Middlesex in the Left Sub-Sector. Relief complete 10 30am. Order of Coy's:- "D" on the Right, "B" in the Centre, "A" on the Left, "C" in Reserve.

20th February 1917 ARRAS.
Fairly quiet. Our artillery bombarded enemy trenches from 10 00am to 10 30am.

21th February 1917 ARRAS.
Quiet day. Trenches in very bad condition owing to thaw. All available men busy in clearing them.

22th February 1917 ARRAS.
Working parties supplied by 7th Sussex and 11th Middlesex to clear trenches.

23rd February 1917 ARRAS.
Quiet day. Only a few rifle grenades sent over. Working parties again supplied for work of re-claiming trenches.

24th February 1917 ARRAS.
Bn. was relieved by the 7th/8th K.O.S. Bn. 46th Bde. 15th Div. Relief complete 9 30 am. Coys. billeted in the MUSEUM. Bn. H.Q.-No.5 RUE des TROIS POMMELLES.

25th to 28th February 1917 ARRAS.
Whole Battn. on working parties by day and night. On the morning of the 26th at 8 30 am, the 11th Middlesex made a raid on the German trenches. They killed a number of the enemy, bombed his dug-outs and brought back 4 N.C.O.'s and 21 men as prisoners.

1st to 2nd March 1917 ARRAS.
Working parties provided. Whole Bn. engaged.

3th March 1917 ARRAS to MONTENESCOURT.
Bn. was relieved in ARRAS by the 9th Bn. ESSEX Regiment. Marching at 6 30pm the Bn. moved to MONTENESCOURT via DAINVILLE and WARLUS.

4th March 1917. MANIN.
Marching at 1 00pm Bn. moved to MANIN via HABRCO and NOYELLE-VION.

5th March 1917. MANIN.
Day spent cleaning up.

6th March 1917. MANIN.
Brigade paraded at 1 00pm for inspection at 2 30pm by Commander in Chief. Very good parade.

7th March 1917. MANIN.
Parades under Coy. arrangements. No. 6424 Pte. L.Cpl. G.ASHMAN (attached 36th F.M. Battery) awarded the Military Medal for gallantry during the raid made by the 11th Middlesex on the morning of the 26th Feb. last.

8th March 1917. MANIN.
Working party found for work in Trenches in Training area.

9th to 11th March 1917. MANIN.
Physical training, B.F., Bombing, Musketry and Ex. Order Drill.

12th March 1917. MANIN.

In the morning, parade according to programme of work. In the afternoon Bn. on the training ground. Positioning relating to attack practice.

13th to 14th March 1917. MANIN.

Battn. on the Training Ground attacking over the Trenches, (Reserve), dug on the side of the MANIN-AMBRINES Road.

15th March 1917. MANIN.

Parades according to Programme of Work.

16th March 1917. MANIN.

Battn. in the training area. 37th Bgde. co-operating on our right .

17th March 1917. MANIN.

Brigade day in Training area.

18th March 1917. MANIN.

Training area.

19th to 20th March 1917. MANIN.

Training area. Brigade attack practice, an aeroplane and dummy tanks co-operating.

21st March 1917 MANIN./ARRAS

Marching at 2 30 pm. Battn. moved to ARRAS and relieved the 7th Bn. East Surrey Regt. 37th Bgde.. Battn. billeted in the museum; Bn. H.Q. No 4. RUE des AUGUSTINE.

Sadler Account:

197. THE BATTLE OF ARRAS. Preparations. Training for Battle. A "Mock"Battleground.

When we left these tunnels we were set to do our training for the battle. Well in the rear of Arras, a piece of ground was found similar to the ground which we had to take on Easter Monday. Staying in a village close at hand we spent a week or so training over this picked ground. I must say it was all very well arranged and all Platoon Sergeants were supplied with photos of the German position which had been taken by our Airmen.

From these photos it was quite possible to see the doorways of the Germans Deep dugouts and even Batteries of German light guns. Everything was brought up to date for this Battle and we were following preparation in a French style. If what we had been doing in the past was of the English style, then it was quite time that we had a change. This time, instead of taking one or two German lines, we were to take so many "thousands" of yards and before the Battle, every man was fully expected to know his job. This is the way in which we were trained over this period. The ground was all marked out, showing all Communication Trenches, both ours and the Germans along with Front Lines etc … also shown were all German Saps and Dugouts, all the German Machine Gun Positions and their Strong Points. First we had the "pleasure" of walking over the ground to see things for ourselves; including our position for the Battle. Each Regiment in the Division was served out with a coloured patch, which was to be worn on the back so that it could be seen from the rear. Each Brigade had its own colour. My Brigade's colour was red and each Battalion had a certain shaped patch; my Battalion's shape being an Oblong. This patch was designed so as to enable us to tell each Battalion from the rear because this attack was planned to be carried out in new way, with different Battalion lines passing through other lines as it progressed. When this happened, these patches came in very handy for recognising just who was who.

199. THE BATTLE OF ARRAS. Preparations. Training for Battle (continued).

Arras was the first Great Battle that was to take place on a large front with the aid of "Creeping Barrages". The Barrage was made up of Shrapnel and Small Shells. Our Heavy Artillery were to be employed doing "Counter Batteries" work on the German Batteries; keeping them from sending over too many shells at us as we advanced and also shelling the German roads so as to stop him from getting up reinforcements. We were also to be getting the help from our Machine Gun Corps., firing a barrage of bullets at the Germans first and second lines, making them keep their heads down. This meant that it made it far from comfortable for them in using their rifles at us. With the help of our Trench Mortars, both heavy and light, the Germans were having a "gay" old time being prepared for them. As the infantry, we carried out the real training for the attack. Instead of rushing "Over the Top", using sections made up from a Lance Corporal and 6 or 7 men as we had done previously; we practiced in the following way. The first thing that was done was that everyone was arranged into their sections ready to start the "sham" battle. Ourselves, we took the second line of advance. Just before the first line of Troops started to advance, Trench Mortars were to put up a barrage on the first German Line, and then our first Line went forward. Ahead of them were our Drummers with their Kettle Drums, which was acting as it was the planned "Creeping Barrage". Everyone had to take notice that they kept within forty yards from the Drums. There was then, at a distance behind, real bursting shrapnel. It being possible for anyone, to being able to follow the bursting shrapnel by the white smoke caused when it burst.

200. THE BATTLE OF ARRAS. Preparations. Carrying Parties with shells.

When the Front Line was moved forward, we moved forward still keeping in Sections. Just past the "mock" German Front Line was a line which was called the Black Line. At this Line we had to lie down for a very long time until the "First" Line had taken its objective. When it was anticipated that this had been done they lit red flares, the signal for us to carry on which we duly did. The Creeping Barrage then played a hundred yards in front of newly won position until we got to where the red flares were sent from. Then at a certain time we passed through that line and carried on going ahead until our objective was gained. Other Troops then followed on in the same way. After going over this ground twice a day for over a week and taking part in more working parties, we were soon to leave for Arras again.

Battalion War Diary:

22nd – 31st March 1917. MANIN/ARRAS
Whole Battn. on working parties for R.E.'s, Northants Pioneers, Trench Mortars and Div. Signals. Most of the men employed in constructing dug-outs.

1st to 2nd April 1917. ARRAS
Working Parties as usual.

3rd April 1917. ARRAS.
Working parties up to the mid-day. In the evening Bn. moved to Cellars PETITE PLACE. Night of the 3rd. was U/V night.

4th April 1917- "V" day. ARRAS.
Bombardment of enemies Trenches commenced. Steady but not heavy.

5th, 6th and 7th April 1917 – "W", "X", "Q" days. ARRAS.
Ditto to 4th April.

8th April 1917- "Y" day ARRAS.
At 11 00 pm. Battn. moved from the Cellars through the caves to BROADWALK and took up position in the trenches for the assault.

Sadler Account:

200. THE BATTLE OF ARRAS. Preparations continue. Carrying Parties with shells.
From the 3rd April we stayed in the Cellars under the Museum for 4 days and, finding a piano in the Cellars, we soon started having a little music and sing-songs etc. … These four days were passed away doing carrying parties etc., carrying up the Flying Pig Trench Mortars as "Iron Rations" for the Germans. After doing four days of hard work, we moved further up towards our Front Line.

201. THE BATTLE OF ARRAS. The Front Line. Close to the Germans. Our Post Duty.
This nature of the Front Line which we were expected to hold was of a type seldom to be found in France as both the Germans and us were holding a village on the left Front of Arras. The Germans were one side of the Street and we were on the other. The road itself was No Man's land and was packed with barbed wire which had been thrown over by both sides. We had no Trenches. The broken down walls acted as our trenches and, here and there, a sort of "Pillar Box" was roughly made from concrete. Each side was very fond of throwing bombs at each other and it was not a very comfortable position to be in without much protection as we found ourselves at such at such close quarters. Sentries used to do their hour on duty in

one of these "Pillar Boxes" and with all the bombs that bursting in these places, or in the nearby area, it really made very little difference to either side. With us being so close to each other, the bombs could worry anyone; British or German.

Heavy Trench Mortars were used by the Germans for shelling the rear and a large number of our men were living in the Cellars one side of the road with the Germans on the other side. Myself, I was staying in a Cellar about 80 yards from the Front Line with a Support Platoon, doing Out-Post Duty every other night. By the side of a small river which was only a few yards wide, we had a Special Out-Post on one side and the Germans had one on the other side. We used to whistle to a post of ours positioned on our Left, every hour, to let them know all was well. Sometimes we would get a return answer of someone whistling back which I fully expect, at times, was the Germans. This somewhat silly game could be carried on in reasonable safety as no one was allowed to give the position of his Post away by firing a rifle round at the Germans.

202. THE BATTLE OF ARRAS. Our Post Duty. Watching Germans on the move.

The Post was only held from "Stand To" at night until "Stand To" at daybreak and six men and one N.C.O. held the Post between these times. The first time that I found myself holding this Post proved rather exciting and, if I had only been allowed to fire my rifle, I expect that I could well have been able to put one or two Germans to a permanent "sleep". This situation came about when I went out to the Post at "Stand To", I was only able to have three men with me, the rest being on a Carrying Party although they were sent out to me on their return. We had only been out there for a short time when we heard the sounds of cracking reeds/weeds just the other side of the river. This was to make us wonder if there were Germans crawling up on us so as to give us a bomb to "share" between us. It was, indeed, a German crawling to another of their Posts but he was taking things steady for the first time in order to see that all was clear. As we were not able to fire, we kept quiet to see what else turned up. It wasn't long before many Germans crossed over the same ground but, instead of crawling, they were walking upright and when a "Star" Light was sent up on the far side, beyond them, it gave us a splendid view. They only stopped and bent their heads forward until the light had died away; then they continued on their journey. All this going on only a few yards from us, but we were not allowed to shoot; not because we were not willing to chance our luck but simply because we were not allowed to.

203. THE BATTLE OF ARRAS. Our Post Duty. Reporting a German Party.

On completing this night at this Post and after getting only a little sleep; the following morning I asked the Company Sergeant Major if I could see the Captain in order to report the details about this Post.

After a short time, I was sent for, to see the "Old Woman". Clearly he wanted to know what I had come to see him about, so I asked him "How is it, we are allowed to stay in a Post with Germans walking about only a few yards away from us and not able to fire at them?" I also asked him what he thought about the situation, if it arose, where it was me who was discovered by the Germans; working with a Party of men around one of their Posts. I asked if he considered whether the

Germans would continue to let me work in peace or wouldn't they have a go at killing me?" His reply to my query as to whether or not I should be allowed to fire from the site of the Post was, "No, you can only fire by going to the right or left of the Post". Perhaps he wanted me to make a fool of myself as, by doing this, I would have been closer to them and in a position where it would have been that much easier for one of them to have a go if they really wanted to have a "dead" shot at me. There was another thing, which I consider could have happened from this Post which would have been to our advantage. I mentioned that just opposite our Post, the Germans also had a position where it was possible to see the German Sentry sitting under a sheet of tin which was acting as cover for him from the rain and which also helped him to try and keep warm. I let this Officer know that if I had my way, I would have had a rifle fixed on that spot and each German that sat under that cover would have received a round from the rifle. I really began to wondered, at times, just what we were out in France for. There was, I considered, far too much "Red Tape" which affected our operations sometimes. This, I think, many of our men came to see for themselves. I believed that when men had to hold a position, such as I have just mentioned, he should be allowed to use his own head and intuition. At the very least, I felt that the man in charge should be able to ask the men in his party as to what their opinions were. We were the ones holding the Post and, supposedly, we were to be visited by an Officer every so often. At this place which I am writing about, we didn't receive many visitors and so we were really the only ones who knew just what was going on.

A Post like this, I felt, should have been held by a Lewis Gun team; the Lewis gun being similar to a machine gun and capable of sweeping the ground in front of the position.

Also I felt that we could have had a better class of Officer in Charge of the Company than we had here. In all honesty, I would not have allowed him to take a dozen boys on a school outing.

204. THE BATTLE OF ARRAS. End of our Post Duty. A Carrying Party to the Front Line. Propaganda Balloons.

After the few days at the end of March and the beginning of April, we left for the Cellars at the Museum in Arras and here we continued on being employed with carrying different things to the Front Line.

Whilst we were on one journey, the Germans sent over a small balloon which was brought down by rifle fire from Troops that were billeted close by. There were several papers attached to this Balloon which we managed to get hold of and, in our Party, we had a man that could read every word of French on the papers.

The papers contained several pages; two of the pages showing how well they were treating French Prisoners, but nothing about the British. The paper also stated that every man who was left behind in England now had three wives and that they, the Germans, would win the War. Further, the message said, they were going to use everything possible to achieve this. We were to find that one of these Balloons came over every so often.

205. THE BATTLE OF ARRAS. Artillery Fire. Bluffing the Germans.

Things around Arras were beginning to get very lively. Not only were out Artillery kindly breaking the news of the forthcoming attack to the Germans but raids were being carried out daily on the German lines and sometimes as many as three raids were carried out in one day. I think that this properly used to worry Old Fritz and it got to the point that he didn't know what to do for the best. I have known our people to use Trench mortars in one part and then carry on and raid another area. After which the Artillery would then concentrate on the position where the Trench Mortars had blown the German wire about; this as if we were waiting in readiness to start a raid. When the raid did take place, it would then be at a different part altogether so that the men who were carrying out the raid would almost be able to do the "job" without having a shell fired at them. Where the wire had been smashed but where there was no raid to take place; this was the spot where the Germans would usually aim to give a good supply of shells, this resulting in them wasting their ammunition. The raids which our troops carried out were done in such an up to date way and, with the aid of a Box Barrage; it was impossible for any Germans to escape. The options which the Germans who were holding their line, inside the Box Barrage, had was to either fight, get taken prisoner or go under.

Most of them appeared to prefer the second, which was to be taken prisoner. It was really wonderful, the amount of British Artillery that would open out when a raid was going to take place. One moment it was as quiet as it could be when, all of a sudden, one would not be able to hear oneself speak and the Germans, for whom the attack was such a great shock, could do little than give themselves up.

206. THE BATTLE OF ARRAS. Moving Forward. Bombardment. Bridging the Trenches.

On the night of the 5th of April, the first and second line Troops, who were taking part in the Battle, moved up to the Cellars in Barbed Wire Square. We moved up there so that we could go straight to the Support Line by using the tunnels. A three day bombardment was about to commence and the Order was for as little movement as possible to take place in the city as everyone expected that Arras was due to have a very warm time from the German Artillery. It was quite expected that the German would set the place on fire with inflammable shells but the city never received any of these and in the end there was very little from the Artillery. For us, enough "Iron Rations" and water were stored in the Cellars to last for several days if anything did happen. Work came to a standstill and the Bombardment was started.

206. THE BATTLE OF ARRAS (cont.) Bridging the Trenches.

I was taking a special part in the Battle which I will now explain. Myself and five men were attached to our Field Company of Royal Engineers for "Bridging" the Lines and making "Strong Points" whilst the Battle was in progress. The same night as my Battalion moved into the Cellars for the commencement of the Bombardment, the Party and myself, with an Engineer, started for our Front Line with as many wooden bridges that were needed to reach over the top of the Trenches. This was done so as to save our advancing Troops from having to jump down into the Trench.

The Royal Engineer in charge of the contract was with us to show us where the Wooden Bridges were to go.

If he had had his way, I think that we should have started the Battle by putting the Bridges across the German Front Line.

207. THE BATTLE OF ARRAS. Bridging. Problems with our Front Lines. A German surrenders.

When I considered that we had gone far enough and had passed several of our lines of Trenches; I decided to ask him, "What line is this. Is this the Support Line or the Front Line?" "No", he replied, "This is our Support Line and it's the next Line where the Bridges have to go". It just so happened though, that the Line where we were actually turned out to be our Front Line and the next Line was the German Front Line! Anyway we were just crossing No Man's Land, on our way to the German Front Line, when one of our Sentries, well to our right, shouted out, "Who are you?" The Royal Engineer shouted "We are only a Party going to bridge our Front Line" to which the Sentry shouted, "You are past our Front Line. This is our Front Line behind you". We were very lucky that we were noticed as our Front Line contained only a Sentry Post here and there. It was proving to be very easy to walk between one of our sentry posts and go wandering on into the German Front Line, as we were finding out. While our Line was held so thinly at this point, an N.C.O. and a man or two had to Patrol the Trenches between each Sentry Post just to ensure that the Germans were not holding the Line as well as ourselves. Whilst writing about our Line being very thinly held, I will recall one occurrence on one night when a German came over to give himself up. One of our Patrols was on their visiting round and he was sitting on the side of our Trench waiting to give himself up. On not seeing anyone for a long time, he was wondering if it was a disused Trench and by the look of his boots and clothes, he appeared to have discovered that he had left a good trench to come and splash about in the mud with us. He was a Warrant Officer and he had apparently not been long outside of one of their deep dugouts.

He was one of those in charge of their Heavy Mine Throwers, known as Heavy Trench Mortars and he enquired as to what damage they had done to our lines. As it was we, would much rather have had his Heavy Gun than him.

208. THE BATTLE OF ARRAS. Making Strong Points. Sing Songs.

A few words now on making Strong Points; these had to be made as and when the Troops pushed ahead.

The Strong Points had to be made in the shape of a Cross so that it was possible to fire the rifles and machine guns in all directions. After finishing the construction of the Strong Point we had to collect what barbed wire we could find and put this around it. Whilst I was attached to the Royal Engineers for this particular "game" or task, we were stationed in the underground caves under the Hotel de Ville until the night before the Battle when everyone moved forward. When my Battalion had moved forward they had brought, with them, the piano which had been in the Cellars at The Citadel, aiming to make the best of the short time before the Battle. This resulted in both the men and Officers joining together with various singsongs. One of the Officers who had been with us in the early part of the War had returned to the Battalion to take charge of the Company once again as we went into Action and the men were very happy. They were looking forward to starting the Battle in jolly good heart and seeing the return of this good leader certainly helped to put some fresh life back into them.

Sheltering below the front line, Sergeant Sadler awaited the opening of the British spring offensive with his platoon.

18

April–May 1917, Arras: The Attack starts Easter Monday then moves to Monchy le Preux. Leave. Cambrai

The 9th April 1917 arrived, it was Easter Monday; preparations were complete, the three day preliminary bombardment was over. The Battle of Arras was underway.

Battalion War Diary:

9th April 1917, "Z" day: ARRAS
Zero hour 5 30 am. General attack was made S. of ARRAS to N. of VIMY RIDGE. The Bde. attacked with the 11th Bn. Middlesex on right, 7th Sussex on left. 9th R.F. behind Middlesex. 8th R.F. behind 7th Sussex.

Battn's objectives were (1) line of strong points from HOUDAIN LANE to HABARCO TRENCH, (2) HABARCO TRENCH, and (3) HULST TRENCH. All objectives taken together with about 220 prisoners and 2 machine guns.

Casualties. 1 Officer killed, 3 wounded; Other Ranks 117.

37th Inf. Bde. passed through us to attack the "BROWN LINE".

Sadler Account:

209. THE BATTLE OF ARRAS. Taking Positions. Preparing for Battle.
On the night of 8th of April, the eve of the great Battle, the Battalion left the Cellars by use of the Tunnels and took up positions in the Deep Dugouts to await 4 o'clock. Things that night were rather quiet in the way of shelling, as I think that we were trying to bluff Old Fritz into guessing what was awaiting him. Preparation for the Battle, early on Easter Monday morning was spent in taking up positions ready for starting off and waiting for the bombardment to commence.

On Easter Monday morning, myself and my working party moved, through the tunnels, to near Arras Station to wait until the first objective had been taken, then we were to start and make our Strong Points.

The most important thing in this sort of warfare was to try and escape the German Barrage which nearly always started a minute or so after ours and generally continued for a long time. Their Barrage was aimed just in front of our Front Line to stop reinforcements from following up. The Germans appeared greatly taken in at this Battle. At ten minutes to four, in the period before Zero Hour and starting off time, No Man's Land was a very busy place. Unknown to the Germans, the first line of our Troops to advance, went forward very quietly and lay close to the German Barbed Wire, and then the Second Line went forward and took their position close to them. Not a sound was heard by the Germans. When the Battle did start, both of the two lines of Troops advanced, together, as far as the German First Line. As we were quite sure the Germans would not shell their Front Line, these two lines escaped the German Barrage and, when these two lines did advance together, it was a sight that the Germans had never seen before. Talk about a Mass Attack; it proved pointless for any German to fire his rifle as our boys they were on them too soon.

210. THE BATTLE OF ARRAS. Battle commences. German Lights and Signals.

Just before the starting of the Battle, at five minutes to four, one might well have wondered to himself if there was a War on; everything was as quiet as could be and it was still dark. Then, on the signal of a very Heavy Gun firing two shells, it was like hell let loose. Every one of our guns sent out its "Message of Death"; not only every gun but every sort of Trench Mortar, both heavy and small, let forth. Also there was the rattle from the machine guns, stationed high in the tops of the houses, as they sent forth millions of bullets. The vibration caused by gunfire was so great that one could notice the trees shaking. In a very short time, smoke clung to the ground like a Gas Cloud and it became almost impossible to see ones hand in front of his face; our Lads were well after them by now. The Gunners on every gun were stripped off and working like niggers to keep Fritz supplied with our "Iron Rations". One would have thought that, if it wasn't for the Shellfire, there was a Fireworks Display going on.

211. THE BATTLE OF ARRAS. German lights and signals. A new kind of Battle. First Objective gained.

Whilst this was happening, the next sight we were to see was the Germans in distress. The Germans started by sending up their lovely Golden Spray. This went high into the air and sent forth dozens of golden stars. Next, came the Red Starlight, a beautiful Red Star used to signal to their troops that all of their Artillery is needed. Following this came their Green Star, which would burst into two Green Stars and meant to the Germans that their Shells were falling short. A large number of these beautiful lights were sent up together, in haste, but our Creeping Barrage was properly frightening the Germans. Up to this time, very few Germans, I would have thought, had had experienced the "pleasure" of watching such a terrible thing. It was not one bit of good for them to try and run away even after the Barrage had passed them. They would only run into death from the great amount of shrapnel bullets flying about. I think that never had the Germans received such a great fright and shock as they did this day. This Battle was a great pleasure to take part in compared to the "old" style of fighting which I had experienced. I can only say that, in comparison to the previous Battles which I had taken part in, this was like spending Easter Monday out on Hampstead Heath. As the Battle progressed, the First Line of Troops to advance, having taken their objective, gave the signal by lighting many Red Flares. This signalled the Second Line to start their advance and it also let our Airmen know how we were progressing. The Creeping Barrage was also stopped from playing a hundred yards in front of the First Objective. The Second Line then started walking to the Front and stopped at the First Objective until, at a given time, when the Creeping Barrage started again they passed through the First Line and followed up the Barrage until their Objective was gained. At this Line, which they were aiming to take, they met in with the German Light Batteries and received shells fired at them at point blank range. Far from pleasant but, unless there was a direct hit, these shells soon go sailing by. What I will say is that I noticed how well the Germans stuck to their guns this day and that they clung to their Strong Points fairly well. However it did them little good because they could see our Troops both to the Left and Right of them and that they also were getting to positions in their rear. This meant only one thing; they had to give themselves up.

212. THE BATTLE OF ARRAS. The German shelling of a Bridge close to our position.

The Station at Arras where we were positioned, ready for making Strong points, was a far from comfortable place to be due to the German shells bursting all around. At one stage we were very lucky that we were not blown to pieces. A hundred yards from us was a large Iron Bridge and under the Bridge was stored, "for cover", a very large supply of shells. Not long after the Battle started a German shell came over from a direction to the left and burst under the left side of the Bridge. It blew not only the shells but the Bridge, high towards the sky. Some of the Bridge was found a great distance away in Arras. The shock of this was terrible.

Also, nearby to our Cellar was a Battery of our 60 pounder Guns which was being used to greatly torment the Germans. The Germans were trying their hardest to find this Battery and it wasn't before too long before that they found it and managed to smash two of the Guns to pieces.

213. THE BATTLE OF ARRAS. Red Cross Station. On to the second Objective.

As soon as the Battle started, I wanted to get above the ground to see what was going on.

I soon managed this although, at times, I received some terrible frights from bursting shells etc.

As soon as the First Objective was gained, we pushed forward, going to the Front in small parties. On the way we passed hundreds and hundreds of German Prisoners and also a few of our walking wounded.

As we got nearer to the Front we could see that we had a German Barrage to get past but, as luck would have it, as we got nearer, the Barrage died down and we were able to carry on. One sight that took my eyes at this Battle was our Dressing Station which, nearby, had a large Red Cross Flag flying. This was a very good idea as there was no need to search Trench after Trench for assistance. Anyone requiring attention could make straight for the Flag. Whilst we were searching the Battlefield to find certain places to start making our Strong Points, I could not help taking notice of what, as one might have considered, the "Clean" Battlefield.

One had to go a great distance before finding a dead comrade. There was only one place which I noticed where six or seven had been caught by a German machine Gun and that was all. I also saw very few Germans lying dead even though a most terrible Battle, as regards Artillery fire, was taking place. At our part of the Front, very little loss of life took place, by this I mean of both our Troops and the

Battle of Arras, 9 April 1917. British infantry moving up to the front line
in support of the initial advance. Copyright IWM (Q 5115).

Germans. The Germans appeared only too pleased to give themselves up in order
to get out of the way of "Hell".

Many of these were so frightened that they were coming in our direction
without any one apparently in charge of them. After a short time of looking around,
we found the place at the First Objective where the first Strong Point had to be
made and we soon marked out the ground and started the work. After about
four hours this Strong Point was finished. Leaving here we again pushed forward,
reaching the top of the "High Ridge"; my Battalion's objective which was the
second objective in the Battle.

214. THE BATTLE OF ARRAS. Second Objective reached. Troop movements.
From the top of this Ridge we were able to look back and see what a splendid view
the Germans had of Arras. We could see all the high buildings, showing up above
all the rest including the Hotel de Ville, the building that had suffered so much. Here
we started making another Strong Point. Things were now rather quiet and we
had the pleasure of seeing the Troops keep coming forward to follow up the Battle.
The German Artillery was very quiet. They had had much of their light Artillery
taken from them and, no doubt, they were now moving their heavy Artillery to new
positions. Our Cavalry had taken up their positions in the rear of us only waiting for
the time to come to go forward. But they were not to be used on this day. After we

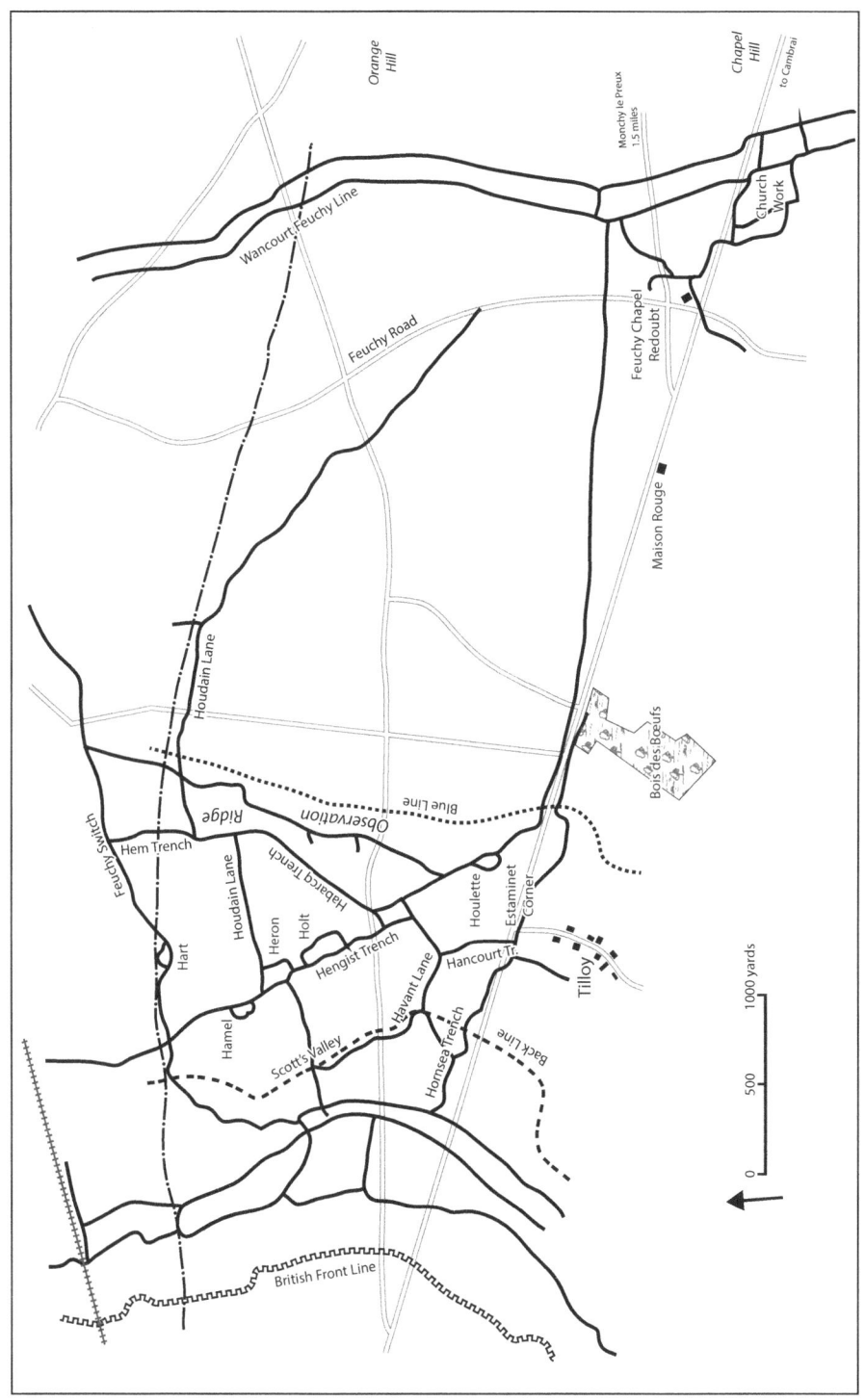

The Battle of Arras. (George Anderson)

had finished our task on top of the Ridge we left the Battlefield and returned to our resting-place for the night, the Hotel de Ville.

Battalion War Diary:

10th April 1917 ARRAS
Captured positions consolidated. 250 men "Standing To" to reinforce 37th Bde. if necessary. Snow storms most of the day. About seven dug-outs in German Front and Support Lines started exploding having been mined by the Enemy before evacuation. The H.Q. moved from German support line to GUILDFORD TRENCH.

For Sergeant Sadler, 10th April meant joining 249 other men on a march which would take them a few miles out of Arras to support 37th Brigade.

Sadler Account:

215. THE BATTLE OF ARRAS. Into Battle again. Lack of German fight. Tanks.
After a few hours rest, at daybreak on the 10th April, we received Orders that we were going forward again; this time to follow another Brigade of our Division. After breakfast we left our Cellars once more and took the main road running to Cambria and never left the road until we reached the place which was the site, for us, of the next stage of the Battle. Here we sat down and waited for the Battle to commence and prepared so that we could make a Strongpoint at this Battalion's Objective. Their Objective was positioned just this side of the little village of Monchy. This stage of the Battle started at 12-20 pm and, from what I saw of this part of our offensive, the Germans showed very little fight. At one particular German Line which they captured, looking at it, one would have thought that nothing had been required to done in order to capture it. This would not have been the case had the Germans really shown any fight. It had heaps of barbed wire entanglements in front of it which had been untouched by shellfire. In fact the charging Troops, from the 37th Division, had to look for places which had been pressed down by a tank or so, before they could actually get past this barbed wire. This day, one or two of our Tanks were on the Battlefield but they could not seem to get going and kept breaking down or going out of action. Hence the road, the Arras -Cambrai Road, which I mentioned, became their place of rest for the day. This day there was very little support from our Artillery as all Guns were moving forward. I did, though, notice one of our armoured motor cars doing some good work.

With all the shells which the Germans were sending after it, it still managed to carry on but I don't think it was ever to return as the Germans were eventually firing at it at point blank range. By this time, a battery of small Field Guns had come forward and the Cavalry were also standing to. Troops from a new Division had also come forward following the Division, which we were supporting, having taken all of its Objectives.

This new Division were to be passing through "my" Division and carrying the fight on. The Cavalry and this Field Battery were waiting to push forward with them in orders to keep the Germans on the run. However this was not to be.

216. THE BATTLE OF ARRAS. Monchy le Preux. The weather. A German dugout.
I could not help taking notice of the little village of Monchy. It was a grand little village; untouched by our shellfire, it had only had the Germans shelling all around it. The new Division which had arrived had now gone into Action, without the aid of our Artillery. With this Battle, it was Monchy which had to be taken. The Troops got into the village but were very soon driven out. They found many of the houses contained German machine guns and it was not long before they had to retire leaving the village still in German hands.

The Germans had reinforced and now had much more Artillery behind them. Up to this point, we had been carrying the Battle to the Germans. Now we had to come to the checking part and possible German counter attack. The weather also set in very badly and it was now snowing very hard.

While the Battle for the village was in full swing, a Royal Engineers Officer ordered me to take my men down a German dugout and to wait until they had pushed ahead. He showed me the dugout and said, "Take your men down there and the others can go down another entrance of the same dug-out". As the dugout had only just been captured, I thought it advisable to see if all was clear. Just near the dugout was a captured Battery of 5.9 Guns and by the doorway to the dugout were two German Bayonets; the only ones which I ever saw captured in this War. I said to my men, "Just stop up here for a minute or two whilst me and another man go down below and see that there are no Germans down there". This done, the two of us started below on our journey and we hadn't been below very long before we had one of the greatest surprises of our lives.

217. THE BATTLE OF ARRAS. Monchy le Preux. A German dugout. Two Germans and souvenirs.
We were walking along a passage when all of a sudden, we noticed, just in front of us, a German jack-boot shoot forward and we knew we didn't have time to play about so decided to rush them and rely on luck.

On doing this we found two Germans lying on two wire beds just behind the door. One of them had been hit with shrapnel across his chest but there was nothing the matter with the other one who said in English "Medicine", by which he meant to say that he was sick. In the dugout we also found, hung up on the walls, dozens of German Hand Grenades. I called down two men and told them to look after the Two Germans while we carried on with the search. I told them that if these Germans were to move then they were to shoot them dead, at once, no waiting. Then we started searching another passage running in another direction.

I went first, holding a lighted candle in my hand, with my comrade nearby ready for action if needed.

We ventured a great distance along the passageway but there were no more Germans to be seen.

We finished up at a German Telegraph Station and what a "grand" place it was; hundreds of pieces of wire in the Operating Room but with all the wires having been cut. When we returned towards our starting place, we found the remainder of the men looking around for souvenirs and there many were to be found: Watches, German Hats, Packs of German Playing Cards, rings etc. and dozens of boxes

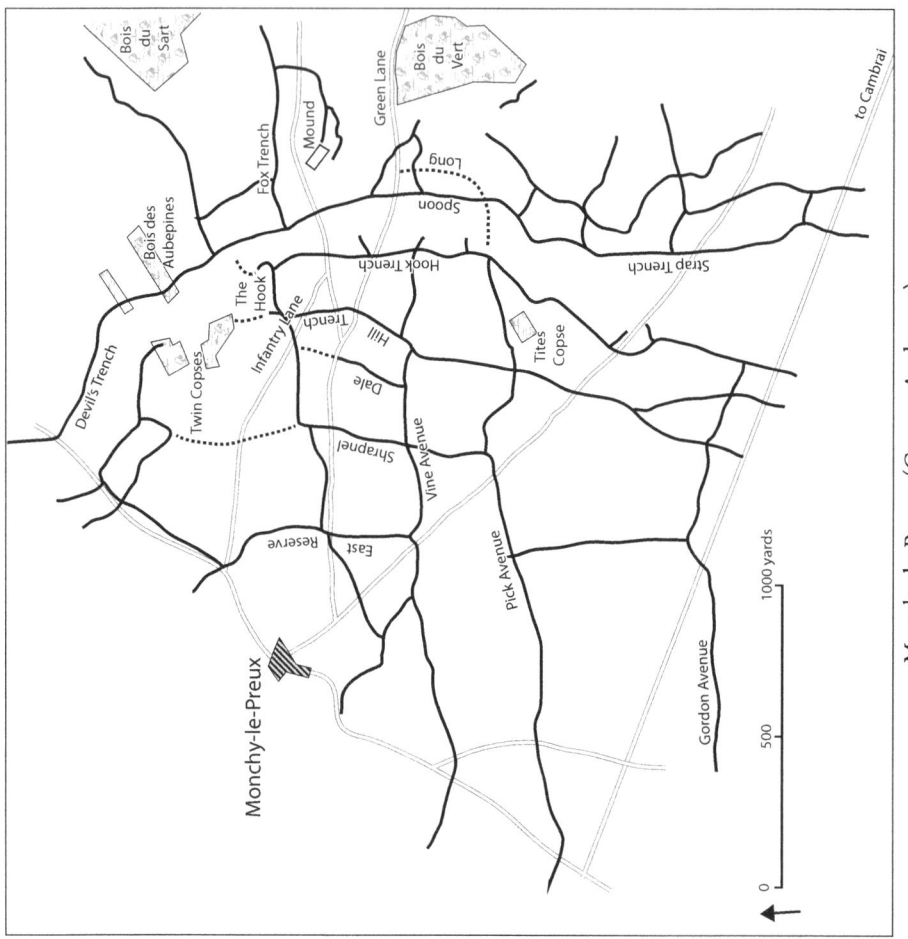

Monchy-le-Preux. (George Anderson)

of cigars. When we left this dugout, we took with us, plenty to smoke and many souvenirs. It was one of the finest German dugouts I had ever seen and it was quite easy for anyone to lose themselves walking around it. The two Germans were taken as prisoners by the Troops who had captured the ground.

218. THE BATTLE OF ARRAS. Weather. Strong Points. Back to Arras.

At about Three o'clock in the afternoon, we were called up to start making our Strong Point and it was snowing now as hard as I have ever seen it snow. This, in some ways, was very lucky for us, as we had to make our Strong Points just a short way off of the borders of Monchy. By this time, one or two of our Field Batteries had come to the Front and Monchy was beginning to get shelled by our guns and things began to get fairly lively. Soon, by hard work, we got a Trench dug and then felt safe under cover. After we had had the pleasure of a few hours' sleep and daybreak had arrived once more, Orders were sent around for us to return to our Battalion, the 9th Royal Fusiliers, at a given time so, after packing everything up, we set out on our journey to find them. The Battalion did not take much finding as they had been withdrawn to Reserves but they were not able to make themselves comfortable in the old German Front Line dugouts. One of the dugouts which had been held by the Brigade Signallers had "gone up" having been mined by the Germans before leaving and nearly all of the men were killed.

Battalion War Diary:

11th April 1917 ARRAS

Bn. moved forward up the CAMBRAI ROAD to take over part of the BROWN LINE from the 37th Bde. Two Coys. at FEUCHY CHAPEL and 2 bivouacking in the open about 300 yds. in the rear. Relief completed by 12 noon. At 6 00pm Orders received that Bn. had to move forward and take over part of the FRONT LINE held by the 112th Bde. Battn. in support, holding a line of Shell Holes from S. of village of MONCHY to the ARRAS-CAMBRAI ROAD. In position by 10 00 pm. Still much snow and rain.

Sadler account:

219. THE BATTLE OF ARRAS. Forward again. Monchy le Preux. Being Shelled. Bad weather.

I, and my party, had not returned for very long before we all received Orders that we were going forward again. At dinnertime we started on our journey and on the way passed Sir Douglas Haig, the Commander in Chief, who was saying a few cheerful words to many. We marched on until we reached some crossroads where we stopped in a large Quarry until more Orders were received. Towards tea-time we were given two bombs per man and I was told that we were going to attack the village of Monchy and we then waited for darkness in order to move forward. Between then and the time when we were to move up, we received a very hot time from the German Artillery. Shells were bursting everywhere except, fortunately, in our Quarry. They struck the edges around the Quarry and everyone was expecting to see one burst in the centre of us. How one of them never did, I can never make out. Later the shelling finished, dark set in and we moved forward by Platoons and took cover for the night in shell holes just outside the village. I doubt if anyone could have received a more uncomfortable night. The snow was four to five inches deep but after moving as much of the snow as possible, we lay down to sleep. In the shell hole, our so called place of "rest", there were six of us who had to attempt to lie down, this proving very difficult so, in the end, we decided that three of us would lie at the bottom of the hole and the other three would lie across the others. In this way we did our best to make ourselves comfortable but as soon as one had fallen to sleep, someone would shout, "Get up, I've got cramp".

If I got up once during that night owing to that complaint, I got up a hundred times. I was jolly glad when daylight arrived and to see that our luck had turned. We found out that we were not required.

220. THE BATTLE OF ARRAS. Monchy le Preux. Not required. Being shelled.

The village had been taken but, owing to the German shelling, all communications had been cut off.

The Battle had taken place over the time that we receiving the "shelling" whilst we in the Quarry.

Our Cavalry had also been in Action for the first time and they had received a very great shock by getting caught in several German Barrages. Horses were returning in large numbers many without riders but, as long as one of the horses had a rider, then the others would follow. It had turned out to be a terrible time for them and, whilst we were stationed in these Shell Holes, we could see many horses just wandering about between our Lines and the Germans. Whilst we were in these holes, there was very little, with regards to Shellfire from the Germans, however at one time we nearly got blown out by our own Artillery. This was reported to our Commanding Officer and a message was soon sent to the rear and the shelling was stopped.

Our shells were seemingly nowhere as good as the German ones with regard to what they were made for. They certainly made a terrible noise coming towards us and when they hit the ground a little earth was sent into the air but there was no crash on exploding like the German shells, nevertheless they were quite enough for us.

221. THE BATTLE OF ARRAS. Monchy le Preux. Back to Arras. Sleep.

Just before tea time this day, a very large mine went up on the outskirts of Monchy which had been timed and set by the Germans. This gave us a little shaking and did much damage to a Regiment stationed close by. After tea, this night, we left for Arras. Fresh Troops had arrived to try and push forward again. It was not a very comfortable journey for us as we were making for Arras as, at times, the Germans opened short and sharp burst of Shellfire on the roads. One could not have seen more traffic on the roads in London, at is busiest, than that which was on this road. Guns, Transport and Troops going towards the Front Line on one side and the Troops who were being relieved, along with their Transport, on the other side of the road.

This night we were to finish up under some caves under Arras.

Battalion War Diary:

12th April 1917. ARRAS./ (MONCHY).
At 3 00pm orders received that Division was being relieved that night. Bn. was not relieved by any other troops but marched off about 8 30pm. to ARRAS. Quartered in the RONVILLE CAVES. Battn. H.Q. Cellar 33 PETITE PLACE.

Sadler Account:

221. THE BATTLE OF ARRAS.(Cont.) Monchy le Preux. Back to Arras. Sleep.
That night we returned to Arras, to our place of rest.

It wasn't long before we were served out with something to eat and drink also given a much needed blanket to keep us warm. After we had had finished our food and drink, we soon settled down for a sleep and, for once in some while, we were able to feel quite safe against shell fire, being so far underground.

This sleep was greatly enjoyed by all and it was a case of them having to call us the next day when breakfast was ready. In the caves it was pitch black except for our own lamps and one was none the wiser as to whether it was daytime or night-time up above. With such a good sleep being quite a change for us, we wouldn't have worried if they had forgotten breakfast for once and just let us sleep on.

The next day, 13th April, was spent in doing as we wished and we were then able to get another good night's sleep.

Battalion War Diary:

13th April 1917. ARRAS
Resting and cleaning up as far as possible.

But on the 14th, the Battalion was on the move again, out of Arras and heading to Mondicourt, for a period of respite, away from the Front Line.

14th April 1917. ARRAS
Marching at 8 30 am. Battn. moved from ARRAS to LATTRE-ST QUENTIN where we billeted for the night.

Sadler Account:

222. THE BATTLE OF ARRAS. Rest from Battle. Germans re-grouped. Rifle Trench.
The following day we were leaving Arras for a short rest. It was slightly different marching away from Arras as opposed to what it had been like marching towards Arras to do Battle. We were able to have our Band in the centre of the Battalion and swing through Arras Station where, only a day or so before, it hadn't been safe for any man to stay in that area for two minutes because of amount of shellfire. After a

long march we finished up at a little village named Mondicourt where we spent ten days and the Battalion also received a few more reinforcements.

Battalion War Diary:

15th April 1917. LATTRE-ST-QUENTIN
Marching at 7 30am. Battn. moved to MONDICOURT. Battn. H.Q. billet. Draft of 86 other ranks arrived in evening about 8 30pm.

16th April 1917. MONDICOURT
Cleaning Up, re-clothing etc.

17th to 21st April 1917. MONDICOURT.
Parades in the morning for Physical Training, arm drill and squad drill.

22nd April 1917. MONDICOURT.
Divine Service in Recreation Room. Draft of 126 Other Ranks arrived from support Bn. about 8 30pm.

23rd April 1917. MONDICOURT.
Marching at 8 30am the Brigade moved to WANQUENTIN. Arrived about 3 00pm and were billeted for the night.

24th April 1917. WANQUENTIN.
Starting at 3 30pm the Battn. moved en masse to ARRAS. 3 Coys. billeted in SCHRAMM BARRACKS and 1 Coy. in MAISON d'ASSISTANCE, PLACE de la PREFECTURE. Bn. H.Q. being RUE de la TERREE de CITE.

25th April 1917. ARRAS.
Bn. marched off at 8 45 pm. Went through Station to the Cemetery thence along Railway to just East of FEUCHY. Turned South along the road. Took over part of the BROWN LINE & HALIFAX TRENCH from 10th Bn. Lancashire Fusiliers. Brigade in support of 35th Brigade which is holding the Front Line.

Sadler Account:

222. THE BATTLE OF ARRAS (cont). Germans re-grouped. Rifle Trench.
Once our ten days here had ended, we made for the Arras Battlefield once more, staying in the Cavalry Barracks at Arras for one night, the 24th, and then proceeding to the Front the following night.

This time we found that the Germans had properly checked our advance and the old style of fighting had to be employed once more with the taking a little bit of Trench at a time instead of thousands of yards. The German Shellfire was terrible. Several people in command had been frightened by messages sent along the Lines that the Germans were massing on the Ridge in order to drive us back and regain the land won earlier. We were then soon to go into Action to get to the top of the Ridge.

Battalion War Diary:

26th April 1917. ARRAS.
Officers patrol sent out in the morning to reconnoitre Front held by the 35th Brigade.

27th April 1917. ARRAS.
Orders received that Bn. was to be in readiness to move forward if required to support in attack being made by the 35th Bde.

28th April 1917. ARRAS.
35th Brigade attacked at 4 30am and recaptured RIFLE & BAYONET TRENCH. Bn. still "Standing To" but no orders to move received.

29th April 1917. ARRAS.
Carrying Party of 150 provided in evening for 35th Brigade.

30th April 1917. ARRAS.
Bn. relieved the 9th Bn. Essex Regiment in support, marching at 8 30pm. Order of Coys. "C" on Right, "A" in Centre, "B" on Left. "D" Coy. lent to O-in-C 8th Royal Fusiliers who were holding Front line.

1st May 1917. ARRAS. Lancer Lane Trenches
Fairly Quiet Day.

2nd May 1917. ARRAS. Lancer Lane Trenches.
Orders received that Bde. was to attack in the morning in conjunction with 37th Bde. on right and in conjunction with the Companys on our left. 9th R.F. were to be on the Right. 8th R.F. on the Left. 7th Sussex in Support, 11th Middlesex in Reserve. Battalion moved off at midnight to take up assaulting positions.

Sadler Account:

223. THE BATTLE OF ARRAS. Germans reinforced. Trying to consolidate. Second Leave.
It appeared that no one seemed to know much about what was going on. This action, on the 3rd. was to cost the Battalion all of its Officers, except two, and nearly half of the men of our Battalion and this just to take a little bit of Trench called Rifle Trench. The Germans were then to make it hell for us until other Troops went into Action on our Right and Left and managed to drive them clean off the Ridge. After this it didn't appear to matter which Troops attacked the Germans, they all met with the same fate. The Germans had gained reinforcements and it now appeared as if we were charging at a stone wall. All we could do was hold on to our newly won position which we did and we consolidated the position then for approximately the next twenty-five days. We worked four days in the Front Line and

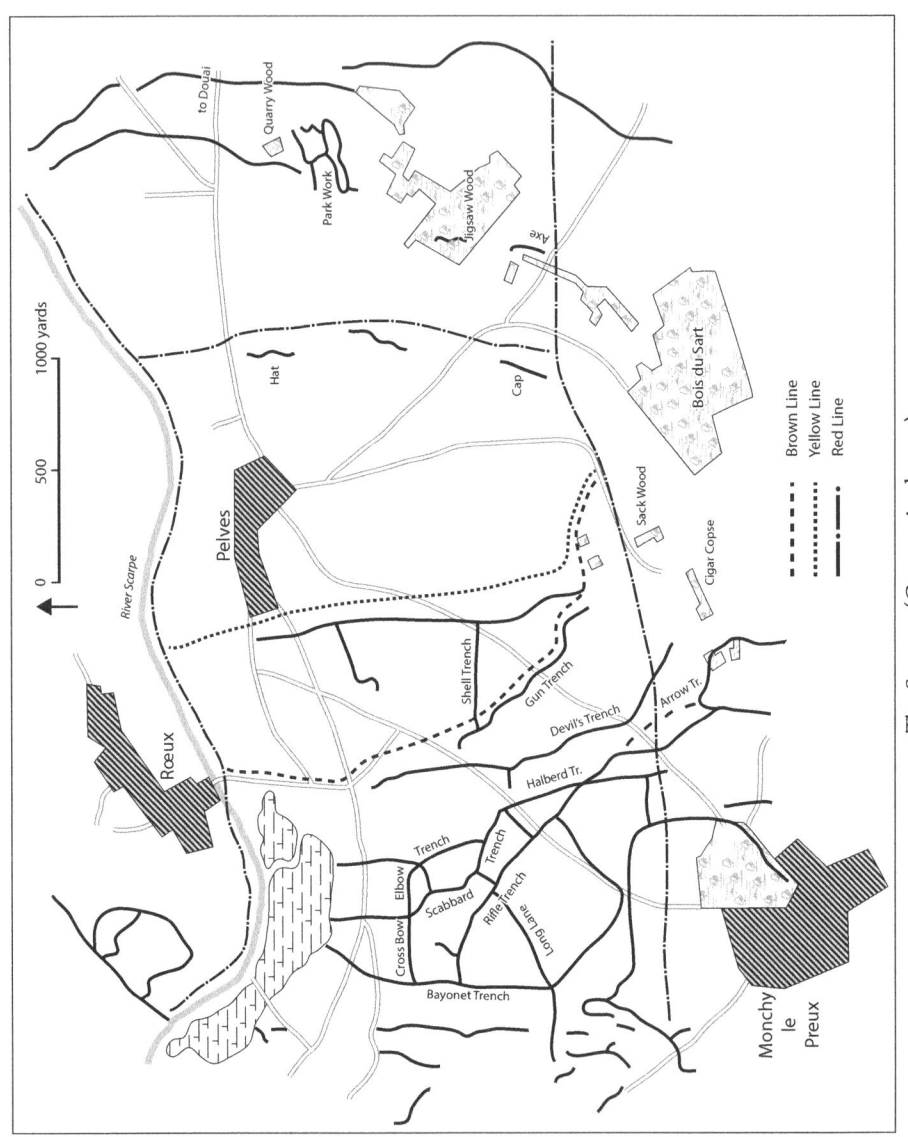

The Scarpe. (George Anderson)

then four days in each of the following Lines which we knew as the Orange Line and Purple Line. In the end we were, what one might call, "Battle worn". However, the Germans little knew that another Great Battle [Passchendaele] and attack was being organised and about to commence at the other end of the British Line. Battalion War Diary:

3rd May 1917. ARRAS TRENCHES.
Battalion in position by 2 45am in BAYONET TRENCH and RIFLE TRENCH (South of ROEUX on S. of Scarpe). Zero hour 3 45am. Objectives of Bn., a portion of RIFLE TRENCH between our right and left of 37th Bde. still held by enemy and SCABBARD TRENCH: BROWN LINE along the ridge in front. 2 Platoons of "A", 2 Platoons of "B" with 2 Platoons of "D", as "moppers", attacked as first wave and reached SCABBARD TRENCH, (with the 8th. Bn. on our left), from PELVES LANE to HARNESS LANE. First wave, (less "moppers"), with remaining Platoons of "A","B" and "D" Coys. as 2nd Wave went on to attack the BROWN LINE where they established themselves. Enemy was reinforced and came up PELVES LANE into SCABBARD TRENCH. 8th Bn. and ourselves were bombed out but we held the C.T. (NEW TRENCH) running from SCABBARD to RIFLE TRENCH. In the meantime, "C" Coy. engaged the enemy still in RIFLE TRENCH with bombs & Lewis Guns. After a hard fight they were driven out and Communication with 37th Bde. was established. At 12 00 noon our Artillery placed a barrage on SCABBARD TRENCH for 10 minutes. 2 Coys. of the 7th Sussex then attacked and captured it. On account of the enemy regaining SCABBARD TRENCH, our people who had gone on to the BROWN LINE were cut off and some of them taken prisoners. In the evening they re-joined the Bn. and informed us that they had been marching on the road to DOUAI when they were caught under our own M.G. fire. The enemy rapidly dispersed and our people were enabled to escape. At 9 45pm under cover of Artillery fire, strong patrols were pushed out towards the BROWN LINE. They came under heavy M.G. and rifle fire. At midnight the Bde. on our right not having advanced and the Companies on our left not having attained ROEUX and the high ground around our flanks in the BROWN LINE were up in the air and the General ordered a withdrawal to SCABBARD TRENCH with strong points in front as our Outpost Line. Trenches consolidated & work on the Strong points continued. CASUALTIES:- Major M.E.COXHEAD (Commanding the Bde.) Killed; Capt. J MacFARLANE. Wounded; Lt. T.B.JONES & 2nd Lt. D.C.FRASER, Missing; 2nd. Lt. RAWLINGS, 2nd. Lt. BURRDETT, 2nd. Lt. HINTON and 2nd. Lt. WOOD. Wounded; – Estimated Casualties -250 O.Ranks. 40 prisoners of 6th S.R. 9th Res. Div. & 2 M.G.'s captured. Many killed. Capt. W.V.L. VAN SOMEREN took over Command of Bn.

4th May 1917. ARRAS TRENCHES
Enemy and our own snipers very busy all day. Intermittent Artillery fire. At evening "Stand To" the Enemy was reported to be massing in the BROWN LINE for Counter Attack. He was dispersed by Artillery, Machine Gun and Lewis Gun fire. Owing to the losses of the 8th and 9th, the two Battalions were combined into one composite Bn. under command of Lieut. Col. ELLIOTT COOPER of the 8th Bn. Starting at

9 30pm, Composite Bn. was relieved by 11th Middx. Regt. Battalion moved back to Trenches in the valley near the gun pits E. of ORANGE HILL. Bn. H.Q. in the Gun pits. Trenches occupied heavily shelled during the night with 5.9's.

5th May 1917. ARRAS TRENCHES
Fairly quiet day. Intermittent shelling.. After dark ½ Bn. moved to trenches in LANCER LANE where we were before moving up for the attack.

6th May 1917. ARRAS TRENCHES
Heavy artillery fire by both sides about 5 00am. Nothing followed. Half the Bn. still in the valley again shelled pretty heavily at night so they were ordered to move to LANCER LANE.

7th May 1917. ARRAS TRENCHES
About 7 00am enemy sent over a large amount of gas shells. One fell in the Trench at LANCER LANE and gassed 3 of our men. 8th and 9th R.F. Bn.'s again separated into different units. Starting at 9 30pm we were relieved by the 7th East Surrey Regt. On relief moved back to RAILWAY TRIANGLE. The Col. came up from ARRAS and took over command of the Bn.

The return to Arras came none too soon. Battle weary, along with his other comrades in the depleted Battalion, Acting Sergeant James Sadler, recalled this:

223. THE BATTLE OF ARRAS.(cont.) Return to Arras and rest once more
When we had finished our twenty-five days, we again left for Arras where we spent two days. During this time we had a great treat by having a bath and clean change of clothes and not, I might say, before time as it was much needed.

Battalion War Diary:

8th May 1917. ARRAS RLY. TRIANGLE.
Busy reorganising & re-equipping the men. Whole Battalion bathed in the baths at GRANDE PLACE ARRAS.

9th May 1917. ARRAS RLY.TRIANGLE.
Reinforcements of 2 Officers and 20 men arrived. Officers- new to the Country. Men-, mostly old Bn. men.

10th May 1917. ARRAS RLY.TRIANGLE.
Starting at 8 15pm. Bn. moved up to the Front Line and relieved the 5th Royal Berks. in sector of Right Bde.

11th May 1917. ARRAS TRENCHES.
1 Platoon of the 8th R.F. attached to us. Bn. H.Q. MONCHY WOOD. Intermittent shelling throughout the day. At 7 30pm people on our right and left made an attack. Enemy brought down a fairly heavy barrage along the ridge in front of MONCHY.

On the left the CEMETERY & CHEMICAL WORKS at ROEUX were captured with 500 prisoners including a Bn. Capt. On the right, TOOL TRENCH was captured with 9 prisoners. Many killed. One wounded prisoner of the 19th. R.I.R. was captured by us. Bn. was relieved by 11th Middlesex. On relief moved back to the GUN LIME PITS.

12th May 1917. ARRAS TRENCHES
At 6 00pm, 11th Middlesex attacked DEVIL'S TRENCH together with people on right and left. Bn. in support if required.

13th May 1917. ARRAS TRENCHES
Yesterday's attack not successful but Bn. not called upon to support. Bn. relieved by 11th Middlesex. On relief moved to ORANGE LINE.

14th May 1917. ARRAS TRENCHES
Slight shelling at intervals during the day.

15th May 1917. ARRAS TRENCHES
Bn. moved back to ARRAS in the evening. Billeted in RUE D'AMIENS& RUE de la TERRE de CITE.

16th May 1917. ARRAS
Day spent in cleaning up and re-clothing the men.

17th May 1917. ARRAS
Marching at 3 30am. Battalion moved to GOUVES via DAINVILLE & WAGNONLIEU. Arrived in Billets 10 30am. Breakfasts en route.

18th May 1917. GOUVES.
Cleaning up and re-organising.

19th May 1917. GOUVES.
Physical Training. Arm Drill. Squad Drill & Musketry.

Sadler account:

223. THE BATTLE OF ARRAS.(cont.) Away from the front. Parading and Leave.
After getting freshened up we again left for the village of Gouves. The first day was spent in cleaning ourselves up and resting. The second day we had to "Blanco" our equipment and make ourselves smart for a coming G.O.C. Parade. Not being able to obtain any "Blanco" for the work we had to fall back on using clay.

Having got all my equipment into pieces and wet with water and clay, I then received Orders to parade at the Battalion Head-Quarters at two o'clock with everything that I possessed and to be ready to start for leave in England. Although a terrible scramble had to take place, I made sure that I was there in plenty of time.

For the next ten days Sergeant Sadler experienced a more than welcome home front leave away from army routine and the inevitable return to the firing line.

19

May 1917-February 1918: From Arras to England and back again, Becoming an Instructor

Sergeant Sadler returned from leave, his first since autumn 1916, on 20th May 1917.

223. THE BATTLE OF ARRAS(cont.). Leave to return home.

On the 19th May, after a long drag to the nearest Railhead, I was soon on the road for Blighty; heading for my 2nd period of Leave from the Front. As things were more up to date this time, it was a fairly comfortable journey and another happy ten days were spent in England. But, once again, at the end of this, England had to be left behind and I was returning back to the Battlefields of France.

224. BACK TO FRANCE. Return to France. Sus-St-Leger and Arras.

Arriving back in France; this time I found my Regiment stationed at Sus-St-Leger for a short rest.

Myself, I was ordered to carry on as Orderly Sergeant and as the heat during the day was very great, long Route Marches were only carried out very early in the morning in full Marching Order but, nevertheless, still wearing Steel helmets. In every march which took place, Steel Helmets still had to be worn. As if we didn't have to wear them enough whilst in the Trenches or near the Line! We had the pleasure, whilst at this Village, of attending the Divisional Sports, 8th June, but not long after we were, again, instructed that we would be on the way back to the Arras Battlefield.

Battalion War Diary:

20th May 1917. GOUVES.
Open Air Service in the morning. Voluntary Service in the evening.

21st May 1917. GOUVES.
Section Drill, Bombing, Musketry.

22nd May 1917. GOUVES.
Platoon Drill, Bayonet Fighting, Bombing. Brigade GYMKHANA postponed on account of wet weather.

23rd May 1917. GOUVES.
P.T., Platoon Drills and Musketry. At 4 00pm the 8th & 9th Bns. Paraded at AGNEZ

for presentation by Div. General of medal ribbons awarded for the operations on the 9th April. The following were presented:-

D.C.M. Sgt T.H. BATT "C" Coy.; 62292 Sgt F.GREENING "C" Coy.

MILITARY MEDAL. 13805 Sgt A.MITCHELL "A" Coy.; 11519 Sgt T.PIMBLETT "C" Coy.; 16417 Cpl P.CARTLEDGE. "D" Coy.; Pte. F.LAMBERT "D" Coy. (Brigade Orderly).

The following N.C.O.s were also awarded the Military Medal for the same operation:-

32300 Cpl A.BIFFEN. "A" Coy. (Wounded). 211 Sgt W.BALL. "A" Coy. (Killed). 3104 Cpl F.STUBBINGS. "C" Coy, 60508 Pte. C.REED. "A" Coy (Missing). 2nd Lieutenant A.E.SIDWELL awarded the Military Cross.

The following Officers, W.O. and N.C.O have been mentioned in Dispatches for their gallant conduct in the Field.:- Major M.E. COXHEAD. (Killed in action); Q.M. and Hon. Lt. G.T.SHELLEY M.C.; 6200 C.S.M. T.W.GRIGGS; Pte. C.W.BLAY.

24th May 1917. GOUVES.
Marching at 7 30am Battn. moved to SUS-ST-LEGER via MONTENESCOURT-HABARCQ-AVESNES-GRANDE RULLECOURT. Arrived at Billets at 12 30pm.

25th May 1917. SUS-ST-LEGER.
Cleaning Up. Coy. Drill and Musketry. Football.

26th May 1917. SUS-ST-LEGER.
Physical training. Coy. Drill. Musketry & Bayonet fighting. 53 O.R. arrived from Depot as reinforcements.

27th May 1917. SUS-ST-LEGER.
Brigade Church Parade in LUCHEUX Woods.

28th May 1917. SUS-ST-LEGER.
Coy. Drill. Bombing, Musketry.

29th May 1917. SUS-ST-LEGER.
Bn. Drill & Bayonet fighting. In the evening Bn. held Sports. Divisional Band was in attendance.

30th May 1917. SUS-ST-LEGER.
Coy. Drill, Musketry, Bombing, Rifle Grenades.

31st May 1917. SUS-ST-LEGER.
Bn. paraded at 8 30am for Route March.

1st June 1917. SUS-ST-LEGER.
Physical training, Bombing, Musketry, Bayonet Fighting.

2nd June 1917. SUS-ST-LEGER.

Bde. Horse Show & GYMKHANA at GRAND RULLECOURT. Bn. won the following places:- 1st. in Cooker Competition; 2nd. in Officers Chargers; 2nd. in Limited Competitions; 2nd. in N.C.O.'s Mounted Competition; 1st. Mess Cart Competition; 1st. Water Cart Competition: 1st. in Officer's Jumping .

3rd June 1917. SUS-ST-LEGER.

Bde. Parade service on the Football Ground at 11 00am. Following N.C.O.'s and men awarded the Military Medal for operations on the 3rd. May:- 40470 Cpl M.E.HART; 4606 Cpl G.WILLIAMS; 10753 Pte. J.HORNET; 4060 Pte. A.L.GUISE; 42357 Pte. C.S.PICKETT; 12014 Pte. A.GREEN.

4th June 1917. SUS-ST-LEGER.

2 Coys. on the Range. 1 coy. on Bombing Ground. 1 Coy. Musketry. Coy. Drill. Arms Drill.

Bde. Sports on football ground in the afternoon. Bn. won the following events and gained places as shown:-

Hurdles: 1st. Sgt Wood, 2nd. L.Cpl. Scobie.; 440 Yds.: 1st. Sgt. Bloyes.; 880 yds.: 1st. 2nd Lt. G.Ln. C.Bandairro. 2nd. Sgt Bloyes.; Long Jump: 2nd. Pte. Burden; High Jump: 1st. Pte. Burden, 2nd. Pte. Dyer; Relay Race; 1st.- Won by 2nd Lt. G.Ln. C Bandairro, Sgt. Bloyes, Sgt. Wood, Drummer Andrews. Tug of War:- (one pull all over) First Round. Easy Pull against M.G. Coy. Second Round:- Pulled over the 11th Middx. Regt. after a hard 12 minute pull.

5th June 1917. SUS-ST-LEGER.

2 Coys. on the Range. 1 Coy. on Bombing Ground. 1 Coy. Bayonet Fighting &. Musketry. Coy Drill. Reinforcements of 6 Officers arrived.

6th June 1917. SUS-ST-LEGER.

2 Coys. on Training area- attack in Open Warfare. 1 Coy. on Bombing Ground, 1 Coy. Bayonet fighting, Bombing & Coy. Drill.

R.S.M. A. STICKLAND awarded the Military Cross for Gallantry in the Field.

7th June 1917. SUS-ST-LEGER.

Route March at 6 30am through WERGNY, LUCHEUX & LUCHUEX WOODS. Bde. Boxing Competition in evening. First Round of Bde. Knockout Football Tournament. Beat the 8th R.F.'s by 4 goals to 0.

FINAL of Tug of War. Pulled over 7th Royal Sussex Regt. after 6 minute pull.

8th June 1917. SUS-ST-LEGER.

Bn. Drill Musketry & Bombing. R.E. Officer instructed Coys. in placing out Working parties. In the afternoon Divisional Sports in Chateau Ground. GRAND ROLLECOURT. Bn. represented the Bde. in the following events & gained places as shown:- High Jump :- 2nd. Place; 880yds:- 2nd. Place; 1 Mile:- 3rd. Place; ¼ mile:- 2nd. Place; Relay Race;- 2nd Place. TUG-O-WAR Semi Final. Pulled over the Northants Pioneers Bn.; Final: Pulled over the 5th Norfolk's after a 4 minute pull. Hurdles and

100 yds.- No Places. Reinforcements of 1 Officer arrived.

9th June 1917. SUS-ST-LEGER.
2 Coy's. attack training in Open Warfare. 2 Coys. on the Range.

10th June 1917. SUS-ST-LEGER.
Parade Service in the morning. 9 30am. Beat M.G. Coy in Semi-Final Brigade Knock Out Football Competition. Score 6-0.

11th June 1917. SUS-ST-LEGER.
2 Coys. on Range. 2 Coys. attack practice in Trenches.

12th June 1917. SUS-ST-LEGER.
2 Coys. on Range. 2 Coys. attack practice in Trenches. Divisional Horse Show and Gymkhana in afternoon at GRANDE RULLECOURT. Battalion represented Brigade and gained places as shown in the following events:-
      Water Cart: – 1st. Cookers: – 1st. Back Games: – 2nd. Limbers: – 3rd.

13th June 1917. SUS-ST-LEGER.
2 Coys. on Range. 2 Coys.-Drill, Bombing & Bayonet Fighting, In the Final of the Brigade football we beat 11th Middx. Regt. Score 1-0. Very good game.

14th June 1917. SUS-ST-LEGER.
Short Route March in morning. In the afternoon the Brigade paraded at SUR for presentation by Divisional Commander of Medal Ribbons. The following were presented: – Military Cross: – C.S.M. A.Brickland; Military Medal & French Croix de Guerre: – 11510 Sgt T Gamblera, 3104 Cpl A. Surridge. Military Medal: – 4560 Lt.Cpl. A.Rivers, 62387 Pte. C.S.Gaskell, 60470 Pte. H.S.Hart, 13204 Pte. A. Green.

15th June 1917. SUS-ST-LEGER.
2 Coys. on Range. 2 Coys. Drill, Bombing & Musketry. 3 New Officers joined Bn.

16th June 1917. SUS-ST-LEGER.
2 Coys. on Range. 2 Coys. Drill, Bombing & Bayonet fighting. Major W.V.L. Van Someren awarded M.C.. Sgts. Buckland and Watson awarded D.C.M. for operations on May 3rd.

17th June 1917. SUS-ST-LEGER.
Marching at 6 00am Bn. moved to GOUVES via GRANDE RULLECORT and AVESNES. Arrived Billets 9 30am.

18th June 1917. GOUVES.
Marching at 8 30pm. Bn. moved to ARRAS. In billets at 9 00am. Men billeted in SCHRAMM BARRACKS. Bn. H.Q. No. 29 PLACE de la PREFECTURE.

Sadler account:

224. BACK TO FRANCE (cont.) Illness.

I was not to reach the Battlefield this time. A good deal of sickness broke out in my Company. We had just managed to reach the Cavalry Barracks at Arras when a Sergeant said to me that he felt bad and I was feeling just about the same myself. I said to him, "Go and have a lie down, I will carry on and do what little there is to do". At 4 o'clock, I had to organise my Platoon for Inspection and I was feeling so ill that I didn't know what to do with myself. After I had carried out the Inspection of the Platoon with the Orderly Officer and the Platoon had been dismissed; I returned to the Barracks to have a sleep.

225. ARRAS. BACK TO ENGLAND. Illness. Hospitalised in England. A return to France again?

That night, the Medical Officer was called to attend to the other Sergeant and, whilst he was doing this, another Sergeant who was with the Medical Officer, asked me, "How are you tonight?" I said that I was alright to which his reply was that it was no good to say that you feel alright when clearly you are not. When I was inspected by the Medical Officer, I was found to be suffering with what was thought to be Trench Fever and I was ordered a hot drink of tea and a rest.

I was told to stay quiet until a Red Cross Car arrived to take both of us to Hospital. After spending a very restless night, and with no car arriving, I decided to take a walk around. When the Sergeant Major of my Company asked me how I felt, I told him that I was feeling much better and really had no great wish to be taken away as it was my turn to go on a General Course. This Course usually lasted five weeks and, as I had only missed three or four days out of the Trenches in two years, I had begun to look forward to it as a great change. However, not long after the Car arrived and so both of us were taken off to Hospital.

225. ARRAS. BACK TO ENGLAND (continued). Hospital in England and a return to France again?

A very few days later, I was in back in England at the Norfolk War Hospital undergoing some electrical treatment followed by a few weeks of being very carefully looked after and undergoing further treatment.

I left there for Aldeburgh Military Hospital to get "polished off " and made ready for Action once more, and then sent, on 18th August 1917, for ten days "sick leave" before, what I thought, was going to be my return to France. After spending a very enjoyable ten days, I returned for my departure from Dover where, as I said, I expected to leave shortly for France once more. This was not to be.

Thus began Sergeant Sadler's eight month absence from the firing line:

226. BACK HOME IN ENGLAND. No return to the Trenches. An Instructor's Course. Dover bombed.

I was not to return to the Trenches for some time, instead I was to have the pleasure of going on an Instructor's Course in England gaining a First Class Instructors Certificate. Following that, I was used as an Army instructor for some time, occasionally getting reminded that a war was still on by the Germans bombing

Dover over the time that I was stationed there. From what I could see of the first German Air Raids that took place, there appeared to be very little notice taken of them. Whenever these Raids occurred, usually at night, we received Orders to dress, lie on our beds until the Germans, having dropped all their bombs, returned and then we went back to bed. I had not been in Dover long before these bombing raids were carried out nearly every night and, at that stage, the Defences of Dover began to improve. From then on, whenever the Germans carried out their raids they met with plenty of Shellfire which, very often, put them off course.

One night whilst I was in Dover we received a bombardment from a German Destroyer. A chum woke me up and asked me what was going on; to which I replied that I thought it was only a gun practice which was very often the case in and around Dover. It wasn't that long after when we heard a shell whistle close by but we took very little notice of this and only fell to sleep once again. We found out the next day the Germans had bombed the place during the night killing one person, a little girl. I had two very narrow escapes from dropping bombs; it appeared that the War and Danger were intent on following me about.

The Dover air raid occurred on 16 February 1918. Thirteen-year-old Gertrude Boorman was the young female victim.

Sergeant Sadler's unexpected absence resulted in his missing long months of trench warfare followed by 12th Division's participation in the Battle of Cambrai (20 November – 7 December 1917). The surprise tank assault supported by a novel predicted artillery barrage breached the vaunted Hindenburg Line thus causing the German high command serious concern. A subsequent German counter-attack (30 November) managed to recapture most of the lost ground, after which both sides consolidated.

Back in Blighty, it is hard to imagine that James ever let a day go by without thinking of his comrades in 9th Royal Fusiliers. Having missed only three or four days out of the line in two years, he was still inexorably linked to the Battalion.

20

March-April 1918: Selected for a Draft and back to France again. Facing the German Offensive – Operation Michael

T he beginning of 1918 found G.321 Sergeant James Sadler M.M., a qualified 1st. Class instructor, still in Great Britain. Initially selected for a draft in early January, he was, nevertheless, due to circumstances arising from the demand for trained NCOs at home, destined to remain in Blighty for the time being.

227. LIFE BACK IN ENGLAND. Warned for the Draft. A 1st. Class Instructor. Training NCOs

I had only been told a day or so previously that I need not worry about going to the Front Line as they considered I had done my bit and deserved a rest. Nevertheless after being warned for a Draft, I took my place with a good heart. I received Orders then to return to my work but I was not anxious to do so because I thought that if I was to be returning to France, I might just as well go sooner rather than later.

In order to make sure I didn't have go, I was ordered to go before the Commanding Officer where he gave me a fine address. He said that he was sorry to think that men with my service at the Front, without a break, should be compelled to return to France when there were a great number of men who had never left the shores of England. I was asked then to remain and carry on with my work for six weeks owing to the Officer in Charge of the Instructors having been injured by falling and reopening an old wound and I was the only First Class Instructor in the place at that time. The new Officer who was due to be taking the injured Officer's place for the time being, wanted a First Class Instructor to stand by him and I was selected.

I let the Commanding Officer know, however, that I was not afraid to take my place in the "Draft" and, whilst I was doing the six weeks, I had the pleasure to instruct several hundred N.C.O.'s from the Training Battalions who had been in the Army nearly as long as myself but who had never crossed the Channel.

One day, one N.C.O. asked me, "Had I ever been across to France?" to which I quickly replied, "Yes".

He then said "From what I see of things, one is just as well off out there as being here" to which I was soon to reply, "Have you just found that out?" I told him, "If and when my turn came to take my place again in another Draft, then the Commanding Officer would not, and should not, stand in my way".

228. RETURN TO FRANCE. Drafted again. Armentières via. Folkestone.

In the meantime I had picked up with a chum of mine, a Sergeant from the same Company as myself.

We had served together in France for nearly two years and I intended to go over there, again, with him.

I instructed N.C.O.s of my own Draft until they had finished their training and then I was fit and ready to take my place on the Battlefields once more. After our training had finished we were given five days leave and I spent five of the happiest days of my life making sure that, if I were unfortunate enough not to return then, they would be five days which I would be able to remember happily, as I was facing my death.

When my time was up, I returned to my Depot and spent two more enjoyable days there. After this, when I left England, I felt that I was leaving in such a good heart and in as good a shape as I had ever left England before. I was quite willing to go and lend the "Lads", a helping hand. Next day was a march to Folkestone where we were very soon on the boat to France where, on disembarking, we were met by Motor Buses and soon at the Infantry Base at Etaples. After spending a night in Tents, the following day all N.C.O.'s were paraded and asked what Battalions they were last in so that they could go back to their Old Battalions.

Once this was sorted, the next day I was, once again, in the Front Line Trenches on part of the Armentières Front around the area of Fleur Baix and Laventie. However, instead of getting back to my old Company, "A" Company, I was sent to "C" Company.

229. ARMENTIÈRES. Back to the Front Line and German raids.

My late Platoon Officer who had been made Commanding Officer of "C" Company had asked me if I would come over to that Company before but, at that time , it had been against my wish.Now, however, as my late Platoon Officer was now Commanding Officer of the Battalion, it was very much a case of going where he sent me. I very soon got used to my new Comrades and was very happy to be with them. As soon as I and my comrades reached the Front Line, we found out that a raid on the German Trenches was taking place at daybreak. (7th March). The men of the Royal Sussex Regiment were already in the Trenches waiting for the starting time and we all expected a warm reception from the German Artillery when the raid started. When the starting time arrived, our Artillery sent old Fritz over plenty of "Iron Rations" and our "boys" were well on the road with the Germans deciding not to return a single shell until later. At this time, whilst we were holding our Front Line, three Germans came over to give themselves up, those being the only three captured during the raid. No doubt this was due to the fact that they were working in front of their Trench when we advanced and could not get back in time. The Germans had begun to get very clever against our raids, just holding certain lines at certain places sufficiently long enough that their men could get to safety alright; this resulting in our Raiding Parties only finding empty Trenches.

230. ARMENTIÈRES. Awaiting a German offensive. Out Posts.

This part of the Front was held very thinly by some of our Outposts and news was fast spreading along our Front of the coming Great German Offensive. As a very great German Bombardment was expected when the Offensive was to start, the Front Line was only held by Outposts here and there. Our main Outpost here was at the end of a Communication Trench and was very strongly made but only held at night so that the Germans could not notice any new movements. Double Sentries were posted at night with other Sentries posted so as to be able to look out in all directions. Everyone had to be awake in case of being suddenly attacked. No one, unless on Patrol, was allowed to walk about at night except in the Post itself and anyone who wanted to visit the Post had to know the Password to give when a Sentry shouted to him, otherwise he would have been shot. The Posts were strongly protected by Barbed Wire run around the Right and Left Entrances which could be used by day. At night, these were shut off by the aid of Barbed Wire leaving only one entrance to the Post which was by way of the Communication Trench. A little way down this Trench a sheet of tin was laid across it so that the Sentry would hear anyone moving about by the tin rattling. It was quite easy for a German Patrol to get in the rear of these Posts and, if the Germans attacked these Posts, no one was allowed to leave; they had to hold the "Post" until their end.

231. ARMENTIÈRES. Waiting for a German Offensive.

All I heard whist I was in charge of this Post was, "The German Offensive starts in the Morning". True; it wasn't long after that it was to start, but not on this Front. When we left these Posts we stayed at a little village in the rear named Sailly- sur- la-Lys, (10th.March); there we were in Reserve. The village was only a short distance from the Front Line and it was seldom, if ever, up to this time, that the Germans had ever shelled this village as this had been a very quiet part of the Front. At one or two houses, here and there, between the Village and the Front Line, the French people were still clinging on to their houses. The Village itself was filled with French people but it had reached the time when they received Orders to depart as our Artillery was trying its hardest to bluff the Germans by keeping up a constant rate of shelling, showing the Germans that we were ready for them. When they actually started their Offensive, the little village started to become a very unhealthy place. Despite that, some of the French people still preferred to risk death rather than move. Whilst we were stationed here, in Reserve, we spent our time making Cable Trenches. These were narrow Trenches, 7 or 8 foot deep and the Cable was laid at the bottom of the Trench which was then filled in. The Cable was then safe against Shellfire. Other Troops were making yet more Trenches and putting up barbed wire entanglements. Everything was being got ready so as to stop the German Offensive when it did take place.

Battalion War Diary:

1st March 1918 ROUGE DE BOUT.

Situation normal throughout the day. Usual working parties of 2 Officers and 190 O.R.'s provided. At 8 20pm the Enemy heavily bombarded the Support and back areas of the Bde. on the left with gas and H.E. shells. His barrage caught our Left Coy. H.Q.'s ("A" Coy.) which sustained direct hits. The heavy fire ceased at 10 30pm. Casualties:- 5 killed, 3 wounded, 5 gassed of "A" Coy.

2nd March 1918 ROUGE DE BOUT.
The Bn. relieved 7th Royal Sussex Regt. in the right sub-sector of right Bde. Left ROUGE DE BOUT at 4 00pm. Relief complete at 6 20pm. Dispositions-"B" Coy.-right front; "A" Coy.- left front, "D" Coy.- in support; "C" Coy.- in Reserve.

3rd March 1918 ROUGE DE BOUT.
Very quiet night and quieter day. At 4 30pm our snipers shot enemy sentry opposite left front Coy.

4th March 1918 ROUGE DE BOUT.
Quiet night. At 12 00 noon and 3 00pm our 6" T.M.'s cut wire opposite Left Front Coy.

5th March 1918 ROUGE DE BOUT.
Very quiet day and little activity on Bn. front.

6th March 1918 ROUGE DE BOUT.
Situation normal-nothing to report. Inter Coy. relief.

7th March 1918 ROUGE DE BOUT.
Day quiet and situation normal, 7th.Royal Sussex Regt. took over part of our front and carried out a raid with Artillery support. Zero hour 4 40am. 3 Prisoners captured. Enemy retaliation-nil.

8th March 1918 ROUGE DE BOUT.
Everything normal-nothing to report.

9th March 1918 ROUGE DE BOUT.
Enemy medium T.M.'s moderately active during day also enemy 77mm guns fired on our Support line and on V.C. corner.

10th March 1918 ROUGE DE BOUT. Right Sub-Sector. (Rt. Bde.).
Enemy 77mm guns active again today during the morning. Instructions received from Brigade that Bn'.s were to be reduced forthwith to battle strength. All surplus personnel were sent back to the Transport Line in the evening. Corps. expected enemy to make an attack in the morning. Starting at 7 30pm the Bn. was relieved by the 7th.Norfolk Regt. Relief complete at 9 20pm. On relief Bn. moved back to billets in SAILLY – Bn. H.Q.'s at THE FACTORY.

11th March 1918 SAILLY.
Expected attack did not develop. Weather & visibility excellent to-day. 5 Officers & 250 O.R.'s employed on working parties. At 6 30pm enemy put shell gas over the railway crossing at SAILLY and fired on Batteries close by.

12th March 1918 SAILLY.
Weather and visibility very good. Same working parties as yesterday provided today. At 10 30pm a hostile barrage was put down in the Support Line of the unit in front of us. Everything normal at 11 00pm. Official notification received that the following O.R. had been awarded the Military Medal for gallantry in devotion to duty. No. 402 Pte. PARKER "A" Company.

13th March 1918 SAILLY.
Visibility to-day excellent. Usual working parties provided today of 5 Officers & 250 O.R.'s. At 7 00pm the enemy shelled a battery situated close to Bn. H.Q.'s. PORTUGESE reported an expected enemy raid or attack but nothing developed.

14th March 1918 SAILLY.
Hostile artillery very active again today, firing in back area. Towards night the situation became normal. Usual working parties provided again today.

15th March 1918 SAILLY.
Enemy batteries again very active. A direct hit was obtained on Bn. H.Q.'s which had to be evacuated between 8 00 and 9 00am. During the afternoon Bn. H.Q.'s was removed to NOUVEAU MONDE in late afternoon near the Church. Situation became normal towards evening. The usual working parties were provided.

16th March 1918 SAILLY.
"D" Coy. was moved from SAILLY and billeted in the vicinity of Bn. H.Q.'s. Steady shelling during the day. During the evening SAILLY Crossroads and Bridge were shelled with 60 H.V. 5.9 shells between 6 00 and 11 00pm. 5 Officers & 250 O.R.'s employed on working parties to-day.

17th March 1918 SAILLY.
Weather and visibility excellent. Usual firing on back area by both sides. Situation normal. Working parties as usual provided.

18th March 1918 SAILLY.
Working parties of 4 Officers & 290 O.R.'s provided for work today under C.R.E & Div. Signal Coy. Situation normal and nothing to report.

19th March 1918 SAILLY.
Very wet day. Slight decrease in Artillery activity especially the firing on back areas. The same working parties as yesterday provided by Regt.

20th March 1918 SAILLY.
Weather and visibility good today. Everything normal-usual working parties provided.

21st March 1918 SAILLY.
At 10 00am the Bn. enbussed at the Church NOUVEAU MONDE for the Reserve area. Bn. billeted at COTTES. All Coys. in billets at 2 30pm.

22nd March 1918 COTTES

"A" Coy. fired on 300yds. Range at AUCHY-LE-BOIS. "B" and "D" Coy. bathed at LILLERS. "C" Coy. paraded in accordance with programme of work. Arrangements were made for Inter Battalion Football Competition.

23rd March 1918 COTTES.

"B" Coy. fired on 300 yds. Range at AUCHY-LE-BOIS. "A" Coy. bathed at LILLERS. Other Companies and N.C.O.'s under R.S.M. paraded according to programme. Inter platoon Football matches 1st.Round were played off. Very keen platoon spirit shown. All leave and Courses cancelled.

24th March 1918 COTTES- LAPUGHOY- BURBURE

Orders received early in the morning that the Battalion was to move to LAPUGHOY. Battn. moved at 11 00am and arrived in billets at 2 00pm. At 8 15pm Orders received that the Battn had to en-bus forthwith at BURBURE. Battn. marched to BURBURE and left in buses at midnight.

The great German offensive, "Operation Michael", had been anticipated as far back as December 1917, but the precise date, time and place had not been determined.

Sadler account:

232. ARMENTIÈRES. On Reserve. Gas Attacks. The German Spring Offensive. By bus to Albert.

After we had spent four days in the Reserves we were due to be going back for a little rest when, just before it was time to leave, the Germans bombarded us with Gas Shells. We had to keep our Gas Masks on for a long time, wearing them as we packed everything up and even when we had to "Fall In" and march away we were still wearing them. However, after marching for some little way, we were able to take them off. This was the day the Great German Offensive started , (21st.March), but we were to head for the "Somme Front" and we were met by Motor Buses and taken to a place near Lillers; "Standing To", ready to move at a moment's notice, in case the Germans tried their luck on that Front. After a night or so and, with nothing happening on the Lille Front, the "Fall In" was sounded by our Bugles and everyone had to parade, at once, in Full Marching Order. Motor Buses then drove up to take us to the Somme Front where we were to lend a hand. (24th/25th March). This night we finished up at Albert and were told that we could make ourselves comfortable as there was another Division between us and the Germans. With that we soon settled down for the night. The next morning we sent out an Advance Guard to find this Division and also where the Germans were. Not a living soul was found between us and the Germans. If the Germans had known, they could have advanced and taken the lot of us as prisoners. We found the Germans quite a mile or two off of Albert. I got to thinking that, due to the divide between us and the Germans, they must have tired of the War, packed up and gone home.

Battalion War Diary:

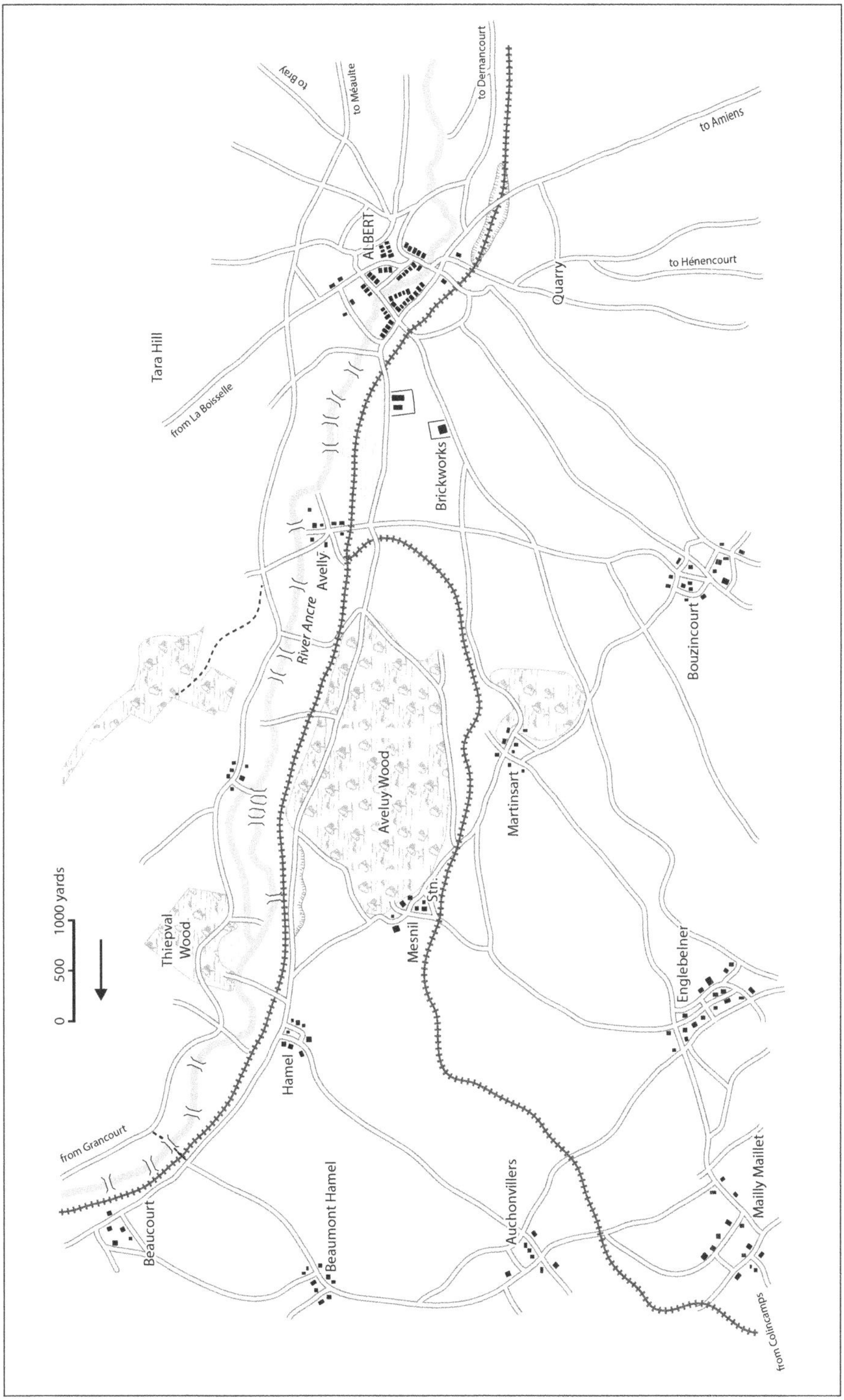

Albert, March 1918. (George Anderson)

25th March 1918 ALBERT via WARLOY and HENENCOURT.

Travelled all night via. ST POL, FERVENT, DOULLENS to WARLOY west of ALBERT arriving there about 9 00am. At 2 00pm Battn moved to HENENCOURT. At 5 00pm Orders received that Battn. had to move up to the Front Line. Reserve personnel left behind. Battn. marched via. ALBERT under Orders to take over line North of MONTABUAM. Soon after leaving ALBERT destination was changed to CARNOY where fresh Orders would be received. At 10 00pm this was again altered and we received instructions to halt by the wayside and await Orders.

26th March 1918 ALBERT AREA/AVELUY.

Waited by roadside 3 00am when Orders were received to move back via. ALBERT and to take up a position on the Western bank of the RIVER ANCRE in front of AVELUY. Battn. in position at 6 00am. Battn. in touch with 7th.ROYAL SUSSEX on the left but there was a gap to the right until 10 00am when the 7th.NORFOLK'S came up and filled it. No sign of the Enemy during the morning but from mid-day onwards he could be seen dribbling forward over the high ground east of the River and down the C.T.'s. During the night the enemy made two determined attempts to cross the bridge over the ANCRE but on each occasion was driven back by M.G., L.G. and rifle fire. At dusk there was much rifle fire from the direction of ALBERT and later we heard that it had been captured by the Enemy.

27th March 1918 ALBERT AREA/AVELUY

At 8 00am enemy again attempted to cross the river but were driven back. At 8 30 am the 7th NORFOLKS on our right gave way closely pursued by the enemy. Our right flank was in the air and we were forced back with the exception of a platoon of "A" Coy. which held on under Capt. BAUDAINS M.C. "D" Coy. was sent forward to counter-attack but they came under heavy M.G. fire and could not reach the River. They established themselves on the front slope of the ridge running from AVELUY WOOD to AVELUY. About 11 00 am a Coy. of the 5th.R.BERKS counter-attacked AVELUY but were prevented from reaching their objective owing to heavy M.G. fire. Capt. BAUDINS was completely surrounded but he fought his way through and reached the high ground near AVELUY. In touch with 7th.Royal Sussex on our left throughout, but no sign of the 7th.NORFOLKS on our right. At 5 00pm the enemy renewed his attacks on our positions from direction of ALBERT. This was accompanied by very heavy M.G. fire and supported by many low flying aeroplanes. Our right was again forced back and a rear guard action was fought. A position was taken up on the high ground in front of MARTINSART WOOD AT 8 00pm. Night spent in digging this line and in re-organising. 5th.R.BERKS took over Right Sector and we the left. In touch on Left with ANSON Battalion of R.N. Div.

28th March 1918 ALBERT AREA/AVELUY.

At 9 00am the Enemy heavily attacked to the left of the BERKS and the right of ourselves supported by heavy M.G. gun fire and numerous aeroplanes. He was completely driven off by M.G., L.G. and artillery fire.

Aveluy today.

29th March 1918 ALBERT AREA/AVELUY

At 1 00am the 6th.BUFFS took over the right sector of the front which the Battn was holding. At 8 00am Orders were received to re-organise the dispositions of the Battn. Posts were established on the Southern edge of AVELUY Wood without opposition. In touch with the 7th.Royal SUSSEX on the left and the 6th.BUFFS. on the right. An attempt to push out a L.G. post down the forward slope south of the wood was not successful owing to two hostile M.G.'s. Commencing at 8 30pm the Battn. was relieved by the 22nd. Battn. LONDON REGIMENT.

30th March 1918 ALBERT AREA/WARLOY.

Relief complete 12 30am. On relief Battalion moved back to billets in WARLOY arriving there 4 30am. At 11 00am Battn. paraded for an inspection and address by Major-General A.B.SCOTT C.B. Divisional Commander. Remainder of day spent on cleaning re-equipment and rest.

31st March 1918 ALBERT AREA/WARLOY

Rifle and L.G. inspections in the morning. Voluntary Services.

1st April 1918 ALBERT AREA./WARLOY

The following casualties were sustained in the recent fighting:-

2/Lieut. E.H.SIMONDS M.M. Killed: 2/Lieut. C.A.HENDRY Missing-believed Killed; Capt. G.L.A.C BAUDAINS Wounded; 2/Lieut. J.H.EELY Wounded; 2/Lieut. A.J.DIXON Wounded; 2/Lieut. L.THOMSON Wounded; 2/Lieut. B.MULLAND Wounded; 2/Lieut. J.S.BENSON M.C. Wounded; 2/Lieut. L.WARMAN Wounded.

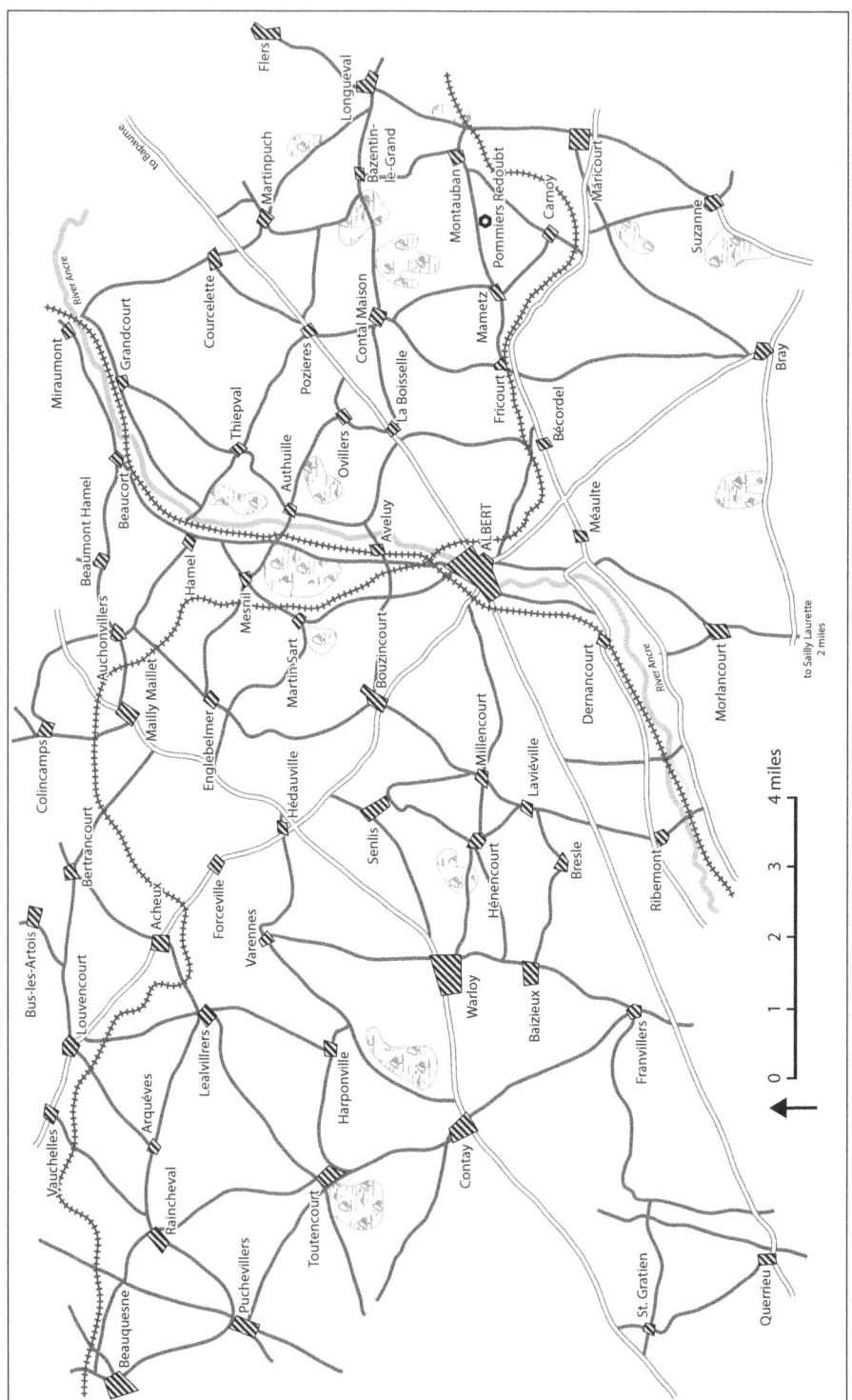

The country around Albert. (George Anderson)

Total casualties to O.R.'s: 187

3 00am: Orders were received that a hostile attack was probable in the morning and that the Battalion had to "Stand to" at 10 00am ready to move. Nothing developed and the "All Clear" was given at 9 00am. Rifle and L.G. Inspections during the morning. Orders received that Bn. was going into the line tomorrow night. Line reconnoitred after dark by C.O and O.in C. Coys.

2nd April 1918 ALBERT AREA./WARLOY. In the Line

Rifle, L.G. and S.B. Respirator inspections. 7 00am: Marching at 7 00am Bn. relieved 7th.Bn. LINCOLNSHIRE Regt. in Left Sector. Left Bde. E. of BOUZINCOURT.

Dispositions:- "A" Coy.- Right Front; "B" Coy.- Centre; "C" Coy. -Left Front; "D" Coy.- Reserve.

3rd April 1918 ALBERT AREA. In the Line.

11 30am. Relief complete 11 30am. Quiet day. After dark- busy wiring the front line and reclaiming trench. Parties supplied by Reserve Bn. and Pioneers to assist.

4th April 1918 ALBERT AREA. In the line.

Quiet morning on our part of the front. At 2 00pm enemy put down a heavy barrage on our flanks. Gas shells being heavily employed. Everything normal by 3 00pm. Weather very wet.

5th.April 1918 ALBERT AREA. In the line.

7 00am.: At 7 00am heavy hostile shelling on our left which had spread by 7 30am to our own front and to our right. Very heavy on BOUZINCOURT. Shelling continued heavy until 9 00am. At 9 05am the S.O.S. was sent up on our right and at 9 10am "C" Coy. and "B" Coy. reported that Enemy were coming over the ridge in front. S.O.S. sent up by "C" Coy. and repeated at Bn. H.Q. by rocket and lamp.. M.G.'s and Artillery put down a good barrage and our L/Gunners and riflemen opened fire. Attack did not develop. Shelling continued heavy at 10 00am but died down on our part of the front towards 11 00am. At 11 45am report was received from "A" Coy. that Enemy had penetrated the line of the 5th.R.BERKS on the right. The C.O. at once sent forward three platoons of "D" Coy. to counter attack this portion of the line over the open. They came under heavy M.G. fire, but gained their objective and worked down the trench for a distance of 300yds. beyond our original right flank where a hostile bombing block was met, strongly held by the enemy. At 1 45pm one Coy. 7th.R.SUSSEX arrived to support us and took over the Res. Line vacated by the platoons of "D" Coy. Remaining platoon of "D" Coy sent forward to reinforce our front line. 2 00-4 00pm.:- From 2 00 to 4 00pm shelling of BOZINCOURT continued to be heavy. "D" Coy. still unable to get in touch with the 5th.R.BERKS on their right. 10 00 – 11 00pm.:-2 Coys. of 7th.R.SUSSEX attached to 5th.R.BERKS counter-attacked to re-establish the line between ourselves and the BERKS. Owing to heavy M.G. fire they failed to gain their objective. At 11 00pm. the 7th.R.SUSSEX relieved the BERKS and took over from us the 300 yards of their trench which we had recaptured. Our casualties during the day's fighting:- 2/Lieut. MASTERTON Killed; 2/Lieut. W. PARR-DUDLEY Killed; 2/Lieut. A.H. TOZER Wounded; 2/

Lieut. E.H.J. SKINNER Wounded; 2/Lieut. C. BAUGH Wounded; 2/Lieut. C. HOWE Wounded; 2/Lieut. R.T. EAGAR Wounded (on duty).

Total casualties to O.R.s: 93.

6th April 1918 ALBERT AREA. In the line.
Quiet day. 6 00pm. At 6 00pm enemy put down a heavy barrage along our front and on rear area. No infantry action followed and everything was quiet by 7 00pm. Bn. relieved by 6th.Bn. R.W.KENTS.

7th April 1918. HENENCOURT.
1.15am. Relief complete 1 15am. On relief Bn. moved back to billets in HENENCOURT. Settled into billets 5 00am. Day spent resting.

8th April 1918. HENENCOURT.
Resting. Whole Bn. bathed under Regt. arrangements.

9th April 1918. HENENCOURT/ ALBERT. In the Line.
Intermittent shelling of HENENCOURT during day. 7 45pm.:- Starting at 7 45pm the Bn. relieved 7th.NORFOLKS in right sub-sector, right Bde. W of ALBERT. Order of Coys.:- "C" Coy.- Right Front; "D" Coy.- Centre; "A" Coy.- Left Front; "B" Coy.- Reserve. Relief complete 12 00 mid-night.

10thApril 1918. ALBERT. In the Line.
From 4 00am to 6 30am the Enemy heavily shelled valley between Bn. H.Q. and MILLENCOURT with 5.9 H.E. and gas. Wind carried the gas to our lines necessitating the wearing of Respirators. Remainder of day quiet. Gas cleared away by 8 00am. Draft of 117 O.R. arrived for the Bn.. All, except 40, are remaining at the Transport lines.

11th April 1918. ALBERT. In the Line.
Quiet night and morning. Considerable hostile aerial activity during afternoon. Two hostile planes brought down. Starting at 9 00pm Bn. was relieved by 13th.R.WELCH Regt. (114th.infantry Bde. 38th.Division).

Sadler Account

233. ALBERT-AVELUY. MARCH 1918. German Offensive. Aveluy Trenches.
Later that day, (26th.March), we finished up at Aveluy Woods and here we had to face German attacks where they tried their very hardest to drive us back. At times they got within a few yards of us and then seemed startled because they had got so close. One time they started coming down a road like they were marching after us in groups of four. This was, though, soon stopped by our Machine Guns and Lewis Gunfire.

We kept receiving Orders that the Left and Right had to Fall Back and that we had to take care and make sure that we never got surrounded. I can never make out, why the Germans didn't follow up their Offensive immediately here as all I can say is that, at this stage, our Army was properly disorganised. It was a major difficulty to get a footing in order to hold the Germans at bay but I noticed that they were prepared to stop on all of the high positions which they had gained over the past three or four days. I could only reflect that it had taken us months to capture these vantage points during the course of the Battle of the Somme in 1916.

Whilst we were here, the Germans broke through the Front which we had been holding just a short while before but, nevertheless we continued working at this Front trying to stop their Advance. After we had done our share in checking the Germans over the next few days, we left for a village in the rear named Warloy, (30thMarch), for four days. From this village we had to work like "niggers" getting some new Trenches dug. The only Trenches we had now were some of our old Reserve Trenches that we had been holding in 1916 and these were a far from comfortable sort of Trench when under a Bombardment.

234. ALBERT-WARLOY-BOUZINCOURT. MARCH 1918. Work Parties. Back to the Front.

The work here was served out to us as Task Work. Each man was given so much to do and his work had to be finished before he left. Whenever he finished his work, he was allowed back to his Billet, going when a number of other men were also finished and when they could return with an N.C.O. in charge of them. By giving the work out in this way, the men did their work with a good heart and very little grumbling was heard. After four days here our work here came to an end and once again, we went back to the Front. This time, (3rd.April), we finished up in the Line just on the left of Bouzincourt, one of the villages which we used to stay in when returning from action in the Somme Battle in 1916. By now Bouzincourt had been smashed to pieces by shellfire and the Germans were advancing and now only a few hundred yards from it. As soon as we got to the Front, my Platoon was shown some Trenches about two foot deep and we had to work all night, getting cover for ourselves. It was much preferred by all of us to dig a new Trench rather than be stationed in one of our old disused Trenches. Things were very quiet and work was done at ease and again, the next day everything was quiet. The Germans were trying to find out a little about where we were by allowing us to walk about just as if there wasn't a War on. By watching where our troops settled, they then knew, for themselves, which Trenches we were holding. This day, towards dark, my Platoon was spilt up, with a Section going to the Left and another Section holding the Line that we had dug; an Officer, myself, and the remainder of the men going to hold one of our Lamp Stations. A nice place this was to hold.We were holding the Lamp Station by posting two Sentry Posts, one on the right and one on the left with each post being supplied with three men and an N.C.O.

235. ALBERT-BOUZINCOURT. MARCH 1918. A German Offensive and Bombardment.

The next morning, (5th.April), as soon as it was light, I thought I would have a wash and shave, as there was a little water in some holes in an old road running by the Station. The Germans kept very quiet until I had finished my wash and shave and then he opened up with a most terrific bombardment which he kept going until about 11 o'clock. All around our Lamp Station one shell was followed by yet another shell. They dropped shells everywhere. I was thinking that, by the sound of the very few of our guns that our Artillery where firing in our defence, that many of them had packed up and were preparing to fall back again.

Then, just about 11 o'clock, overcame the Germans in Full Marching Order looking as if they had it in mind to stay for good. They received a very great welcome from us. The men were mad keen to be after them and only a very few Germans succeeded in getting into our Trench, well on our left. Our Company in Reserve, "D" Company, were put into extended Orders and were soon after them, driving them out of another Regiment's Front. The Germans restarted their bombardment again about 2 o'clock and when they finished things went quiet again for a short time. However, just before dusk, another bombardment started on our left and, by the time that had finished, the bombardment had reached Our Front again. It was a terrible time; shells were falling all around us. It got so hot with shellfire that I was ashamed to have to send my two Sentries to their Post so I said to them, "Take cover in the Lamp Station and I will keep a good Look Out myself".

236. ALBERT–BOUZINCOURT. MARCH 1918. The German Offensive. Being relieved. The weather.

The main thing was to look out for SOS Rockets etc. … If a signal of Distress went up just in front of us we had to go to their help. The Officer in Charge of the Station kept sending up to me to find out if we would be able to get to the Front if anything happened. I had to send back the message that we would never be able cross over to help them owing to such terrible shellfire. I told him that it would pay us to hold on where we were. I thought to myself that if he wanted to know anymore, then he should come and see for himself just as I was doing. I will confess that I was expecting my last to come at any minute and this had been why I decided to stop the others from doing their turn of Sentry duty. I really didn't see why a dozen men should be out and facing such terrible shellfire when one was enough. As it was, we were not called upon to go and help. Later the same night, the Germans sent over many heavy Trench Mortars aimed at the end of a Communications Trench. All the Troops were moved from that quarter until we were called to hold it and then, to make it more cheerful, it started to rain as hard as ever it could. Also, later on this same evening, we were getting relieved and my Officer and myself sat down; in the rain, to study the map in order to find the best way out and to plan the roads which we then decided that we would take. We got relieved and had started on our journey when we met with another Platoon. My Officer and the Officer of this Platoon decided to change our Plans and the journey, which should have taken an hour or so to do, took us, in all , about ten hours. It was a wonder we ever reached the village of Henencourt alive.

237. ALBERT 1918. Trench Digging

At this village, I was thanked for all the good work that I had done in the past four days. We were stationed and carried on in this area of the Front until July, working so many days in the Trenches and so many doing work in the way of digging new defence lines. The continuing German Offensive had and was to make very much work for us.

The German offensive, having reached the limit of its success, ground to a halt on 5 April.

21

April–July 1918: Retreat

As Sergeant James Sadler observed, the German advance had created a great deal of work for him and his comrades, coupled with the unwelcome prospect of further retreat. No doubt too distracted to record the day-to-day details in his personal diary, the Battalion war diary provides the best narrative of this critical time of defence and withdrawal:

12th April 1918. WARLOY. MIRVAUX.
Relief complete 1 15am. On relief Bn. moved back to billets at WARLOY. Settled in billets 3 00am. Notification received that a big attack was expected today by the Enemy in AMIENS and that from 4 45am Bn. had to be ready to move at ½ hours' notice. Reveille 4 00am. Nothing developed and at 9 00am the front was reported clear. Bn. marched at 12 30pm to billets at MIRVAUX, halting on the way for Baths at CONTAY. Settled in billets at 5 30pm.

13th April 1918. MIRVAUX.
Day spent resting and cleaning up. C.O. inspected the new draft of 117 men at 1 45pm. Mostly boys under 19 years of age.

14th April 1918. MIRVAUX.
Coy. parades in the morning. "A" Coy. on the Range. Voluntary Church Services in afternoon and evening.

15th April 1918. MIRVAUX.
Coy. parades in the morning. "B" Coy. on the Range. The following N.C.O.'s awarded the Military Medal for conspicuous gallantry near ALBERT:- 19100. Sgt. BIRD; 50277. Cpl. WARREN; 69392. Pte. HAYES.

16th April 1918. MIRVAUX.
Coy. parades in morning. Inspections of Transport by C.O.

17th April 1918. MIRVAUX.
Usual Coy. parades. "C" Coy. on the Range. 2/Lieut. F.KNIGHT awarded Military Cross for conspicuous gallantry near AVELUY. Capt. J.H. LEGGE M.C., Medical Officer, left the Battn. for 37th.Field Ambulance. Lieut. E.R.SATHER of the U.S. Army took over his duties.

18th April 1918. MIRVAUX.
Coy. parades. "B" Coy. on the Range.

19th April 1918. MIRVAUX.
Marching at 2 00pm the Battalion moved via BEAUCOURT to HARPONVILLE. All under canvas. Settled in by 5 30pm.

20th April 1918. HARPONVILLE.
Large enemy attack expected to be made today by enemy on Third Army Front. Bn. under ½ hours orders to move. Nothing developed beyond artillery fire.

21st April 1918. HARPONVILLE.
Voluntary Church services in the morning. 400 men in working parties near WARLOY. Battn. allotted Baths at CONTAY.

22nd April 1918. HARPONVILLE.
C.O. & Officers "C" Coy. reconnoitred the Front which the Battn. will shortly be taking over. Marching at 4 00pm the Battalion moved to LEALVILLERS taking over billets vacated by 7th.Bn. ROYAL FUSILIERS. Settled in billets by 5 30pm.

23rd April 1918. LEALVILLERS.
Under- mentioned N.C.O.'s and men awarded Military Medal for conspicuous gallantry near AVELUY & ALBERT: 34788- Lt.Cpl. C.HOLDEN; 41258- Lt.Cpl. G.POTTER; 13140- Lt.Cpl. H.JACKSON; 47422- Pte. H.REVELY; 16505-Pte. C.DENNIS; 1267- Pte. H.BEASLEY; 60723- Pte. J.HAMMOND; 20290- Pte. S.CROSSLEY.

Marching at 5 00pm Battalion took over Reserve Bn. Right Bde. from 1st.Bn. 3rd.NEW ZEALAND RIFLES Brigade. in area between ENGLEBELMER and MAILLY MAILLET. Relief complete 8 00pm.

24th April 1918.ENGLEBELMER and MAILLY MAILLET:Lines.
Our artillery active between 3 00am and 7 00am. Coy. Commanders reconnoitred front of both Bns. in the line.

25th & 26th April 1918.ENGLEBELMER and MAILLY MAILLET:Lines.
Quiet except for bursts by our artillery throughout the night. 200 men working on front line each night.

27th April 1918.ENGLEBELMER and MAILLY MAILLET:Lines.
Both artilleries active. "B" Coy. had 4 casualties in wood N. of ENGLEBELMER. 250 men working on C.T.'s. (Communication Trenches).

28th April 1918.ENGLEBELMER and MAILLY MAILLET:Lines.
Usual harassing fire by our artillery throughout the night. Service for R.C.'s in the morning.

29th April 1918.ENGLEBELMER and MAILLY MAILLET:Lines.
Usual night firing by our artillery. Bn. should have been relieved to-morrow by 6th.Bn. THE QUEENS, but Relief cancelled.

30th April 1918.ENGLEBELMER and MAILLY MAILLET:Lines.
Quiet day. Capt. G.la C. BAUDAINS awarded the D.S.O for conspicuous gallantry and devotion to duty near AVELUY. Lieut. J.M.LEA awarded the M.C. for conspicuous gallantry near ALBERT during the Counter Attack by "D" Coy. on the 5th.inst.

1st May 1918. ENGLEBELMER and MAILLY MAILLET: Front Line.
Marching at 8 00pm, Bn. relieved 7th.SUSSEX and part of 5th.R.BERKS on front line. Front readjusted and is now held with one Bn. in Lines, one in Support and one in Reserve. Relief complete 11 45pm. Dispositions:- "A" Coy. Right Front; "B" Coy. Left Front; "C" Coy. Support; "D" Coy. Reserve.

2nd May 1918. ENGLEBELMER and MAILLY MAILLET: Front Line.
Quiet night. Our artillery active at intervals during the day particularly in the early morning.

3rd May 1918. ENGLEBELMER and MAILLY MAILLET: Front Line.
Div. Commander came round the sector in the morning with the Brigadier. Quiet day.

4th May 1918. ENGLEBELMER and MAILLY MAILLET: Front Line.
Quiet night. Enemy shelled our Support Line at intervals during the day with 77mm guns. Infantry relief in evening starting at 10 00pm.: "C" Coy. relieved "A" Coy.; "D" Coy. relieved "B" Coy.; "B" Coy. relieved "C" Coy.; "A" Coy. relieved "D" Coy.

5th May 1918. ENGLEBELMER and MAILLY MAILLET: Front Line.
Artillery action during early hours of the morning. From 3 00pm to 4 30pm Enemy registered on Reserve Line with 4.2" guns.

6th May 1918. ENGLEBELMER and MAILLY MAILLET: Front Line.
Quiet day. Starting at 8 30 pm. Bn. was relieved by 5th.BERKS. Relief complete 12 15am Pouring with rain all night.

7th May 1918. ENGLEBELMER and MAILLY MAILLET: Front Line.
On relief Bn. moved back to billets in ACHEUX. Settled in billets 5 00am. Day spent in resting.

May 1918 began with the 9th Royal Fusiliers holding the line to prevent further enemy advances. Their efforts were succeeded by a further withdrawal of 4 kilometres to Acheux. Otherwise, it was business as usual – working parties.

Battalion War Diary:

8th May 1918. ACHEUX.
Whole Bn. bathed under Regimental arrangements.

9th May 1918. ACHEUX.
Bn. under ½ hours' notice to move from 3 00am as a German attack is expected this morning. L.G. limbers ready loaded in case of a move. All clear given about 7 00am. Whole Battn. out on working parties-cable burying. In the evening "A" Coy. had to move up to the trenches in front of MAILLY, to act as nucleus garrison, which were manned in case of hostile attack.

10th May 1918. ACHEUX.
Working parties in the morning. Football match in the evening against 36th. F.A.,(Field Artillery), Bn.. Lost 5-1.

11th May 1918. ACHEUX.
Usual working parties under Divisional Signals.

12th May 1918. ACHEUX.
Voluntary services for those able to attend. At 1 00pm- "B" and "C" Coys. march off to provide working parties previous to relieving 7th.ROYAL SUSSEX in the Intermediate System in front of MAILLY. "D" Coy. and Bn. H.Q. marched from ACHEUX at 7 45pm. Bn. relieves 7th.ROYAL SUSSEX in the Intermediate System. Relief complete 10 30pm. Heavy shelling of MAILLY by enemy as Bn. passed by the outskirts. 2 Officers and 30 men of "D" Coy. remained behind to do special training for a night raid at an early date.

13th May 1918. MAILLY.
Quiet day. Nothing to report.

14th May 1918. MAILLY.
"D" Coy's. Raiding Party came up in the morning and were billeted in cellars at MAILLY. At 6 00pm, Raiding Party moved up to our Front Line. Intention was to rush hostile M.G. Post kill the enemy and obtain identification. Bn. H.Q. moved forward temporarily to H.Q. of 7th.ROYAL SUSSEX. At 10 00pm raiding party crawled out to place where M.G. had been previously located. On arrival there, no gun was to be found so party went on towards German's front line. Enemy evidently saw them and opened fire on them with 2 M.G.'s. At the same time enemy sent out two parties, each about 30 strong with the evident intention of working round the flanks of our party. Bombs were thrown at these enemy parties and 9 were killed. Owing to hostile M.G. fire, Party was unable to advance and secure any identification. Casualties: 1 O.R. wounded, 1 O.R. died of wounds, 1 O.R. missing believed killed. 2/Lt. A.C. HEYES was in charge of the party with 2/Lt. J.O.BOWRY.

15th May 1918. MAILLY.
Quiet morning. Div. Commander came round about noon. As soon as it was dark a party went out under 2/Lt. J.O.BOWRY to find man missing from raiding party and if possible obtain identification from dead Germans. Found the body of our man in No Man's Land but, owing to the presence of strong hostile patrols which were out, party was forced to return.

16th May 1918. MAILLY.

Quiet during the morning. Slight hostile shelling of Intermediate System between 2 00pm and 3 30pm.

17th May 1918. MAILLY.

Heavy artillery fire from 6 00am until 7 00am. chiefly on our right. Otherwise nothing report.

18th May 1918. MAILLY.

Quiet during the day. Bn. should have relieved 7th.ROYAL SUSSEX but owing to a re-arrangement of Div. Front, the Relief was cancelled.

19th May 1918. MAILLY.

About 1 00am enemy started heavy gas shelling of MAILLY. (Mustard). Shelling was heavy until 3 00am when it slackened any gradually ceased. Causalities – NIL. At 1 00pm enemy again gas shelled MAILLY. Not quite so heavily as in the morning. All quiet by 11 30pm. No Casualties.

20th May 1918. MAILLY.

German attack expected in the morning from statements of prisoners. Bn. was relieved by 6th.Bn. THE QUEENS. Relief complete 1 30am.

21th May 1918. MAILLY.

On relief Bn. moved to positions on PURPLE SYSTEM N.E. of MAILLY. From 3 00am onwards Bn. was prepared to "Stand To" in view of the expected attack. Apart from artillery fire nothing developed and "All Clear" was given at 7 30am. Starting at 9 00am Bn., (less "B" Coy.), moved to billets in ACHEUX. Settled in billets by 12 00noon. "B" Coy. remained behind as nucleus garrison. MAJOR H.A. SCARLETT D.S.O. left Bn. to take over temporary command of 7th.NORFOLK Regt. MAJOR C.O. SKEY D.S.O., M.C. joined the Bn. and took over duties of Coy. Second in Command.

Capt. D. PARKINSON joined the Bn. and took over Command and payment of "C" Coy.

22nd May 1918. ACHEUX.

50 men on work under Div. Signals, cable buying. In evening "D" Coy. back to move up to PURPLE SYSTEM to relieve one Coy. of the 5th.R.BUCKS there.

23rd May 1918. ACHEUX.

50 men out again-cable burying. Started work at 4 00am and finished at 8 30am.

24th May 1918. ACHEUX.

Bn. due to be relieved to-morrow by 7th.Bn. LINCOLNSHIRE REGT. 17th.Div..

German Attack expected in the morning. Prisoners state that it was postponed from 21st.inst. to 25th.inst. for an unknown reason.

25th May 1918. ACHEUX.

From 3 00am, Bn. under quarter hours' notice to move up to the PURPLE SYSTEM. L.G. Limbers packed and mules in harness ready to move. Apart from artillery fire nothing developed. Marching at 11 50am the Bn, (less "B" & "D" Coy.) moved to BEAUQUESNES via. LEAVILLERS- ARQUEVES- RAINCHEVAL and VAL-VION. Settled in billets at 3 00pm.

26th May 1918. BEAUQUESNE

Voluntary Services in the morning. "B" and "D" Coy's arrived in billets at 11 00am having been relieved in PURPLE SYSTEM by Coys. of 7th.LINCONSHIRES.

27th May 1918. BEAUQUESNE

Coys. busy cleaning up.

28th May 1918. BEAUQUESNE

"A" and "C" Coys. started training- Musketry and Platoon Training. Both Coys. finish on the Range. No. 20201- Pte. FRANCIS awarded the Military Medal for gallant conduct during the operation on the 14th.inst.

29th May 1918. BEAUQUESNE

All Coys. training in accordance with programme in musketry, drill , platoon training and night patrols. "C" Coy. carried out field practices on 300 yards range. The under mentioned Officers and W.O of the Bn. have been mentioned in dispatches for their distinguished conduct in the field. Lt.Col. W.V.L. van SOMENSEN D.S.O. M.C.; Major. H.A.SCARLETT D.S.O.; Major C.O.SKEY D.S.O. M.C.; Capt. W.H.SHEDAL; R.S.M. A. STICKLAND M.C.

30th May 1918. BEAUQUESNE

Training as usual in Musketry, etc., Orders received that Bn. was to move to LEALVILLERS tomorrow for working parties.

31st May 1918. BEAUQUESNE/LEALVILLERS.

"A" Coy. on range. All Coys. had S.B. Respirators tested in gas. "B", "C" and "D" Coys. bathed . Brigadiers inspected transport at 2 00pm. Marching at 5 15pm, Bn. moved to LEAVILLERS via. VAL VION, RAINCHEVAL, ARQUEVES and BELLE EGLISE. Took over billets from 6th.QUEENS. Settled in billets 7 45pm.

1st June 1918. LEALVILLERS.

No orders received for working parties so carried on with training in billets.

2nd, 3rd & 4th June 1918. LEALVILLERS.

300 men out each day digging a switch tunnel N.E. of MAILLY MAILLET. Hours- 9 15am to 4 30pm.

5th June 1918. LEALVILLERS.

Marching at 5 45 am Bn. Moved to BEAUQUESNE. Settled in billets 11 00am.

6th June 1918. BEAUQUESNE

Division under orders to move at short notice. Coy. training from 10 00am to 6 00pm. All Coys. on Range. 5th.ROYAL BERKS beat the Bn. 2-1 in Brigade Knock-out Soccer Competition.

7th & 8th June 1918. BEAUQUESNE

Coy. training 10 00am to 6 00pm. Division on G.H.Q. reserve.

9th June 1918. BEAUQUESNE

Brigade Church Parade 9 00am. "A" Coy. on Range in afternoon. Bn. likely to move out any time, probably South.

10th June 1918. BEAUQUESNE

Coy. Training 10 00am to 6 00pm.

11th June 1918. BEAUQUESNE

Parades finished at 12 noon. Brigade Sports in afternoon. Bn. won following events:- Drums Competition, Assault at Arms, Tug of War, Places gained as shown in following events:- 1st.& 2nd.in High Jump- 2nd. in 100 yards,2nd.in 880 yards.

12th, 13th & 14th June 1918. BEAUQUESNE

Coy. Training 10 00am to 6 00pm.

15th June 1918. BEAUQUESNE

Divisions returned to "V" Corps yesterday and are to relieve 35th.Division at an early date in AVELUY Sector. C.O. and Coy. Commandant go up to reconnoitre the line. Capt. H.R.BROOKE wounded.

16th June 1918. BEAUQUESNE

Voluntary Service In the morning and evening.

17th June 1918. BEAUQUESNE

Marching at 9 10am Bn. moved via PUCHEVILLERS- TOUTENCOURT and HARPONVILLE to bivouac area between HARPONVILLE and SENLIS arriving here at 2 00pm. Halted for dinners and teas. Marching at 8 30pm Bn. moved to SENLIS and BOUZINCOURT to front line- Right Bn. of Corps. Relieved the 19th. Bn. D.L.I., (Durham Light Infantry), 31st.Division. Dispositions: – "A" Coy. Left Hand, "C" Coy. Right Hand, "B" Coy. Left Support, "D" Coy. Right Support. Quiet during relief except for a salvo of gas shells about midnight in vicinity of Bn. H.Q.'s. .

18th June 1918. BOUZINCOURT: In the line.

Relief complete 1 10am. Quiet night & quiet during the day.

19th June 1918. BOUZINCOURT: In the line.

Quiet day except for a few light T.M.'s which fell near Support Line of Right Front Coy. "Chinese" attack was made at intervals during the night in portion of AVELUY

WOOD held by the enemy. 2/Lieut. W.G.LONG wounded, 2 O.R.'s killed and 6 O.R.'s wounded from enemy retaliation.

20th June 1918. BOUZINCOURT: In the line.
Enemy T.M.'s active around sector of Right Front Coy. in retaliation for our 6" Newton Mortars at intervals during morning and afternoon.

21st June 1918. BOUZINCOURT: In the line.
Considerable artillery activity during the night in support of raids on our right and left. Starting at 10 00pm. Bn. was relieved by 7th.ROYAL SUSSEX. Regt.

22nd June 1918. BOUZINCOURT: In the line.
Relief complete 1 10am. On relief Bn. moved back into Brigade Reserve in rear of BOUZINCOURT. Under mentioned W.O.'s and N.C.O.'s of the Bn. have been awarded the Meritorious Service Medal for their good work in the field. 6390- C.S.M. J.GRIGGS; 2093- Sgt. W.MONK; 413 L/Cpl. A.H.NASH.

23rd June 1918. REAR OF BOUZINCOURT
About 2 30am V11a was shelled with gas shells & 5.90. There was considerable activity during the evening. Working parties of 288 men for active work provided under 70th. Coy. R.E.. 5 Men of "A" Coy wounded when returning from working party.

24th June 1918. REAR OF BOUZINCOURT
Dull windy day. Our artillery active. Vicinity of ENGLBELMER shelled. The usual working parties were found.

25th June 1918. REAR OF BOUZINCOURT
Bright Sunny day. Conditions normal. Bn. relieved the 5th.ROYAL BERKS in the left front line. Coys. disposed as follows: – "D" Coy. Right Front, "B" Coy. Left Front, "A" Coy. Right Support. "C" Coy. Left Support. Relief commenced at 9 45- Complete at 12 45am. Enemy were quiet during the day.

26th June 1918. REAR OF BOUZINCOURT
Weather still good. Enemy apparently registering on our left front. Working parties from 5th.ROYAL BERKS were employed on digging at SAUCHIEHALL SUPPORT –almost obliterated. Two enemy M.G.'s located by our patrols. Blue X shells fell in vicinity of Bn. H.Q.'s about 10 30pm. Box Respirators were worn.

27th June 1918. REAR OF BOUZINCOURT
Considerable amount of work done by companies. Laying Trench Boards, cutting grass, constructing T shelter, etc. Enemy artillery fairly active 20 mins. Attack put down on Front and Support lines. Increased aerial activity. The C.O. went to Transport- sick. MAJOR. COSKEY D.S.O., M.C. took command of the Battalion.

28th June 1918. REAR OF BOUZINCOURT
18th.Div. in conjunction with Special Coy. R.E. sent over gas and gas shells on

enemy front at 12 15am, 2 30am & 3 00am. No immediate retaliation on our front. BOUZINCOURT was shelled at intervals throughout the day. Considerable aerial activity. One of our balloons was brought down by E.A.(Enemy Aircraft) about 4 15pm. Cases of influenza on the increase. Capt. PARSONS went down sick. Considerable amount of work done by Companies.

29th June 1918. REAR OF BOUZINCOURT
Weather still bright and sunny. 2/Lt. BARNES reported having died at HAURE suffering from influenza. Conditions normal. Considerable aerial activity during evening. 6 bombs were dropped near Battalion H.Q. about 11 00pm. "A" and "C" Coys. moved to bivouac area between SENLIS and HARPONVILLE. Moved off at 10 15 and 10 30am. "D" and "C" readjusted their dispositions. Bn. front now held by 2 Coys. and Bn. H.Q. Two Platoons in SAUCHIEHALL TRENCH; 2 Platoons in SAUCHIEHALL RESERVE and 4 Platoons in BOUZINCOURT TRENCH. Our shells reported dropping short on front one line. One M. Gunner killed.

30th June 1918. REAR OF BOUZINCOURT
Conditions normal during the day. Considerable aerial activity. Bright sunny day. Lt. SAUTHER (U.S.A.M.R.C.) went down sick. Replaced by Lt. HAYES (U.S.A.M.R.C.) at 2 30pm. Rations were dumped on the roads by the Reserve Bn. H.Q. and parties dribbled across the track from Bn. H.Q. Apparently they were not observed by the Enemy and no shells were sent over. Between 9 00pm and 9 35pm there was an unusual calm. Hardly a shot was fired during this period. At 9 35pm our barrage came down and the attacks by the 37th.Brigade to capture the high ground in W 15 & 21 were launched. Our guns were firing consistently until 11 30pm when it was reported that things were fairly quiet. Shortly after 9 35 the enemy put down a barrage on AUCHY and MATINSART WOOD but it was not until 11 10pm that the enemy artillery gave any particular attention to BOUZINCOURT when it was reported that the area in front of BOUZINCOURT was being heavily shelled. At 12 30am all was quiet except for desultory shelling and occasional M.G. bursts. No casualties were reported on our front. 2/Lt. BOWRIE went down sick and 2/Lt. HUNTER came up to replace him.

July 1st 1918. BOUZINCOURT
Quiet day. Between 8 00 & 9 00 pm, two EA (Enemy Aircraft) flew up and down the line on our left at a low altitude dropping lights. At 9.15 pm the S.O.S. went up on our right and extended to left and right of us. Heavy bombardment on our left and right- less intense on Bn. Front. By 10 40 our front was quiet. No infantry action took place on our front.

July 2nd 1918. BOUZINCOURT
2 00 am.: S.O.S again reported on our right. Bn. Front heavily shelled. All quiet at 3 00 am. The remainder of the day was comparatively quiet. Brilliant sunshine.

9 00 pm. It was reported that 40 Germans had been seen, (wearing full equipment), to cross the road at W156.9.4. Companies were warned. At 8 30 pm. an E.A. flew up and down the front on our right, dropping lights. At 9.20 pm. heavy bombardment

commenced. S.O.S. reported on our left and right. Shelling was extremely heavy on our front. At 10.15 – all quiet on our front. Orders for relief received.

July 3rd 1918. BOUZINCOURT
Relieved by 5th.Royal Berks. By 3.30 am. moved to bivouac area behind SENLIS. Battalion moved up again in the evening to Reserve lines behind BOUZINCOURT taking over the Trenches vacated by 7th.R.Sussex.Bn.. In position by 12 30 midnight.

July 4th 1918.BOUZINCOURT
Quiet night. Our own Artillery busy. Quiet during the day.

July 5th 1918. BOUZINCOURT
At intervals during the day the Enemy sent over "crashers" on to the SENLIS Crossroads. Half the Bn. out at night on working & carrying parties under the R.E.'s. (Royal Engineers).

July 6th 1918. BOUZINCOURT
Quiet during the morning. About 2 00 pm. enemy sent over a considerable amount of gas shells in vicinity of Bn. HQ. A large number also fell in vicinity of the Trenches. Appeared to be a new kind of gas. Usual working and carrying parties during the night.

July 7th 1918. BOUZINCOURT
Quiet night & day. Usual working parties. Enemy attack expected shortly on this part of the front, due to take place between the 10th. & 15th July. Division due to be relieved on the night of 10th/11th.

July 8th 1918. BOUZINCOURT
Quiet night. Usual working & carrying parties.

July 9th 1918. BOUZINCOURT
Reconnoitring parties came up during the morning from the 9th.Bn. Duke of Wellington's Regt. 32nd.Inf. Brigade. 17th.Div.. Enemy artillery active during the afternoon in counter battery work.

July 10th 1918. BOUZINCOURT to TOTENCOURT WOOD
Bn. was relieved by the 9th.Bn. Duke of Wellington Regt. and moved to TOUTENCOURT WOOD.

July 11th 1918. TOUTENCOURT WOOD.
Coy's were settled in new mess by 4 00pm. The day was spent in cleaning up & inspections. A draft of 2 Officers and 123 OR arrived from the back/low Reception Camp. A violent hailstorm occurred during the evening. Many of the tents were flooded.

July 12th 1918. TOUTENCOURT WOOD.
Coy's were at the disposal of Company Commanders for reorganisation.

July 13th 1918. TOUTENCOURT WOOD
Coy's. At the disposal of Coy. Commanders. Part of the Transport moved off at 1 45. By road to FAMECHON. 10 00 pm- detailed instructions received concerning move.

July 14th 1918. FAMECHON
Remainder of the Transport moved off at 3 40.am. En-training at RUGAL.
    Personnel moved off at 7 30 am. Order:- "D","C","B","A"," HQ".. The starting hour was passed at 7 50am.
    Bn. en-bussed at point north of RUBEMPRE moved off at 10 00 am. Route:- RUBEMPRE – PIERREGOT – RAINNEVILLE – AMIENS – NAMPTY – TILLIS LES CONTY – CONTY – FLEURY – CONTRE – FREMONTIERS.
    Bn. de-bussed outside FREMONTIERS and marched to FAMECHON where billeting was completed by 4pm.

July 15th 1918. FAMECHON.
Company's carried out training as per programme. Warning Order for move received at 2 45 pm Transport moved off by road arriving at ORESNAUX about 12 midnight. Battalion paraded at 6 45 pm. and en-bussed on POIX FREMONTIERS Rd. at western entrance to FREMONTIERS at 7 15pm.
    Route:- FREMONTIERS – CONTRE – FLEURY – CONTY – LE BOSQUEL – ESSERTAUX – ROSSIENOL – ORESMAUX. Battalion in billets by 10 00 pm.

July 16th 1918. ORESMAUX.
Coy's. were at the disposal of Coy. Commanders for inspection and cleaning of billets. News concerning German attack in CHAMPAGNE received. Enemy bombing planes active during the evening. 8 bombs were dropped outside the western edge of the village about 12 midnight.

July 17th 1918.ORESMAUX
Coys. Carried out training as per programme. Rain interrupted training during the morning. Flies in the village very troublesome.

July 18th 1918. ORESMAUX
Coys. Carried out training as per programme.

July 19th 1918. ORESMAUX.
Coys. carried out training as per programme. News of French Brigade's counter attack received. Established on SOISSONS – CHATEAU THIERRY Road.

July 20th 1918.ORESMAUX
Training according to programme. Thunderstorm during the morning interfered with training.

July 21th 1918. ORESMAUX
Church parades for all denominations were held during the morning. A football match

was played against the 5th French "C" Command Regt. Result 8-5 in our favour.

July 22nd 1918. ORESMAUX
All SBR's were tested during the morning. Coys. Carried out the usual training.

July 23rd 1918. ORESMAUX
Usual training. A Lewis Gun instructor from the IV Coy's. School reported for duty. A draft of 26 OR arrived.

July 24th 1918. ORESMAUX
Usual training:-Range practice, Lewis Gun training, Route March, Drill, PT etc.. Draft of 11 OR arrived. "A" and "D" Coys. to usual construction Trench activities in ORESMAUX & ESSERTAUX.

July 25th 1918. ORESMAUX
Usual Training. Tactical schemes carried out by "B" and "C" Companies. on CHAUSSOY – EUGANY road. Inspection of Draft.

July 26th 1918. ORESMAUX
"A" and "D" Coys. carried out tactical scheme. "B" Coy. were on the Range. "C" carried out the usual training-Route March, Drill, Lewis Gunning, Marching etc.

July 27th 1918. ORESMAUX
Usual training. The G.O.C. 12th Div. presented medal ribbons to 11 O.R. who had not been previously presented. One Company attended the parade.

July 28th 1918. ORESMAUX
Voluntary Church Parades were held for all denominations. Brigade Boxing competition took place on the football field at 5.30pm. The Battalion won all weights.

July 29th 1918. ORESMAUX
"A" Coy. were attached to Range. "B" & "C" carried out tactical scheme on CHAUSSOY – EUGANY road. "D" Coy. carried out the usual training.

July 30th 1918. ORESMAUX: VIGNACOURT
Bn. moved by train to VIGNACOURT leaving ORESMAUX at 12 noon. Arrived LOUGICHY at 2 00 pm. by marching route. En-bussed at 4pm. arrived at VIGNACOURT 6 00pm. Transport moved by road.

July 31st 1918. VIGNACOURT
Coy's. were at the disposal of Coy. Commanders for inspection. PT etc.

Morlancourt today.

Sadler's account:

235. AMIENS 1918. Preparing for the Offensive.

Finally, after several months of Trench digging, our Great and Final Offensive was to start and, because of that, we were soon to leave all our work of the past few months in the rear. Before our Offensive started we had the pleasure of going to support the French when they started their Great Offensive. This was only a few miles to our rear. However, we were not called to take part in it because it turned out to be such a great success. Our Artillery went to the Front Line and gave them a hand for four days and the French were delighted with their help. After a very enjoyable time staying in Baizieux, a French village which very few British Troops had seen, we again left for our own Front this time by Motor Buses and, after a very short time, we finished up in some Trenches on the left of a road running into Morlancourt . Here we found things rather lively.

July 1918 was drawing to a close. The succeeding month would see a dramatic turn of events as the Allies commenced a series of offensives that would send the enemy reeling and destabilise his front. The first major breakthrough would occur on British Fourth Army's front with Sergeant Sadler and 9th Royal Fusiliers at the sharp end.

22

August 1918: Advance Towards a Decision

For 9th Royal Fusiliers the first days of August were on of preparation for the Amiens offensive. Little actual combat was experienced prior to 8th August, the scheduled date for the first assault of the "100 Days" offensives.

Battalion War Diary:

August 1st 1918. VIGNACOURT
7 00-9 00 am.- Company Route Marches. 10 00-12 30pm.- Coy. Parades. Div. Boxing Tournament in evening at which the Bn. Won the Featherweight, a special prize in the Welterweight and were runners up in the Middleweight.

August 2nd 1918. VIGNACOURT
C.O. and Coy. Commanders were due to reconnoitre part of line held by 53th.Div. But Lorries were not available. Adjutant sent up in evening to reconnoitre area held by 8th Bn. London Division.

August 3rd 1918. VIGNACOURT-BAIZIEUX.
Bn. en-bussed at 7.10 pm. and proceeded to BAZIEUX, de-bussing about 1 mile from the village. "A" & "B" Coys. billeted at in BAIZIEUX. "C" & "D" at LASSVILLE TRENCH about 5 kms. E of village.

August 4th 1918. BAIZIEUX.
Special Anniversary Service for all those able to attend. 30 men supplied for work under the R.E.s.

August 5th 1918. BAIZIEUX
Quiet day. Usual working party.

August 6th 1918. BAIZIEUX-FRANVILLERS
Orders received that Bde. were moving back into Coy. Reserve but, during the afternoon, this was cancelled and we were to be held in readiness to relieve a Bde. of the 18th Div. which had been attacked early this morning. At 9 00 pm Orders received that Bn. was to move forward to FRANVILLERS, S. of BAIZIEUX. C.O. attended conference at Bde. HQ. Bn. to take part in a large attack at an early date.

August 7th 1918. FRANVILLIERS-MORLANCOURT.
Settled in billets in FRANVILLERS at 2.30 pm. Coys. busy throughout the day organising for the attacks. C.O. and Officers "C" Company reconnoitring. Marching at 8.15 pm Bn. moved to HEILLY to assembly position and behind British Support

Line immediately South of BRAY – CORBIE RD., S.E. of MORLANCOURT. Heavy hostile shelling of roads and tracks as we were moving up.

Capt. D PARKINSON and Lt. ORTON MC. wounded and major portion of 2 Platoons were causalities. Lt. AYSFORD was wounded.

Sadler Account:

236. ALBERT 1918. German Bombardment. Preparing for "The Offensive".
The Germans never seemed to think that their shellfire was enough for us so they started bombing our Trenches; this time with the help of their airmen. When these bombs were dropped and exploded, they made holes quite 12 feet across. Although, as it happened, it was now only four days off of the starting of our Great Offensive; we had not been told a word about it. Everything was kept perfectly quiet. During the three days which we spent in this Trench, the Germans seemed to show a great need to occupy a certain part of our Front, not far to our left. They sent over strong forces to raid our Line. When they had gained their Objective they continued to hold out until they were driven out by a counter attack Then, for a short time, our men again had the pleasure to hold this Front once more but, again, it wasn't long before the Germans were over and attacking this part of the line. This time, we were ordered to get everything packed up ready to move, and all of us thought that we should soon be after the Germans to drive them out once more. However, this was not to be the case as, later that night, we left the Trenches for a little village in the rear , Franvillers, arriving at the village about midnight where we soon got to sleep, not thinking about what was in store for us. The next morning, first, we received Orders to pack up all of our private property and to put it in our Great coat pockets. Our Great Coats were to be handed to the Section Commanders and tied up in bundles of ten. What we then had to wear was what was called New Battle Orders, which involved wearing our packs on our equipment instead of using our haversacks. The haversacks also had to be done up like the Great Coats, in bundles of ten, and passed on to our Section Commanders. We could only guess, after we had done this, that there was some "dirty" work coming off for us shortly.

234. ALBERT 1918. Preparing for the "Great Offensive". 8th August 1918.
We were told that the Germans had again been driven out of our Front by a Counter Attack and that this part of the Front was going to be our starting point in the Great Offensive which was taking place, the next morning, on the 8th.August 1918. This was the first we were to know or hear about it. The remainder of this day was to be a day of great excitement; having different plans of the coming Battle shown to us and being shown what was our Objective and how to recognise it by a road running into Morlancourt. This, it was explained, was to be the Right Flank of the whole Attack with ourselves acting as the "Pivot" of the start of the Great Offensive. We were told that we were being well supported by the Artillery and that we were also getting the assistance of our 12th .Division Artillery which had also lent the French a hand in their Offensive. We were also to be receiving great help from the Tanks, having three of these to support each Company's Front and with another one positioned in the Support Line. We had to learn different signals as to what to do

when the Tank was needed and what the Tank would signal if it was out of Action and also there were a good number of signals for other purposes. This was a day of Orders for everyone; first from one Officer, then another, then the Company Officer.

235 ALBERT 1918. Orders and Preparations for Advance.

Our Company Officer at this time was a gallant Officer, a gentleman in every way and was much liked by all.

He was a Company Officer who would like to spend much time with his men, as he always liked to feel that they properly understood what they were about to undertake. Along with the earlier Orders we also received Orders on how to hold our Objective when it had been gained. This was because, at this stage of the War, the Germans were getting rather clever as regards to not giving many of their positions away to our airmen.

The Germans had a Front Line much the same as us but not far in the rear they also had Posts here and there, made in such a way that it was very difficult for our Airmen to trace. By organising and working in this way the Germans saved themselves many heavy Bombardments from our Artillery. Our way of holding newly won ground was to hold it by Section Posts. These were little Trenches dug here and there and these had to be held by a Section Commander who may have been a Lance Corporal or a Corporal and about a further 6 men. If the ground had to be held for any length of time, these Posts were joined up and by that it made a Front Line Trench and the Platoon in Support would do likewise and by that form the Second Line.

Before we had finished our preparation for the starting for the Battle, we were supplied with much extra equipment. We received many Flares and bright pieces of tin which were to be used so that we could signal to our brave airmen. We were not supplied with Bombs, Mills bombs, because none were to be had at this time but, for these, we were depending on what could be found in the Trench which we were starting from as we headed into the Battle. There was really no need for us to take a large supply of bombs, etc., as we were going to have Supply Tanks following us up.

236. ALBERT 1918. 7th to 8th August. Advance. Artillery in Support.

This was the first time I had seen such Tanks take their part in Battle and they were carrying a supply of all things which might be needed; Ammunition, Bombs, Water, Iron rations and Barbed Wire. The very last thing that was supplied to us was Rations for two days. Just after we had collected all of these things came the time for us to commence our march to our Staring Positions ready to take our part in the beginning of the Great and Final Offensive. I shall never forget that night of the 7th to 8th August 1918 as long as I live.

Battalion War Diary:

August 8th 1918. BRAY-CORBIE Rd.
Large attack being made today by the 4th Army. The Brigade has been lent to the 18th. Div. for the operation and is operating S. of the main BRAY-CORBIE RD. Parties

are co-operating. Bn. in forming- up places at 2.30 am. Bn. attacking on the left of the Brigade's Front (BRAY-CORBIE Rd.) inclusive of 7th. Royal Sussex on the right. 55th.Bde. on our Left. Zero at 4 20 am.

Tanks started moving forward at Zero minus 20 mins. and the Infantry at Zero minus 10 mins. Artillery of all Calibre opened heavy barrage along the Front of the attack at Zero.

A dense mist prevailed at Zero and it was impossible to see 10 yds. as a result Sections, Platoons, Coys. and Tanks became somewhat mixed up.

By 8 00 am the mist had lifted and it was observed that the first Objective had been gained by "B" Coy. on the right and "D" Coy. on the left. "A" Coy. on the right and "C" Coy. on the left passed through and gained the second objective.

The 53rd.Bde. of the 18th.Div. passed through us to the third Objective which they gained. They were driven out however by a German counter attack and by the afternoon the Bn. found that it was holding the Front Line. All troops in front of the Bn. had been driven back. Bn. held on to their Objective.

Hostile shelling died down towards the evening and the Bn. consolidated the lines it had gained. Troops on our right were in position but on our left the situation was not quite clear. Touch was eventually gained with 5th. ROYAL WEST KENTS.

Casualties to Officers:-

Killed: – Lt. WE HILL, 2nd/Lt. R.T. EAGER, 2nd/Lt. A. NICHOLSON.

Wounded: – 2nd/ Lt. C.S.R. SIDEY, 2nd/Lt. J.A. DAVIES.

Missing: – 2nd/Lt. A.L. HUNTER.

O.R. (Other Ranks) killed or wounded estimated at 350.

Captures made by the Bn.: 300 prisoners, 30 M.G. (machine guns), 8 T.M. (Trench Mortars), 9 Anti-Tank Guns.

Owing to casualties the Bn. was organised into 2 Companys.- No 1 commanded by Lt. T. CHARTER. No.2 commanded by 2nd/Lt. HARRUP.

Sadler Account:

We had Orders to "Fall In" ready for marching away about 6 o'clock and it was not long before every road was packed with Troops going to the Front; all of them to take up their positions in the same way as ourselves. However, having travelled some distance things began to change. Some branched one way and some another and one could really tell that there was a Battle about to take place. Our large guns, 9.2's, were sending over a large number of Salvos to the Germans. On the word of Command, all of the Batteries would fire all together; this was enough to make anyone jump if he had allowed his mind to wander off onto something else rather than just looking and waiting for the heavy guns to fire. Many of the Gunners who were "Off Duty" came across to greet us and to wish us all the best of luck. We marched on and on until we got within reach of our light guns; the 18 Pounder Field Guns. Then Orders were sent back to get into Artillery Formation, 100 yards between each Platoon, and whilst the message was being sent to the rear, we were told to "Fall Out" and rest for a short time.

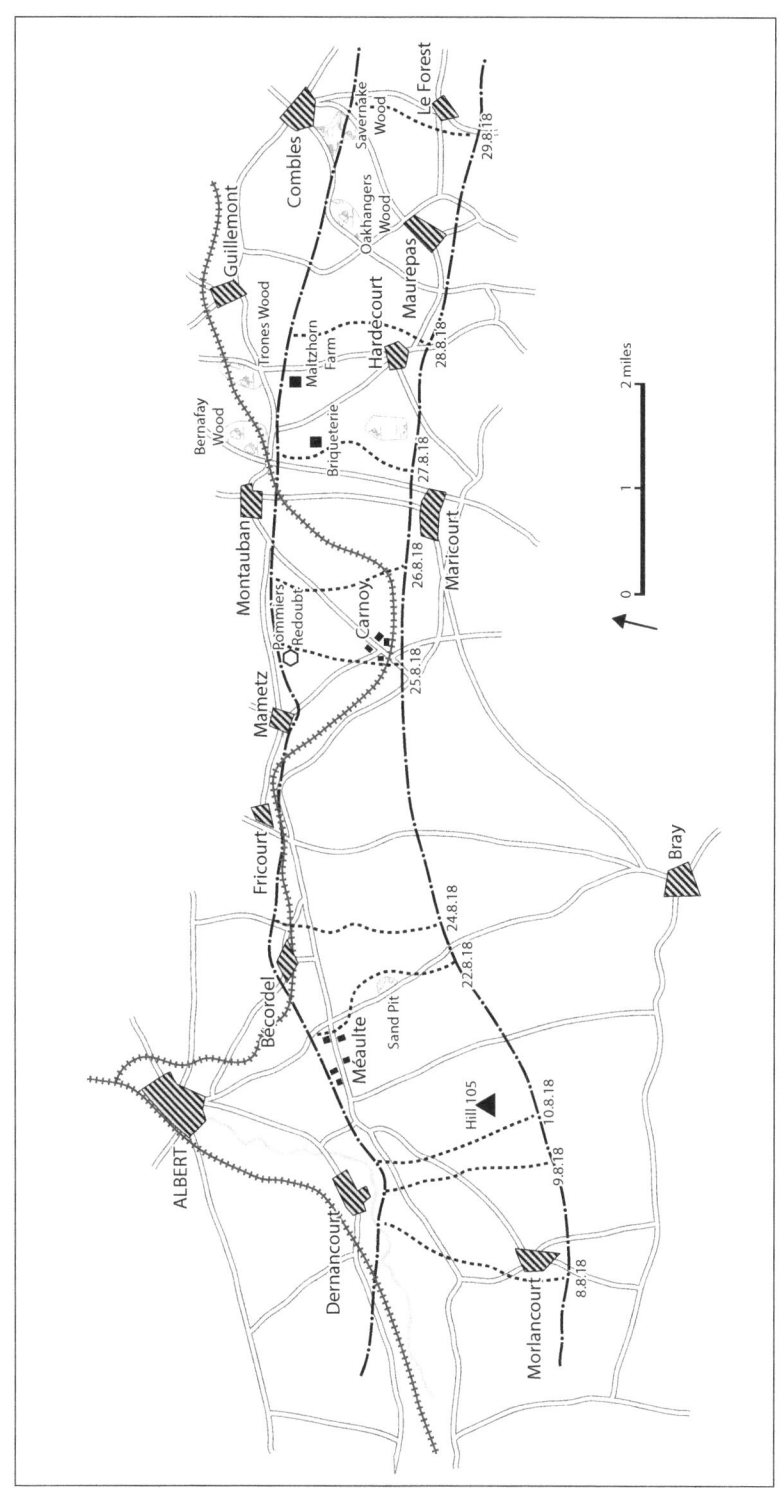

Morlancourt through to Hardecourt-aux-Bois: the advance August 1918. (George Anderson)

237. ALBERT 1918. 7th.August. Continuing the Advance.Advancing under shelling.

Whilst we were enjoying our rest, two of our SOS rockets were seen to go up at Our Front and many more followed. It would have surprised anyone to know just how many guns fired at all at once. Things now began to get very lively. Why our SOS rockets were sent up; I could not say. We wondered whether the Germans were making another attack on our Lines but I think, myself, that the reason they were sent up was because the Front Line Troops fancied that these rockets said something and so we sent them up to make sure. The SOS rockets going up though didn't really improve things for us and, as soon as our guns opened fire, it wasn't long before the Germans were sending back plenty of Shells which were to put some of our Guns out of Action. This was to make it very uncomfortable for us as we were, at that stage, going up a specially made Track which I am sure the Germans knew just as much about as we did. When things quietened down again, we "Fell In" and started, once more, on our journey with shells beginning to burst all around us. We had not gone a great distance when the Germans sent over a very large inflammable shell which burst only a few yards from us. The large flame it created lit the whole place up for a great distance around. This shell started trouble for us as, no doubt, the Germans had someone looking out and could see us making headway along the Tracks towards the Front. We began to think that the Germans must have found out news of our Great Offensive; most likely from the men who they had captured on their two raids on Our Lines. Anyway, they must have known something big was about to be starting as we were followed everywhere by these inflammable shells. The shelling got so heavy that we had to take shelter in an old Trench until things went quiet again. It was costing us the services of too many men who were getting wounded.

238. ALBERT 1918. 7th.August. Advancing under Shelling.

When things had gone quiet again we started moving forward. We hadn't got very far before another shell came over and burst close to us again. This time our Gallant Leader, the Company Officer, was very badly wounded along with several other men. By now we had met a Guide but, like most of the Guides, he himself wasn't too sure of his way and it was only after he had taken us a few miles out of our way that we finished up in a newly dug Trench, dead tired. Here we were told we could sit down and rest. We soon quite understood this wasn't the right Trench as things were far too quiet and we found out we had yet another mile to go before we were to reach our intended destination. Just as we had started to get nice and comfortable, the Order was passed along to "Get Up and Lead On" and I must say that we were all beginning to get fed up with our approach towards the Battle. As we were getting nearer to the Line we were intended for, we didn't seem to find any "Made Up" tracks and we were to finish our journey walking up a very badly knocked about road.

239. ALBERT 1918. 7th August. Advance but how far?. The role of a Guide.

Not only were Shells now falling either side of us but also the "Road" was also being well swept by German Machine Gun fire and again we had to take cover in a ditch along the side of the "highway". Once again, when things went quiet, we "Led On" once more. The next message that was sent to the rear was to tell everyone to hurry to get by a certain part of the road because the Germans, at times, opened out short and sharp bursts of Artillery fire. About a hundred yards past this we were again shown another Trench where we settled down for a time. Again we were left wondering if this was our stopping place. Yet again, after we had got nicely settled down, the Order was again passed along, "Get Up and Lead On" which we did; moving along the Trench to the Right. Here the Trench was about two foot deep with another foot of mud at the bottom. Finally, the Order was sent along to "About Turn" and "Lead Back" to the part of the Trench which we had just left. At this place we were told to settle down for an hour or so before the starting time of the Great Battle. Up to now we had received a terrible time getting to this Trench; this mainly due to the Guide not knowing his way. The reason for this was that most of the Guides, who were sent to show relieving Troops the way in, had not got the slightest idea of the Roads themselves. The Guide wasn't to blame. The one who sent the Guide was the one to blame. A man acting as a Guide should have had the "pleasure" of going over the ground several times before taking charge of leading Troops to their Positions his role was a very responsible one when he was called upon to lead many men.

240. ALBERT 1918. 8th. August – Advance to Battle.

This wasn't the only thing which we had to put up with before 4 o'clock; the starting time of the Great Battle.

As soon as we tried to get an hour or so of sleep, the Order came along the Trench to look around the Trench for Bombs and Picks and Shovels and, not long after this, we received a terrible time from the German Artillery which, again, made us think that he must have known what was about to take place. After about half an hour or so, things again went quiet and we got up as close to each other as possible in order to get warm and try and have a sleep once more. At five minutes to four we were going to take up Positions in No Man's Land by Sections in Artillery Formation. Two of our Companies were taking the lead and we were keeping in Sections until they had taken their Objective then we had to pass through them and go on to take our Objective which I thought was a grand idea. All we had to do now, if we were unable to sleep, was to start thinking of the beginning of the Battle and not one of us could imagine what we were going to receive by way of a reception as we prepared to advance.

The anxious moments drew on until ten minutes to four when, again, the Germans started a most terrible bombardment of small shells; all bursting in No Man's Land.

241. ALBERT 1918. 8th. August – Going into Battle. Over the Top.

At this point everyone was expecting to hear the rattle of the Tanks coming forward but they were not to be heard and it was only a minute or so before we had to take up our positions ready for Battle. Still the Germans were sending over thousands of shells and, anyone who had never seen shellfire before would never have thought it possible for any man to cross over No Man's Land under such terrible fire. The smoke from the Germans bursting shells made it impossible to see a good yard in front. Five minutes to four, the Order came along the Line to "Go over the Top" and lie in Sections, ready for starting off. I would have thought that never have any Troops ever had to go and lie in the open under such terrible shellfire. All we could think was we would be very lucky if we ever reached the German Front Line. Our own Artillery was doing its best to bluff the Germans by not firing back any shells and these five minutes, in No Man's land, waiting for our Artillery to give up the Signal to go ahead by starting an instant and terrible bombardment; seemed more like years to us than minutes. We knew now, alright, that the Germans were aware that we were coming after them. As it happened, on that day, they were getting ready to attack us but, of course, we were not to know. However, they soon found out which it was to be. We were after them first and it was impossible for them to see us coming because of so much smoke and mist.

242. ALBERT 1918. 8th. August – Advancing into Battle. The German Front Line.
Crossing over to the German Front Line, I was to receive one of the greatest shocks of my life.

At Four o'clock everything started in full swing and once more we stepped forward with the aim of causing the Germans a very unpleasant time. I must say that, up to now, they were also causing us a terrible time but we were not all destined to be killed by his terrible Barrage. After we had passed their Barrage we had little to worry about, or so we thought; having two Companies in front of us. At last the German barbed wire was reached which had been untouched by our Artillery fire. It looked very much as if it had only just been put out as it was barbed wire made in a similar way to the French concertina wire and there was no doubt, it had been run out in a hurry. We really thought that we didn't have to worry about this as we quite thought that the German Front Line must have already been taken by our advancing Companies. At last , though, we were to get over the wire only to receive one of the greatest surprises of our lives when, within two or three yards from the German Trench, we found that we had run up against a German Machine Gun Post.

This opened out with a burst of fire, the bullets hitting one or two of the men before they could lie down.

There we had to lay with bullets striking the ground near our feet. Not only did we receive showers of bullets but also many dozens of hand grenades. We found we were in a very tight fix. If we had had some bombs we could have chanced putting the Gun Post out of action but we could not have known that we were as close as we were. We could only tell this by how far they were able to throw their hand grenades.

243. ALBERT 1918. 8th August – Taking the German Front Line. Tank Support.
When the machine gun stopped firing for a short time we rushed to our right and, owing to there being so much smoke about, it was impossible for the Germans to see us. At this time we were also able to hear one of our Tanks moving about but we were unable to see it. As luck would have it, we found the German Trench to the Right empty and we soon got to the rear of the Machine Gun Post. On the road

running towards Morlancourt we found a few more men of another Division; also three of our Tanks stationed on the Road.

While we were talking to the men in command of the Tanks; all of a sudden we heard shouting and much rifle and machine gun fire. We rushed around to the opposite side of the Tanks for shelter and got ready for Action. This noise turned out to be the Germans from this Strongpoint of the Machine Gun Post who had decided to turn about and made a rush for us. They found out they were up against stronger Forces than themselves and they had to pay for it. At last many of them shouted out "Camarade" and, if it hadn't been for an Officer shouting out, "Why can't you see they are holding their arms up? Stop firing", not one of them would have been taken Prisoner. As it was there was only one or two who were shot and in the end we considered we had had our own back on them. They had frightened us, it's true and we had done the same to them. After getting over this particular piece of trouble we were able to push forward with all of our men who could be collected together and with the aid of the three tanks. I must say the Tanks did some very good work. They went on ahead and tripped along from one end of our advance to the other, using their guns and machine guns but most of the Germans were soon off when they heard the sound of the Tanks. The Germans were far from fond of such creatures and with this we were able to walk ahead with only a few stray bullets being fired at us.

244. ALBERT 1918. 8th.August – Observations on a newly won Trench.

It wasn't a great length of time before we had won our Objective. I noticed, in many of the newly won Trenches, much of our own equipment. Whether there had been any raids by us at this part of the Line and our men had been driven out before they had time to collect their equipment, I could not say. The equipment could, though, have been left there since our enforced "retirement/ withdrawal", in March. When at our Objective, I had another very narrow escape. Myself and a Sergeant, a chum of mine, were ordered to Post an "Out Post" in front of our Objective to keep a good Lookout whilst the men were digging the Sectional Posts. He said, "Coming for a look round?", and I decided to go with him. When he said "I know where there is a Trench, over here, which will make a good Out Post", I followed him to take a look. The Trench was amongst some high wheat and wire netting had been spread over the top of the Trench on short stakes. Over the top of this net, some wheat had been sprinkled by the Germans so that our Airmen would not be able to notice the Post. We noticed the Post all right. What we didn't notice was what was in the wheat nearby.

245.ALBERT 1918. 8th.August – Resistance North of Morlancourt. A casualty.

We had only just reached the Post and were about to jump down to take up our Position when we were greeted with a sharp outburst of machine gun fire. We found out that the Germans were taking cover in the wheat close by. Anyhow we had only just jumped into the Post for cover when one of the men was caught by a bullet from the machine gun. This had hit him in the arm and cut an artery. As I had a little idea of what to do with such a case, we soon tied a bandage tightly above the wound but then the man came over very faint. I walked around the Post to see if I could find anyone who could go and fetch some Stretcher-Bearers. To my surprise, I found all the rest of the men, except for the four of us, had left the Post and so I had to go and look for Stretcher-Bearers myself. I found our own Stretcher-Bearers were busy taking wounded men away and because of that they were unable to offer any assistance. This being the case I set off to another Regiments Front, The Royal Berkshires, which was a Battalion in support of us. On meeting one of their Officers I asked him if it was possible for me to have their Stretcher-Bearers for a short time because one of our men had had an artery cut and I explained that, if it had only been a wound, then I would not have bothered him. This Officer was only too pleased to let me have them, so we set off and returned back to the Post. I began to wonder if we were going to find the Germans holding the Post on our return, but everything went well and we were able to reach our wounded man. The Stretcher-Bearers redressed the wound and the man began to come round and after a short time he was able to get to the Dressing Station without the aid of the Stretcher-Bearers.

246 ALBERT 1918. 8th.August – Morlancourt. The opposing German Troops.

Soon after this we left this Post and, as I had lost sight of the remainder of the Out Post party, I proceeded back to the place from where the Sergeant had initially asked me to come with him. Here we started working to make a little bit of cover for ourselves as the German's deadly shrapnel was causing a large number of our men to be wounded. Another Brigade from another Division had followed us up and was trying to take the village of Morlancourt but the Germans were making them fight for every inch of ground. This Brigade was not managing to take much ground from the Germans on, this, the first day of the Battle. Towards dark, this night, the Germans made a Counter Attack and managed to drive this Brigade back a little so that some of the ground which they had won during the day was recaptured. We found out that we were up against some of the finest Troops the Germans had got. It turned out that they were the Germans 27th. "Storming" Division; especially trained Troops which they used for attacking purposes. These Troops generally came to the Front, made their attack and then went back to the rear again. They were trained to undertake attacks but not for holding the Lines. I could never remember meeting such big and strong looking German Troops and they tried their very hardest to ensure that they would not to give up any of their ground to us.

247. ALBERT 1918. 8th.August – Morlancourt. Tanks – A possible counter attack.

What I did notice during this day's Battle was the fact that the German Troops did not mind meeting us too much but it was our Tanks which they did not like facing. They knew very well that the bullets from their rifles would not manage to stop one of them. Our Tanks had done some very good work this day and were really the means by which we got to our Objective. When dark set in, on the night of the 8th.August, we quite expected an attack from the Germans on our Front and we received the Order several times that the Germans were massing for a Counter attack. As luck would have it for us, no attack took place and we enjoyed a fairly quiet night. By this time we also had a fairly good Trench for cover. The following morning we were troubled at times by German machine gun fire coming from the direction of the Post which I had visited the day before. As there was another stage of the Battle taking place in the afternoon, this machine gun fire had to be stopped, if at all possible, in order to give our advancing Troops a chance of going ahead. A Sergeant and one of our men went to the Front to see if this machine gunner could be found and also to carry on with the sniping. About four o'clock in the afternoon, two of our Tanks were seen coming to the Front and the Gunners from the German Light Batteries were trying their very hardest to put these Tanks out of action. Small shells were bursting all around but they could not seem to get a direct hit. This afternoon our tanks were on the Scene before the Infantry.

Battalion War Diary:

August 9th 1918. MORLANCOURT
Quiet during the morning. Work of consolidation pushed on with. A hostile M.G.'s nest which was holding out on our left was causing considerable trouble. During late afternoon, Sgt. S BARTON with 3 men went out to silence it and if possible to capture the post. The manoeuvre was completely successful and has succeeded in capturing 1 Officer, 3 MG's, and 30 men. By 5 30 pm. the attack was continued by the 35th.and 37th.Inf. Bde. of the 12th.Div. N. of the BRAY-CORBIE road and by units of the 58th.Div. S. of the Rd.

MORLANCOURT was captured and the Bn. was ordered to the area E. of MORLANCOURT to try and consolidate a line of Trenches behind the 37th.Inf. Bde. This was done without opposition.

Sadler Account:

248 ALBERT 1918. Morlancourt. Getting a German Post to surrender.
It wasn't long before our advancing Infantry were seen coming forward by Section and, although they were keeping under cover as much as possible, it was not too long before they were noticed by the Germans and a Barrage was at once opened out. A great number of our Troops had passed before the Barrage was opened out and they were beginning to give the Germans a very trying time. Not long after this attack had started, I was sent for by an Officer and told to bring six men with me to report to him so, collecting the first six men who were close at hand; I set off on my journey. The Officer ordered me with my six men to go out and get the German Machine Gun Post to surrender. This was the same post as I have mentioned before where the Germans had given us such a shock in the wheat field. We set off on our journey and it wasn't long before we got as close as possible to the Post under cover. I decided to use my six men as my covering Party and I got them to take up Positions where they would be able to see the German Post and also be able to fire when ordered. I explained to them before starting what I was going to do. I knew that, if I wanted to get the Germans to surrender, I had to make myself seen to them and get them to be watching my movements. I told my men that my intention was to get as close to the German Post as possible and then I was going to stand straight up and beckon them to surrender. What I wanted them to

do was watch the Germans at the Post and, as soon as they saw a German put his rifle to his shoulder, to try and shoot at me, then they were not to wait but fire straight at them.

249 ALBERT 1918. Morlancourt. Getting a German Post to surrender (continued).

It very much depended on them as to whether I was going to be giving my life up or not. I must say that the men, with me, were well up to the "game" and capable of achieving our desired result. When I considered that I was close enough to the German Post, which was only a case of a few yards, I stood up and beckoned to the Germans to get out of the Post by lifting my hands towards the sky. Then, by bringing my hand towards my head, I signalled that I meant for them to get out of the Post and come towards me. After doing this, not a single German moved and I could see there were quite 20 to 30 of them only a few yards from me. I could also see the German's machine gun with men by it, ready to fire. That took my eye and I decided to act. I took my rifle, which I had leaning against me, and fired straight at the man nearest to the machine gun and made sure that he wouldn't worry me anymore. My six men opened fire at what Germans they could see. I had offered the Germans the chance to surrender which they had not taken so, with our Action, it was one way or the other. After our outburst of rifle fire, I tried them again by standing up for a second time. This time a German answered my signals by jumping up out of the Trench and coming towards me.

250. ALBERT 1918. Morlancourt. A German Post surrenders.

I walked forward to greet him and he turned out to be a German Officer. His first words to me were "I am the Officer in Charge of the Post". I said to him that I didn't care who he was but he was to get his men out and to get over there to a place which I was pointing at. The German Officer soon ordered the men out of the Post and, as the Germans got up out of the Post, they made towards me holding their hands out for me to shake hands with them. I showed them where I wanted them to go and told them to get on with it. After they had all moved on past me, the Officer stayed and walked in with me. From what I could make of what he was saying, his mind was wandering towards London. He spoke one or two words about London. I took him to the Officer who had sent me and my men out to get the Post to surrender. After he had saluted our Officer, he again informed him that he was in charge of the men. Up to this point we had captured 34 Germans and the 1 Officer and all of them seemed happy and reasonably content to think that they had been taken prisoner.

Our Prisoners were handed over to two of our men to be taken to the Detention Camp. Myself and my Party of men; we returned to the Post to get the captured machine guns. We had the pleasure of bringing two of these back. I picked up one of the guns which I found to be so hot from being fired so much that I had to drop it quickly. Two Germans lay dead near the guns. They had been caught by rifle fire. After looking around to see if there was anything else that we could find to keep in remembrance, we left the Post to take up our position once more.

251. ALBERT 1918. 9th.August. Morlancourt captured.

The Battle which had taken place this afternoon was a great success and included the surrounding of Morlancourt and it wasn't long before we were called upon to go forward and support the Advanced Troops.

When we started moving forward the Germans were only sending over a shell every now and then. I fully expected that they were busy in putting the majority of their guns into new positions. It seemed to me that we marched for miles before we came to the end of the newly won ground. On our journey we passed many square holes that had been cut by the Germans and which contained German machine guns but no Germans.

Passing over the site of this new battlefield, I do not think that I saw more than half a dozen dead Troops and that included both our Troops and the Germans. This night we finished up digging more Section Posts, not a great distance from the outskirts of Morlancourt. This turned out to be a very hard night's work, digging for cover. The Germans did not really worry us but certainly did not intend to let our Troops settle in Morlancourt and did this by sending over very heavy shells. Up to this stage, all we had in Morlancourt was an advanced Dressing Station and it was a far from healthy place to be carrying wounded.

Battalion War Diary:

August 10th 1918. MORLANCOURT

Hostile shelling active all day against our new position E. of MORLANCOURT. Heavy gas shelling commencing at 10 00 am. Bn. moved back to the old British Front and support line N.W. of MORLANCOURT and reverted to the 36th.Inf. Brigade.

Sadler Account:

252. ALBERT 1918. Action or Not? Advancing Troops. Being relieved from Battle.

It was not to be very long before another stage of the Battle was to take place. After working hard all night, we intended to get a little rest for the following day before it came to daylight. However it wasn't long after daylight when we received Orders that we were again going forward but this was not to be the case. I think the reason why we, as a Battalion, did not go into Action was because we were not strong enough in numbers. We could only muster one Company's strength out of the four who had advanced the previous day. The Battalion was now only 150 men strong. Anyway for our troops, everything was packed up ready for action and, about four o'clock in the afternoon, Tanks were again seen coming to the Front. Not long after, the Infantry were to be seen following up, again advancing in Sections. As they passed by our Posts, we wished them all the very best of luck and all the men seemed bright and cheerful. It wasn't long after that before the Germans started shelling all the low ground in the rear of us to make sure that no more Troops were being massed, but by this time it was too late. From the position where our Posts were placed, we had a grand view of the Battle. It was grand sight to see the Troops advancing by Sections and, every now and then, a very large smoke or gas shell would burst well in the rear of the advance. It wasn't a long time after that we received news that their Objective had been gained. This time we were not to be called upon to Support; instead Troops stationed too the rear of us came forward to go to their support. This night we were to receive a great surprise for, on receiving Orders, these were that we were going to get relieved when dusk set in so, about 9 30 this night, we left our Posts and made tracks towards Morlancourt . Passing along the edge of the village, we finished up near our starting point for the Great Offensive where we settled down in some old Trenches and soon fell asleep. As it was nearly daybreak before we arrived at these Trenches, sleep was needed more than food.

So after two days of continuous action, Sergeant Sadler and comrades found a brief respite from the relentless advance to victory that would force Imperial Germany to seek terms.

23

August–September 1918: Driving the Enemy back

It was during the second week of August that the German Army, reeling from the Amiens push, was in full retreat, as Allied was maintained.

Battalion War Diary:

August 11th 1918. MORLANCOURT
Settled in new position about 3 00 am. Day spent in resting.

August 12th 1918. MORLANCOURT
Day spent in resting. Marching at 9 00pm. Bn. moved forwards and relieved the 6th. Queens, 37th.Inf. Bde. in the front line N.E. of MORLANCOURT preparatory to taking part in an action tomorrow in conjunction with the 7th.Royal Sussex. Draft of 36 new and 36 old men arrived from Reception Camp during the night and were formed into a third Coy. under 2/Lt. G. GUYATT MM.

Sadler Account:

253. ALBERT 1918. Morlancourt. – Back to the Front.
We spent about 24 hours at these Trenches, (Aug. 11th.), and with new reinforcements having arrived, we received further Orders that we were going back to the Front once again. We were also told that we were going to be taking a certain part in a coming Battle, this even though we were tired out. We started on our long journey back to the Front. It seemed a great pity to have been brought such a long way back for only a few hours. After doing this journey we finished up in an old German Trench, well to the left of the Posts where we were last time. Every action in this Battle had been fought so as to push forwards and in towards the rear of Albert. It was about this time the Germans started to fall back from Albert.

Battalion War Diary:

August 13th 1918. N.E. of MORLANCOURT
Relief complete 4 30 am. At 4 55 am the 7th.Sussex on the right and ourselves on the left attacked under cover of an artillery barrage to capture the new position of high ground in front of our present lines.
　　Our operation was successful but, as the result of a German counter attack, the 7th.Royal Sussex were driven back to their original line. The Bn. maintained its position and swung round to its right flank to gain touch with the Sussex in the old

front line.

Our casualties: – 4 O.R. wounded.

August 14th 1918. N.E. of MORLANCOURT

Between 2 30 am & 4 00 am hostile artillery was very active on our position of the Front. At 3 45 am our own artillery replied vigorously at our request and by shortly after 4 30 am all was quiet.

Intermittent hostile shelling during the day. Enemy reported to be retiring E. of ALBERT. Strong patrols pushed out opposite our own Front to gain touch with the enemy. Found him in occupation of a trench about 300 yds. away. This was being strongly held.

August 15th 1918. N.E. of MORLANCOURT

Very quiet day and night. Our new position being consolidated and wired.

Sadler Account:

254. ALBERT 1918. August 13th. -Attacking Again.

This being the Pivotal Point of the Great Offensive, we had to work our way round to keep pace with the Right Flank so, all of the attacking done from our Position, was done in order to push forward and to get to the rear of the Germans and surround as many of them as we could.

The Germans were keeping well out of sight and it was a puzzle to know exactly where they were. We knew they were still holding their Trenches on our left rear and with that being so they were on the other side of Albert on the top of a great ridge. It was to be a grand sight to watch the flashes from our own guns on our left as we went forward. The old German Trench which we were now holding was, though, far from being a comfortable health resort. The Germans were busy for several hours after we arrived, sending over very large Gas shells and compelling us to wear our gas masks at intervals. The next morning we were to be gaining a little more ground from the Germans. The action of this part of the Battle was taking place on our right but, in the end, finished up at Our Front. As the troops to the right were swinging round, we had to join the newly -won ground up to our Front by digging across No Man's Land.

255. ALBERT 1918. Morlancourt. Wiring. Aerial Bombing and Shelling.

At four o'clock the next morning, the Battle started with a terrible outburst of Artillery fire. We made our way out into No Man's Land and took cover in shell holes on the top of the Ridge. From these shell holes we dug towards each other to make our new Front Line. The Troops to our right were driven back by some strong forces of Germans but, owing to us having a grand view of the German position ahead of us, we received Orders to hold on. This night I received Orders to take out a party of men to put up barbed wire around the front of the new posts. The first night was spent in putting up much wire and everything was fairly quiet however, the second night was completely the other way about. After we had started and done an hour or so of work, the Germans opened up a terrible rate of shellfire. Whether a German

Patrol had noticed a large Party of us, out and about, wiring and had made the mistake of thinking we were getting ready for another attack, I could not say but, how we managed to get back to our new Posts to take cover without having a man wounded, I do not know. To make it even more "cheerful", one of our Airmen came over to drop bombs on the German Front Position and these very nearly finished up by falling on top of us. We received the shock of five terrible crashes, one after the other, and when we took shelter in the Posts; we nearly got blown out again by a large shell bursting just in the rear. The Germans were making sure that we should have something to face if we were undertaking another attack. He kept up the shelling all night, including firing a great number of gas shells. Towards the usual time of our attacking, which was about 4 o'clock in the morning, the Germans started using every kind of gun that he had and we received a very warm time for an hour or so. We all expected to see the Germans over and after us.

256. ALBERT 1918. Around Morlancourt. An escape for a Ration Party.

All the sentries received Orders to keep a sharp look out but with the smoke caused by the bursting shells and the gas; it was impossible to see a yard or so in front of us. When it began to get properly near daylight and the shellfire had begun to quieten down a little, the Sentry, who was doing his hour on duty, shouted out, "Here they are, coming". My Officer and myself jumped up on the Fire Step ready for action when he called out to our men, "Don't fire yet as it may be one of our Ration Parties". What he was thinking was that they could well have been taking rations to the Posts when the bombardment started and, having stayed at the Posts for cover, and owing to the amount of smoke, lost their sense of direction. This actually turned out to be the case and it was indeed very lucky for the Ration Party that this thought had crossed this Officer's mind or they may have all been killed. When the Officer and myself had initially jumped up; it is true that we could see moving objects ahead but with the smoke it was impossible to see if they were British or Germans. It was never found to be advisable to wait until whoever it was got too close before opening fire. One never knew what was following on behind.

257. ALBERT 1918. Around Morlancourt

When it was eventually possible for the Germans to see for themselves that no more Troops were likely to be coming forward, he finished shelling our Trench and started shelling all the "dips" in the Rear.

It was certainly not the Germans intention to let any Troops mass in these "dips" whatsoever.

This night we left this Trench for a few days to go back to some more Trenches in the Rear where we were to receive our reinforcements. This was the last action that we were to see in this grand position.

Battalion War Diary:

August 16th 1918. N.E. of RUSEMONT

Quiet day. Starting at 10 00 pm. The Bn. was relieved by the 7th Norfolk's, 35th Bde. Relief was completed 11 45 pm. Our relief Bn. moved back to trenches immediately

N.E. of RIBEMONT, near the Sugar Factory.

August 17th 1918. N.E. of RIBEMONT
Settled in our new area by 2 00 am. Coys. Bathed during the morning in the River ANCRE. During the afternoon the Bn. was reorganised into 4 Coys. of 4 platoons each, Draft of 6 Officers and 150 O.R. arrived.

August 18th 1918. N.E. of RIBEMONT
Cleaning up and inspection parades during morning. Clothing parades in the afternoon.

August 19th 1918. N.E. of RIBEMONT
Inspection parades. Musketry & L. Gunnery. Draft of 2 Officers and 80 O.R. received.

Sadler account:

257. ALBERT 1918(cont.). Young reinforcements arrive on 17th. Honours for Company Sergeant.

On getting back to the rear, we were made up to strength by a large number of Northumberland Fusiliers, all young chaps, of around 18 years of age, who turned out to be some very smart young men. Whilst we were at these Trenches we spent a day or so in training our new comrades. Various messages were read out to them on the good work the Battalion had done in the past. The next day I was called to our Company Head Quarters and told that we would be going to the Front Line again tomorrow night and that I should have to carry on with the duties of Company Sergeant Major. This was owing to fact that the Sergeant, who should have been taking the Position, was being "Left Out" to receive the "Honour" for capturing the machine gun post and prisoners in the wheat field which I have mentioned earlier. The best part of this was that this Sergeant, plus one or two men out of the six men who I had taken on that venture, were to be commended for doing "Good work in the Field" under me!

Battalion War Diary:

20th August 1918.N.E. of RIBEMONT.
Usual parades during the morning. C.O.'s and N.C.O.'s in charge of Coys. reconnoitre the trenches held by the 6th.West Kent's Reg. Same trenches that we occupied when the 7th.Norfolk s relieved us. Marching at 8 30 pm Bn. relieved the 6th.West Kent's in the right sub-sector of the Left Bde. Front. Relief complete 1 30 pm.

Sadler account:

258. ALBERT 1918. Morlancourt. Further Advances. Preparations and Maps.

As I was now in the position of acting Company Sergeant Major, I had to go and look at the Trenches which we were about to take over. On arriving at the Trenches, having taken with me an amount of stock and stores etc., I found it was the position we had left last time that we had been in the Line. I could guess that we were not going to be there too long before going forward. After I had taken over all the stores required, I left to join my Company and to return to the Trenches again.

Later the same day, on returning and having just had time to have tea, it was time to "Fall In" and as a Company we proceeded to the Trenches by Platoons. I will say that it was a very long journey to the Trenches but it turned out to be very quiet one. As soon as we reached the Trenches the men received Orders to start on improving the Trenches, which they carried out all right. When all Platoons had taken up their correct Positions, I had to walk around and visit all Platoons of the Company and report that the Company was present. The night turned out to be a fairly quiet one, all except for our machine guns which were stationed nearby. They kept up a constant rate of firing on the road behind the German Lines; this causing, at times, the drawing of German shellfire as they searched for our guns. The next morning all Officers were called to attend Company H.Q., such as it was, and here we were handed a smoke and the Company Officer remarked, "I have some good news for you". It wasn't long before we were handed new maps showing the ground, which we were about to take.

Battalion War Diary:

21st.August 1918. N.E. of RIBEMONT
Enemy artillery active carrying out harassing fire from about 4 00 am to 5 00 am. Quiet during the day. Heavy gas shelling by enemy from 9 00 pm onwards. Gas shelling continued throughout the greater part of the night being very heavy at times.

22nd. August 1918.N.E. of RIBEMONT
Bn. taking part in joint attack today. Formed up in assembly positions in front and behind our front line by 4 00am. Zero hour 4 45am. Commencing at Zero, Artillery of various calibres put down a heavy barrage and the Infantry commenced moving forward. Tanks were co-operating but they were late in arriving. The 18th.Div. were operating on the Bde.'s left and 35th.Bde. on the right. In the Bde. sector the 9th.R.F.'s were operating on the Right and the 5th.Royal Berks. on the Left as far as the first objective. From 1st to 2nd Objectives the 7th.Royal Sussex were on the Right and the 5th.Royal Berks were on the Left. Bn. attacked on a 2 Coy. frontage, each Coy. having 2 platoons on the first wave and 2 in the 2nd.wave. "A" Coy. on the Right and "B" Coy. on the Left attacked and captured the first objective of the Bn. "C" Coy on the right and "D" on the left then "leap frogged" through and took final objective. Frontage allotted to the Bn. was 1000ft in depth of advance 2500 yds. 5th. Royal Berks captured and cleared the village of MEALUTE. 7th.Royal Sussex passed through the Bn. and took the Bde.'s final objective. Bn. in touch on right with 7th.Bn. Norfolk's Regt.

Captured by the Bn.:- 100 prisoners, 12 M.G.'s and 4 T.M.'s.

Casualties:- Officers:- Lt. H.H.D.KIDMISTER M.C.; 2/Lt. L.F.WADE, Killed;- 2/Lt. T.O.BOWRY; 2/Lt. H.A.REYNOLDS, Wounded.

Casualties to O.R.:- 78.

Sadler account:

259. ALBERT 1918. Morlancourt – Advancing under shelling.-22nd August.

Next we had to mark our Maps with the position where the attack was to be taking place at 4 o'clock the following morning. We were going to have to lie in the Open at five minutes to four, by Sections, ready to push forward and we were also going to have Patrol or Liquid Fire Shells on our right flank to show us our direction. I had more to do in sharing out stores etc. for the coming Battle and, when this was finished, rations arrived and these had to be served out. Throughout this day and night, I was to get very little time to myself. At about half past three in the morning, I received Orders to get the Company ready to take up their positions as another Regiment wanted this position because they were passing through us and going on a short distance ahead. We took up our places ready for Action and had to lie quietly for half an hour before going ahead. By now the Germans were commencing their usual early morning shelling and it was to be one of the most uncomfortable half hours one could ever spend; lying out in the Open with shells bursting all around.

About five minutes to four, the shelling got so heavy that we had to take to the Trench for cover. This we found was a little better than lying out on the ground. At last 4 o'clock arrived. Our Artillery again sent forth a terrible creeping barrage and, also, overcame the first "spreading" fire shell to show us our direction.

This shell did not really do us any good as it fell short and burst between us all and in doing so put several men out of action.

260. ALBERT 1918. Advancing. German Barrage and Gas Shells.

After we had passed through the German Barrage things went fairly smoothly and we were able to keep in Sections instead of Extended Order. The other Regiment then passed through us and went ahead. We then kept in Platoons until we had taken our Objective. Whilst we were on the Road to our Objective, I noticed that the Germans had cut a great deal of wheat and, where they had left it undisturbed; we were greeted with a large number of Gas Shells. The Germans were quite well aware that the Gas would hang about in the long wheat but this was to make very little difference to us. It was true we had to wear our Gas masks but, as we knew it was not altogether a very dangerous sort of gas, we only adjusted the nose-clip and mouth piece and left the mask itself, hanging loose so that we could see what lay ahead. What was to prove more dangerous to us, were several of our own guns which were firing their shells at short range. They were sort of putting up a creeping barrage all of their own and this at a very dangerous distance behind the correct Barrage as the shells were landing just about at the distance where we had to follow up. It was far from comfortable to walk ahead with shrapnel bullets striking the ground all around us, knocking little pieces of turf out of the ground. This was not only kept up for a hundred yards or so but for the whole journey and caused many of our men to be wounded.

261. ALBERT 1918. Advancing. Taking Prisoners. Reaching Objectives.

We were only delayed once by a German strongpoint which, after a very short time, surrendered. However, the men would not take them Prisoners without first having a shot or two at them. This was, they felt, just to let them know they were prepared to kill and that they were not to be played about with. As this Strong Point had caused us trouble the men wished to do the same to them. We mustered quite 30 prisoners from this Post and, after this; we had a clear road ahead until our Objective was reached; our Objective being a deep Sunken Road. I noticed the Germans had cut out "fire-steps" in the banks of the Sunken Road and had tried to do their very best to hold it but it was really only a case of holding their hands up, in surrender, when we got to them. Once the German prisoners were got away, we started the men to digging Section Posts, 50 yards apart on the far side of the road then another Regiment, (5th Royal Berkshire), passed by us and went ahead and took their Objective with very little trouble. As Acting Company Sergeant Major, it was my job to find out where the Company Officer had decided to make his Head Quarters. He said that he had noticed several deep dugouts which had been started in the Sunken Road and had decided to make one of these his Head Quarters. A place such as this was far from what I would have wished for as I had seen enough of Sunken Roads and knew very well that the Germans liked searching such places with their shells.

262. ALBERT 1918. Advancing. Captured German Dugouts. Duties as Company Sergeant Major.

The Company Officer and myself, however, walked along the Sunken Road to try and find the best dugout and, as we had Royal Engineers with us during this attack whose task was to test deep dugouts before we entered, it was not long before we came into contact with two of these Royal Engineers. The Officer asked them to test a dugout for him which they did but the so called "Dug Out" did not require much testing as it was found to be only four steps down in the ground. No doubt the Germans had quite intended to stay for an extended period and to make themselves very comfortable but they had been "turned out" before they had been given very much time to do a lot of deep digging to complete the dugout. Although the doorways of the dugout were facing in the direction of the Germans, it was quite good enough to be able to sit in and do writing etc. especially when it had a blanket hung up over the doorway.

As for myself, I was having nothing to do with starting to make any new dugouts. Being a fairly deep Sunken Road, I decided to make a place in the bank on the other side of the road where I knew it would be impossible for German shells to cause a nuisance by coming down through the entrance. My chum and myself set to work and cut a place out in the bank so that both of us could sit in it comfortably. Then we took a trip around to try and find one or two sheets of tin which we felt we needed to use a roof in order to cover the place. I had writing to do nearly all of the time, marking out Trench Strength Rolls and serving out rations at night-time.

263. ALBERT 1918. Organising Troops. Advancing with Tanks.

In the end we made a nice little shelter for ourselves and throughout the day the Germans kept fairly quiet. I then had to sort out the men by sending a few here and there and, after this, I had to count the strength of the Company and send a report into Battalion Head Quarters. Once all this had been done I knew just how many men we had lost in the Battle. In all, my Company had only 20 men wounded but not a single man had been killed. In all my time in France, I could never remember going into Battle with so few men being put out of action. We had one or two Tanks at this Battle but, as we were meeting very few Germans, they went over to our Left Flank to give help as they were having a much harder time than us in taking the village. However, they were able to keep up with us the whole way and we both joined together at our Objectives. Whilst at this Sunken Road, just after we had captured it, I was looking well ahead to see just what could be seen and had the pleasure of witnessing a very grand sight which was taking place involving one of our Tanks; quite two miles ahead. I could see one of our Tanks cruising along the top of a high ridge, from one end to the other.

The man in charge of the Tank certainly seemed intent on having good look around and I must say that I considered that it was a very plucky thing to do; being willing to take his Tank so far ahead, alone, on a journey like that was very risky thing to undertake.

264. ALBERT 1918. Advancing with Tanks. Rations. Taking Cover.

The main reason as to why a journey like that was a very risky thing to undertake was that the Tank was more than likely to have met with a German Light Battery of Guns. These could very soon have put it out of action by being able to fire at it at point blank range. I have no doubt the Officer in Charge of the Tank found out much important news and also sure that both the Officer and men would have given the Germans a very hard time had anything happened to the tank. It would have really surprised most people to have seen the great amount of traffic on this Sunken Road when it reached dark that night, especially as we were not a great distance from the Germans. There were Royal Engineers bringing up rolls of wire, iron stakes etc. in Large General Service Wagons and besides these there were a large number of Ration Limbers taking rations up to the Troops on our Right. It was truly wonderful what work could be carried on whilst it was dark.

Whether the Germans could hear the rattle of the Wagons or Limbers this night I could not say; but the next day they spent much time on ranging their guns on this Sunken Road and they found that they were able to drop shells right on the centre of the road. Due to this, the Sunken Road never became a very good "Rest Camp" for the Company Headquarters but we were still able to hang on to this Sunken Road. At times it was impossible to hold on to our little shelters and we finished up by digging a deep narrow Trench in the side and close up to the bank of the road so that, when the Germans started shelling directly on the road, we were able to take cover in this Trench.

265. ALBERT 1918. Another Battle. Watching the Advance.

This night another Battle was to be taking place to our Front and Right but it was intended to give the Germans a surprise by starting this battle at mid-night instead of at daybreak. We were asked if we would give up our little shelter to the Royal Medical Corps. To be used as an advanced Dressing Station which we were pleased to do. Whilst this was taking place we took to our "Trench".

The following morning the Germans received another great surprise by a new Battle starting, this time on our Left and, after this, we were no longer the Pivot of the Offensive. This time the Battle took place on the other side of Albert and from our position it was a great sight to see the Battle in progress as our Troops drove well into the German position. They were moving into what was the area in front of the new battle, taking into account the direction from which they had started. The men who were advancing were making towards us. What a great sight it was to watch the Battle start and to see the bursting shrapnel getting closer and closer and the Infantry following it up. This Battle clearly greatly worried the Germans as they were so afraid that, whilst this one was going on, another might commence from our direction. We were all to have a fair supply of shells in this Attack as the Germans didn't seem to care about the idea of necessarily concentrating all of his Artillery on the "New" Battle.

266. ALBERT 1918. Artillery moving forward. Further Battle preparations.

This night, it would have greatly surprised the Germans if they had been able to seen just what was going on at our Sunken Road. Our Artillery were coming to the Front and taking up position in the Sunken Road and also in front of us. The best of it was that they were bringing up large supplies of shells in broad daylight and it wasn't very long before the Germans started to make things very uncomfortable with their shellfire.

Their "Five-Nines" were bursting each side of the road and when they fired their small batteries, they were well able to hit the centre of the Road.

Battalion War Diary:

23rd. August 1918. N. E. of RIBEMONT

Quiet during the night. Day spent in consolidating. Hostile Artillery showed considerable activity. 2/Lt. L.CLARK wounded.

24th August 1918. N.E. of RIBEMONT

Bn. under orders to move forward at short notice in support of an attack made by the 7th Royal Sussex and 5th.Royal Berks. in conjunction with units on flanks. Village of BÉCOURDEL & BECOURT captured. Bn. not called upon.

Sadler Account:

266. ALBERT 1918 (cont.). Artillery moving forward. Further Battle preparations.

This day all Officers and N.C.O.'s were again called to the Company Headquarters to hear the news of another Battle which was due to take place. This was supposed to have been taking place at 2 o'clock this day, (23rd.August), but things were rather lively and three of our small "Whippet" Tanks, who were sent to the Front to test the German's strength, found it far from comfortable. So much so that only one of these three small Tanks had the pleasure to return. Between the time we were called to Company Head Quarters and the time the Battle was due to commence, I had an hour or so of sleep and when I woke it was nearer to four o'clock than two.

267. ALBERT 1918. Preparing to go into Battle. Rations.

By the time it had got to four o'clock, no news had arrived as to what time the Battle was going to start but I had a great deal to do in charging about from Platoon to Platoon seeing to different things that we were to be needing in battle. This involved such things as serving out flares and tin plates and SOS rockets.

Later that night we were told the battle was going to take place at two o'clock the following morning and we were told to leave this position at Midnight. Then, just before starting for the Battle, the following day's rations arrived extra late and we had a scramble to get them served out in time. A message was sent to me to say that, if the Rations could not be served out in time, we were nevertheless to go on and leave them. We were not to be late in taking our position for the Battle. As it was, we managed to get everything served out in time and, at midnight; we left to take up our positions with both sides being very quiet with regards to sending shells over at each other. After a very long drag, every man was so tired that no doubt they could have even fallen asleep whilst marching along and, I must say, the "few" hands who had been taking their place in the various Offensives since the start of the War were really getting greatly War weary and worn and thoroughly sick and tired of the word, War. However, it was not a little bit good any of us grumbling, it had to be done and as the Battle approached we were expecting a very warm time as we were getting between the high ridges that had been the old Somme Battlefield. Knowing this only made soldiers, such as myself even more sick of War as we had been over this ground before in 1916 and the area and villages were still piled in heaps from those Battles.

Battalion War Diary:

25th August 1918. FRICOURT

At 2 30am Bn. passed through the Units in the front line under cover of artillery and M.G. barrage and advanced on a front of 200 yds. to a depth of 2000yds. All objectives taken. Bn. now holding a line from the S.W. edge of FRICOURT- S.W. to the BUIS FRANCAIS inclusive. 120 prisoners, 1 M.G. & 24-27 howitzers captured.

18th.Div. co-operated on the left and the 58th.Div. on the right. Infantry on the flanks. Patrols pushed forwards on the left and reached the eastern edge of FRICOURT and patrols pushed out by the Bn. along the N.W. edge of MAMETZ reported the village clear. 35th.Bde. was sent forwards too as new advanced guards to the Bn.. They defended the high ground to the North of MAMETZ. Pack animals and all Officer's chargers sent up to the Bn.. Bn. ordered to Assembly Positions N.E. of BECORDEL- BECOURT. In position by 6 00 pm.

Sadler account

268. ALBERT 1918. Back over old ground. Awaiting Battle.

Every now and then, one would see hundreds of crosses together and these crosses only served to make us remember earlier times; reminding us of our Comrades who were once fighting by our sides.

Everything looked quite unearthly to us "Old Hands", however we were able to take up our positions and we lay in the open, by Sections, for quite half an hour without having a German Shell sent over towards us.

What few Shells the Germans were sending over were going well behind us. Whilst we were in this position, waiting for the Battle to commence, we were told that we were not having a Creeping Barrage this time. We were informed that all of our Artillery were going to shell the first Objective for a certain length of time and whilst this was going on we had to wait .Then this Barrage would be lifted and aimed at the Second Objective; due to be taken by the second line of troops to advance. Ourselves, we were due to be taking the First Objective. Our Objective was the Second of two roads and we were told we should be able to tell the road because there were Railway Lines running up the side of it.

269. ALBERT 1918. News of the Front Line. Moving Forward.

After this, the Company Officer and myself spent our time talking to the Troops who were holding the Front Line.We did this to find out all of the news and, if the Bombardment had been started whilst we were at the Front Line, then we were going to be going over with the Front Line instead of taking our position between the First and Second Lines. It had always been my wish to be in the Front Line as one was more likely to escape the German Barrage. All of a sudden our Bombardment started on the First Objective and we all moved forward without receiving a single shell from the Germans. Just after we started moving forward, a German machine gun started sending a few bullets at us but they soon packed up and moved away before we could reach them. These were only a few Germans who had been left behind to bluff us as being part of the Germans rear guard action. We continued on and on with our advance without seeing a single German until we reached our Barrage Line. Here we had to lie and wait quite twenty minutes before the Barrage lifted on to the second Objective. At times, the shells were falling short and we found it far from comfortable waiting for the Barrage to lift.

We were rather close to all this and, if I hadn't passed a remark to our Officers, we may well have been closer still. I told them that I thought it would be for the best if we turned back a short way as the Shells were bursting only a few yards away from us and, at times, they were nearly blowing us in the air. Anyway we found an Old Trench close by and waited until the shellfire lifted.

270. ALBERT 1918. Advancing Under Barrage. Evidence of German Retreat.

The worst part of it though was that the Barrage didn't lift. Several of the Guns still kept firing at the same position but, nevertheless, we had to go on whether the shellfire lifted or not. It wasn't that long before we came to a roadway but, with the smoke from the shellfire, it was impossible to see anything so we tried to see if we were on the right road with the aid of torchlight. At last, we ended up feeling for the Railway Lines with our hands and, as luck would have it, we found them and so we considered that we were at our Objective.

However, we were unable to find any Troops on our Left and we began to wonder if we might end up getting surrounded. Any rate we settled down in an old Trench running alongside the road and waited until daybreak as it really wasn't safe to move too far; this due to the fact that, at times, many of our own shells were bursting rather too close. When daylight arrived we took a trip around to find out as much we possibly could as to what was taking place. Not many yards away from our Trench was a German Battery of "Five- Nines" and a very deep dugout. We took a trip down into the dugout to see what was below and, by the look of things, whoever had been in it at the time of the commencement of this Battle had made a very quick move, leaving things upside down. The guns were in grand condition. On the road was a German Wagon which must have been passing through when our bombardment started and, clearly, one of ours shells had burst close by it.

271. ALBERT 1918. Rediscovering our Old Trenches.

On this road were several of our own dugouts; ones which we had made and which had been captured by the Germans when our "Withdrawal/Retirement" of March and April had been taking place. We could see by the bandages and blood lying about that the Germans had been using the dugout as a Dressing Station. These dugouts contained many of our own wire beds and tables and it could be seen that many of our shells had burst near the doorways and had very nearly blocked these dugouts up. Anyone could see that the Germans had decided to make themselves comfortable here as they had also started work on a very large dugout which looked as though it was eventually going to be a German Head Quarters. This was positioned at the corner of four crossroads and was well covered over with chalk so that its entrance did not catch our Airmen's eyes.

This position was, though, very similar to many others and there were many stores which could be seen lying about that had once belonged to the British Tommy. Our Company Officer decided though that he would not undertake to enter any German Dugout and instead elected to stay on the Road itself. We managed to find a table and two chairs, from one of the German dugouts, for him and he said that enjoyed the fresh air treatment. He was, it was felt, so afraid that, if he entered a dugout to get a little rest, it would be mined and that he could well get blown to pieces.

272. ALBERT 1918. Roll Call. Advances to our Left. Further German Retreat.

As for myself; I had to make out my Trench Strength Roll and so had to take a trip around to see how many men I could find. I knew, though, that we could not have many men missing, if any, as I hadn't yet seen a German at this Battle. The

Company Officer told me that, so far during this Action, only two German prisoners had been captured and they had been taken by another Company. When I had finished my Trench Roll, I discovered that we were in fact only seven men short and they could be accounted for as being slightly wounded by our own Shellfire. However, we could see that the Germans were playing a splendid Rear Guard Action. What did take my eye particularly on this morning was seeing the Troops advancing on our Left. They were due to have started the same time as ourselves but they were only just coming forward. They were marching to the Front in Sections with their rifles and bayonets slung over their shoulders in the same way that they had been trained for Battle in the rear of the line; this was instead of how it should be done when they were about to tackle the real thing. The sun was shining on their bayonets in a way which set them off and marching in such a fashion as if nothing, whatsoever, was going to be interfering with them.

In all my time in France I had never seen anything like this in an Attack.

The German Army was becoming completely disorganised and there was no doubt that they were looking to retire to safe quarters. Owing to the fact that we had such a long march to reach our next objective, it wasn't very long before it was reported that the Germans had in fact retreated. Soon many of the "Heads" of our Army were to come forward to The Front.

Battalion War Diary:

26th August 1918. N.E. of BECORDEL. BECOURT. FRICOURT and MAMETZ
At 1 00 am. C.O. was sent for to attend a conference at Bde. HQ. At 2 00 am. the Bn. marched from assembly position through FRICOURT and MAMETZ to old trenches N.E. and S.W. of the MAMETZ – CARNOY Rd. In position by 4 30am. Bn. and Bde. observed hostile artillery active from 4 00am. onwards.

At 4 30 am, 7th. Royal Sussex and 5th. Royal Berks pushed forwards ahead of our Bn. front for a distance of 1000yds. where they were held up by M.G. fire. About 6 00 pm, the Enemy was observed to be withdrawing closely followed by our troops. Bn. had orders to move forward on receipt of Orders but was not called upon.

Marching forward, Acting CSM Sergeant Sadler and his men prepared to meet the enemy in the still novel conditions of open warfare.

24

27-28 August 1918: Advance and Wounding

S adler Account:

273. ALBERT 1918. Advances of our Guns. Cavalry Scanning. Placed on Brigade Reserve.

Not long after this, everything which we had available for use in warfare started to be brought forward.

The roads were, again, packed with Traffic. Guns of every size were coming to the Front and dozens and dozens of Motor Lorries were carrying shells for the guns. When the word was given by the Artillery Officer for the guns to be put in position, the Gunners soon got to work and had their guns, once again, ready for action. Now, they didn't worry about covering the guns up from view; all they really wanted to do was to get on with the good work. It wasn't long after that several, especially selected, cavalrymen were sent to the Front to find out just how far the Germans had fallen back but they were unable to go very far before they met with the German's rear-guard. They were greeted with showers of bullets from the German's machine guns and, soon after this, the Germans tried to bluff us by sending over many shells. We could tell the shells were being sent over randomly, not actually being aimed at hitting any particular object. Nevertheless their shells were unable to miss and almost bound to hit someone or something as there was so much movement going on. This particular afternoon, further Infantry came to the Front and were to be going ahead of us; getting as near to the German rear guard as possible but they were to be doing this without much aid from our Artillery.

Battalion War Diary:

27th August 1918. FRICOURT and MAMETZ
At dawn the 37th.Bde. advanced through the 36th Bde. which became Bde. in Reserve. Day spent in resting. Draft of 132 O.R. arrived. At 11 00pm. Bn. moved forwards to assembly position behind the Front Lines held by 6th.Buffs., W. of FAVIERS WOOD.

Sadler Account:

274. ALBERT 1918. Sleeping. Still on Call. Back to the Front.
As for ourselves, we were put in Brigade Reserves and we retired a short distance to take cover in an old Quarry with the aim being to get as much rest as possible. Nevertheless, we had to keep everything packed up; ready to move at a moment's notice. None of us really required much "rocking to sleep" as we were dead tired

and the strain of being constantly called for Battle was becoming terrible. That night I had several attempts to get to sleep but every time, just when I was managing to get to some rest, the Company Officer wanted to see me at the Headquarters. I really started to wish that I could lose this job as Acting Company Sergeant Major. After I had been called about a dozen times, I finally managed to get an hour's sleep and it really was only just for about an hour. At midnight I was called again and I woke up with such a start and still felt so tired that I began to wonder if it was actually twelve o'clock midnight or twelve o'clock noon.

Anyway, I received the Order to get the Company paraded immediately and to be ready to move off.

It wasn't to be long before we started off towards the Front once more. Never, I considered, could Infantry have had a more trying time than that which we had been going through since the "Big Offensive" had started. We had been battling against the enemy almost continually whilst getting only a few minutes sleep every now and then. We were beginning to feel that we really didn't care what was to become of us.

So we started on our journey to the Front and were marching by Platoons until, just before daybreak, when we were shown our position and just where we had to get ready in order to take our part in another phase of the Battle.

275. ALBERT 1918. Taking Cover. Other Troops passing through. Our Guns. Battle awaited.

After lying out in the open for some time, we received Orders to take cover in an old Trench as other Troops were waiting to pass through. They had not yet taken their Objective owing to having been held up by the German's rear guard. We were quite able to tell this for ourselves judging by the great number of machine gun bullets that were to be passing over our heads. The old Trench in which we were taking cover was not in view of the Enemy but down in a dip between two ridges. All the time the Germans were searching for massing Troops and because of that, every now and then, a shell would burst only a yard or so from our Trench. To make things even better for us; two of our 60 pounder guns then came and stationed themselves close by and the Gunners started worked like niggers to supply the Germans with "Iron Rations". Never, I think, did I ever see guns positioned as close to the Front as these two were. It wasn't long before all Officers and N.C.O.'s were called to the large shell hole which we called Company Headquarters, here to receive news of the Battle once more and, although we marked out our maps, we were not sure exactly when the Battle was to be taking place.

276. ALBERT 1918. Awaiting Battle-Trench Repairs. Reinforcements allocated.

We were informed that we had to be ready to move forward at any minute. This was to be as soon as the Infantry in front of us had gained their Objective. They were trying to do without the aid of any of our Artillery and it was turning out to be very slow work for them. Whilst passing away the weary hours at this trench we repaired the Trench so that we could sit down in comfort, not knowing how long we were likely to stay there and we managed to have a little bite to eat which was our, so called, breakfast. All that we had to think to about was when will our next part in the

Battle start. Dinnertime arrived and we were still to be found in this old trench. After Dinner, some if not all of us, managed to have a bit of a sleep whilst sitting up in the trench. On waking, it was teatime but still no news of us starting into Battle. After tea, a young Officer who was staying alongside me, decided to get one or two men from his Platoon to fetch some wood and sheets of tin so that he could construct a little shelter. Meanwhile, about 50 men arrived as reinforcements and I had the task of serving them out to different Platoons and rearranging the Company. This also meant that I had to make out a new Company Roll Call for the Company Officer and myself. I started to think that some sort of cover was needed if one was to be called upon to reorganise a Company at the Front.

On finishing this job, the Rations arrived and I had to see to them being served out.

277. ALBERT 1918. Awaiting Battle. Battle Orders. Preparing to move.

When I had finished that job, I went to see the young Officer in the shelter which he had made. I will say that considering conditions, he had made a very good job of it. Quite up to date, really, including a table etc. … Anyone would think we were liable to be spending a week in this Trench. When the Officer remarked to me, "I think we shall be all right for the night and perhaps we'll be able to have a sleep." I replied "Yes", whilst thinking to myself, "Yes, if we are very lucky!" I was only to have just a short time in this Shelter before I was called to Company Head Quarters where they had also made a cover in their shell hole. I received Orders to call together all Officers and N.C.O.'s with maps. The time, then, was a quarter of an hour before midnight. To cheer me up even more, the Company Officer then said, "You will have to hurry up a bit as the Company has to be made ready to Parade; they are to move off at 12.15 am." With this an almighty scramble started. It was far from being cheerful news for all the men as they had settled down for the night and many of them were fast asleep. Not even the Company Officer appeared to be very cheerful over the thought of the coming battle.

What few minutes we had, were spent in marking out our maps showing our Objective and, when we had finished, we wished each other well, hoping that we would meet with the same good luck that we had had during our last Battle. After this all the men had to be called and ordered to get dressed at once. Every man carried this out as quickly as possible. In a very few minutes we were off again on our way to the Front.

Battalion War Diary:

28th August 1918. HARDECOURT AUX BOIS.

Bn. in position by 3 00am. At 4 55 am. Bn. attacked along whole Bde. front under cover of our artillery and MG barrage. Attack successful to an average depth of 2000 yds. and all objectives taken including the village of HARDECOURT. In touch with 1st. of 11th. CAMBRIDGESHIRE on Left and 1st.of 2nd. LONDON on Right. During the advance the Bn. came under heavy MG fire.

Casualties to Officers Capt. E.C.DUPRES- Killed. 2/ Lt.'s W.C.LONG and F.O.BINGHAM- Wounded.

Casualties to O.R. (Other Ranks).:- 150

Captured. 50 prisoners of German Bn. Guards Divisions. & 6 M.G.s

Many Germans killed. Hostile artillery very active during the afternoon and evening with H. E. (High Explosives) and Gas.

Sadler Account:

278. ALBERT 1918. Advancing to Battle. Start Time 4 00a.m. Artillery Bombardment.

It took us over three hours before we were in position ready for Battle. We were to receive much luck whilst we went on our way. The Germans were searching, with their shells, all of the low ground looking for any massing of Troops but, as we were marching ahead, the Germans shells were dropping in the rear. When we did, eventually, manage to get to the Front, we found things were very quiet. We were able to lay in comfort for quite half an hour before the time it was due for the Battle to start, the starting time of the battle being four o'clock, with our Advance taking place at five to five. Even in this time of waiting, so many of the men, being dead tired, were able to fall asleep and forget the strain of the forthcoming Battle. The men who could not sleep could only wait for the outburst of our Artillery. From the outburst of our Artillery we were always sure of the correct time of starting, a watch never being required. When at last four o'clock arrived; our Artillery started as one gun and away we went on our "journey". As we moved forward, I was in charge of the Company Head Quarters men who only numbered eight but, this time, as we were taking the Second Line, I was quite fully aware that we should meet the German Barrage which was starting to commence.

This being the case, it was my wish to hurry ahead for a short distance in order to try and escape it.

279. ALBERT 1918. German Shelling. Caught and injured by a shrapnel shell.

All of a sudden the Germans sent over a shell which burst into a large yellow flare. With the aid of this flare, it was quite possible to see all that was going on for a great distance all around and it wasn't long after this that shells stared coming from all directions. I still very much wanted to keep well up with our front line of Troops when the Company Officer said to me "Don't be in too much of a hurry". I looked round to speak to him and, in that instant; a shrapnel shell came from the left direction and burst in the air only a few yards from us. This shell did much damage. The "bullets" from the shell spread all around us, one bullet catching my steel helmet which made a perfectly round hole through the steel rim of my helmet and finished up making a very deep groove in my skull. Another shrapnel "bullet" hit the pouches of my equipment, went through it and finished up in my chest and another "bullet" or piece of casing of the Shell hit my left leg, tearing away a large piece of flesh. Having received my "share" of this shell, I soon realised that it was to be impossible for me to continue into Battle and, although it was increasingly difficult for me to move far, I knew that it wasn't going to be much good for me to stay lying out in "No Man's Land" with shells bursting within only a few yards of me.

After I had pulled round a little and wasn't feeling quite so dazed from the effect of the hit in the head, I struggled into a deep German Trench which was close at hand. However, whilst I was sitting here, another shell came over and nearly blew the Trench in on me.

280. ALBERT 1918. Seeking out Stretcher Bearers. Being looked after.

It was then that I had the "pleasure" of meeting up with two or three more wounded comrades but, after spending very little time there, I decided to get around the Trench somehow and look for the Stretcher-Bearers. Not one of my wounds had been bandaged up and they were causing me a great deal of pain.

My right eye was closed up by the blood, which was clotting, flowing from my head but, the worst wound, and the one which was causing me the most pain, was the one in my chest as the shrapnel had caught my ribs and the blood there was also clotting inside. Although I felt myself to be in terrible condition, I managed to get a good way down the Trench where I was lucky enough to meet with two Stretcher Bearers who, seeing me nearly finished, bandaged my head up and put me on a stretcher before starting to carry me away.

Although they did their very best to carry me as steadily as they could, the shaking about was terrible.

However, once they got me into safer quarters, they then started to bandage my chest and leg up.

What made our "trip" worse for me was that so many of the Trenches ran in all directions and, therefore, the ground which we had to go over was uneven with many turns to be made. It was starting to become very hard work for the stretcher bearers with me on the stretcher so, when we came across these trenches, I decided to get off of the stretcher and they helped me through this part of our journey.

281. ALBERT 1918. Being taken to a Dressing Station. Meeting Old Chums.

The Stretcher Bearers actually had no idea where our Dressing Station was as it was such a great distance from the Front, but, having known them for a very long time, I was feeling quite happy to be having two good chums by my side. At times they would light a cigarette up and put it in my mouth and also gave me water to drink which served to greatly freshen me up. Several times they passed the remark, "Poor Old Sergeant, we are going to be losing one of our very best friends from the Action". I was never to forget this pair of faithful Stretcher-Bearers. Great chums of mine during the long time that I was in France. However, this day was to be the day that we were to be parted and I said to them, "Cheer Up, I will be able to write to you when I get back to Blighty"' You can be assured that the good old word "Blighty" was able to cheer up any badly wounded man. It was after we had been on our "journey" for about an hour that we met up with a man walking towards us. The Stretcher Bearers asked him where the nearest Dressing Station was and, with the man pointing in a certain direction, we continued on our way and before too long before we noticed the Regimental Red Cross Flag flying and we were soon to arrive at the Dressing Station.

Hardecourt aux Bois, Chimp Valley.

Hardecourt aux Bois.

282. ALBERT 1918. German Stretcher Bearers. Field Dressing Station.

Here I was to meet several more very old comrades who I had known all the time that I had been in France.

Many of my old friends came round to greet me for the last time. One of them handed me a drink of hot tea and, although it contained neither milk nor sugar, it was very acceptable and another of them gave me a lighted cigarette. The Medical Officer pinned a label on me and as my wounds were already neatly bandaged up they did not redress them. The Officer then wanted to know how things were going on with regard to the Battle but I was unable to tell him. By this time many German Prisoners were coming back to the Station on their own; some with Red Crosses on their arms which meant that they were German Stretcher-Bearers.

I did know that the Germans at times used to put this band round their arms so that, on being captured, it gave the impression that they were Stretcher-Bearers when they were not. Using this "trick" they thought they would have more pity shown to them as Stretcher-Bearers were unarmed men. Four of these German Prisoners were called over to carry my stretcher and they seemed only too pleased to do so. After wishing my chums "Goodbye, and the best of Luck", the four Germans then carried me the whole of the journey to the Advanced Field Dressing Station without resting and whilst on the journey it started to rain very hard.

One of the Germans who was wearing a Great Coat took it off and very kindly covered me up with it in order to keep me dry. I must say they did their very best for me and it wasn't very long before the Field Dressing Station was reached.

283. ALBERT 1918. Waiting for Transport to Casualty Clearing Station.

Here my Stretcher was put on the ground I had to wait quite twenty minutes until a Red Cross Car arrived.

I really needed another drink but, at this stage, was not allowed one by the R.A.M.C. men due to the hit and wound in my chest. I began to suffer a great deal more pain. Whilst I was lying there one of the R.A.M.C. men was complaining about having no rations. Hearing this, I said to him, "Undo my pack," which was being used as the pillow for my head, "in it you will find my rations, have them." I knew there was no way that I would be able to eat them but he was very pleased to accept them. Even this though was not to get me a drink. What refreshment I got came from them dipping one of their fingers in water and then putting that it in my mouth. They were only doing what was right and what they knew would cause me no harm. At last a Red Cross car arrived and I was carried out and put in the car. When the car started its journey, travelling over shell holes, it became too much for me and I soon went off to sleep; remembering no more until after I had been operated on at the Casualty Clearing Station.

Wounded and in-transit to the rear, acting Sergeant Major Sadler's long active service experience was over. The long road to recovery from injuries sustained would be his next major battle. For their part, 9th Royal Fusiliers seized Hardecourt aux Bois from the enemy.

25

28 August 1918: Onwards Christian Soldier, Wounded. Out of the War and Recovery prior to Discharge

A s 28th August 1918 drew to a close, Sergeant James Sadler found himself badly wounded in a Casualty Clearing Station ward.

Sadler account:

284. OUT OF THE WAR. Operated On. Visited in Chest Ward.

I woke up to find myself in a bed once again but I was in terrible pain.

Standing on the right hand side of the bed and close to my head was Sergeant Major Saunders, the Officer who had undertaken the Operation, and, alongside him, the Charge Sister of the Chest Ward.

Although I was only just alive, I knew something had to be done to my chest because I was having such difficulty in breathing. I told the Charge Sister that I was unable to breathe and Major Saunders said something to the Sister and she undid the bandages to try and relieve the problem for me but that really didn't seem to do any good. I asked the Major if I could have a smoke and, even though smoking was not really allowed in the Chest Ward, he did not refuse but lit a cigarette and gave it to me. I will say that everything in the way of kindness was shown to me here. After the "Major" and Sister had left my bedside, I was greeted with a few cheerful words from the Army Chaplain who wanted to know where my home was in England along with several other things. When he finished, he knelt by my bedside and offered up prayers; something which I shall never forget. Although I was unable to move, as I was still so tender from my wounds and the cutting from the operation which I had just undergone, I was still able to hear.

Once the Chaplain had left my bedside I received another visit from the Sister.

285. OUT OF THE WAR. After the Operation. Waiting for the Train.

When I asked her for something to drink, the Sister would hear nothing of it but she did give me a feeder containing water, not to drink, but it was there so that I could wash my mouth out. I promised her that I wouldn't drink any of it and I never did. I started thinking that the Sister was quite right in not letting me drink and, with that, I did not go against her wishes but I can vaguely remember the Sister coming to me the same day and saying, "What are you doing with that water?". I seem to remember telling her that I was only bathing my hands to keep cool but I really had no idea of what I was doing. In a day or so, I began to pull round a little; only a night seemed like a week. All the time I just could not seem to make out where I was. I kept thinking that I was still lying out on the Battlefield instead of being in bed. For three days I was looked after very well by our good, kind-hearted Sisters who will always be remembered with affection by the men who had served and who were injured at the Front. Although these gallant Sisters had to work very hard, they always greeted everyone with a pleasant smile and did whatever was in their power to comfort any badly wounded "Tommy". Soon after this, though, I began to pull round and I left for the 12th . General Clearing Station; wishing all my kind friends here "Good Luck" before leaving them.

286. OUT OF THE WAR. Transport to Hospital. My wounds and their effect.

I was to travel on the Red Cross train and, as a Special Chest Case, had to be carefully handled. Whilst I was on the train I was given, tea and thick slices of bread and butter and made myself as comfortable as I could and was quite content, eating and drinking as much as I was able to. When our journey was finished, eight "Special" Cases were taken away first and we were put into two cars and soon driven to the Hospital. That night, two of us finished up in a large tent; with the remainder of the men in the tent who were suffering from sickness but not actually wounded. Here I was to spend a terrible night but I must say that those amongst the sick men who were actually able to get up, did all that they could possibly do for us. Next morning they organised and sorted us out once more. I was able to have the pleasure of leaving the tent and going into a special Chest Ward where this time I was attended to by "Tank Sisters". As it was, I wasn't there very long before my wounds were redressed. When I got to see my body wounds, I asked one of the Sisters just what exactly they had been trying to do and whether they had tried to cut me in two.

The biggest wound from the operation was nearly a foot long and the wound which had resulted from being caught by part of the Iron Shell had four large stitches in it. In all I had 27 stitches in my body and it was a far from pleasant sight to for me to see. However, the effects of most of the wounds seemed to worry me only a little although the tightness of the stitching on my chest wounds caused me a great deal of trouble as it affected my right lung and my breathing.

287. OUT OF THE WAR. Journey back to England. Le Havre to Southampton.

After several more days of careful treatment I was, eventually, able to travel back to England although, whilst on this journey, much was to happen regarding my condition. Whilst travelling to Le Havre on the Red Cross Train I desperately wanted to get up and have a walk around as it was as much as I could do to breathe whilst lying down. I asked a passing Orderly if I could get up but, instead of him giving me an answer, he called the Sister in Charge. The Sister came by and told me that she would not be able to accept any responsibility for allowing me to get up in my present condition. I told her that, after having asked the Orderly, if he had only given me an answer, I would have been quite happy to obey his orders. I was promised that they would have me taken from the Train as quickly as possible at the end of the journey and they were true to their word. On arriving at Le Havre, I was soon being carried to the Red Cross Hospital Boat and I put into a "cot" but the heat on the boat was extreme and, I considered, it was not improving my health. I began

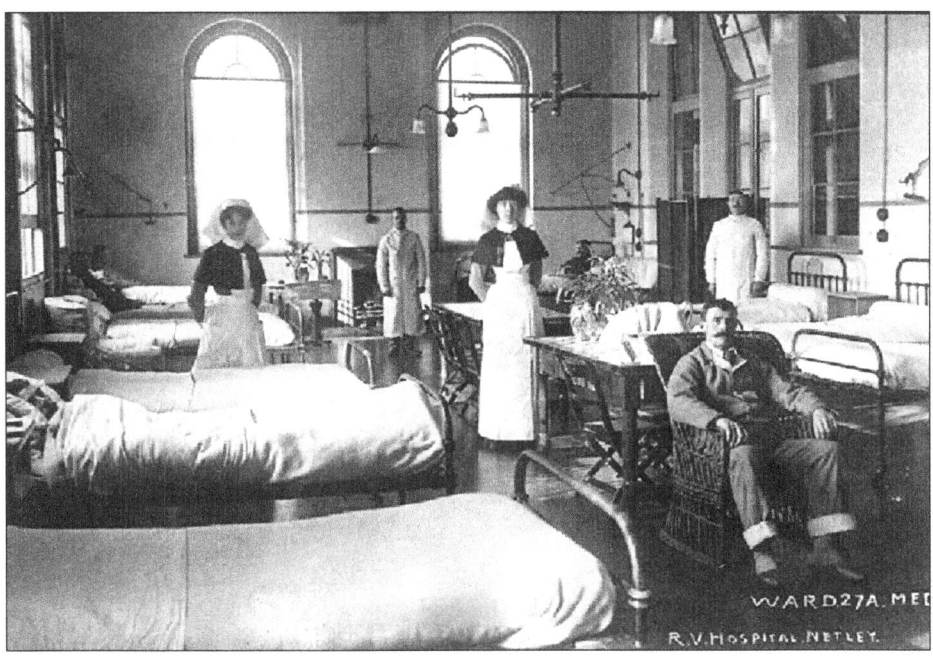

A Ward in the Southampton War Hospital at Netley where James was
treated for his wounds on return to England in summer 1918.

to get very restless and it wasn't very long before I decided to take a chance and
try my luck at having a walk. On looking around I could see that there was nobody
around who could stop me. I got up and, by helping myself along from cot to cot,
I managed to get right down to the other end of the Boat. Eventually though I was
stopped and asked if I was generally allowed to walk about by myself and then it
was not long before I was put back to bed and, soon after, I was given something
to send me off to sleep.

288. RETURN TO ENGLAND. Disembarking. University War Hospital, Southampton.

When I woke up I found that we were lying off Southampton and there were three
Hospital Boats waiting to be unloaded. As it turned out, we were to be the last to
be unloaded and it was between 8 and 9 o'clock before I was finally taken ashore.
On disembarking, I was then to receive another ride in a Red Cross car with me
and another chap sharing the journey with the man who was in charge of stretcher
cases accompanying us.

He kept asking me many different questions and, in the end, as politely as I
could, I asked him not to ask any more of me as I was finding that I was unable
to answer him. At last we arrived at The University War Hospital in Southampton
where, as ill as I was feeling, I could not stop myself from smiling at the wonderful
Sisters who were soon making me very comfortable. I was soon off to sleep again
and, when I awoke towards morning, the first thing which was handed to me by the
Night Sister was a nice cup of hot milk. Later that morning, my Lady Doctor came

James Sadler's Medal Card as held in the National Archives.

to visit and to take a look at my wounds and I was then moved to the warmest part of the Ward. I was given a bed rest which meant that I could sit up in bed. I became a "sitting up" case and was to remain one for many weeks. I really couldn't have received any better treatment; everything possible was done for my comfort. For three weeks I was fed on a milk diet, after which I had a change and went to living on a chicken diet for what seemed a great many weeks.

289. HOME IN ENGLAND. University War Hospital. Stitches removed.

The day the Sister took the stitches out of me, I had a cover put over my face so that I was unable to see what was going on. She started by taking the eleven stitches out of my head wound and then came the four from the wound under my heart. Then followed the removal of the twenty three stitches which had resulted from the wound which had required the long operation; these were of a very large size. After the Sister had taken out about a dozen, I asked her if she could wait a few minutes whilst I had a blow. She replied that she was taking them out as carefully as possible but, unfortunately, could not help hurting me. As she said, they were the largest stitches she had ever had to take out. They were extremely large silk stitches. Following this, she and the Charge Sister got to work and finished the job. I just had to put up with the pain which was quite something. This pain resulted from the fact that the stitches were nearly out of sight, having been pulled into my flesh by the pressure of my body which had built up on them. All this time I only really wanted to know how many more there were to take out as I was longing to get the job over. Once all the stitches had been taken out you could never believe what a great change it made. Whilst the stitches were in it was a case of being able to breathe every now and then; after they had gone, I was, once again, able to breathe as well as I ever could.

James Sadler entry recorded on a page in the Roll of Individuals awarded Great War medals. The exact dates which James saw action on the Western Front are given here. It is extremely poignant to note the details relating to L.Cpl. William Spry, the first soldier recorded on this page.

290. HOME IN ENGLAND. University War Hospital. Being Operated On.

What was then to cause me terrible pain was the tetanus injection which I was given in my arm to try and prevent Lock Jaw. This was to turn poisonous in my arm. There followed three weeks of great pain, and I begged my Lady Doctor to operate on it which she agreed to do. A very short while after "sending me to sleep", she opened up my arm and put a tube in it in order to drain the poison away. I came round to find that the pain had gone and I was just in time to receive a very good dinner and able to take no notice of what I had undergone. This was to be the case until the following morning when my arm had to be redressed, the rubber tube taken out, cleaned up and put back in. Once again I was in for some more pain. The Sister who carried out the job was, thankfully, very, very quick at her work and so I was only to suffer for a short time. Once my arm got better and the effects of my wounds became less, I was able to leave my bed for an hour or so every day but it was to prove very uncomfortable getting about as I had become so used to sitting up in bed for so long. I found, for some considerable time, that I just could not stand upright and began to wonder if, indeed, I would ever have the pleasure of walking upright again. It was then to come as a great surprise when my Lady Doctor told me she was going to send me home for good. This meant that I was soon to be discharged from the Army altogether.

291. SOUTHAMPTON TO SWANAGE. Discharged. Duty Done.

It was, however, some weeks after this before I received my discharge papers and during that time I was to suffer several dangerous attacks from the effects of my chest wounds which resulted, on one occasion, in having to have the Doctor called in twice in one afternoon. However, I started to grow stronger once again, and from then on I was less troubled. After, eventually, getting "finished off", I was ordered to attend a Medical Board and, without any trouble whatsoever, I received my Discharge from the Army as a Disabled Soldier. In a very few days, I was to leave Southampton for Swanage where I was able to undergo further treatment if it was needed and I had the real pleasure of wearing civilian clothes again. This really was a most welcome change as, since enlisting on 13th August 1914, I had been wearing little else excepted my Army uniform.

So in finishing ... Now, I am pleased to think that I have done my duty, and done my duties well, for my King and Country.

James undoubtedly followed the remainder of the war's progress during a lengthy convalescence. It would be inconsiderate to him and his comrades to leave their story at this point.

26

September–November 1918
Advance Towards Armistice: the War
to end all Wars reaches a Conclusion

With Sergeant Sadler convalescing in Blighty, 9th Royal Fusiliers carried on with its part in the general Allied offensives in which the Belgians, French, Americans and the entire BEF would be involved. No doubt James would have been with them in spirit.

On the 28th and 29th August 1918, the Battalion captured Maurepas, after which it went into reserve. Early September 1918 was spent in billets at Carnoy and Mametz with orders to move at short notice. Receipt of orders that they would "be taking part in a large attack at an early date" arrived on 16th September, after which the Battalion moved to Saulcourt and on the 18th at 5 30am, captured Epehy, a fortified village fronting the Hindenburg Line. Relegated to brigade reserve, they received orders that the Division was to be "moving North to another Army area" on the last day of September.

Embussed and debussed throughout early October, the Battalion arrived at Vimy Ridge in Third Army sector. From there, 9th Royal Fusiliers continued their role in the great advance capturing the enemy front and support Lines against minimal opposition. Now in full retreat, the Germans were, according to the Battalion diarist, "still putting up some considerable opposition", with the Battalion's companies however achieving rapid gains in northernmost limits of the Hindenburg Line. On 13th October, the Battalion was relieved and moved to rest billets at Henin Lietard. Moving forward again on the 17th, they liberated Raimbeaucourt and entertained the inhabitants at a Brigade concert held in a German cinema.

There was, however, still work still to be done, Lecelles village, on the French side of the Franco-Belgian border there next objective. Captured on 22nd, they underwent heavy shelling, subsequent progress held up by fierce machine gun fire, near Flagnies, which the enemy appeared to be holding in strength. Nevertheless, during the next four days, 12th (Eastern) Division, in co-operation with 58th (London) Division, continued the advance against the retreating foe. Relegated to the reserve on 27th October, 9th Royal Fusiliers were relieved by a battalion of 52nd (Lowland) Division. Settling into billets in nearby Flines, they carried out company and platoon training, HRH The Prince of Wales paying a visit on 7th November. From these billets the Battalion marched (10 November) to Landas where they received word of the Armistice the following day.

This was simply recorded in the Battalion War Diary:

11th November 1918. LANDAS.
Notification received at 9 00 hours that Germans had signed our Armistice and that

hostilities would cease at 11 00 hours. Brigade Thanksgiving Service on the Village Green at 11 00 hours. No other parades.

27

1919: A Footnote: After the Armistice: the 9th Royal Fusiliers (Service) Battalion disbanded

"Routine" or "As usual" were common war diary entries following the Armistice, This, in all likelihood, meant tactical training exercises; indeed the only descriptive entry for this period reads as follows:

12th November 1918. LANDAS.
Carried on with Platoon Training.

The 9th.Royal Fusiliers (Service) Battalion were, from late November 1918 through the succeeding months until disbandment, involved in battlefield salvage and clearance operations near Cambrai. Nevertheless, those troops of the Battalion and Division, who remained in France, also found time to entertain themselves with numerous sporting events such as Football, Cross Country Running, Boxing, Paper Chases and Tugs of War and there were many different Educational classes organised for the men in order to prepare them for their return to civilian life.

The 9th Royal Fusiliers (Service) Battalion continued to operate as a unit until disbandment on 6th June 1919 when the last remaining troops embarked on the S.S. St George at Dunkirk.

The final war diary entries were composed by Battalion CO Lt. Col. W.V.L. Somerson DSO, MC:

16/6/1919. Dunkirk. Embarked on S.S. *St George*
17/6/1919. Arrived at Southampton. Remained at Contingency Rest Camp.
18/6/1919. Arrived Hounslow.

The Battalion's Task Complete.
The 12th (Eastern) Division had been disbanded slightly earlier on the 22nd March with Major-General H. W. Higginson bidding the troops who had been under his command farewell as follows:-

On relinquishing command of the 12th Division I wish to express, to all ranks of every unit and department, my deep sense of gratitude for their unfailing support, loyalty and comradeship during the past eleven months during which it has been my privilege to have the proud honour of being its Commander.

The months of May, June and July 1918 were ones of constant vigilance and hard work in the trenches owing to the expected renewal of the German Offensive. During this period the Division distinguished itself in several successful raids which were made on a considerable scale.

On the 8th August 1918 you attacked with the rest of the Fourth Army and during a period of constant hard fighting and attacking, almost daily, you drove the Enemy from position to position to VENDHUILE which you reached on the 30th September, a distance of 26 miles from your position on the 8th August.

You were then transferred to the First Army and went into the line near LENS on the 6th October.

The following day the Enemy was in retreat in front of you and you drove him back in daily encounters until you reached the line of the River ESCAUT, a distance of 32 miles from your starting line on the 27th October, and were relieved there on the 29th.

This is your record of the 6 months preceding the Armistice.

Previous to this the Division has played a prominent part in many famous Battles. Its achievement at LOOS, THE SOMME, ARRAS and CAMBRAI were worthy of its best traditions.

Between May 1915, when the Division first landed in France, and the 11th November 1918, the Division has lost 2,103 Officers and 46,038 Other Ranks in action. This testifies that your laurels have not been lightly earned and to the gallantry and devotion to duty shown by you who have survived the great ordeal and by those brave comrades who have given their lives for Our King and Country and who, by their sacrifice have won immortal fame.

In a few weeks the Division will cease to exist but wherever our fortunes may lead us in the future, we shall all remember, with pride, the days when we fought in the 12th Division and will still retain the spirit of comradeship and loyalty to each other which has carried us to Victory in this Great War.

I wish you all good luck and God-speed.

H.W. Higginson. Major-General. Commanding 12th Division.
16th March, 1919.

Appendix I

Outline of the organisation of the Army into which Private G321 J. Sadler enlisted in 1914

On enlisting Private G321 J.Sadler found himself as a member of "A" Company of the 9th (Service) Battalion of The Royal Fusiliers.

The Battalion was attached to the 36th Brigade, formed during the Great War to fight on the Western Front as part of the 12th (Eastern) Division.

This consisted of the following Battalions:

8th The Royal Fusiliers (City of London Regiment); 9th The Royal Fusiliers (City of London Regiment); 7th The Royal Sussex Regiment; 11th The Duke of Cambridge's Own (Middlesex Regiment).

The following gives, in rough outline, the structure, starting from the top, of the Army's Organization at the start of the Great War.

Unit	Commanded by	Generally consisting of	Approx. No. of Troops
ARMY	General or Field Marshal	2 Corps ; H.Q.'s & Army Troops	40,000 to 80,000
CORPS	Lieutenant-General	2 Divisions; H.Q.'s & Corps Troops.	20,000 to 35,000
DIVISION	Major-General	4 Brigades; H.Q.'s & Divisional Troops	12,000 to 18,000
BRIGADE	Brigadier-General	4 Battalions & H.Q's;	3,000 to 4,000
BATTALION	Lieutenant-Colonel	4 Companies; (A, B, C, & D). & H.Q.'s	800 to 1,000
COMPANY	Major or Captain	4 Platoons;& H.Q.'s	160 to 200
PLATOON	Lieutenant or 2nd Lieutenant	4 Sections (No's. 1 to 4)	40 to 50
SECTION	N.C.O. or Lance Corporal	1 Corporal + Privates	10 to 14

At times this underwent some changes as the War progressed; Companys in a Battalion being reduced from 4 to 3 and Brigades reducing from 4 to 3 within a Division.

Appendix II

Seniority of Rank in the Army into which
Private G321 J. Sadler enlisted in 1914

The following is the Order of Ranks held within the British Army during the 1914-18 conflict.

RANK	Abbreviation
Field Marshal	Fld. Marsh.
General	Gen.
Lieutenant General	Lieut Gen.
Major-General	Maj. Gen
Brigadier-General	Bgde. Gen.
Colonel	Col.
Lieutenant-Colonel	Lieut. Col.
Major	Maj.
Captain	Capt.
Lieutenant	Lieut.
2nd Lieutenant	2nd. Lieut.
Sergeant Major	Sgt. Maj.
Sergeant	Sgt.
Corporal	Cpl.
Lance Corporal	L.Cpl
Private	Pte.

In Infantry Regiments during World War I, a Sergeant generally held the rank of Platoon Sergeant and was 2nd in Command of a Platoon.

The Company Sergeant Major, C.S.M., was the senior non-commissioned soldier of a Company with special responsibility for administration of supply of ammunition, discipline and standards etc. and was often responsible for evacuation of the wounded and collection of prisoners of war.

Appendix III

James Sadler M.M.'s position in the British Army 1914–18

Army

In France and Flanders during 1914-18, the size of the British army became such that it was subdivided into five Armies. The following gives the chain of command downwards from each of these Armies.

Corps

The Corps were not permanently attached to any particular Army nor were the Divisions beneath them attached to any particular Corps.(The number of Corps under the command of the Army was generally two, but may well have been increased if an Army was to be undertaking an offensive operation).

Division formed 21.08.1914, Army Order 324 (about 20,000)

12th (Eastern) Division: Comprising 35th Brigade, 36th Brigade; 37th Brigade; Engineers; RAMC; Cavalry; Motor Machine Gun Battery; Sanitary & Veterinary Units.

Brigade (4,000)

36th Brigade: Comprising 9th Royal Fusiliers, 8th Royal Fusiliers; 7th Royal Sussex; 11th Middlesex –(about 4,000 men)

Battalion (1,000)

9th Royal Fusiliers (Service), (about 1,000men)

One of four Companies (A, B, C and D) (240)

Company (about 240 men)

One of approx.16 Platoons (60)

Platoon (60 men)

One of approx. 64 Sections (14)

Section (14 men)

The Individual (1)

Soldier-Infantry (James Sadler MM).

Lightning Source UK Ltd.
Milton Keynes UK
UKOW06n1527130116

266333UK00006B/71/P